Ernst Wilhelm Hengstenberg

History of the Kingdom of God under the Old Testament

Ernst Wilhelm Hengstenberg

History of the Kingdom of God under the Old Testament

ISBN/EAN: 9783337134754

Printed in Europe, USA, Canada, Australia, Japan

Cover: Foto ©Lupo / pixelio.de

More available books at **www.hansebooks.com**

HISTORY

OF

THE KINGDOM OF GOD

UNDER THE OLD TESTAMENT.

TRANSLATED FROM THE GERMAN OF

E. W. HENGSTENBERG,

LATE DOCTOR AND PROFESSOR OF THEOLOGY IN BERLIN.

IN TWO VOLUMES.

VOL. II.

EDINBURGH:
T. & T. CLARK, 38, GEORGE STREET.
MDCCCLXXII.

CONTENTS.

SECOND PERIOD—THIRD SECTION.

THE PERIOD OF THE JUDGES; FROM JOSHUA'S DEATH TO THE ELECTION OF SAUL.

	PAGE
§ 1. Chronological Survey,	1
§ 2. Introductory Remarks,	10
§ 3. Principal Events,	15
§ 4. The Civil Constitution at the time of the Judges,	67
§ 5. The Condition of Religion,	71

FOURTH SECTION.

FROM THE ESTABLISHMENT OF ROYALTY TO THE DIVISION OF THE KINGDOM.

§ 1. Events from the Election of Saul till his Rejection,	75
§ 2. From the Rejection of Saul to his Death; or, Saul and David,	89
§ 3. David and Ish-bosheth,	106
§ 4. David King over Israel,	110
§ 5. The Life of Solomon,	124

FIFTH SECTION.

FROM THE DIVISION OF THE KINGDOM TO THE BABYLONISH CAPTIVITY.

§ 1. Rehoboam and Jeroboam,	139
§ 2. Abijam and Asa in the Kingdom of Judah. Nadab, Baasha, Elah, Zimri, Omri, and Ahab, in the Kingdom of Israel,	156
§ 3. Jehoshaphat,	197
§ 4. Ahaziah in the Kingdom of Israel,	204
§ 5. Joram in the Kingdom of Israel and in the Kingdom of Judah,	212
§ 6. Jehu, Jehoahaz, Jehoash, Jeroboam II., and Zechariah,—the five Kings of the Dynasty of Jehu,—in the Kingdom of Israel. Joash, Amaziah, Uzziah, in the Kingdom of Judah,	232
§ 7. History of the Kingdom of Israel to the time of its complete Dissolution,	238
§ 8. Judea under Jotham, Ahaz, Hezekiah,	242
§ 9. From Manasseh to the Captivity,	247

SIXTH SECTION.

JEWISH HISTORY FROM THE CAPTIVITY TO THE DESTRUCTION OF JERUSALEM.

	PAGE
§ 1. The Babylonish Captivity,	252
§ 2. The new Colony on the Jordan to the completion of the Building of the Temple; or, Zerubbabel and Joshua,	292
§ 3. Ezra and Nehemiah,	308
§ 4. From the Death of Nehemiah to the time of the Maccabees,	338
§ 5. The time of the Maccabees,	366
§ 6. The Jews under the Supremacy of the Romans,	388

ESSAY ON THE LIFE AND WRITINGS OF HENGSTENBERG.

BY REV. W. B. POPE,
PRINCIPAL OF THE WESLEYAN COLLEGE, DIDSBURY, MANCHESTER.

MORE than a quarter of a century has passed since Hengstenberg's *Commentary on the Psalms* opened the present series of translations. From that time until now the "Foreign Theological Library" has given the works of this eminent expositor to the English public with unfailing regularity. Hence no German name is so familiar in England as that of Hengstenberg; certainly none is so thoroughly identified with all that is sound and honest and loyal in German theology. And this prominence among ourselves corresponds very fairly with his prominence on the Continent. In many respects, and in some departments, of which a slight account will be given in these pages, Hengstenberg has been the foremost man in Lutheran Protestantism for nearly a generation. No one has for a long time departed, leaving a more sensible blank, whether in his own country or in ours. And now that his last and posthumous work appears before the English reader, it seems not inappropriate to accompany it by some notice of his life and labours. As a biographical memorial, these pages will be brief and fragmentary, for the simple reason that nothing like a memoir of this eminent man has yet appeared. But, as a tribute to his character, claims, and work, it will aim at least at being complete and faithful,—the uncoloured and honest expression of respect for services which have laid the English theological public under very great obligation.

Ernst Wilhelm Hengstenberg was one of a noble band of men who came in with the present century, and are about this time reaching the term of human life and passing rapidly away. He was born at Fröndenberg, in Westphalia, where his ancestors for several generations, indeed from the fourteenth century downwards, had figured largely and made themselves memorable in the local annals. A line of political Hengstenbergs are found leading the movements of a feudal aristocracy; and these are matched by an equal line of ecclesiastical Hengstenbergs, in unbroken succession, from Canonicus Hengstenberg, who gave his heart and soul to the Reformation, down to the present day. The father of our subject, a man of considerable endowments and large attainments, occupied several pastoral charges, and showed some zeal and energy, especially in the department of education. A firm friend of the Union between the Lutheran and Reformed Churches, he was a theologian rather of the Reformed or Calvinistic than of the Lutheran type; and, moreover, was something of a modern "humanist," having no very profound convictions on religion, and giving himself up very much to classical literature. The son of such a father had the ministry always kept before his view, was trained in the Reformed system of doctrine, and received an early bias towards the Union. In the last respect paternal influence was happily neutralized or lost in other and stronger influences, of which more hereafter. A good mother lived long enough to watch over him up to maturity; and this was a special blessing to a youth who began life under the conditions of a diffident nature and an unsound constitution. Until seven years of age the lad was not permitted even to read,—a restraint, however, for which he made swift amends when he fairly began. Almost entirely confined to the room by lameness, he contracted the habit of steady poring diligence in study. From that time to the end of his life he was among his books daily, from five or six o'clock in the morning until eight in the evening, with the exception of about three hours' intermission. He was accustomed to attribute much of his success to the troubles which inured him to a sedentary life so early, and to the necessity which this imposed of exceeding strictness in exercise and diet. "I have scarcely," he said to his brother on his deathbed, "during life known for a single day the feeling of perfect health, and have done what I have done simply through having been obliged to keep my body under stern discipline." This must be taken into account hereafter, when the prodigious amount of his literary labour comes under notice.

Young Hengstenberg was at this early stage comparatively self-taught. His father was in failing health, and left the youth very much to his own resources,—not, however, without watching him and noticing his advancement. "He will be a professor," he used to say, with more than the usual fond presentiment. He might well indulge the prophetic instinct when such evidences of his son's diligence met him as the following:—"The astonished and amazed countenance of my father is still before me," says the same brother, "as he took from my brother's hands a little honorarium, which he had received from a Leipzic publisher for the translation of a Latin author, I think Aurelius Victor. The manuscript had been at once accepted by that firm, little dreaming that the author had just entered his seventeenth year." The same authority tells us that his brother Ernst was confirmed by his father in October 1819, and adds some remarks which it is a pleasure to quote. "On the same day was the baptism of his brother Edward, who died at Berlin in 1861 as Consistorial Counsellor. Ernst was his godfather, and watched over his youth, as also over mine, with a tenderness and fidelity the remembrance of which will never be effaced. Piety was a fundamental feature in his character always, especially in relation to his own household, every member of which may say, 'As he loved his own, he loved them to the end.' Next day he went to the University of Bonn, and passed his examination with great credit."

Just at that time the German youth were enthusiastic in their patriotic fury against France, and zeal for the regeneration of the Fatherland. The fruits of that seedtime of Prussian revival the world has lately seen. In Bonn the *Burschenschaft*, or confederation of German youth, Hengstenberg joined and co-operated with most heartily; he helped to keep up its dignity, and received from it in return a wholesome preparation for the discipline of public life. He also derived benefit to his health from the diversion thus afforded to his overtaxed mind, and the stimulant to bodily exercise. Meanwhile he pursued his studies with diligence, chiefly in a philosophical and philological direction. Before reaching his twentieth year he had finished a translation of Aristotle's *Metaphysics*, as evidence of his success in the former branch. It was in the latter, however, that he was destined to win most distinction; and an edition of an Arabic author, *Amrulkeisi Moallakah*, in a Latin translation, and illustrated by notes, gave earnest of his success in oriental studies. This was his testimonial essay for the Doctorship of Laws, and proved to all the world that he had not studied under Freytag in vain, and that he would in due time become a high oriental authority himself. Arabic he studied rather as a cognate of the Hebrew, and for the sake of the biblical learning, to which he already began to devote himself. For though not as yet brought under the influence of personal religion, and with only an indefinite idea of consecration to the service of the gospel, he was impelled by a strong instinct to give the first-fruits of his intellectual vigour to the sacred languages. It would not, perhaps, be wrong to say that he was already under the guidance of the good providence which directs the early energies of men who have a great work to do. Hengstenberg's sphere of labour was to be preeminently the Old Testament; and before his twentieth year he had laid the broad and deep foundations of an eminence in Hebrew, and its kindred dialects, which not even the most learned of his numberless enemies ever despised or disparaged.

One effect of his remarkable success as an oriental editor was the high opinion of Sylvester de Sacy, who recommended him to the Bâsle Missionary College as every way competent to give instruction in the Eastern languages. Accordingly he removed to Bâsle, where the Spirit awaited him who leads the sincere student into all truth. Hengstenberg spoke of this period nearly half a century afterwards, when opening his heart to the readers of the *Kirchenzeitung*, as the time of his conversion and of the beginning of his Christianity. "I had been engaged at Bonn," he says, "in seeking goodly pearls, but I had not yet found the pearl of great price." It appears, however, that his theological principles were somewhat in advance of his religious life. For when his tutor, the well-known Professor Brandis, put into his hands Schleiermacher's new book, the *Glaubenslehre*, a system of Christian doctrine, he read it with profound interest, but soon returned it with the remark: "I shall not remain what I am; if indeed I did so, I should never be a theologian; but to that man I shall never betake myself." This shows two things,—first, that the youth was discontented with himself and his own character; and, secondly, that he was able, beyond most of his contemporaries, to sound the depths or the shallows of Schleiermacher's theology. Considering that he was a mere youth at the time, and had not been very carefully trained in systematic theology when younger, this was a remarkable exhibition of precocity. Schleiermacher was then rising to the height of fame and influence. The book which young Hengstenberg thus threw from him was fascinating almost the whole world of German Protestantism, and literally inaugurating a new era of religious thought. Its influence was destined to divide the old from the new, and not only to stem, but to arrest and turn back, the tide of Rationalism. Had the youth been previously entangled in the snares of the Illuminists, it is probable that he might, like many others, have hailed Schleiermacher as his saviour. But, fortified by a strong and determinate bias towards pietism in sentiment and orthodoxy in creed, he saw only the negative and unreal elements in the new theology of dependence. He perceived plainly, or rather felt, that Schleiermacher's God was not the triune God in personal manifestations to the human race; that his Christ was an ideal being, who accomplished only an ideal atonement; that in his hands the entire face of theology was changed, and man had become in a wonderful manner the centre of religious truth. He perceived how the subjective spirit of the new Christianity trifled with the objective facts, and was disposed to subordinate the firm external word to the internal consciousness of feeling. It may be gathered that he left Bonn with a rooted conviction of the truth of the Bible as a record of God's dealings with the human race, and with a full preparation of heart for the reception of those personal influences which the associations of Bâsle would soon bring to bear upon him.

In the missionary institution of that place he remained only a short time, but long enough to find what he called "the pearl of great price." Hengstenberg was not a man given to much self-revelation; and it was at a season of unwonted freedom of spirit, when the approach of the end released his tongue from restraint, that he spoke of this period of his conversion. The details of his call and personal consecration are not at our command; nor do we need them. His whole life bore testimony, clear, consistent, and unvarying, to the reality of his devotion to the Person of Christ,—a devotion which he entered upon at Bâsle. He became what in Germany was called a Pietist,—what in England would be called an earnest Christian. To this pietistic, fervent, experimental type of religion, the soul of which is the personal relation of the believer to his Lord, he was faithful to the end, notwithstanding some appearances to the contrary. It classed him with bodies of men from whom, as to their doctrine and religious observances, he recoiled with something like aversion. It allied him, for instance, in spirit with Neander, and Tholuck, and Stier, from whom, as evangelical disciples of Schleiermacher, he kept at a doctrinal distance. But to this we shall have to return.

Hengstenberg very soon reached the goal of his ambition and the scene of his long labours, the University of Berlin. This new foundation was fast becoming the glory of Prussia. It had not undergone the usual lot of such institutions, that of a gradual victory over prejudice and attainment of popularity, but took its place at once amongst the foremost factors in modern Christendom. The ministry who had charge of the education of the country, with a wise forethought gave every encouragement to young men of ability wherever found. Hengstenberg was one of those who profited by this patronage. He had obtained a Doctorship in Divinity at Tübingen,—another illustration of precocity, remarkable even in that region of early maturity, reminding us of the youthful veterans of our own universities in the sixteenth and seventeenth centuries. To attain this degree he must have worked hard in theology, at least in biblical theology, to which he seems to have devoted himself, as soon as his mind became truly Christian, with a concentration that never relaxed. Thus graced, he found his way to Berlin, and underwent the severe ordeals which test the ability of a candidate to become a private teacher of theology. Shortly afterwards, in 1828, he became ordinary Professor, and took the rank and position which he held to the end. Thus we find him, at an age when most of our students are looking out upon life, and pondering their vocation, in the dignity of a teacher of the most difficult science in one of the most important universities of Europe. No sooner was he settled in this post than he became settled in another respect. He married a lady of high birth and connections, who thus contributed materially towards securing his access to high society, and extending his influence among those who would otherwise have been inaccessible. It may be said here that this wife was a most faithful sharer of his joys and sorrows for thirty-two years. His home was in all respects happy, save indeed that Providence disturbed its peace by a succession of bereavements. Though he was left all but childless in later life, his children while spared to him were a source of the purest satisfaction. The fidelity with which he watched over the sons of his own generation entrusted to him was rewarded by the goodness of his own. His family was from the beginning well ordered. In due time his house became one, and not the least favoured, among the many centres in Berlin to which the cultivated in Church and State were attracted. His open hospitality will long be remembered; and still longer his more unostentatious but more influential private receptions of the students, for whom a certain portion of the day was always reserved. In this last respect Professor Hengstenberg was only complying with a familiar and kindly usage in the German universities. How perpetually do we fall in with grateful reminiscences placed on record by students under such men as Olshausen, Stier,

Schmid, and especially Tholuck, who did so much by their private and unreserved influence towards reinforcing and confirming the public influence of their Chairs!

When Hengstenberg began his public career in Berlin, the aspect of theology, and of religion generally, was very gloomy. The expectations excited some dozen years before by the fresh tide that had been poured into German thought and life by the war of freedom had been to a great extent disappointed. Sanguine men had hoped that the vulgar rationalism was effectually checked, and that the chastised nation would return to a simpler religious faith. A noble future of sound development was expected for the evangelical Church of Germany. It was thought, moreover, that this development would be greatly assisted by the Union which had been brought about, under the influence of King Frederick William and his ministry, between the Lutheran and the Reformed Confessions. This Union, it is true, had rather been imposed upon the Churches than matured as the growth of healthy tendencies from within; but it was hoped that it would nevertheless be consolidated in due time, and that, as a peace-offering to the tercentenary of the Reformation, it would be accepted of God and approved of men. The result was not what was hoped, though only what might naturally have been expected. The Union increased the division, and gave occasion to the old enemy to blaspheme. Confession waged war with confession. The spirit became manifest which, in Silesia and elsewhere, made Old-Lutheranism resist all attempts to bring it into concert with Calvinism; and the Government, already greatly embarrassed, was beginning to find out that this would be a question of long continuance and of endless difficulty.

Evangelical Germany, divided amidst contradictory opinions, was much less able to resist the common foe of rationalism. The theological schools which began to be fashioned under the influence of Schleiermacher, and which afterwards split into two camps, that of the orthodox and that of the rationalists, had nothing strong and definite enough wherewith to encounter the practised adversary,

skilled in the tactics of nearly a century. An internal, and
subjective, and ideal religious system was not palpable enough
for rough aggression, or even defensive warfare; at any rate,
it had not yet put forth its strength, and its Neanders and
Tholucks were men of might who had not yet found their
hands. The orthodox Lutheran confessional divines, who
have since done so much to restore systematic theology in
Germany, were only beginning to form a consolidated party;
and as yet the wonderful Lutheran divines of the sixteenth
and seventeenth centuries slumbered on the shelves. Meanwhile the rationalists, whether more or less unfriendly to
supernaturalism, had the fatal prerogative of the highest
learning and the highest places. The old and vulgar rationalism of Röhr and Bretschneider was in the ascendant in
some seats of learning. In Halle, eight hundred young
divines, the pride and hope of Germany, sat at the feet of
Wegscheider and Gesenius, gathering up and surely remembering every word and every argument against tradi-
tionalism or the faith, catching the subtle influence of every
innuendo and every sally of wit, and receiving into soil only
too fruitful the plentiful seed of a no less plentiful harvest.
The times seemed very unpropitious. Some hope there was
in the pure and earnest godliness which Pietism nurtured in
southern Germany, and which found its way, through the
influence of individuals, into all the centres of the north.
But Pietism was hated most cordially by the leading states-
men of the day, and by the leading professors also. The
former were busy with the formularies of worship, but exceedingly anxious to keep out of those formularies the living
spirit that would have given them their value. They seemed
to have lost sight of the truth that a sound confession, a perfect liturgical service, and an evangelical life breathed into
both, and working upon the world by love, make up the
notion of the Christian Church. The dignitaries who taught
theology were too often thoroughly sceptical as to the fundamental documents on which all depend. The Old and New
Testaments were disintegrated; their unity surrendered and
broken up into mere collections of literary fragments; criticism played havoc with the text; Rationalism cleared away

all the miracles and the mysteries; and a hard and literal grammatical interpretation made the residue harmless to the conscience and the peace. Things seemed to have reached such a pass, that truth and fidelity cried out aloud, and almost in despair, for some champions who could meet the adversary with equal learning and with equal pertinacity. Such champions there were, and the organizations were ready through which they might rally the dispirited forces of evangelical Germany. The Government were to feel their rebukes, and the universities to come under their influence, —slowly, indeed, but surely, as we have since happily proved.

Hengstenberg was scarcely firm in his seat before he made it very manifest that he had fixed his decision and taken his definitive place in the great struggle of the day. Though his natural disposition was tranquil, and even phlegmatic,— though his early tastes and predispositions were all in favour of retirement and solitary study,—though the traditions of the office he held would, if followed, have confined him to a continuous course of learned dissertation more adapted to the recluse student than to the arena of public controversy,—yet there was something stronger than all these motives that gave him such an impulse to religious controversy as never relaxed its impetus till his dying day. He became known, as soon as he was known at all, as the acknowledged defender of the documents of Scripture, especially the Old Testament, and the avowed enemy of all temporizing and compromise, whether in the domain of literature, or in the affairs of the University, or in the conduct of the State. This stedfast persistence in one course has scarcely a parallel. It must have been the result of some very powerful influence. That influence, we have no doubt at all, was nothing less than the strong confidence of a deeply religious spirit. No power other than divine grace could have enabled him to hold out so well and so long, through good and through evil report, until his name became the very synonym of desperate fidelity to scriptural truth and the inspiration of the Holy Ghost. Some of his views he changed in the course of a long life, as will be hereafter seen; but in his loyalty to the word of God he never varied. Moreover, the things in which he changed were matters of isolated opinion,—questions which, with regard to the tenor of his life, were subordinate. In the great object of his life—instruction in Scripture—he never wavered. It is true, also, that he did not always maintain the meekness and gentleness of spirit and word that became the defender of divine truth; but his offences were venial when viewed in the light of that strong devotion to what he thought the word and will of God which never knew a stain. The testimony of all who knew him bears this out: that of his foes is reluctantly given, that of his friends most enthusiastically, to the same effect. Dr. Kahnis, one of Hengstenberg's younger friends and disciples, says: "There can be no manner of doubt that the foundation of Hengstenberg's theology was the living fellowship with God of a converted Christian." But this is not saying enough. Many a true-hearted Christian rejoices in divine truth for himself, but leaves others to defend it, or defends it fitfully, and with conciliatory zeal. Hengstenberg had the priceless blessing of a clear and deep conviction. It is impossible to question for a moment that he really believed in what he so resolutely defended, and had a sublime confidence in the literal truth of every portion of the word of God.

But it is time to consider distinctly, though briefly, the three departments of apologetic service to Christianity in which Hengstenberg was pre-eminent, and through which he has earned the gratitude of his own age and of posterity. These three were—his professorial chair; his editorship of the *Kirchenzeitung;* and his defensive and exegetical writings.

As professor of theology, Hengstenberg was not distinguished by any remarkable ability; that is, he was not pre-eminent in the professional qualifications of a lecturer. His teaching was concentrated on biblical theology,—a department which he selected with a wise regard to his own preparations and aptitudes. He was thoroughly equipped with what may be called the instrumental and technical learning that this branch of theology specially requires. He gave continuous courses of lectures on the Old Testament, and on the New, the substance of which, especially so far as concerns the Old Testament, reappeared in his writings. As a lecturer, he

b

had not the charm that attracted multitudes to the feet of some of his compeers. He was very much bound to his manuscript, and dispensed with the advantage of a direct personal address. He never swayed his audience by extemporary eloquence, or established between himself and them the electric current which free colloquy produces, but of which the paper is too often a non-conductor. What he lacked, however, in this respect, was abundantly made up by the indescribable vigour of a profound conviction expressed in unfaltering words. Whatever Hengstenberg was or was not, he knew nothing of vacillation or wavering. He was always decided, and therefore decisive. Wavering judgments he had no place for, either as a lecturer or as a writer. He did not simply guide his pupils on the way towards conviction, and conduct them through a process of investigation, which might or might not end in the determination of truth. He sat in his chair as a teacher, even when his years were immature. And he never changed that character. It may hardly be said that he gathered round him a school. He was not enough of a systematic theologian for that. But he trained, or assisted in training, a number of able men, some of them not much younger, and not much less influential in after years, than himself. Hävernick, Keil, Caspari, Philippi, Schultze, Kahnis, with many others, may be said to have been more or less moulded by him, so far at least as their attitude towards rationalism and their views of the Old Testament theology were concerned. Seated so very young in the chair, many of his own contemporaries, so to speak, were his pupils; and men who are grey-headed speak of Hengstenberg, lately gone, as their master with profound respect.

It has been observed that his house was thrown open daily, and always with perfect freedom of access, to his pupils. There was an hour devoted to them, the benefit of which many now living refer to with gratitude. His nature was affectionate, confiding, and singularly disposed to attend to little details. His knowledge of men and things, growing rapidly as it did in consequence of his editorship and large acquaintance in Berlin, made him a good adviser. His counsel was always at the disposal of those who sought it. Nor was he tenacious as to his prerogatives, or unduly solicitous that his pupils should adhere to his opinions, or take his part in the many controversies in which he was constantly engaged. Though exceedingly impatient of unsettled views, and peremptory in his refusal to encourage discussion for the mere sake of looking at all sides of a question, he was content to let others, even his own pupils, differ from himself, provided they did not diverge from the truth. He allowed a wide latitude so far as concerned agreement with his own judgments, while the line was very sharply drawn so far as it concerned the word and truth of God. He had in this respect his reward. What he sought not was given to him. Few men of this generation have more firmly knit to themselves and to their views the mind and sentiments of others. Some there were, and are, who carried their deference to the master too far, and looked to Hengstenberg's dicta as their oracles; but a far greater number did no more than justice to his clear teaching. He saved many from sheer infidelity, and many more from the mediating theology, which is little better; indeed, great as were his services in other respects, it is exceedingly probable that in this branch of service he effected his most essential and permanent good. His conversation, as described by those who were familiar with him, was not sparkling or humorous, or even ingenious; no book of table-talk could be constructed from the remembrances of it. His strength was, to repeat the assertion, the transparent honesty of his convictions, and their simplicity. There are a great number of theological teachers in Christendom, and there are many who far surpass Hengstenberg in multifarious learning and literary grace, but there are not many who equal him in pure and perfect belief of what they teach.

Hengstenberg's most obvious influence on the affairs of his own time, and on its religious tendencies, was exerted through the medium of the *Evangelische Kirchenzeitung*, a bi-weekly paper which was issued in the interests of Lutheran orthodoxy. This journal was dedicated at the outset to the defence of Christian principles against all kinds of heresies

and all kinds of errors. It had no particular mission for
or against any particular manifestation of modern thought,
but was a champion against all comers from the regions of
rationalism, and a watchful asserter of all kinds of neglected
truths. It was projected by a band of earnest men, among
whom the von Gerlachs and Tholuck were prominent.
Hengstenberg, about twenty-five years old, was chosen as
the editor. He undertook the service with a generous enthusiasm, and conducted it with a fidelity, that did great honour
to him. For forty-two years he was its impulse, director,
and leading writer; it was, in fact, his organ, intermediate
between the professor's chair and his expository writings.
Through it he spoke to the age in clear tones,—sometimes
harsh, sometimes melodious, but always certain and true to
the gospel. Rationalism, disguised and undisguised, whether
taking the form of infidelity or that of indifference or that
of mediation, he pursued with unsparing animosity. He followed it in all its ever-shifting forms, tracked it through its
manifold mazes, and encountered it without fear wherever it
appeared,—in the court, in the family, in literature, in science,
in hymn-books, in catechisms, and the sermons of the day.
The journal helped him in his lectures, and the lectures
helped him in the journal; thus, material being provided for
each, neither suffered from the unusual combination. Those
who have been accustomed to see that most venerable of all
Protestant journals, will remember Hengstenberg's annual
Vorwort, which, as regularly as the year opened, was looked
for by all parties as the oracles of a very different potentate
were looked for in France. He spoke as from a throne.
" What will Hengstenberg say?" was the common question,
on the emergence of every new subject of interest. These
Prefaces touched on every imaginable subject: all the struggles
of the Union, all the innumerable discussions between Church
and State, all the literary phenomena that teemed with every
year, found their place in them. A collection of these annual
addresses would be the history of the last generation in
brief.

It has been said by a not very friendly critic, that Hengstenberg in his journal united the utmost servility to the

ruling powers with a spirit of the most demagogical independence. With regard to the former part of the compound his defence is comparatively easy. In the year 1830, soon after the paper began, he published a vigorous article, in which the Government was sharply rebuked for permitting Wegscheider and Gesenius to hold the word of God and the doctrines of the Church up to contempt.' In doing this he imperilled his own position in the University, and thus gave no small pledge of his sincerity. What tried him still more was the fact that, by this and similar protests, he exposed himself to the imputation of bigotry, and gradually but surely alienated from himself the fellowship, if not the confidence and respect, of such men as Neander. So far was he from being thought a sycophant or time-server, the parallel between John the Baptist and him—comparing, of course, the greater with the less—was very frequent in the public comments upon his conduct. At a great cost of feeling—for he was naturally disposed to peace and private study—he continued his attacks on all sorts of abuses to the end. He said to his brother on his deathbed: "They thought me a kind of Hercules, always in my element when in wars and difficulties. How little they knew my nature! How often have I longed for rest, as the servant for the shade, or the hireling for the end of the day! But it was my calling to oppose the weak and accommodating spirit of the time." His testimony to himself is confirmed by the documents that remain, as well as by the evidence of many witnesses, both friendly and adverse. No man of our century spoke so strongly and for so long a series of years against the abuses of the day both in high places and in low.

His relation to the Church and State, and to the Union already referred to, will do something to explain both charges. In one sense his vehement devotion to the union between Church and State would tend to give the semblance of courtliness and secularity to his views, while his ardent Lutheranism, especially towards the end of life, made him a cold friend and finally a declared enemy of the other Union between the Lutheran and Reformed Confessions. His sentiments as to the relation between the civil power

and the religious were moulded by the Old Testament. He
was rooted and grounded in the theory of a Church bound
up with and sanctifying the State. With regard to these
points it may be said that he was unfaithful to his early self,
and that here, though here alone, an exception is found to
the law of unchangeableness which governed his life. He
was brought up under Reformed influences, but became in
the course of years a High Lutheran,—a remarkable change,
as they will admit who study the grave differences between
the Confessions. His views of the theocracy were fashioned
by the Old Testament, and in harmony with Calvin's, as he
experimented with them on the civil estate of Geneva; but
he became in due time what, to us at least, appears to have
been a servant of the State, and the faithful administrator
of its legislation. A Pietist in early life, and an evangelical
lover of good men to the end, he nevertheless came to distrust the Union by which Germany has striven to heal the
breach of the divided Confession inherited from the Reformation. He would rather have the Lutheran Church in a
Lutheran State than the Union which would efface the distinction and exhibit the State as tolerant. Doubtless, if
this were the fit occasion, it might be shown that the Union
sacrificed principle to peace; that it made the articles of
concord too simple and few, especially in regard to the
ordination pledges of the ministry; that it compromised too
much on both sides to lead to any good result; and that a
universal laxity, with the occasional variations of hypocrisy,
would necessarily follow. It might be urged that on these
accounts Hengstenberg did well to oppose it so strenuously.
Suffice that he did oppose it, though without helping in any
perceptible measure towards solving the difficulty. He was
no reformer, no legislator, no system-framer; he had not the
profound sagacity and ready contrivance of an ecclesiastical
statesman: and therefore, while the *Kirchenzeitung* provoked much agitation and helped forward the strife on these
questions, it lent no aid towards amendment and reconstruction. It may be said, in passing, that the journal was in his
hands until death folded them, and that he left it, with his
dying blessing, to another guide of his own selection. He

held it to the end as a duty, and said among his last deathbed words, "One of the benefits of heaven is this, that I shall have no more *Vorwort* to write." He ended, as he began, in the spirit of duty; and his relation to the *Kirchenzeitung* is certainly one that has no parallel in journalism, religious or otherwise. No paper has had so long a career in the advocacy of the same interests, and certainly none was ever conducted by the same editor and controller so long. In other respects it was like most others, of various ability, alternately tranquil and stormy, and occasionally offending alike against charity and sound judgment. In the reckoning of Hengstenberg's life and labour it is certain that the *Kirchenzeitung* must have a prominent place.

But it is as a commentator on Holy Scripture, and defender of the authority of the biblical documents, that this great man will keep his hold on posterity. It is in that capacity that he is known among ourselves. Hengstenberg accomplished a great deal, even in a country where there is an order of men always accomplishing prodigies; and one of the secrets of his enormous amount of work was the unity of his life as spent upon a single subject. He was literally *homo unius libri*, and of one portion of that book. The Old Testament was his sphere through life. In it he was strong; in any other he was like other men, and inferior to many. In the vindication and exposition of the Old Testament he was in his own day pre-eminent. His earliest discipline pointed that way. Oriental studies engaged his attention long before they are usually entered upon; and the consequence was, that he was fully equipped with the apparatus for a vigorous prosecution of his task before the work of his life began. Thus two errors were avoided,—first, he did not occupy his time and squander his energies in the pursuit of multifarious learning, like some prominent German names of the present day; and, secondly, he did not take up a great subject in middle life, when the specific learning and tastes demanded by it are more difficult of attainment. Of course there were some drawbacks: doubtless his mind was by this concentration somewhat cramped; his New Testament studies were sacrificed to a great extent, as the works written upon it indicate; and his strictly miscellaneous acquirements were perhaps kept within a narrower range than was expedient. But these drawbacks scarcely deserve mention by the side of the great service that he was able to render to the defence and study of the ancient Scriptures.

His first work was a bold challenge thrown down in vindication of the authenticity of the books of the Old Testament that were at that time especially contested. Several able and learned dissertations were gathered together and published as *Contributions towards the Introduction to the Old Testament*. This was mainly an apologetic work. Rationalism had attacked the ancient Scriptures as a whole, and certain portions, such as the Pentateuch, the unity of Isaiah and Zechariah, the authenticity of Daniel. These essays, considering when and by whom they were written, and the wide range and minute character of the learning brought to bear, were very remarkable, and stamped the writer's fame at once. But it was as a startling vindication that they created the deepest impression. In Germany, much more than in England, the writings of the old economy were surrendered, so to speak, to rationalism. The revival of comparatively sound views, under the stimulating leadership of Schleiermacher, had almost entirely left the Old Testament out of the question, as if it were a hopeless province, inaccessible to light. The general estimate was that Judaism was a monotheistic belief of a people who supposed themselves favoured by Providence; who vaingloriously ascribed their history to a special concentration of the regard of Heaven upon their petty selves; who imagined a descent of the Divinity for the purpose of giving them their laws,—laws which, while they borrowed much from the surrounding nations, were carefully ordered so as to give back nothing in return, but to exclude the rest of the world from their benefit; who supposed their peculiar religious enthusiasms to be the result of an immediate afflatus of the breath or Spirit of God; who would be content with no lower an authorship for their holy books than that Jehovah Himself, using certain men as His mechanical instruments. Rationalism poured unmeasured contempt on all these pretensions, and undertook to show that the history of the Jews was like every other history in what was good in it, inferior in some respects to some; in fact, that the Hebrew documents could not stand in the judgment when brought to the bar of either criticism, or morals, or history. It was necessary that some one should arise who could exhibit the evidences of authenticity which the texture of the books themselves afford, and which the annals of other peoples suggest in confirmation. Hengstenberg could do this well, and did it. But others were capable of the same service, and had in some sense performed it. What was peculiar to him was the exceeding boldness with which he avowed the unity of the Scriptures, the dependence of the New Testament on the Old, and the absolute necessity of faith in both if faith in either was to be maintained. He saw with clearness the whole compass and fulness of the issues involved. He saw that the stream of revelation must be traced up to its fountain; and that, if the fountain was not pure and divine, no streams issuing from it could be heavenly and undefiled. He saw that the entire literature of religion stands or falls with the early documents which are its elements and alphabet: that if these individual books were not written by the men to whom the later Scriptures ascribed them,—if they do not record facts that are historical,—if the New Testament inspiration is not really an approval and guarantee of an Old Testament inspiration,—if the Scriptures of the old and new covenants contradict each other,—if, in short, there is not a perfect unity in the grand and complete record,—then Christianity is undermined and ready to fall, bringing down with it the hopes of mankind. All this he saw, with perhaps a deeper insight than most men; and if he even exaggerated the expression of the principle, it was a venial fault. It is hard to deny that he was right in staking so much on the genuineness and integrity of the Old Testament.

The work of Hengstenberg has surrendered much of its goodly material to other builders, who have made a better use of it than even he did. Hävernick, for instance, one of his pupils, systematized his facts with some skill; and he in his turn has been methodized and set before the public in a perfect form in the *Introduction to the Old Testament*, published by Keil, one of the noblest representatives of the spirit of the older master. Hengstenberg, as an apologist for the Old Testament, will of course never be obsolete. His works will be read still,—perhaps more than ever, when the supreme importance of the Old Testament comes to be acknowledged as it ought, both in Germany and in England. But it is well known that the ground of attack has since shifted, and that the dissertations referred to exhibit only a partially obsolete aspect of the question. The rationalists of the days of Hengstenberg's early work were modest in comparison of what they are now. They did not then take the whole Bible to pieces, disturbing all dates, shifting all authorship, and reducing the whole to a constellation of nebulæ, if that were possible, the scanty nuclei of which are left to the faith of believers, be their worth what it may. To us it seems that a long age divides us from the time when the most earnest opponents were content to deny the Pentateuch to Moses as a whole, to separate Isaiah and Zechariah into parts, and assign the book of Daniel to a Maccabean date, without denying the historical foundation of the Old Testament as a whole. For the more recent developments of scepticism we need new Hengstenbergs, who will need the same loyalty and concentration, with learning adequate to meet a much more extensive assault. The tendency at the present time seems to be to bring down the books of the Old Testament to one period of wonderful fertility, when a thousand scattered myths and legends and mouldy documents were woven into that amazing fabric by men who suppressed their own names, and thought to honour Jehovah by inventing a series of colloquies between Him and His imaginary servants, extending over many ages, and by declaring that a succession of institutions was founded, and historical events took place, during centuries that knew nothing of them. Such astounding theories as those now broached to account for the historical books of the Jewish legislation have of course some basis of argument to rest upon; in fact, there are a multitude of evidences which by ingenious torture may be made to serve in their defence. The new and rising race of apologists will have to do more than Hengstenberg ever dreamed of doing; but he has, by his integrity, by his happy use of materials gathered from every source and spoiling all kinds of Egyptians, by his skill in directing many lights upon some one dark place until its darkness vanishes, and, above all, by his serene confidence that God was on his side, set a noble example to the younger generation.

We pass to another sphere of service, which, as more permanently important as well as more congenial to the devout student, occupied the greater part of his time,—that of biblical exposition. Here, again, Hengstenberg is a man of the Old Testament,—it may be said, exclusively such; for the books he published on the New Testament, the *Commentaries on St. John's Gospel* and *the Revelation,* were commended to him by their analogies with the old covenant. A writer on Daniel could not fail to feel himself drawn towards the Apocalypse; and it is the peculiarity of Hengstenberg's *Gospel of St. John* that it is really an exposition framed on the principle of illustrating the evangelist from the Old Testament. Valuable as these works are in some respects, they do not display the abilities of a master in New Testament exposition. That the author thought differently of them—that is, that he had a higher estimation of their value than of the value of some other of his expository works—says but little. Writers of books of unequal merit are proverbial for reversing their hands, like the patriarch, and laying the right on the wrong, but without any divine sanction for their preference. But of this more hereafter.

His most important, ablest, and most influential work is the *Christology of the Old Testament,* exhibiting, in the second edition especially, with a rich and interesting variety, the Messiah in the Old Testament in the light of the Christ in the New. This was followed by a *Commentary on the Psalms,* which for a long time was, both in Germany and in the English translation of this Series, the leading book for the preacher's use, combining in a remarkable way the results of adequate learning in the unfolding of the structure, and the materials of profitable application. A monograph on *Balaam and his Prophecies* appeared in 1842;

then the *Canticles* and *Ecclesiastes*; then followed the *Commentaries on the Revelation* and on *St. John's Gospel*. Lately to these has been added a very valuable *Exposition of Ezekiel*; and, finally, as a posthumous production, the present volumes on the *History of the Kingdom of God in the Old Testament*.

Various estimates have been formed of Hengstenberg's value as an expositor of the Old Testament; and estimates must needs vary so long as widely different theories are held of the relation of the New Testament to the Old. He does not in this department exhibit an absolutely unvarying fixedness of principle throughout his life. The earlier editions of his commentaries differ in a very considerable degree from the later in some very important respects,—not, indeed, affecting the evangelical tone of his exposition, but his conception of the relative value of the Old Testament theology. There is a school of evangelical expositors of the ancient covenant in whose judgment Hengstenberg's views are, or rather were, at an earlier period, too little regulated by the principle of historical development in divine revelation. He was said to have been always too anxious to find everywhere the full truth of divine doctrine, scarcely disguised, and thus to have gone far towards effacing the distinction between the Old Testament and the New. He was also charged with unduly spiritualizing the predictions, and losing sight of the historical bases of events. But there does not seem much ground for these charges, especially as directed against his works when issued in their final form. There can be no doubt that Hofmann's original and most suggestive volumes on *Prophecy and Fulfilment*, written on principles diametrically opposed to those of Hengstenberg, had the effect of making him more careful in the realization and exposition of the facts interwoven with all predictions. Nor can it be doubted that the works of another very eminent writer, Oehler, especially his *Prolegomena to the Biblical Theology of the Old Testament*, influenced considerably his estimate of the progressive character of revelation from Mosaism to Hebraism and prophetism. But Hengstenberg, like all voluminous writers, must be judged by his works in their final form. And the volumes which we now introduce will show that his conception of the Old Testament is distinguished by the very qualities which have been found wanting by his censors,—a comprehensive view of the order and progression of divine truth, and a careful historical sketch of all the dispensations. As to his facility in finding consummate truth in the Old Testament, we should be disposed to hold him to be right where these critics would hold him to be wrong. We believe also that a kingdom·of grace and truth has never been absent from the earth; that the divine-human Person of Christ is more conspicuous in the old covenant than most theologians admit. We embrace heartily, against half the world, our expositor's noble views of the Angel-Logos of the old economy, and of the essential divinity of the Messiah, not obscurely revealed by the prophets, though they did not understand their own revelation. We also think that the Holy Ghost has a history in the Old Testament which is the prelude and the germ, or more than the germ, of His history in the New. In fact, as to the question between Hengstenberg and his very severe critics, we should be drawn by our deepest convictions to side with him, and to wish that he had defended himself more copiously than he did from the assaults of which his exposition was the object.

Hengstenberg was not at any time a systematic theologian, but biblical theology was cultivated by him with great ardour. Biblical theology, however, to be of any service, must be systematized; and here it was that our expositor failed. He was only an expositor, or, if he entered upon the discussion of the doctrines derived from Scripture, it was only in detached essays and monographs. Had he given a few years of his strength to the construction of an Old Testament biblical theology, he might have accomplished one of the most deeply needed tasks of the day. There is no book that thoroughly exhausts, or even fairly exhibits, the doctrinal system that was gradually completed before the volume of inspiration ended. All that has been done amounts only to what Oehler called his able little book, *Prolegomena*. The mention of this last name reminds us of the great loss which this branch of theology has sustained in the premature death of this distinguished man, who, like Hengstenberg, has devoted himself ardently to the old covenant. The student who should desire to understand the bearings of the whole subject could not do better than read carefully, in addition to his *Prolegomena,* his admirable Essays on *Prophecy,* and kindred subjects connected with the Old Testament, in *Herzog's Encyclopedia.* If, besides these, he has acquainted himself with Hofmann's treatises already referred to, he will have a just conception of the wonderful extent, difficulty, and superlative importance of the department of theology which is based upon an exposition of the Old Testament Scriptures.

In the New Testament, Hengstenberg selected St. John for his exposition. The Apocalypse he took great delight in, as being an Old Testament prophet, as it were, risen again, and thus a confirmation of the views which guided him in his investigation of the doctrines of the old covenant. He had no doubt that the one evangelist wrote this book and the Gospel, and he set himself to detect and indicate in order the multitude of allusions to the ancient Scriptures which St. John's works contain. Thus he would make it appear that that apostle, who is generally supposed to have least of the spirit conventionally ascribed to the Old Testament, and to be most evangelical, and tender, and mystical in his tone of mind, dwells more than all others in the ancient circle of ideas. The commentary on the Apocalypse has not secured much acceptance in England. It robs the millennium of its awful meaning for the future, makes it "past already," having been simultaneous with the thousand years of the German ascendency, a gigantic exhibition of Church and State. Here and throughout the book the author spiritualizes away all that clashes with his great theory of a theocracy already set up among men, and varying in its forms. It is only right to say that the earlier parts of the book, the Saviour's own letters to the churches, is expounded with much power, and that the whole work is pervaded by a profoundly reverent spirit, as well as enriched by many most valuable quotations from other authors, and especially from the less known comments of Bengel.

The *Commentary on St. John* occupied a long time, and

was very closely bound up with the writer's personal experience and hopes. Its peculiarities are very striking. It omits much of the kind of learning in which others abound, and supplies the place by much that is found in no other. Though the Gospel never quotes the Old Testament formally and directly, save in such general reference as "The law was given by Moses," Hengstenberg makes it bear incessant reference to the ancient economy. He will see the waters of the early reservoir reappearing through all the conduits of the New Testament, and not least of all in St. John. Perhaps this was the reason why he took such pleasure in it, and anticipated for it so hearty a reception. It was the first connected work that occupied his thoughts, and its Old Testament colouring gave it a fascination. St. Matthew, as might be supposed, was a favourite Gospel; but he never succeeded in satisfying himself with his exposition. The Epistle to the Romans he lectured upon, but not with such results, either to his own mind or to his readers', as to warrant publication. St. John's Gospel he minutely elaborated. He intended it to be much more acceptable to the public, and much more influential on the higher classes, than it ever became. He was heard to say that he thought his *Psalms* would at any rate give him joy in eternity, but that the *Gospel of St. John* would command the attention of learned and simple alike. It was honest toil; in the sweat of his brow he had cultivated an old field in a new way. But the work was never popular in Germany, not even so popular as it is in its English form.

It was natural that Hengstenberg's theory of allusion to the Old Testament should be somewhat exaggerated. For this we are prepared by the preface, which says that "in no Gospel are the allusions to the Old Testament so abundant, so delicate, so mysterious, so profound, as in John: those only who have lived in the Old Testament thought and phrase can immediately detect them." At the very outset the tendency is observable. Other expositors and investigators have shown—Niedner, to wit—that the Philonic Logos is a very different being from the Johannean, and in that point Hengstenberg has all the argument with him. When, however, he asserts that the evangelist had no reference to any pre-existent operation of the Logos, but even in the beginning of the prologue refers only to the incarnate Word, and that the terms *light* and *life* are to be interpreted simply of the Messianic salvation, because those words have such a meaning in the ancient Scriptures, who does not feel that the theory is carrying the expositor away? So also he is quite justified in pouring a New Testament illumination into every verse and clause of the Shepherd idyll, Ps. xxiii.; but when, inversely, he makes the ancient idyll interpret every verse and clause of the Good Shepherd's words in John x., we feel that the expositor is misled again, and begin almost to sympathise with the cavils of his critics, who would convict him of finding too much truth in the old covenant. So also it is as perilous as it is unjustifiable to interpret the "eating my flesh and drinking my blood" by the voice of ancient Wisdom crying, "Come, eat of my bread, and drink of the wine which I have mingled." In his zeal to establish identity of authorship, the cabalistic employment of numbers and symbols, and all the minutiæ of mystical allusion, as found in the Apocalypse, Hengstenberg seeks to trace in the Gospel, and sometimes not without success. But for the excessive adoption of this principle the reader has only to consult the subtle and elaborate comment on the Samaritan woman, who by some preconcerted divine arrangement was prepared to be a symbol of the idolatry and pollution of Samaria. Indeed, this is but one instance out of many.

The Gospel, which was written to teach all men what and how to believe, which ends with the most remarkable victories of faith in illustration of its own principle, has been more instrumental than almost any other part of Scripture in instigating doubt; especially has this been the case within the last two decennia, and therefore every good commentary on St. John, which deals fairly and fully with its few pressing difficulties, should be welcomed with deep gratitude. Rich as is our orthodox Johannean library, it may be said that the sceptical is as yet still more rich. This of Hengstenberg is, as it respects its apologetic part, of great value, and therefore is a great gain. It should be read very carefully on the Paschal question, on the variations between the Synoptists and St. John, on the genuineness of the discourses assigned to our Lord, and on the last chapters generally. Again and again we have read Hengstenberg's solution of the difficulty as to the harmony between St. John and the three in the date of the crucifixion, and each time with a deeper sense of the solidity of his argumentation. The same cannot be said—at least we should not say it—concerning the connection between the anointing at the supper in St. John and that of St. Luke. Hengstenberg's scheme of the family relations of the Lord's friends at Bethany is not exactly original; but he has made it such by the copiousness of his argumentation on the subject. According to his reading of the gospel narrative, our Mary sitting at the feet of Jesus, the symbol to all ages of the absorbed devotion of a pure and ethereal contemplation, was the reformed sinner whom Simon condemned in his heart. That Simon was the husband of Martha, who, only in part grateful for his healing, could not bring down his soul or raise it up to the level of his duty to Christ. The details of this enforced harmony, which Origen and Augustine redeem from utter contempt, while its adoption by the Romish expositors makes it in its doctrinal aspect suspicious, we must leave to the reader of Hengstenberg's commentary. One point alone demands further notice here. While Hengstenberg invests Mary with the characteristics of the converted Magdalene, he also invests the converted Magdalene with the charm of Mary's devotion. Hence the interpretation of "for she loved much," which in our expositor's comment is made to mean that her forgiveness was in a very important sense the fruit of her love.

Hengstenberg had to the very last to feel the effect of this unhappy exposition. On the one hand, the sceptics assailed him for making such great concessions in so hard and inconsistent a manner. Strauss, in particular, wrote "The Half and the Whole!" an essay in a periodical to pour ridicule upon the tortuous combinations of the exegete to arrive at the simple fact which scientific criticism discerns at once. The cry was everywhere, so to speak, "Is Hengstenberg among the rationalists?" He could bear this kind of attack—he was used to it; in fact, it added zest to his life, and gave him the stimulus he wanted. But there was another kind of impeachment not so easy to be borne. His evangelical friends mourned over the defection from the doctrine of justification by faith alone, which they thought they discerned in his words. This gave him a severe pang. But he was never known to shrink pusillanimously from the consequences of a position honestly taken up. The *Kirchenzeitung*, which had always been known by all as the *Evangelical*, became the organ of his defence, for the first time in the service of its editor's orthodoxy. But his defence made matters worse. In 1866 there appeared in the paper an essay on the Epistle of St. James, which had been delivered as a lecture, and was then, according to his custom, reproduced in the journal. The reconciliation of St. James and St. Paul, easy enough when essayed in simplicity of purpose, he made rather mystical, and, many of his best friends thought, with a certain disparagement of St. Paul's doctrine as generally received. So far did resentment and suspicion go, that the man who had for so many years been the watchword and bulwark of orthodoxy, was virtually condemned by an ecclesiastical court, from which issued a warning to the clergy, directed against his error. He was on all sides bewailed as an apostate in heart from the great principle of the Reformation. His more express justification of himself appeared in his paper in an essay entitled "The Sinner." Without renouncing the exposition of the lecture on St. James, he expanded the thought of degrees of faith, as well as of degrees in the forgiveness of sins and justification. He maintained that faith laid the foundation for the first access to Christ, and was the instrument of the first participation in forgiveness; but that faith must then proceed onward through love and the good works flowing from love, in order to be capable of appropriating Christ more and more perfectly, and of drawing more and more abundantly from the treasures of grace concealed in Him.

Whoever is acquainted with the shades of distinction on this subject which the contest with Rome renders necessary, will be prepared to find that such an essay as this did not allay the disaffection. The excitement was in fact increased, and extended its influence to a wider circle. Many who had hung on his words were offended; some of his own former pupils, to whom his writings were little short of a confession of faith, now were constrained to write against their master; and conferences, of which he used to be the very centre, were now assembled to renounce him and his doctrine. Though he resolutely maintained his innocence of any intentional abandonment of the fundamental principles of the gospel, and assumed the air of one who was perfectly tranquil on the subject, it is well known that this agitation embittered his latter days, and it is suspected that it had something to do with his comparatively sudden departure. The whole circumstance is to be deplored; for it is certain that Hengstenberg did no more than follow out to their just conclusion certain exegetical results, which a deeper pondering would have shown him to be worthless; and, on the other hand, it is equally certain that he did not abandon the guiding principles and the deepest convictions of his life. We have again and again indicated that, in our judgment, he was not a systematic theologian, or to be trusted for the definition of doctrine. While desperately faithful to the foundations of the Christian faith, and expert in defending those foundations from assault, he had no constructive faculty, and never added a stone to the superstructure of dogmatics. He had not the wisdom which was so necessary for the combination of scientific with biblical theology. He knew not the secret—the important secret—of controlling his biblical results by systematic definitions, and of moulding systematic definitions in the light of Scripture. There is an analogy of Scripture, there is an analogy of faith: each is of the utmost importance in its own sphere; but it is their mutual relation, harmony, and control that constitutes the highest gift and the most important qualification of a teacher of theology.

This, however, requires a little further explanation. In a volume lying before us, *The Christian Doctrine of Justification and the Atonement*, by Albrecht Ritschl, the matter is exhibited in a striking light by one not very well disposed towards orthodoxy. Ritschl asserts that Hengstenberg, as the head of a party, strove to bind his followers to the dogmatic definitions of Old-Lutheranism while not really faithful to them himself, and that it was only an accident which brought to light at the end the secret inconsistency of his life. This is a grave charge, coming from a man of such eminence as Ritschl, especially as his work is published in English for circulation among us. But it is a reckless charge, and one that has no real foundation. Dr. Ritschl is perfectly correct in asserting that "*for* she loved much" does not specify the reason of the woman's forgiveness, but indicates the reason for inferring that she was forgiven. And he is right also, to a certain extent, in his allegation of Hengstenberg's inaptitude for dogmatic distinctions. But if he were perfectly unbiassed, he would be ready to admit that the worst passages of the censured essays only approximate to what seems like a variation from the Lutheran doctrine of justification by faith. And against that seeming variation must be set the strong, clear, unfaltering assurance given by Hengstenberg himself, that throughout his whole life the doctrine of the Reformation had been held by him explicitly and implicitly; that this precious truth had been continually the very food of his soul, and would be to the end. There are men whose testimony to their own sincerity ought to be an end of all controversy; and there are times when that testimony is enough to outweigh a great amount of plausible argument and evidence. Hengstenberg was such a man, and his dying confessional was such a time. For ourselves, we are deeply convinced that the question with him was not a doctrinal one, but an ethical. He regarded the love which flows from forgiveness as "the fulfilling of the law;" that is, as the gracious spring and strength of all those acts of devotion and obedience which secure the complacency of the Redeemer and the rewards of grace. Giving a rather wider meaning to the terms "forgiveness" and "justification" than Lutheran dogmatics would warrant, he intended to teach that the internal righteousness and sanctification of the soul, and consequently its internal acceptability in the sight of God, goes on increasing in proportion as love increases. Firmly convinced, but most erroneously, that the Mary of loving devotion and the Mary of much forgiveness were one and the same, he stretched the language of systematic theology to meet the case of the imaginary compound of those two. For the rest, there may be degrees in the sin forgiven, in the depth and fervour of the sense of forgiveness, in the expression of that sense, and in the capability of responding to the Lord's love: all this may be admitted in harmony with the express words of the Simon-parable, and without the least infringement of the true elements of justification by faith.

Before leaving the commentaries of Hengstenberg, one more remark may be made as to their very practical and devotional character. From beginning to end he aimed at unfolding the word of God as a text that cannot be understood save by the spiritual mind, and in relation to spiritual uses. Not that he stands alone in this: he was but one of a large and increasing school of exegetes, whose pietism has done much to redeem exegesis from the frightful scientific aridity that once was its leading characteristic. He was not, perhaps, the founder of this school; but he certainly was, or rather is—for though he is gone, his works have not in this sense followed him, but are with us still—the most interesting example of it. Let the reader make the experiment: let him take the commentaries in this Foreign Theological Library, and find the driest subject—if any can be dry—and follow the expositor, he will find that, while the scientific and the lexical and the dogmatic meaning are fairly brought out, the spiritual is never forgotten. Sometimes, indeed, the proportions are not perfectly observed, but that is not often the case. And the effect is enhanced by the insertion of striking observations taken from the older writers. Hengstenberg does not often make his own practical observations: he defers in this department to Bengel, and the rich old mystical Berlenberg Bible, and the Speners and Arndts. These, once more, are interwoven with the commentary proper in a very profitable way; and this style is, on the whole, much better than that adopted in the conglomerate expositions of Lange's Series, for instance, where the critical and the doctrinal and the homiletical are kept mechanically apart. The perfect commentary is, wherever it can be found, the perfect fusion of these. Hengstenberg has aimed at this, and fairly succeeded. His works are very valuable to the preacher,—more valuable to him, perhaps, than to the systematic theologian or the miscellaneous biblical student. What he remarks in his last exegetical preface is a kind of manifesto that will suit them all :—" The time is no longer distant when every pastor worthy of his calling will make it a rule of life to read his chapter daily, as in the original text of the New Testament, so also in that of the Old Testament. The exposition of Scripture must meet such a laudable custom, which is formed even in education. There is a want of such exposition of the books of the Old Testament as truly corresponds with the requirements of the clerical office. The author has here earnestly aimed at this object. How far he has succeeded it is not for him to judge, but for those for whom he has written. It will depend very much on this whether he has succeeded in edifying, without going out of his proper sphere, by the introduction of ascetic considerations."

The last work of this indefatigable servant of Christ and of His word was that which is introduced by these preliminary notices. The veteran ends with the strain, to the music of which he attuned his life at the beginning. It might have seemed a superfluous thing to go over the track of the Old Testament history again after so many separate excursions in that territory, especially as the works of Kurtz and Keil, written on the same principles, were fresh before the public; but the author exercised a wise discretion in closing his life with this work. It is a final manifesto of his fidelity to the principles of his career, on the one hand, while, on the other, it is the depository of many a retractation, unconsciously made, of former errors, and of many a concession to fair and honourable criticism upon his works. The reader of these wholesome and readable volumes will be amply repaid, especially if he studies and ponders them. They contain a lucid account of the progressive history of the revelation of God's will, with invaluable side references to the adverse criticism of infidelity. It is wholly disencumbered of the apparatus of heavy learning, and made interesting and readable by all.

Reviewing the long series of Hengstenberg's writings, dispassionate critics will agree that they combine more of the qualities that recommend this class of works than those of any other writer who has appeared in this century. In every one of those qualities—in learning, in grace, in exactitude, in profoundness, in spirituality, in finish—he is surpassed by some other author or authors who might easily be named, but there is no other who unites them all as he does. And if to the list of his known works were added a few volumes—the number might be made very large—selected from his terse and vigorous lighter essays, his importance as an author would be very much increased. There is one drawback, that the earlier works were not subjected before his departure to a stern revision. The apologetic works might have been greatly improved; the *Commentary on the Psalms* might have been recast to advantage; and, generally, an edition of Hengstenberg's works from his own revising hand would have had a value that cannot now be attributed to them as a whole. Still there is not one of them that the theologian, rightly instructed, would like to miss from his shelves.

Hengstenberg declined rather suddenly. It has been seen that from the beginning his constitution was not sound, and that he had rarely known the satisfaction of spending a day entirely without pain. All the details of his sickness and death were in strict keeping with the tenor of his life. Some one spoke to him, when he lay ill, of the services he had been able to render to the Church. "Ah!" he replied, with a well-known wave of his hand, "that is all nothing! If any one will glorify God in me, let it be for this, that I have laboured more to fear God than cared to fear man, which is a strange thing in these days." He was full of peace, and greatly desired to depart. "From infancy," he remarked once more, "I have longed for death. When I first came to the knowledge of saving faith, and learned my vocation, this feeling retired; but the homesickness never altogether left me." Before his last communion, he was asked if he was ready to forgive all who, during the campaigns of life, had injured or grieved him, and answered, " I know none to whom I have to forgive anything. I am deeply thankful to all men who have admonished me to hold fast my fidelity in watchfulness and prayer." These words obviously had reference to the misunderstanding as to his fidelity which has been already mentioned; so does the following. He was questioned as to whether he departed in the simple faith which he had taught throughout his course. " Yes, verily do I! The blood of Christ and His sacrificial death have been my only consolation in life, and shall be my solace and hope in death." All the holy affections of his renewed nature were exhibited most impressively during a severe affliction. His charity was made perfect, as also his patience; both were delivered from every hindrance to their finished exercise, and saved from every taint of imperfection that both others and himself had mourned in them before.

As to his patience, it had been severely tested always. Hengstenberg had known severe trials. Five children had been followed to the grave, as also his faithful wife, the mother of them all. His eldest son, Immanuel, died at the age of thirty-three. He was a man like-minded with his father, his faithful companion in arms, and bound up with all his literary labours. It may be supposed, therefore, what a deep sorrow is implied in the dedication of the third volume of his *St. John:* " To the pious memory of my son Immanuel, born 30th Sept. 1830; slept in the Lord, 4th Oct. 1863. He was deeply engaged with me in this work, which occupied him shortly before his departure." This had been a very heavy calamity, the precursor of the disruption of all ties on earth; but the amazing energy of the veteran did not yield. He had serious thoughts of giving up the *Kirchenzeitung*, as well as of renouncing all other engagements. But a stern sense of duty and desire to be useful chained his limbs again to the oar, and, with a smitten heart, he continued every work on which he had been engaged; and not till the immediate approach of death did he make arrangements for a successor in the editorship of the journal.

In March 1869 he was attacked by inflammation, which

was followed by nearly three months of dropsy and great physical distress. Bereavement came again before death. His son John was removed, and then his only grandson was laid in the grave. "My God, this also!" he cried, and, folding his hands, looked steadily before him in amazement of heart. But he was spared any spiritual conflict. He had "strengthened his brethren," he was now himself strengthened. "My soul," he said, "is like a deep ocean, full of the voice of God's praise and honour." Refusing to receive the narcotics they pressed on him,—"with perfect clearness of soul I would go into eternity,"—he departed in peace.

At the funeral solemnities in Radensleben, a sermon was preached by Pastor Wölbling on Gen. xxxii. 28, in which it was forcibly shown how applicable the words were to the faithful man who had gone: who wrestled with God in prayer and faith, and prevailed; who wrestled with man also for the faith of Jesus, and likewise prevailed. Another tribute was paid, that of Rathusius: "Suddenly has been called from us a man who was the most distinguished and important Germany had for the interests of the Church, without distinction of Confessions, as men of all Confessions will admit." Such was the general strain of reference in the evangelical papers of Germany. All parties were united in the honour of one whose memory was held in esteem even by those who shrank from his severity and hated his religious earnestness. His friends were enthusiastic in their tributes: those who had suffered his fair fame to be beclouded before their eyes by prejudice artfully excited, or hasty and ill-advised resentment, forgot everything but his lifelong devotion to the truth. The man most spoken against, or most discussed, at any rate, in Lutheran Germany, was perhaps the object of a more unanimous expression of reverence and respect than any man who has departed during this century. "For forty years," says Dr. Kahnis, "so-called public opinion has connected with the name of Hengstenberg all that it feels to be distasteful in relation to our return to the faith of our fathers. Pietism, dead orthodoxy, obscurantism, fanaticism, Jesuitism, league against all enemies of progress, and whatever other name may be given to the spirits of night that progress first invents, then fears, and finally fights against. Whatever has been alleged of every representative of the faith of the Church in any age, the name of Hengstenberg is in a certain sense the representative of it. He recapitulated all their evils. And this was not an accidental circumstance. The present time has no ecclesiastical theologian who, with such energy, such perseverance, such unsparing hardness towards himself, fought against the tendencies which are the favourites of the age." The same disciple and friend says again, turning to the contemporaries of this champion of the faith: " How various are the notions which the fellows of Hengstenberg formed of him! Many who knew him only by his Old Testament writings pictured him with the simple dignity of Abraham, or the imperial spirit of Moses, or the flaming zeal of one of the prophets. To others he appeared like a true reformer,—like a genial Luther or a stern Calvin. Others thought that one of the great polemics of the sixteenth and seventeenth centuries had returned. Others, remembering the sympathy with the Herrnhuters which he had always manifested, thought him a Pietist. Some, finally, regarded him only as an ecclesiastical politician, never led by feeling, but swayed always by motives of ecclesiastical expediency. Every one of these was more or less right in his estimate of the character of Hengstenberg. But the combination of the whole in him was something altogether different."

These observations may be extended to the personal character of this venerable man. As his works were of a peculiar order, and as the general estimation placed him in an isolated and unshared place, so his character as a Christian man was stamped with an impress of distinct individuality. He seemed predestined to combine opposites in himself. He was of a phlegmatic and inert constitutional tendency, and yet no man ever led a more impetuous and earnest life. He was thoroughly affectionate, and his nature was pervaded by tenderness, which beamed through every expression and action; yet he conveyed to the world around the notion of unyielding austerity, and was a man of war through life. He cherished a fervent devotion to the person of Christ, and his religion was altogether of an emotional character, having never lost the tinge of its earliest Pietism; yet he came to distrust theoretically what he practically exhibited, wrote some severe articles against Pietism in its relations to the Church, and never indulged in much free utterance in religious things. Rejoicing in a subjective internal experience as rich as most Christians know, he yet never ceased to magnify religion in its objective and internal character,—until the last, when the approach of death seemed to give him back a certain childlike simplicity, and he talked with effusion of divine things. Among his last words were, for instance, "No orthodoxy without pietism, no piety without orthodoxy;" and this beautiful combination, which is undoubtedly the perfection of the Christian estate, he probably, if all the truth were known, had been seeking to realize through life. His charity abounded, and showed to all men, and in all the relations of life, its best fruits; and yet his judgments were often intolerant, his invectives piercing, and his spirit as a controversialist sometimes intolerably harsh. He "took the sword," and used it freely. For the sake of much heroic service done, we must forgive, even as his Master forgave, much that was intemperate in his warfare. Moreover, it must be remembered that he paid the penalty of any offence of this kind. He did not indeed "perish by the sword," but he keenly suffered; and in due time the weapon of others was used for his chastisement, and in order to the perishing of his uncharitableness. His fine character blended at the last all Christian perfections, and lost its unevenness in the unity of a perfect love.

His relations to the Christian Church and its Confessions were marked by the same peculiarity. He was born and brought up under Reformed influences; was confirmed under pietistic; but subsequently gave himself up wholly to the Lutheran creed. Yet the two abandoned elements never ceased to co-operate forming his doctrinal judgments: they wove into a fabric their unobserved threads while he was unconscious, and the result was a remarkably composite theology. The *Formula Concordiæ*, which made so noble an attempt to reconcile the conflicting tendencies and thoughts of the Reformation, he never accepted thoroughly; but his heart was faithful to the Augsburg Confession, which carried with it, as he thought, at least, his full and unwavering convictions. But he was not a dogmatic divine. Systematic theology he never thoroughly understood, and certainly contributed nothing to its modern forms. The works of the first generations of Lutheran systematic theologians—the Quenstedts, and Calovs, and Hutters, and Gerhards—he either never read or never understood. They never moulded his thinkings, as any one may see, for instance, in the theological essays appended to the volume on Ecclesiastes, especially that on the sacrifices of Scripture. In fact, with all his strictness as an advocate of the faith, he was not himself absolutely bound to any Confession. His theology was essentially biblical: the Scriptures were the norm and standard of truth to him. Tolerant enough, and even lax with regard to some points of confessional theology, he was exceedingly tenacious and even bigoted when the infallible standard was in question. It was as an advocate of Scripture that he uttered his most peremptory decisions; and it was in the name of the word of God that he condemned so unsparingly the manifold errors of the day. Dr. Kahnis remarks on this subject: "By the kingdom of God he did not understand the Lutheran Church, nor the kingdom of Protestantism, but the believing world as it pervades all the Confessions. With his strong realism, which always demanded a firm foundation, he required in the Church immoveable authorities and fixed norms. The authority of authorities, the norm of norms, was to him the Bible. A theologian who seeks in Scripture the unbending rule appointed of God and written by His Spirit, will be strongly disposed to insist upon the authenticity, credibility, and integrity of every jot and tittle of that word. We have seen, however, that Hengstenberg pressed this requirement of fixed norms beyond the demands of the Reformers and orthodox teachers of Lutheranism, and involved himself thereby in inextricable difficulties. In this legal position to the Bible we may find the principle of that categorical tone which he assumed in the *Kirchenzeitung*. It was not given to him to exhibit facts according to the laws of historical objectivity, to investigate them in their inmost motives, to deal gently with developing movements, to bear with the weak, to repel kindly the error. Things under the moon have commonly two sides; but Hengstenberg approved of no mixture. The grey must be either white or black; the green must be blue or yellow. In criticism he saw only unbelief, in speculation only self-deification, in mediating theology only the theology of halves, in the Gustavus-Adolphus union only a blending of belief and unbelief. Hengstenberg showed his own peculiar strength and idiosyncrasy when he painted the shady side of Church and State in apocalyptic colours, and poured out threatenings and promises accordingly. But, after all, he who loves the truth must confess that in this fearless and unsparing treatment of friends and foes, kings and people alike, there was something exceedingly grand, which suggested a parallel with the witnesses of the old covenant." This passage fairly represents the general feeling with regard to Hengstenberg among the orthodox of modern Germany. They admire his principle of deep devotion to the word of God, but seem to sigh over it as a hopeless ideal. They reverence the simple grandeur of the censures which, in the name of the truth, were denounced on error; but think that it savours also of Old Testament severity, and entangles men in hopeless difficulties. But there can be no doubt upon one point,—that men of such unbending firmness and simplicity of faith are the pillars of the modern Church, and, under God, the only hope of Christendom.

In Germany, however, all things religious and confessional are complicated by their relations with the Union between the Churches. This was through life a chronic embarrassment to Hengstenberg; indeed, it was in some sense an hereditary one. Almost every principle, save that of charity and peace, warred in his mind against the Union. He was not what might be called a rigid Lutheran, and yet sufficiently so to make him recoil from a surrender to any scheme of compromise with the Calvinistic Confessions. He was in spirit much attached to some of the doctrines of the

Reformed Churches, but not enough to reconcile himself to
their infusion into public formularies and rubrics. However, as a devoted adherent of another union,—that of
Church and State,—he was constrained to accept what was
an accomplished fact. Hence, in the ten years of conflict
between the unbending Silesian Lutherans and the Union,
he was obliged to consent to what he did not in his secret
soul approve. But it was the national Church that he sided
with, not the Union as such. In the year 1844, his annual
Vorwort showed how gloomy were his views of the Union,
and that he was fast preparing to be its opponent. After his
experiences of the General Synod of 1846, and the revolutionary year 1848, the ceaseless vacillations of the Government, he took a very decided attitude of hostility to it. But
these are questions with which the memorial of Hengstenberg has more to do in Germany than in England.

The same may be said of his specific views as to the
relations of the Church with the State in Prussia. It has
been remarked that Hengstenberg held very high and in
some respects very peculiar opinions on this subject. They
were opinions which largely influenced his practice, and gave
a tone to his writings. Through his paper he was a perpetual censor of public affairs,—one whose voice was heard,
directly or indirectly, on every subject, rising shrill and
clear above the din of strife. Like an ancient prophet in
the theocracy, he brought the principles of divine truth to
bear on every question, not shrinking from its application to
any persons involved, from the highest to the lowest. It
would need a tolerably extensive acquaintance with the
various history, domestic and civil, of his fatherland, to
understand how great a power he was in this capacity of
advocate-general. He judged every question of politics and
morals, education, divorce, trades' unions, international commerce, from a purely scriptural point of view, and therefore
often came into serious collision with public sentiment,
whether expressed by philosophers or by the common people
His conservatism was consistently, even with chivalrous
consistency, carried into everything. Obedience to the
throne was closely allied with obedience to the King of

kings. He distrusted the popular voice in government, whether in the making or in the administering of laws. In ecclesiastical matters he was no friend to the massing of men together in presbyteries and synods, though, as may be supposed, his expedients for abolishing such a large representative element were of a rather grotesque description. He loved to dwell in the times and scenes of God's manifestation of Himself through select agencies. The ideal was always present to him of the one God acting through one instrument, revealing His purposes and plans to the silent thinker and earnest pleader, while passing by the tumultuous assemblies of the rulers of the Church. In fact, he lived in a modern and unrealizable theocracy,—an ideal which most men besides himself saw to involve an anachronism. It was not a hierarchy in the State that he wanted, nor a merely preaching synagogue, nor a temple of ritualistic offering. His theory was faithful to the universal priesthood as acknowledged by the State, and in one sense constituting the Church itself. In this, and in many other respects that might be indicated, he was a remarkable combination of Luther and Calvin, by turns the one or the other preponderating, but the latter having the ascendency.

For nearly fifty years this noble-minded scholar and Christian instructed his generation, exerting an influence not surpassed by that of any other man upon his own country, and, through the translation of his works and the echoes of his influence, influencing the Christians of other lands. He is gone, and his works follow him. His works also remain, and it is long before they will cease to be standards of authority. In time, however, they will cease to be such; but his name will for ever take high rank among those who have devoted their lives to the *Testimony of Jesus*, to its vindication and enforcement, both in the Old Testament and in the New.

HISTORY OF THE KINGDOM OF GOD

UNDER THE OLD TESTAMENT.

SECOND PERIOD—THIRD SECTION.

THE PERIOD OF THE LAW; FROM MOSES TO
THE BIRTH OF CHRIST.

THE PERIOD OF THE JUDGES; FROM JOSHUA'S DEATH TO
THE ELECTION OF SAUL.

§ 1.

CHRONOLOGICAL SURVEY.

IN no part of sacred history is chronology of greater importance than here. The view taken by each one of the condition of the Israelites during this period must be essentially different, according as he comes to the conclusion that the contents of 1 Sam. i.–vii. run parallel with those of Judg. xi.–xvi., so that the two one-sided accounts supplement each other; or assumes that they both refer to different times, and Eli first attained the dignity of high priest after Samson was already dead, or, as some believe, a considerable period later, so that between the judges and Samuel there would be a gap, a space of time of which we know nothing at all. We must therefore begin with the chronology. This question has been considerably facilitated by Keil, in his chronological examination concerning the years which elapsed between the exodus of the Israelites out of Egypt and the building of the temple of Solomon, in the *Dorpater Beiträgen zu den theologischen Wissenschaften*, 2d vol., Hamburg 1833, p. 303 ff., which has its best analogy among the ancients in the close translation and acute examination of the different views by Vitringa in the *Hypotyposis hist. sacræ*, p. 29 sqq. The intermediate researches of Joh. Dav. Michaelis have only served to complicate the matter. Bertheau also, in his *Commentary on the Book of Judges*, Leipzic 1845, and Ewald, in utter ignorance of the researches of Keil, have only obscured the question by a multitude of new chronological fancies.

We have a firm starting-point for chronological inquiry in 1 Kings vi. 1, according to which 480 years elapsed between the exodus of Israel out of Egypt and the building of Solomon's temple. It cannot be the task of the chronologist to harmonize this statement with that made by St. Paul in Acts xiii. 20, in a discourse which he held in the synagogue at Antioch in Pisidia, where he makes the period of the Judges to have lasted only 450 years. Vitringa supposes that the chronological statements in the apostle's discourse are glosses interpolated afterwards in an unsuitable place. This view is based on the fact that the chronological determination in Paul is merely a passing one. For the apostle's object, accuracy was not demanded: he was not called upon to oppose and correct the chronological view then prevalent. For him, it was enough to give the historical view—a general chronological substratum. A century more or less was of no importance to him. That he has no intention of encroaching on the sphere of the chronologists, and putting them in fetters, he expressly declares by the ὡς, *towards, about*, which takes away the support from all those who make his statement the starting-point of chronological calculations, and likewise from those who charge the apostle with a chronological error. The 450 years exactly agree with the numbers of the book of Judges from the first slavery to the death of Eli, recorded in the books of Samuel, which it was then the custom to reckon together, without considering that some of the periods might run parallel and thus include one another. Hence our only task is to bring the general chronological statement in the books of Kings into harmony with the particular determinations in the historical books. The following reasons make it necessary to disclaim a chronology definite and accurate in every single point:—1. Some chronological data are entirely wanting in the Old Testament, viz. the determination of the time which elapsed from the first division of the land of Canaan to the first hostile oppression—that of the Mesopotamians. Likewise the statement of the year of Samuel's judgeship and Saul's reign. 2. On glancing at the chronological accounts of the book of Judges, we are at once struck with the circumstance that the numbers are so often *round*, more frequently than is generally the case in chronologically accurate history. Half of the numbers are of this kind, such as 10, 20, 40, 80, 7. But this discovery only attains its full significance when placed in connection with the whole historical character of the book of Judges. Taking this fact into consideration, it appears to us *à priori* improbable that it was the author's intention to give a chronology accurate to the year and day. For this the author is far too little of a chronicler, far too much of a prophet. Studied chronological precision would be at variance with the care with which in the historical representation he leaves out everything not subservient to his main object. These defects, however, are of comparatively small importance. The periods left indefinite are but few—only the two already mentioned; and even with regard to them, we have data which enable us to form an approximate determination. Nor must we allow the *round* numbers in the book of Judges to lead us astray. For in the definite numbers which are mixed up with them, such as 18, 22, 23, we have a guarantee that they are only put there when the definite number came very near the round one— 40, for example, for 39 or 41; and this want of precision can exercise the less influence upon the whole, since the too much and the too little almost balance one another when such a course is pursued for a long period.

We shall now turn to particulars, beginning with a chronological survey, and then going on to discuss the various difficult and doubtful points. The 480 years are divided thus:—

The time from the exodus out of Egypt to the death of Moses,	40 years.
From the death of Moses to the distribution of the land (compare the earlier observation),	7 years.
To the invasion of the Mesopotamians,	10 years.
From the beginning of the bondage to the Mesopotamians to the death of Jair, the separate dates in the book of Judges, ch. iii. 8–x. 3, together amount to	301 years.
So that from the exodus out of Egypt to the death of Jair we get a sum-total of	358 years.

We now find in the book of Judges a series of parallel dates, Israel being attacked simultaneously by the Ammonites in the east and by the Philistines in the west. We shall here follow the latter chronological stream. The oppression by the Philistines lasted in all 40 years; comp. Judg. xv. 20. Of these, the *first* 20 years are the last 20 of the 40 years' priesthood of Eli. The acts of Samson belong to the *last* 20. The period ends with the victory over the Philistines under Samuel. These 40 years added to the 358 make 398.

Hence there still remain 82 years of the sum-total. Of these, 40 belong to the reign of David, and 3 to the reign of Solomon until the building of the temple. Thus we get a remainder of 39 years for the judgeship of Samuel and the kingship of Saul.

Let us now turn to the other chronological series. The oppression by the Ammonites lasted 18 years, according to chap. x. 8. Jephthah was judge for 6 years, Ebzan for 7, Elon 10, Abdon 8. The whole series makes 49 years. They came to an end in the time of Samuel's judgeship. Jephthah's appearance takes place under the pontificate of Eli, shortly before the appearance of Samson. The victory over the Philistines under Samuel takes place in the last year of the judge Elon. We shall now consider separate particulars.

1. Many have thought it necessary to lengthen the time between the (first) distribution of the law and the invasion of the Mesopotamians (Bertheau, for example, computes the time from Joshua's death to the invasion of the Mesopotamians at forty years), from misapprehension of the passage

Josh. xxiv. 31, and Judg. ii. 7, according to which the Israelites served the Lord as long as Joshua lived, and the elders, who lived long after Joshua. These words are not to be so misapprehended as to lead us to suppose that the Israelites were absolutely faithful to the Lord up to the moment when the last of the elders died, and were absolutely unfaithful from the time that his eyes were closed. They are not inconsistent with the fact that the depravity had already begun to germinate in the last years of Joshua, and in a short space of time acquired so much power that punishment became necessary. This punishment does not presuppose the complete apostasy of the whole nation, but rather implies the contrary by its mildness and short duration. Here also we see how perilous it is to reason immediately from the universal to the particular. That the period cannot have been much longer, appears with certainty from the fact that Othniel, who set Israel free after eight years' bondage, was a valiant hero already in Joshua's day, at the time of the occupation of the land; comp. Josh. xv. 17, Judg. i. 13.

2. Throughout the whole period from the invasion of the Mesopotamians to the death of Jair, the chronological reckoning proceeds quite simply. One date does not cover another. The events are all narrated in chronological succession. Only the victory of Shamgar over the Philistines occurs in the intermediate period between the Moabitish and the Canaanitish oppression, in which Israel on the whole enjoyed rest, as appears from the circumstance that Judg. iii. 31 neither gives the date of this act of heroism, nor records the fact that Shamgar judged Israel.

3. The most important questions relate to the time towards the end of the period of the judges. First, whether the oppression of the Philistines succeeded that of the Ammonites, or whether they were simultaneous. We decide unhesitatingly in favour of the latter view. Judg. x. 7 speaks decidedly for it. We are first told how the children of Israel did evil again in the sight of the Lord, and especially how they served the gods of the Philistines and of the Ammonites; and then we read: "And the anger of the Lord was hot against Israel, and He sold them into the hands of

the Philistines, and into the hands of the children of Ammon." Then there follows a full account of the oppression by the Ammonites, Israel's repentance, and their deliverance by the hand of Jephthah, ver. 10–xi. 33. Chap. xiii.–xvi. are occupied with what the Israelites had to suffer from the Philistines, and with the help vouchsafed to them by the Lord. If the oppression by the Philistines had only occurred after that by the Ammonites, how could the author put them together, as he does in chap. x. 7, even placing that by the Philistines first? That the oppression of the Philistines in x. 7 is not distinct from that in chap. xiii.–xvi. is self-evident. For if they be separated, it follows that in the first oppression by the Philistines we have no account whatever of the subsequent course of events, or of the saving mercy of the Lord, which is quite at variance with the character of the book, whose author in the very introduction represents the merciful deliverances as the object of his writing, no less than the righteous oppressions, and who elsewhere records sin, punishment, repentance, and deliverance, in regular succession, observing the same course even in the Ammonitic invasion.

4. If the beginning of the oppression by the Philistines be definitely fixed, the question arises as to its end. Its duration is set down at forty years in the book of Judges. These forty years, however, reach beyond the events which are recorded in the book of Judges. For Samson, with whose death the book of Judges concludes, was only beginning to deliver Israel, chap. xiii. 5; he judged Israel in the days of the Philistines twenty years, chap. xv. 20. When he dies, the power of the Philistines is still unbroken; his deeds were rather proofs that the God of Israel *could* deliver His people, prophecies of future deliverance, than themselves calculated to effect it. If we now turn from the book of Judges to the contiguous books of Samuel, we find ourselves here again upon the same ground on which the author of the book of Judges left us. In chap. iv. we find the Philistines at war with the Israelites; and the misfortune of the latter reaches its highest point in the fact that the ark of the covenant is taken by the Philistines,—an event in conse-

quence of which Eli dies. There can be no doubt that the oppression of the Philistines, to which this battle belongs, is the same of which the book of Judges treats; for otherwise the one would want a beginning, the other an end. But the oppression by the Philistines in the books of Samuel lasted twenty years after that catastrophe. It was brought to an end by the great victory which the Lord gave to the Israelites, after they had earnestly turned to Him under the influence of Samuel, 1 Sam. vii. 14. According to this determination, the last twenty years of the forty years of Eli's priesthood fall in the time of the oppression by the Philistines; the *last* twenty years of the oppression by the Philistines, which are left quite void in the books of Samuel, are filled out by the deeds of Samson narrated in the book of Judges. According to chap. xiii. 5, the Philistines reigned over Israel already at the time of Samson's birth. While still a youth, Samson began his exploits, chap. xiv. 4. Assuming his age to have been twenty years, the end of his twenty years' judgeship, which began with the death of Eli, borders on the beginning of Samuel's judgeship, which was based on the decisive victory over the Philistines. Thus everything was in the most beautiful order. For the space of twenty years, the second half of Eli's pontificate, Israel is in complete subjection. At the end of this time the climax of misfortune is reached by the taking away of the ark of the covenant. Then Israel rises again. For twenty years Samson makes the Philistines feel the ascendency of the God of Israel, supplemented by the reformatory activity of Samuel, which prepares the way for a lasting and complete victory. This victory takes place immediately after Samson's death. At the time when Israel's hope is carried to the grave with Samson, it re-awakens more gloriously with Samuel. The objections which have been brought against this arrangement may easily be set aside. It has been thought strange that nothing is said of Eli in the book of Judges; nothing of Samson in the books of Samuel. To this objection the true answer has been given by Joach. Hartmann, *Chronol.* S. 157: " Eli non nominatur in historia judicium, quia ipsi cum militia; Simson non nominatur in libris Samuelis, quia ipsi cum ecclesia et Samuele nihil negotii fuit." Notwithstanding the clear and definite statement at the very beginning of the book of Judges, it has been too often forgotten that it was throughout not the author's intention to give a complete history of this period, but that he only occupies himself with a certain class of events, with the acts of the judges in a limited sense, the men whose authority among the people had its foundation in the outward deliverances which the Lord vouchsafed to the nation by their instrumentality. In this sense Eli was by no means a judge, although in 1 Sam. iv. 18 it is said that he judged Israel for forty years. Eli was high priest, and merely exercised over the affairs of the nation a more or less extended *free* influence, which had its origin in his priestly dignity. Hence the author of the book of Judges had nothing to do with Eli; and we are not at liberty to conclude, from the fact that he does not mention him, that Eli's activity was no longer felt in the time of which he treats. And the author of the books of Samuel had just as little to do with Samson. His attention is fixed on Samuel, whose activity stood in no relation to that of Samson, had nothing whatever to do with it; and he mentions Eli only because his history was so closely interwoven with that of Samuel. If this be apprehended, the second objection disappears of itself. According to this view, the first book of Samuel was not so much a continuation of the history, as a partial repetition of that which belonged to the period described by the book of Judges. The book of Samuel takes up the thread of the history where the author of the book of Judges lets it fall, towards the end of the forty years' oppression by the Philistines, in 1 Sam. vii. But it was not enough for the author's aim to describe the new formation of things as established by Samuel, without repeating certain preparatory events which the author of the book of Judges had no object in communicating. Before narrating the decisive appearance of Samuel, he feels it necessary to make us acquainted with his personality and the circumstances of his appearance. It is clear that the author only speaks of Eli with reference to Samuel, from the whole manner of his representation. The most important events—for example, the manner in which the high-priesthood passed over from the family of Eleazar to that of Ithamar—he entirely omits. Finally, it has been objected that, according to this computation, the activity of those judges named in the book of Judges after the oppression of the Ammonites would coincide with the judgeship of Samson, and in part with that of Samuel. But this objection is based on an unhistorical conception of the office of judge. The judges were judges in Israel, each one belonged to the whole nation; but none was judge over all Israel, with the exception of Othniel in the very beginning of the period: most of them acted only among single tribes, or among a few neighbouring tribes. The judges enumerated in Judg. xii. 8–15 acted only among the eastern and northern tribes, which were not involved in the oppression of the Philistines.

5. The only point of controversy which now remains is the determination of the length of Samuel's judgeship, which began with the end of the oppression by the Philistines, soon after the death of Samson; and of Saul's kingship. With regard to this we have no definite and explicit statements. That it is not possible to go much beyond the thirty-nine years at which we have already estimated this time, nor to attribute forty years to the reign of Saul alone, by reason of the general statement in Acts xiii. 21, which probably includes both Samuel and Saul, appears from the combination of several circumstances, for which we must refer to Keil, S. 358 ff., since the chronology here has not grown together with the history, as in the former examinations.

As a guarantee for the correctness of our chronological calculation, we have not only 1 Kings vi. 1, but also a second passage, Judg. xi. 26, where Jephthah says that Israel dwelt in the land east of the Jordan, conquered in the last year of Moses, for 300 years, until he fought against Ammon. Our calculation gave 318 years from the death of Moses to that of Jair, after which came the Ammonitic invasion. Bertheau is obliged to confess that his chronological computation stands in glaring opposition to these two general statements, and in so doing has passed judgment on it. From the exodus out of Egypt to the building of the temple he calculates more than 600 years. This large number of years he gets by calculating, on his own responsibility, forty years for "the sinful generation after Joshua," by denying the synchronism of the Ammonitic and the Philistic oppression, and extending the judgeship of Samson, which he estimates at forty instead of twenty years, beyond the oppression by the Philistines.

§ 2.

INTRODUCTORY REMARKS.

The leading points of view for the history of this period are given by the author of the book of Judges himself, in chap. i.–iii. 6. In many respects it bears a similarity to the forty years of the march through the wilderness. It also is to be regarded as a time of temptation. God's palpable grace, as it had been experienced by the nation under Joshua, was in some measure withdrawn. The nation was left more to its own development, that it might gain a more perfect knowledge of itself. For the godlessness which was rather suppressed than rooted out soon asserted itself in its peculiar form; Nature freed herself from the burdensome restraint which had been laid upon her, and threw off the elements which were foreign to her. As a matter of course, the godlessness was accompanied by idolatry, the expression of it peculiar to the age. Yet, even in the time of its deepest degradation, the nation still retained so much piety that it did not openly revolt against the Lord, but sought to combine the heathen vanity with its own worship. The choice of Israel was shown just as much, perhaps even more than in the deliverances, by the fact that punishment invariably followed sin. If this had ceased to be the case, Israel would soon no longer have been Israel. By punishment sin was always recognised as such; and when only the beginnings of repentance were visible, God's mercy removed the punishment. The nation scarcely got beyond the beginnings during this period. The rapidity with which they always sink back into their old sins, shows that they had not yet made very much advance, that this period could only have been preparation for another, that there must be a reformation, built on more solid grounds than the former ones. Towards the end of the period there stepped forth the man whom God had prepared for this purpose—Samuel, the counterpart of Moses. From his ministry we first learn to understand the character of this period. It was intended to prepare the ground for the reception of the seed which he was to scatter. Before he could succeed, like a second Moses, in bringing the law nearer to the heart of the people, they must become thoroughly acquainted with the carnal wickedness of their heart by long and painful experience, as had been the case under the *first* Moses. For centuries they must sigh under the oppression of sin and its consequences, that they might joyfully welcome the deliverance, and willingly submit to the regulations which secured to the new reformation a firm duration. But the fact that Israel passed through all these heavy trials without fundamental injury, that after every grievous fall they still rose up again, that Samuel found in them a point of contact for his vigorous reformation,—all this shows that the efficacy of Moses had not been in vain, that it had penetrated to the innermost soul of the nation, and there implanted truths which were indestructible. Divine seed is like oil, which, however much it may be shaken together with water, still comes to the surface again. And for individuals who find themselves involved in severe struggles with their corrupt nature, it is very consolatory to see this truth confirmed in so grand a way in the history of this time.

But there is justice in the remark of Ewald: "This long period is one of many new experiences, but not of new truths fully recognised and accomplished; its greatness consists in the spiritual possessions which it has already won." To maintain these against all temptations, this was the task. Progress belonged to a later time. In this period the standpoint of the ἐκλογή was purely conservative. That which here asserted itself as progress went for nothing.

It is generally supposed that the author of the book of

Judges represents the fact that the Israelites, in opposition to the command of Moses, failed to exterminate the Canaanites, but allowed them to dwell among them, and intermarried with them, as one of the main causes of the corruption among the Israelites. But on closer examination we find that throughout the whole introduction no blame is attached to the Israelites on this account; the non-expulsion of the Canaanites is not made a reproach to the Israelites, but is attributed to *divine,* not *human* causality. That the author attributes the incomplete conquest of the land under Joshua to innocent incapacity, we see clearly from chap. i. 19, "And he drave out the inhabitants of the mountain, but could not drive out the inhabitants of the valley, because they had chariots of iron;" which does not, however, exclude the probability that individual idleness and want of faith had something to do with it. Nor can the non-expulsion of the Canaanites be made a direct reproach against the Israelites after Joshua's death. According to chap. ii. 21, they wanted the requisite power, because the Lord had withdrawn His promises of victory as a punishment for their apostasy. Most probably the Israelites were never deficient in the desire to expel the Canaanites utterly. Their own interest was too much involved in it. The point of view from which the author regarded the incomplete victory over the Canaanites under Joshua may be better seen from chap. ii. 22 ff., iii. 1. (Chap. ii. 21 shows plainly that the expeditions recorded in chap. i. belong to Joshua's time, and that afterwards nothing more of any importance was done against the Canaanites: "I also will not henceforth drive out any from before them of the nations which Joshua left when he died.") According to these passages, a considerable remnant of the Canaanites was left for the trial and eventually the punishment of the Israelites,—a theory which agrees excellently with the character of the period of the judges. Sin in man can only be completely rooted out by making him pass through temptation, by giving him outwardly the opportunity for its development. Without struggle, no victory. In contact with the world, the people of God must prove themselves to be such; gradually and through many a severe fall they must become ripe for their vocation. It was from this point of view that the choice of a land for Israel had been made. It has been justly remarked, that if the intention had been to spare Israel the struggle, to give them a quiet retired life, calm development, and peaceful relations, a less suitable land than this could scarcely have been chosen,—a land bordering on the sea, much disturbed, influenced in many ways from without, adapted for intercourse with other countries. Intercourse with the Canaanites also gave the Israelites abundant opportunity for strife. That they stood the temptation badly was to be expected beforehand, since human nature is so constituted, that the inner alienation of a people from the world is slow to follow their outer withdrawal from it. The sensuous religion of the Canaanites found a powerful ally in the heart of the Israelites; it exactly answered to the demands of their nature. The easy unrestrained life was far more congenial to them than that enjoined by Moses, circumscribed by the strict requirements of the law, and demanding continual self-sacrifice; comp. Josh. xxiv. 19. The splendour and the luxury which prevailed in the centres of Canaanitish commerce had the effect of making them ashamed of their poor mode of life. The inspiration which had arisen under Joshua disappeared more and more in proportion as the objects which had called it forth were withdrawn. Israel became secularized. The consciousness and the inner wall of partition which separated them from the Canaanites disappeared. Now was realized in them the eternal law by which he who is called and chosen by God, when he surrenders himself to the world, is punished by the world. The instruments of temptation were transformed into instruments of punishment. God had already bound the rods before the evil had been perpetrated. The Canaanites became to Israel in reality what, in accordance with the threats of Moses and Joshua, they were to become to them in event of their apostasy—snares and nets, pricks in their sides and thorns in their eyes.

The servants of divine justice were established not only on all the borders of their land, but also within it. But just as that which was already attained by Israel intellectually and spiritually at last got the upper hand in spite of all perilous fluctuation, so likewise the external. Under Joshua they had conquered the high places of the land, and these the Canaanites never were able to reconquer. From these heights, in the course of centuries, they finally succeeded in conquering the valleys also, which the Canaanites had retained for a long time. However much appearances might be against it, yet in the end it became manifest that the land was really conquered under Joshua.

The leadings of divine providence were shown not only in this preparation of means for temptation and punishment, but also in the fact that the original constitution of the Canaanites continued throughout the whole period, which made it impossible for them to offer permanent resistance to their enemies in the usual way. Each tribe was well organized in itself, but an external firm bond of union was wanting which should keep the twelve tribes together. This was especially the case after the mere personal authority of Moses and Joshua had ceased, the latter of whom named no successor. As long as they remained faithful to the Lord, and as often as they returned to Him, this was not felt to be a misfortune. We see this plainly in the history of Joshua to the time of the assembling of the whole nation shortly before his death, and of the war against the Benjamites in the beginning of the period of the judges, in which "the congregation was gathered together as one man." If their faith were strong, the invisible Ruler rendered them infinitely more help than they could have had from a visible head; but if their faith were lost, if the living God became transformed into a mere abstraction, all the disadvantages of this form of government became apparent. The twelve tribes fell asunder, the externally weak bonds by which they were united were loosened, self-interest asserted itself, and the nation became an easy prey to the enemy. If they then humbled themselves before God, in His wisdom He gave them help which was only *temporary*. The bond of union formed by individual judges was in every case dissolved on their death. First in connection with a vigorous reformation, and firmly-established regulations for the security of its permanance, was a standing earthly representation of the divine supremacy given to the nation in kingship. "It was better," says Ewald, "that human kingship generally should not come while the men were still wanting who could have established it in the right way."

The long series of heathen attacks to which we see Israel exposed during this period, is only rightly understood when we find its main cause in the heathen aversion towards Israel as the nation of the Lord, which, beginning at the time of their elevation to this dignity, runs through the whole history. That assumption of being the only chosen, that self-isolation, which seemed to the heathen consciousness to be an *odium generis humani*, was at all times an incentive to bitter hatred for those nations with which Israel came into contact. Almost all the wars which Israel had to undertake were religious wars. Where would it be possible to find an example of such ineradicable hatred between two nations, continuing for centuries with unabated violence? Amalek attacks Israel already in the march through the wilderness, because they declared themselves to be the people of God, Ex. xvii. 16.

The history of the time of the judges first appears in its true light when we regard it as not purely external, but as having a lively reference to our own hearts, and to the relations of the present, when it forms a mirror in which we see the image of man in his depravity, and of God in His righteousness and mercy. This history then forms a rich source of edification to us. We shall now first notice the separate events of this period in succession, and then conclude with remarks on the civil constitution and the religious history.

§ 3.

PRINCIPAL EVENTS.

1. The two events which are narrated in the appendix to the book of Judges, as examples of the licentiousness which prevailed during this period, belong to the time shortly after Joshua's death. This determination of time can be subject

to no doubt, since, according to chap. xx. 28, Phinehas, the contemporary of Joshua, was then still high priest. The first event, the making of an image by Micah, is worthy of special note, because it shows us the transition from the pure worship of Jehovah, as it existed in the time of Joshua even among the masses, to idolatry, to which the inwardly faithless portion of the nation abandoned themselves far into the period of the judges, but in such a way that they always sought after some mediation between it and the worship of Jehovah. Here we have not to do with the ἐκλογή, but rather with such as represent the worse tendency. Micah, who first had the image made, is a thief, upon whom the curse of a mother rests; and the Danites, who appropriate it in a thievish way, are rude associates bent on adventure. And yet we find Jehovah here, and nothing but Jehovah. At a later period, persons of their disposition would certainly have given themselves up to the worship of Baal and of Ashera. Private worship—in this also we see that we are still near the God-fearing and legal time of Joshua—appears throughout as an imitation of the public worship of Jehovah, which alone makes its origin comprehensible. There are four objects named as having been made by Micah,—a graven image, a molten image, ephod, and teraphim. But we infer from several passages that these objects, though separable, were joined together. The cast served as a pedestal for the image. With the ephod the image was clothed, and in the pocket of the ephod were the teraphim. The image served as a substitute for the ark of the covenant in the sanctuary; the ephod was an imitation of the ephod of the high priest; the teraphim served instead of the twelve precious stones which formed the foundation of the Urim and Thummim, a spiritual thing, and were present in the חשן. Instead of the high priest, Micah hires a Levite. At the close of the narrative it is stated that the image of Micah remained among the sons of Dan until the day of the captivity of the land. To this determination of time another more obvious one runs parallel, from which it receives its light, viz. all the days that the house of God was in Shiloh. Since the tabernacle of the covenant remained in Shiloh till the capture of the ark by the Philistines, and was then transferred to Nob, the "captivity of the land" can only refer to that Philistine catastrophe. Just at this time we find a most suitable opportunity for the abandonment of the illegal worship in Dan. Towards the end of the period of the Philistines the great reformation under Samuel took place, in which every illegal worship was laid aside; comp. 1 Sam. vii. 4.

The second event, the war of extermination against the Benjamites, caused by the shameful deed of the inhabitants of Gibeah, is remarkable in so far as it shows us that in the time immediately after Joshua the national unity still continued among Israel. The nation rose up with great energy *en masse*. We find the basis of this still existing national unity in the continuance of a considerable fund of pious disposition. That the lusts through which Israel afterwards fell into sin were already at that time springing up, we learn from the example of a whole town, which in moral degeneracy had already sunk to the depth of Sodomites, and from the conduct of the Benjamites, whose horror of sin is so weak, that it is outweighed by a morbid sense of honour, by displeasure,—conduct which arouses the interference of the whole nation in what was supposed to be the private affair of the tribe. In the mass of the nation, however, this horror is exceptionally strong. They fear lest they should call down the judgments of God upon themselves in omitting to punish the wickedness. Bertheau excellently remarks: "The community indeed waged war—a fearful war—against their own flesh and blood; but when under the kings do we find Israel so unanimously, vigorously, and earnestly undertaking the most difficult warfare for the highest possessions? Here we feel the influence of the elevated time of Moses and Joshua." It appears strange that the tribes at first suffer a double defeat, notwithstanding the righteousness of their cause and the fact that they fought in the service of the Lord and at His command. We find an explanation of this on a closer consideration of the account in ch. xx. 18 ff. At first they only go up (to the place where the ark of the covenant was, and the high priest), and *ask*. Then they go up, and *weep* and ask. Finally, they go up, not merely ambassadors, but all the sons of Israel, the whole nation, and weep and sit there before the Lord, and fast and bring burnt-offerings and peace-offerings. In this gradation we have the explanation of the varying result. At first they are impenitent, then there is a slight beginning of repentance, and finally it is complete. To the righteousness of the cause, which Israel thought sufficient, was now added individual righteousness, and the victory was theirs. The event affords a glimpse into the working of God's retributive justice. Lightfoot makes an excellent remark on this subject, only that he takes too narrow a view of the guilt of Israel, when he makes it to consist mainly in not punishing the illegal worship of which the former narrative treats. Postquam deus usus erat Benjamine ad exsequendum judicium suum contra Israelem ob non punitam idololatriam, utitur porro Israele ad puniendum Benjaminitam ob Gibeam judicio non permissam. In an awful manner the divine retribution was made manifest in what befell the Levitical concubine, who may be regarded as a type of Israel. She had been faithless to her husband in secret, and must now serve to satisfy the coarse desires of the inhabitants of Gibeah, till she dies. The conduct of Israel towards the Benjamites has been very falsely judged, when it has been attributed to motives of barbarous cruelty and revenge. The question in chap. xx. 28, "Shall I yet again go out to battle against the children of Benjamin my brother?" shows how far the thought of carnal revenge was removed from the people, even after they had sustained the most trying loss. They would willingly have given up the thing, but thought it necessary to fulfil the duty pointed out to them by the Lord, that the curse might not pass over from those who were guilty to them. This is evident from the words which they use to the Benjamites before the commencement of the battle, "that we may put away evil from Israel," which contain a verbal reference to the command so frequently reiterated in Deuteronomy; comp. Deut. xiii. 5, xvii. 7. After what happened, we find an expression of the deepest sorrow in chap. xxi. 3: "O Lord God of Israel, why is this come to pass in Israel, that there should be to-day one tribe lacking in Israel?" They weep before the Lord. That what was done to the Benjamites was חרם—the same on a large scale as was now done to the evil-doers on a small scale—appears from chap. xxi. 11, according to which the inhabitants of Jabesh in Gilead were punished with the חרם, because they drew back from the holy war, and by their refusal to take part in punishing the sinners revealed their own love for sin. "And this is the thing that ye shall do, Ye shall utterly destroy every male, and every woman that hath lain by man" (תחרימו). The analogous treatment of the inhabitants of Jabesh is here expressly characterized as a curse. This and the proceedings taken against Benjamin are based on the passage Deut. xiii. 12 ff., which forms the key to the whole thing. We here learn how an Israelitish town, which had incurred the guilt of worshipping other gods, was cursed with all that was in it, after the deed had been carefully investigated,— men and cattle were slain with the edge of the sword, and all the spoil burnt, "that the Lord may turn from the fierceness of His anger, and show thee mercy, and have compassion upon thee, and multiply thee, as He hath sworn unto thy fathers." "Quod admodum rigidum et severum mandatum, illi jam exsecuti sunt," says Michaelis. In the account of the treatment of the Benjamites and of the inhabitants of Jabesh-Gilead, we have verbal reference to this law, in accordance with the invariable habit of the authors of the book of Judges and the books of Samuel, who never actually quote, but have the law constantly in their mind, and by verbal reference to it indicate their judgment. Thus the Israelites acted as servants of divine justice. It is true that in the law there is no express mention of the worship of other gods. But the ground of their punishableness is their secession from the living and holy God, and this revealed itself in both cases by unmistakeable signs. And when this was the case, it was possible even at that time to conclude with certainty respecting the existence of the special declaration regarding putting away strange gods, which was expressly named in the law. The rulers of the nation quote the authority of the law, not only in the punishment, but also in that which they afterwards do for the restoration of Benjamin, in the measures which they adopt to make the weak remnant a new seminary. The words, "that a tribe be not destroyed out of Israel," in chap. xxi. 17, which they give as a reason, rest upon Deut. xxv. 5, 6, where, as a motive for the decree that the eldest son of a Levirate marriage should take the name of the deceased, we find, "that his name be not put out of Israel." They avail themselves of a conclusion *à minori ad majus*, reduce the small to its idea, and hence infer the large: if the Lord therefore cares for the individual, how much more ought we to interest ourselves in the preservation of a whole tribe, and do everything to further it! Thus the actions of the rulers were at that time regulated in every respect by the law, and especially by Deuteronomy, which, in accordance with its whole object and character, must necessarily have the *primas partes*. The firmness with which the law was rooted at that time also appears from the ingenious means adopted by the rulers of the nation, on the one side, not to break the oath made to the Lord, that no Israelite should give his daughter to wife to a Benjamite, and, on the other side, to provide for the preservation of the tribe of Benjamin. This difficulty could not have arisen, if the Mosaic law prohibiting marriage with the Canaanites had not still been regarded as sacred and inviolable. The Benjamites would only have had to take Canaanitish wives. But this expedient does not even seem to have occurred to the rulers. It is a question of some importance whether by the feast, which, according to chap. xxi. 19, was annually celebrated in Shiloh, and at which, by the decree of the rulers of the nation, the Benjamites were to steal wives for themselves, we are to understand a local feast of indefinite origin, or the passover-feast, a feast of the whole nation. If the latter be proved, it follows that it must have been kept throughout the whole period of the judges, and at the same time we learn that we are not at liberty to conclude from the author's silence respecting religious arrangements—a silence which was necessarily connected with his tendency—that these arrangements did not exist. In favour of the feast of the passover, we have, among others, the following arguments:—(1.) The designation, *the* feast of the Lord, חג יהוה, not *a* feast of the Lord, as it must have been termed if a particular festival had been meant. The feast of the Lord is in Shiloh, the elders say. This leads to the passover, the principal and fundamental feast of the Israelites, which is always meant when the feast κατ' ἐξοχήν is spoken of. (2.) The circular dance performed by the daughters of Shiloh at the feast also leads us to suppose that it was the passover; for this has reference to Ex. xv. 20, the circular dance of the Israelitish women under the direction of Miriam, which occurs within the seven days of the passover. Probably this dance was performed on the second day. That it took place on the principal day of the feast, we can scarcely suppose. (3.) The ימימה מימים. This occurs in the law of the passover, and of no other feast, Ex. xiii. 10: "Thou shalt therefore keep this ordinance in his season" (ימימה מימים). And elsewhere it is only to be found where an allusion to the passover is unquestionable, or at least most probable; comp. afterwards. (4.) If the Benjamites were in Shiloh at the feast of the passover, their presence could excite no remark, and the stratagem could be carried out much more easily. That the Benjamites themselves took part in the celebration of the feast, and had come to Shiloh independently of the plan which they then took occasion to carry out, appears from chap. xxi. 20. In Shiloh itself the elders speak to them. Their advice to them is not, Come to Shiloh, etc., but merely, "Go and lie in wait in the vineyards." We are still met by the question, how to explain the circumstance that the nation assembled in the cause of the Benjamites in *three* different places, in Mizpah, Bethel, and Shiloh. Further, how are we to reconcile the statement in chap. xviii. 31, that during the whole period of the judges the tabernacle of the covenant was in Shiloh, where we meet with it in the books of Samuel towards the end of this period, with the fact that all at once we find the ark of the covenant in Bethel during the Benjamitic war? The following is the simple solution. The nation assembled first of all in Mizpah, not in Shiloh, because this place was not only more in the centre of the land, but was situated specially in the territory of the Benjamites. The court was to be held among the guilty race, in order that, if they did not submit, execution might immediately follow. After the breaking out of the war, in which the Lord was to be leader, the ark of the covenant was brought to Bethel, generally, because this lay in the country of the Benjamites, near to the scene of battle, but particularly, because this place was consecrated by the history of the patriarchs. That there was no permanent sanctuary there, and that the sojourn of the ark of the covenant was merely temporary, appears from the express statement in chap. xxi. 4, that the people built an altar there, that they might offer up sacrifices. After the two defeats, the people assembled in Bethel. Thither also they repaired after the close of the campaign; and on this last occasion we have clear reference to that event of earlier times by which the place was consecrated. "And the people," we read in chap. xxi. 2, 3, " came to the house of God, and abode there till even before God, and lifted up their voices, and wept sore; and said, O Lord God of Israel, why is this come to pass in Israel, that there should be to-day one tribe lacking in Israel?" The very circumstance of אלהים occurring in a connection where in other places we always find Jehovah, points to Genesis. At Bethel, where in Jacob God blesses his posterity; where, on the journey to Mesopotamia, He tells him, " And thy seed shall be as the dust of the earth; and thou shalt spread abroad to the west, and to the east, and to the north, and to the south: and in thee, and in thy seed, shall all the families of the earth be blessed;" where, after the return from Mesopotamia, Israel is told, "Be fruitful and multiply; a nation and a company of nations shall be of thee;"—the people give utterance to a bitter and grievous complaint of the contrast between the idea and the reality. Now, after the cause of the temporary abode of the ark of the covenant in Bethel had ceased, it was brought back to Shiloh. Thither, as the place of the sanctuary, the people also repaired, for the time of the passover was come. The celebration of the passover formed the keystone of the whole event. After the grievances had been removed, the feast of the covenant was kept. Then all returned to their homes. The final conclusion to be drawn from the two events narrated in the appendix to the book of Judges is, that although the *good* principle was at that time still predominant, yet the *evil* principle had already begun to assert itself, and with such power, that even at that time it was necessary to sever whole diseased members from the body.

2. The first enemy to whom the Israelites succumbed was Chushan-rishathaim, king of Mesopotamia, who is mentioned not only in the book of Judges, but also in Hab. iii. 7, when in the victory over *him* the prophet finds a pledge of future assistance against the enemy, and judgment on them. In this passage he is merely called Cushan, but there is an allusion to his surname—Rishathaim, twofold wickedness—in the words, "I saw the tents of Cushan *in affliction*" (under punishment). This surname is probably of Israelitish origin. Chushan-rishathaim corresponds to Aram-Naharaim,—Aram of the twofold river, Chushan of the twofold wickedness. This fact, in connection with that recorded in Gen. xiv., shows that already, long before the familiar period of the great Assyrian, Babylonian, and Persian monarchies, kingdoms arose and perished in central Asia; and there, in very early times, a strife began for the possession of the coast-land. Here was attempted, but with transitory result, what was afterwards accomplished by the more extended and firmly-rooted power of the Assyrians and Babylonians. The apostasy of Israel, which had this punishment for a consequence, is thus described in Judg. iii. 7 : "And the children of Israel did evil in the sight of the Lord, and forgat the Lord their God, and served Baalim and the groves." In accordance with the prevailing assumption, Ashera is identical with Astarte, the personification of the feminine principle in nature, in conjunction with Baal, the male principle. But it is more probable that Astarte is the goddess herself, and that Ashera is her image or symbol, mostly consisting of sacred trees or groves; hence the LXX. ἄλσος, the Vulgate *lucus;* comp. Bertheau on this passage. But there is no doubt that we can here look only for the beginnings of this worship, which proved so seductive for the Israelites,

and prevailed throughout their whole territory. Othniel became the deliverer of Israel,—the same who, according to chap. i. 13, had been active in the conquest of Canaan under Joshua. In chap. iii. 9 we read of him: "The Lord raised up a deliverer to the children of Israel, who delivered them. And the Spirit of the Lord came upon him, and he judged Israel, and went out to war." The words, "And the Spirit of the Lord came upon him," have frequently been understood here and elsewhere merely of the physical power and courage which are given by God for the good of His people. But this opinion is decidedly wrong. Otherwise, how could we account for the fact that this Spirit of the Lord is imparted only to servants of Jehovah? Here, as in the prophets, and throughout the Scriptures, the extraordinary gift rests upon the ordinary. This χάρισμα, like every other, has πίστις for its necessary foundation. This does not, however, exclude many weaknesses. Even in those gifts which are of a more internal nature, the amount is not always in proportion to the measure of faith. The deliverance by Othniel took place after eight years' servitude. It was succeeded by a rest of forty years. It has frequently been assumed that Othniel judged the Israelites for the whole of these forty years. But this view, which is scarcely consistent with the age of Othniel, rests upon a misunderstanding of chap. iii. 11, 12, where the words, "and Othniel died," must be taken in close connection with what follows: "And the children of Israel did evil again in the sight of the Lord;" equivalent to, And the children of Israel continued to do evil after the death of Othniel. If we suppose that the death of Othniel followed the forty years of rest, and that the apostasy was subsequent, no time is left for the latter, which was certainly a gradual development. For the punishment, the new oppression by the Moabites, followed immediately after the end of the forty years. Hence the apostasy must have taken place during the forty years; and since the death of Othniel, whose pious zeal kept the nation true to the Lord while he lived, is made one of the causes of it, this must have occurred a considerable time before the expiration of the forty years. The invasion of Cushan is the first and last oppression originating in the territory beyond the Euphrates during the time of the judges. The subsequent attacks were made by those nations dwelling in the more immediate neighbourhood of Israel: the *Canaanites*, who took advantage of the weakness of Israel to recover their old supremacy; the *Ammonites* and *Moabites*, who were related to the Israelites by race, and grudged them the beautiful inheritance which had been bestowed on them by the grace of their God; the *Midianites*, and other peoples of the desert, who would willingly have exchanged with them; and, finally, the *Philistines*, who cherished in their hearts a peculiarly deep hatred towards Israel.

3. First, there was a servitude of eighteen years to the Moabites. They were delivered by the Benjamite Ehud, who by cunning gained a private audience of the Moabite king, and slew him. This act has been very severely censured; and we certainly cannot assume, with the older theologians, that it was done by the express command of God. Judg. iii. 15 states nothing more than that Ehud was raised up and strengthened by God for the deliverance of the Israelites, the choice of means being left to himself. Let it be observed that with respect to Ehud nothing is said, except "the Lord raised them up a deliverer," not, as in Othniel's case, "and the Spirit of the Lord came upon him," with special reference to the *act*. The demand that the author should expressly have condemned the act is based on a total misapprehension of his tendency, whose object was not to glorify and criticise human instruments. His glance is only directed to God's faithfulness and mercy, which remain always the same, whatever may be our judgment concerning the act. But though, humanly considered, the act is by no means justifiable, yet it is very excusable. Ehud is described as a man who was left-handed. From Judg. xx. 16 it seems to follow that the brave men among the Benjamites took pride in neglecting their right hand, and in using the left, which was radically weak. We have there a description of 700 men who were left-handed. This probably had its origin in their name. They sought by this means to meet the derisive remarks called forth by it. The

scene of the event was the former site of Jericho. On this important spot, which secured them an entrance into the country, the Moabites had set up a fortified camp. Studer's opinion, that the event occurred east of the Jordan, in the proper land of the Moabites, is quite incorrect. It is remarkable that in ver. 19 we read, "And Ehud turned again from the quarries" (graven images), and afterwards, "And Ehud escaped while they tarried, and passed beyond the quarries (graven images), and escaped unto Seirath." The Moabites had set up their idols as watchers and protectors on their borders; comp. the פסילים in Deut. vii. 25. Ehud came from them with his pretext of a message to the king, and passed them again in his flight, after having accomplished his design. The graven images were as little able to hinder his escape as to prevent the death of the king. Their impotency became manifest on this occasion, and Ehud took the opportunity of calling upon the Israelites to throw off the strange yoke. They lent a ready ear to his summons, and the land had rest for eighty years.

4. The *Philistines* made an inroad into the country, but were driven back by Shamgar, a valiant hero. Besides the Canaanites, the Philistines were the only nation whose territory was promised by God to the Israelites, and that because they had taken possession of Canaanitish land with hostile intention. But the occupation of their land was a difficult undertaking; for the Philistines inhabited the low country, where they could make the most of their skill, which consisted in chariots of war, against the Israelites, who were not accustomed to fight in this way. True, Judah, under Joshua, captured the three Philistine cities, Gaza, Askalon, and Ekron, Judg. i. 18, but they were not able to keep possession of them, ver. 19. The five princes of the Philistines remained unconquered, comp. Judg. iii. 3, and the Israelites were obliged to relinquish the hope of supremacy over the low country of the Philistines, as well as over the Phenician coast-towns. It lay in the nature of the thing that the strife between the two nations should continue throughout the whole history. When we read of Shamgar that he slew 600 Philistines with the goad of an ox, which served

him for a lance, we must remember that these Philistines were not proper warriors, but a mob eager for plunder, who took advantage of the humiliation of Israel, and expected no opposition whatever. The boldness of an individual reminded them of the saying, "Ex ungue leonem," and life being dearer to them than booty, they fled in wild disorder. It is not stated that Shamgar *slew* the 600 men, but only that he *smote* them. And the fact that the deed is attributed to him alone does not altogether exclude the participation of others, but only their independent participation, such as could have enabled them to contest the honour of the deed, the success of which was due to him alone. We have only to compare what is told of Saul in 1 Sam. xviii. 7. With regard to the time of this act of Shamgar, it cannot have occurred during the eighty years of rest, but in the period of servitude to the Canaanites described in chap. iv. The Philistines here took advantage of the opportunity to make incursions on the land, just as they afterwards did in the invasion by the Ammonites. We infer this from the short notice itself. For at a time when the power of the nation was unbroken, the Philistines would not have ventured to act in this way, but only to invade the country with a well-equipped army. And we are led to the conclusion still more definitely by the song of Deborah, when, in chap. v. 6, Shamgar and Jael are associated as representatives of the melancholy past. In this passage Jael is no other than the wife of Heber the Kenite, mentioned in ver. 24, notwithstanding the contrary opinion of Ewald and others. The reason that the time of oppression is named after *her* in conjunction with Shamgar—her to whom Israel was so deeply indebted—is to do her honour. From the time which succeeded the years of rest, the author first of all narrates Shamgar's isolated deed of heroism, which had no permanent result, and then goes on to describe the grievous oppression and the great deliverance.

5. The *Canaanites* had recovered themselves in the lapse of time, and in particular had founded a mighty kingdom in Hazor, which had been conquered and destroyed by Joshua. Jabin, the king of this city, oppressed Israel grievously,

through his general Sisera, for a period of twenty years.
The name Jabin seems to have been common to all the
kings of this empire, Josh. xi. 1. Jabin was able to take
the field with 900 chariots of war,—a very considerable force,
since Darius had only 200 in his army, and Mithridates only
100. Yet the principal strength even of his army consisted
in the cavalry and infantry, and the war-chariots were
merely accessory; the Canaanites, on the other hand, appear
to have had no cavalry, and but little infantry. Then we
must take into consideration that Jabin was not king of a
single town, but probably ruler of all the Canaanites in
North Palestine, especially the inhabitants of the plain of
Jezreel, who by their war-chariots were so terrible to the
Israelites already at the time of Joshua; comp. chap. xvii.
16. Chap. v. 19, where several kings are mentioned, seems to
point to a confederacy of Canaanitish princes who marched
against Barak. The oppression of the Israelites cannot be
regarded as complete, for, according to chap. iv. 4, they
still had their own administration of justice; and the description
in the song of Deborah points only to a condition of
painful insecurity, called forth by the incessant inroads of
the Canaanites, against whom they were no longer able to
stand in the field. The oppression does not seem to have
extended to Judah at all: throughout the period of the
judges this tribe seems to have had less to suffer, and to have
continued more in undiminished power. Israel was delivered
by Barak, who acted, however, under the guidance of an
inspired woman, Deborah. According to chap. iv. 8, after
Deborah had summoned Barak to deliver Israel, he replied,
"If thou wilt go with me, then I will go; but if thou wilt
not go with me, then I will not go." Deborah answered,
verse 9, "I will surely go with thee: notwithstanding the
journey that thou takest shall not be for thine honour; for
the Lord shall sell Sisera into the hand of a woman." This
dialogue is generally misunderstood, as if Barak here revealed
his cowardice, and Deborah taunted him with it. Studer
unhesitatingly calls Barak the representative of the cowardly
spirit which at this time had taken possession of the Hebrews.
The LXX. have taken the correct view. After the words

contained in the original text they add, ὅτι οὐκ οἶδα τὴν ἡμέραν, ᾗ εὐοδοῖ κύριος τὸν ἄγγελον αὐτοῦ μετ' ἐμοῦ. Barak knew that in the warfare of the Lord's people nothing is done by human strength and courage, but that higher consecration and calling are necessary; these he perceives in the prophetess Deborah in a higher degree than in himself. It is therefore humility, and humility which is not without foundation,—for his standpoint was really a lower one, he is not to be compared with a Gideon,—but not want of courage, which induces him to urge her to accompany him. There is no scorn in her answer. She merely points out to him that after the victory he will not be at liberty to judge differently from now,—to ascribe to himself what belonged to a woman, and at the same time to God. She draws his attention to God's design in obliging him to lean upon a woman, or in choosing a man who required to depend on a woman. This was none other than to bring the ποῦ οὖν ἡ καύχησις; ἐξεκλείσθη clearly to the consciousness of the nation. When help comes through women, the glance which so readily remains fixed on the earth must be directed to heaven. If the honour belong to God alone, there will be the greater inclination to thank Him by sincere repentance. The fact that Barak was here directed to Deborah rests upon the same law by which Gideon is instructed to retain only 300 men of the whole assembled army: the women Deborah and Jael belong to the same category as the ox-goad of Shamgar. At all times God delights to choose out the small and despised for His service. What great things did He not do by means of the poor monk Luther! At the command of the Lord, Barak is obliged to blow the trumpet loudly on Mount Tabor. This is the usual way in which the deliverers begin their work in the book of Judges. The act has been misunderstood when its object is regarded as the assembling of the nation, so that the blowing of the trumpet would be like our alarm-bell. That Mount Tabor, where Barak was to blow, was not the place of assembling, appears from ver. 10, where it is said to have been Kadesh. The meaning is plain from Num. x. 9: "And if ye go to war in your land against the enemy that oppresseth you, then ye shall blow an alarm with the trumpets; and ye shall be remembered before the Lord your God." This makes the blowing of the trumpets a symbolical act, by which an appeal was made to the Lord. He Himself had prescribed this custom. Therefore as certainly as the nation heard the sound of the trumpet, so certainly might they expect that the Lord would be with them. In this way they must have been filled with holy courage. We find this decree first carried out in Josh. vi. 5, where the object cannot possibly have been to assemble the nation. That the act had reference only to the relation towards the Lord, appears from the relation of the משכתי in ver. 7 to the משכת in ver. 6, which necessarily leads us to infer that the משך in ver. 6 has a twofold meaning. The prolonged notes are intended as an appeal to God. Then, ver. 7, "And I will draw unto thee Sisera, the captain of Jabin's army." First God, then Sisera; first the helper from heaven, then the enemy on earth. The author indicates the point of view from which the victory is to be regarded by a hidden reference to the Pentateuch, which is characteristic of him. In chap. iv. 15 he says: "And the Lord discomfited (ויהם) Sisera, and all his chariots, and all his host." An allusion is here made to Ex. xiv. 24, "And the Lord troubled (ויהם) the host of the Egyptians;" and we are reminded that the present discomfiture, effected by means of the sword of the Israelites, is no less wonderful than the former, which was the immediate work of God, the result of fearful natural phenomena. If we mistake the reference to the Pentateuch, the expression appears inappropriate, especially on account of the addition לפי חרב, which has led many to attribute a different meaning to the words. But in other places where the המם occurs, the reference to the Pentateuch is unmistakeable: for example, 1 Sam. vii. 10; 2 Sam. xxii. 15; Josh. x. 10. The flying general Sisera turned into the tent of Jael, the wife of Heber, of the Midianitic tribes of the Kenites, which had accompanied the Israelites on their march from the wilderness to Canaan and had settled down there, in the most southern part of the country, close to the borders of the wilderness. But Heber had separated with his horde from the tribe, and had established himself in North Palestine. Befriended by this tribe, and hospitably received by Jael, Sisera believed himself secure, but was slain by her while sleeping. Here also the older theologians have attempted to justify what is unjustifiable. For although Jael by this act proves her faith in Jehovah, the God of Israel, yet the act itself is not praiseworthy. The commendation bestowed on Jael in Deborah's song of victory, Judg. v. 24, is only an expression of the gratitude which Israel owed to her, or rather to God, who gave the success. Israel rejoiced in the deliverance vouchsafed them, without taking part in the deed itself. They were not called upon to pass judgment, but only to show gratitude.

This song of Deborah in Judg. v., whose genuineness has recently been very decisively defended by Ewald, Studer, and Bertheau, and is now, after some passing attacks, acknowledged even by the boldest critics, is clearly to be regarded as a counterpart to the song of the Israelites after the passage through the Red Sea. The introduction, in vers. 4, 5, is a verbal reference to Deut. xxxiii. 2, the introduction to the blessing of Moses, and to Ex. xix. 16, the account of the phenomena which accompanied the giving of the law; just as "they chose new gods," in ver. 8, is taken from Deut. xxxii. 17. It is of special importance, because it shows us that the leading point of view from which the author of the book of Judges regards the history of this time is not one arbitrarily devised and introduced by himself, the product of a later time, but the same from which those who were living in the midst of this time themselves regarded the events. The author begins with the covenant which the Lord had made with Israel; he then goes on to depict the sad state of dismemberment which has resulted in consequence of the breaking of the covenant and the worship of strange gods; finally, the deliverance vouchsafed to the nation by the grace of God. Here we have the same principles which lie at the basis of the author's representation. Those who acknowledge the genuineness of the song, and at the same time maintain that the tendency of the Israelites to idolatry during the time of the judges cannot be regarded as a relapse into their old habits of evil, as the author from his later standpoint supposes, but must be attributed to the fact that the religion of Jehovah was not separated from natural religion until a later time, are guilty of great inconsistency. We here find the strongest contrast between Jehovah and the idols; the worship of the latter is regarded as a culpable apostasy from the plainly revealed and clearly recognised truth. The acknowledgment of the genuineness is also irreconcilable with the denial of the activity of the prophethood before Samuel. The song has throughout a prophetic character. Even if the author had not stated that Deborah was a prophetess, it would be evident from this song.

6. After the Israelites had enjoyed rest for forty years, they were grievously oppressed for seven years by hordes of the Midianites,—those who had their dwelling east of Canaan in the neighbourhood of the Moabites, and against whom a war of vengeance had been waged as early as the Mosaic time,—the Amalekites and other Arab Bedouins from the districts between Canaan and the Euphrates. It was a kind of migration; the wilderness rose up against the cultivated land. But the tribes were so successfully repulsed, that they remained quiet during the rest of the time of the judges. Here, as throughout, except in relation to the Canaanites, the Israelites were the aggrieved party. Throughout their history we find them only defending themselves, as became their position, not attacking and conquering. Hence they have a right to be heard when they attribute the only exception to higher motives. We learn the severity of this oppression, not merely from the relation in chap. vi. 1 ff., but also from the first chapter of the book of Ruth; for the coincidence of the circumstances narrated in the two accounts shows that the history of this book, which is generally wrongly placed in the time of the judges, belongs specially to this period. Both tell of a great famine. In the book of Ruth it is said to have continued for a number of years, so that the Israelites were obliged to transfer their habitation to a foreign land. It cannot, therefore, have been caused by failure of the crops, which would equally have affected the neighbour-

ing country of the Moabites. Elimelech leaves Bethlehem on account of the famine. According to Judg. vi. 4, the host of the Midianites extended as far as Gaza, and therefore over the district in which Bethlehem lay. After ten years, Naomi learns that the Lord has visited His people, and returns to her fatherland. The oppression by the Midianites lasted for seven years, and some time had to elapse before the land could quite recover the effects of it, and attain to the flourishing condition in which Naomi found it on her return. Here also matters take their regular course, and history proves itself an inverted prophecy. First the sin, then the punishment, then the sending of a teacher of righteousness, the raising up of a preacher of repentance, the ordinances of God for the spiritual redemption of the nation, which formed the condition of their external redemption, and finally this external redemption itself. The instrument employed by the Lord for the internal deliverance is not expressly named, but only characterized as a prophet whom the Lord sent to the children of Israel when they cried to Him against Midian. His discourse, as summarily given in chap. vi. 8–10, rests entirely upon the law, and in the words of it contrasts the mercy of God and the ingratitude of Israel. With regard to the effect produced by it, nothing is definitely said; but the result clearly shows that it did not pass over without leaving some traces, for the external salvation was immediately prepared. We are not, indeed, entitled to assume a fundamental and complete change. The measures which Gideon had still to take against the worship of Baal prove the contrary. But God did not demand more than the beginnings of repentance. Where these were present, progress was furnished by contemplating the mercy which God displayed in the salvation of His people. God called Gideon to be the deliverer of the nation, of the family of the Abi-ezrites, a branch of the tribe of Manasseh, whose head, it seems, was Joash, the father of Gideon. Not without an object does chap. vi. 15 lay so much stress upon the circumstance that the family of Gideon was the poorest in Manasseh, and that he was the youngest in his father's house. Even rationalistic expositors have been forced to acknowledge the tendency of the narrative in this respect. Studer says, p. 174: "Jehovah chooses the youngest son of an obscure family of the small tribe of Manasseh to be the instrument for delivering His people, that His power, which is mighty in the weak, might be the more glorified, and that all might recognise that man can do nothing in his own strength, but that, by God's assistance, the greatest result may be produced by the most insignificant means." Strangely enough, he makes this tendency a proof of the mythical character of the narrative, as if God's dealing in this respect did not remain the same through hundreds and thousands of years; as if the previous deliverance had not been effected by two weak women, as narrated in the song of Deborah, which he himself declares to be genuine. In Gideon's dealings with the angel of the Lord, the main point to be noted is that here, as is universally the case in the post-Mosaic history, anything extraordinary concerning events and man's relation to them rests upon the analogy of the Pentateuch; which was *à priori* to be expected, since it exactly corresponds with the universal relation of the patriarchal-Mosaic time to the later, which has in no respect an independent root, but is built throughout upon the foundation previously laid. The appearance of the angel of the Lord presents a striking affinity to Gen. xviii. Gideon demands the same expression of his miraculous power that Abraham prescribed to the angel of the Lord, that he might be certain he was not deceived. The mode of this has its type in Lev. ix. 24. When Gideon makes his weakness a plea for declining the commission, the angel of the Lord repeats to him the great word, כי אהיה עמך, spoken to Moses in Ex. iii. 12,—a point of union which, owing to the peculiar usage of the כי, cannot be accidental, referring to the earlier glorious confirmation of this promise, and to the former actual refutation of the theory that a man must be originally great in order to do great things. When Gideon is convinced that he has looked upon the angel of the Lord, he fears he must die. In ver. 39, "Let not thine anger be hot against me, and I will speak but this once," Gideon borrows the words literally from Gen. xviii. 32, and excuses his boldness by recalling that of Abraham, which was graciously accepted of God. Together with this dependence, which might easily be traced still further, we have throughout great independence, proving that the agreement is not due to later authorship, but has its foundation in fact. It would be interesting and important to follow this relation through the whole history of revelation up to the New Testament,—the more, since, roughly and externally apprehended, it has furnished a handle for attack; whereas, rightly treated, it offers very significant apologetic particulars. The question arises, how the first sign which Gideon here receives, the consumption of the sacrifice offered to the Lord, is related to the second which is granted at his request, the bedewing of the fleece. At first glance, the first seems to make the second superfluous. But, on nearer consideration, it is apparent that they have a different meaning, and refer to a different object. By the first, Gideon is made certain that it is really the angel of the Lord who has spoken to him; by the second, he is convinced that the Lord, who has given him the commission, is really able and willing to make the work of deliverance successful. In both cases the sign presupposed the weakness of Gideon's faith. If his spiritual eye had been perfectly clear, the apprehension that it was the angel of the Lord who spoke to him, which he had at the very beginning, as the אדני in ver. 15 shows, would have developed into perfect certainty even without a sign. If the weakness of his faith had not made him inconsistent, the certainty of his commission would have given him the certainty of its accomplishment, and the second sign would have been unnecessary. But since it was his sincere wish to do the will of God, notwithstanding his weak faith,—since his demand for a sign was an actual prayer, "Lord, I believe, help Thou mine unbelief," having its origin in the deep and inward conviction that he could do nothing without God,—therefore God condescended to his weakness. The sacrifice which Gideon offered up in the night, after the appearance of the Lord, has much that is striking. "Sacrificium hoc," says Lightfoot, "fuit miræ et variæ dispositionis, oblatum noctu, loco communi, a persona privata, adhibitis lignis e luco idololatrico, ipsumque idolo fuerat destinatum." Only on superficial consideration has this act of Gideon's been regarded as a violation of the Mosaic constitution, or a proof that the sacrificial arrangements of the Pentateuch had not yet taken root at that time. These arrangements referred merely to the ordinary course of things: they laid down the rule, from which exceptions were to take place only at the express divine command. Gideon received such a command. A violation of the law would only occur if a standing worship had been set up in Ophrah. The transaction was therefore exceptional. It had a symbolical meaning. It was an actual declaration of war on the part of God against idols,—a prophecy that their supremacy over Israel was now at an end,—a manifesto that God would now demand again what had been unjustly taken from Him. The transactions after Gideon's act—his supposed outrage on the sanctuary of Baal—had become known, show that the constitution of the time of Moses and of Joshua still remained unaltered. Joash, the head of the family of the Abi-ezrites, has the *jus vitæ et necis*. The people turn to him with the demand that Gideon should be punished, and he threatens death to all who should lay hands on Gideon. In the account contained in Judg. vi. 29, 30, of the course pursued by the inhabitants of Ophrah after Gideon's deed—" And the men of the city said one to another, Who hath done this thing? And when they inquired and asked, they said, Gideon the son of Joash hath done this thing. Then they said unto Joash, Bring out thy son that he may die; because he hath cast down the altar of Baal," etc.—we have an unmistakeable reference to Deut. xvii. 5. Here we read: " If there be found among you any that hath gone and served other gods, and worshipped them, and it be told thee, and thou hast heard of it, and inquired diligently, and, behold, it be true, and the thing certain, that such abomination is wrought in Israel; then shalt thou bring forth that man or that woman, which hath committed that wicked thing, unto thy gates, and shalt stone them with stones, till they die." It does not appear that this reference belongs only to the narrator, whose object it is by this means to point to the strangeness of the circumstance, that the attempt was made to do to the servants of the Lord what, in accordance with the law, was to be done to the servants of idols. Numerous traces lead us to conclude that the worship of Baal, which is here regarded as what it really was in its inner nature, a direct antagonism to the worship of God, was not intended as such by those who practised it, but that, embarrassed by syncretistic error, they identified Baal and Jehovah. With this idea, they supposed that Gideon had transgressed against Jehovah, and hence they made the law of Deuteronomy the basis of the punishment. From the battle against the spiritual enemy of his nation, with which Gideon appropriately began his work, he received the name of Jerubbaal—opponent of Baal. This name served for a perpetual memorial to the nation, reminding them that they could only enjoy the love of God by completely renouncing the idols which robbed Him of His honour. In the sign by which Gideon, in the face of danger, is assured of divine help, a symbolical meaning is apparent. The fleece is first wet by the dew, while everything else remains dry; then it remains dry, while everything else is wet, כל הארץ. Dew is, in Scripture, the symbol of divine mercy. The fleece, in contrast with the rest of the earth, denotes Israel. Thus Gideon was taught, by a living image, the truth that it was God alone from whom Israel had to expect times of refreshment, that God alone was the Author of their misery. The latter was no less encouraging for Gideon than the former. For if the misery of Israel had its origin in God, the great power of the enemy need cause them no anxiety. The prophetic meaning of the sign rested upon its symbolical meaning, as Lightfoot has well shown in the words: " Signum Gideoni ostentum in madido et sicco vellere vera Israelis imago fuit, madidi rore doctrinæ (more correctly, gratiæ) divinæ, quando totus mundus reliquus erat siccus, nunc vero sicci, quando totus mundus reliquus est madidus." If Israel's salvation and misery proceed only from the Lord, and are dependent on the nation's attitude towards Him, things must necessarily happen as they did: the apostasy of the nation must be followed by the deepest misery, while the dew of mercy and salvation fell upon the rest of the nations. The question arises, why Gideon first called together a great multitude of the people, then from the 32,000 chose only 10,000, and finally retained only 300 of the 10,000? Apparently he might have selected the 300 brave men at the very beginning. The object was, according to the way narrated in the history, by intentionally reducing the large number to a small one, to show clearly that God would be the Deliverer. This point of view has commended itself even to critics like Studer, who says, "The fact that the author makes Gideon intentionally diminish his army to a small number has a didactic aim, which is definitely expressed in chap. vii. 2. The lesson, which had already been taught in the call of Gideon, that Jehovah makes use of the very weakest, in order by this means to glorify Himself, and to free man from the delusion that he is able to do anything in his own strength, was intended to be manifested in the way in which the victory was gained over the Midianites. How deeply this religious consciousness became rooted in the nation, we learn from the many analogous utterances in the prophets, down to the Apostle Paul, who found a new confirmation of the above doctrine in the means which God employed for the spread of Christianity, 1 Cor. i. 25 ff." But this point of view is not the only one. How can it explain the fact that Gideon, by a wisely-chosen test, selects the very bravest 300 of the whole number? If this were the only point of view, he would rather have chosen the weakest and most cowardly. The event is therefore intended to teach a second lesson. It is all the same to God whether He helps by many or by few; but the few through whom He helps must be true men, such as have received from Him the *spiritus fortitudinis* in the carnal and spiritual battles of the Lord. And these are less different from one another than might appear. This second point of view is the more obvious, since it is only by accepting it that we can explain the unmistakeable reference which the event bears to Deut. xx. 8. According to this passage, when the people are ready to march to battle, after the priests have inspired them with courage, the officers call out, " What man is there

that is fearful and faint-hearted? let him go and return
unto his house, lest his brethren's heart faint as well as his
heart." In accordance with this injunction, Gideon speaks
thus at the command of the Lord: " Whosoever is fearful
and afraid, let him return and depart early from Mount
Gilead;" chap. vii. 3. Gideon learns that the time to
attack Midian has come, when, at the command of the Lord,
he repairs with a companion to the hostile camp, and there
surprises the guards narrating and interpreting an unfortunate dream. The symbolism of this dream, a cake of barley-
bread overturning the tent, has, it seems, been carried still
further by Studer in one point. While the sense is generally interpreted thus, " the poor and despised nation of the
Israelites will carry the day," according to him the meaning is, " the despised husbandmen will completely defeat the
tent-dwelling nomads." Only by taking this particular view
can it be explained why *bread*, the characteristic symbol of
agriculture, should be selected; while in the usual opinion
only the *property* of the bread, the fact of its being made of
barley, comes into consideration. Gideon's victory over
Midian is also frequently cited by the prophets as one of the
most glorious manifestations of divine grace, one of the
clearest pledges of future deliverance: comp. Isa. ix. 3,
x. 26; Hab. iii. 7. On the great invasion of the land of
Israel by the sons of the desert, in the time of Jehoshaphat,
Israel prayed, " Do unto them as unto the Midianites . . .
Make their nobles like Oreb and like Zeeb; yea, all their
princes as Zebah and as Zalmunna;" Ps. lxxxiii. 9, 11.
The two former were the leaders of the Midianites, the two
latter their kings. That Gideon after the victory should
have declined the dignity of kingship, and that not from an
individual reason, but because it came too near the honour
of the Lord who alone was King in Israel, seems strange
at a first glance. Was not kingship in Israel constantly
represented as a blessing, even in the promises to the patriarchs, as the aim to which its development was tending?
And how could kingship be supposed to be incompatible with
the theocracy, since Moses, in Deut. xvii., expressly prescribed what was to be done in the event of the people choos-

ing a king for themselves? But these difficulties disappear as soon as we consider that Gideon does not reject kingship *in abstracto*, but a concrete kingship,—kingship in the sense in which it was offered to him by the nation. He felt deeply that kingship in this sense was not a form of realizing the dominion of God in Israel, but rather opposed to it. Ascribing the victory over Midian not to God, but to Gideon, the nation believed that by choosing him their king, they would in future be able to overcome their enemies without God. It was natural, therefore, that Gideon's heart should revolt against the proposition,—the more, since he was convinced that if it were God's wish that the important change should take place, He would give some definite sign; which was not yet the case. While declining the reward offered him by the nation, Gideon asks only for the golden ear-rings of the spoil that was taken. In chap. viii. 27 we read, "And he made an ephod thereof, and put it in his city, even in Ophrah; and all Israel went thither a whoring after it: which thing became a snare unto Gideon, and to his house." Here it is quite plain that Gideon imitates Aaron. In the same way Aaron had formerly asked the people for the gold ear-rings. "And he made an ephod thereof," corresponds to Ex. xxxii. 4, "And he made it a molten calf." Gideon believes himself at liberty to follow the example of Aaron, in so far as his undertaking is not in express opposition to the letter of the law. His intention is not to make an image of the true God, as Ewald has recently supposed, still less to make an idol: the use of language forbids us to understand a statue by the אפוד, as even Bertheau has acknowledged; but the image which, he confesses, is not to be found in the narrative, he adds on his own authority, though the personality of Gideon is opposed to it. According to ver. 33, it was only after Gideon's death that the Israelites fell back into the worship of Baal. If we follow established phraseology, we can understand by the ephod nothing but a copy of the ephod of the high priest. Without doubt Gideon thought he was doing nothing wrong in having it made, but rather intended to give a proof of his piety. He wished to have something sacred in his own possession, and thought he could satisfy the wish, in this rather gross way, without violating the law. In itself his undertaking was not exactly at variance with the letter of the Mosaic law, which only prescribes that there should be but one place for offering up sacrifices, and not, as Bertheau thinks, that there should be but one sanctuary in the wider sense. But we find no trace of sacrifice having been offered up in the sanctuary of Gideon. It cannot be denied, however, that he himself here betrays an element of religious egotism: his private sanctuary alienates his heart, more or less, from the common sanctuary of the nation; and even if the matter contained no danger for *him*, yet, out of consideration for the weakness of the nation, he ought to have desisted from the undertaking, which only too soon made the new sanctuary an object of exaggerated and separatistic love. In the sanctuary of Gideon, he himself was honoured. Thus, by a deviation, apparently so small, the foundation was laid for a series of divine judgments which are described in chap. ix. Gideon's crime drew down divine punishment on his family, who took pride in exalting the new sanctuary. The instruments of this judgment, the Sichemites and Abimelech, were punished for the guilt thus incurred, through one another. It is only his interest in these judgments that induced the author to continue the history of Gideon up to his death, which is quite at variance with his usual habit.

7. Gideon's victory over the Midianites was followed by a rest of forty years, during which he died. Idolatry, which was unable to make any progress during his lifetime, reappeared in great strength after his death. In chap. viii. 33 we read: "As soon as Gideon was dead, the children of Israel turned again, and went a whoring after Baalim, and made Baal-berith their god." It is of importance to investigate the origin of the name Baal-berith, since it leads to remarkable results respecting the nature of idolatry and its position with respect to the worship of Jehovah. The worship of Baal-berith is here attributed to Israel generally; but we find from chap. ix. that it belonged specially to Sichem and its environs. From chap. ix. 46, it follows that the temple

of Baal-berith was not in Sichem itself, but in the neighbourhood. Ver. 6 contains a more exact determination. The inhabitants of Sichem, the adherents of Baal-berith, assemble to choose Abimelech as king, at the same place where Joshua had last assembled the nation immediately before his death, Josh. xxiv. 1, 25, 26, where he had erected the monument of stone as a token of the covenant which the nation had made with Jehovah and had solemnly sworn to keep. The name Baal-berith now becomes clear. We can no longer entertain the idea of an open antithesis to the worship of Jehovah, but only of a syncretistic worship of Jehovah. It is plain that the place could not be sacred to those who had apostatized. Apostasy was hidden under the mark of piety. Faithlessness veiled itself in the garment of loyalty. The law respecting the unity of the sanctuary was met by the argument that it was right to honour the place which the Lord Himself had honoured. The reason why the author enters so fully into the history of Abimelech lies, as we have already indicated, in the remarkable examples of divine retribution which it contains. The author himself draws attention to this tendency, by quoting the prophetic words of Jotham, the youngest and only remaining son of Gideon (his brothers had all been slain by the base Abimelech), in chap. ix. 20, which contain a reference to Num. xxi. 28: "Let fire come out from Abimelech, and devour the men of Shechem; and let fire come out from the men of Shechem, and devour Abimelech;" also by his own reflection in vers. 23, 24: "Then God sent an evil spirit between Abimelech and the men of Shechem; and the men of Shechem dealt treacherously with Abimelech: that the cruelty done to the threescore and ten sons of Jerubbaal might come, and their blood be laid upon Abimelech their brother, which slew them; and upon the men of Shechem, which aided him in the killing of his brethren." Finally and most decisively he indicates this tendency by his concluding observation in vers. 56, 57: "Thus God rendered the wickedness of Abimelech, which he did unto his father, in slaying his seventy brethren: and all the evil of the men of Shechem did God render upon their heads: and upon them came the curse of Jotham the son of Jerubbaal." "First," says Studer, "the avenging Nemesis strikes the inhabitants of Sichem, who had revolted against Abimelech. Unexpectedly attacked and conquered by him, they are abandoned to destruction, together with their city. Divine retribution then overtakes Abimelech himself on his way from conquering Sichem, towards Thebez which had also revolted against him. For during the siege a woman struck him on the head with a piece of a millstone, so that he died a most ignominious death by the hand of a woman, and his adherents dispersed." With regard to the extent of Abimelech's supremacy, we cannot place any reliance on the words in chap. ix. 22, "And Abimelech reigned three years over Israel." It is a prevailing custom in the book of Judges to attribute to Israel what concerned only a part of the nation,—a custom due to the author's vivid apprehension of the unity of Israel. Abimelech was always an Israelitish ruler, even if he had but a few tribes under him. We could only infer from the passage that it was the author's opinion that Abimelech reigned over all Israel, if instead of "over Israel" he had said "over all Israel." The way in which Abimelech attained to kinghood, by the choice of the men of Sichem, speaks against his supremacy over all Israel; also the fact that these chapters treat almost exclusively of North Palestine; and that, according to ver. 21, Jotham found a safe place of refuge in the tribe of Judah. But, on the other hand, we must not limit the supremacy of Abimelech to Sichem alone. He had another residence, and could raise an army to wage war against Sichem. The following is the most probable conclusion: Sichem was at that time the principal place of the tribe of Ephraim, as it was afterwards when the tribes assembled there after the death of Solomon, and when Jeroboam made it his place of residence. Hence, in being chosen as king of Sichem, Abimelech acquired dominion over the whole tribe of Ephraim. But this tribe always maintained a certain superiority over the neighbouring ones,—a circumstance which prepared a later foundation for the kingdom of the ten tribes. Thus Abimelech's recognition by the Ephraimites might involve his recognition by the other tribes also, without our being able to give any exacter definition of the extent of his kingdom, which is remarkable as the first attempt to found kingship in Israel.

8. Abimelech was succeeded by two judges, Tola and Jair, of whose acts we know nothing. Oppressed by the Ammonites, the trans-Jordanic tribes chose Jephthah as ruler for life. He had previously distinguished himself by expeditions against the Ammonites, and now conquered the enemy in a decisive battle. His joy at the victory was embittered by a vow he had made. Before going out to battle, he made a vow that if the Lord should give him the victory, he would offer up to Him the person who would first meet him on his return home. And when his daughter was the first to come and meet him, he considered himself bound by his oath, while the daughter calmly submitted to her fate. With regard to the nature of this fate, and what Jephthah's vow really was, there are two different opinions. According to one, Jephthah offered up his daughter as a burnt-offering. Josephus, Justin Martyr, Chrysostom, Jerome, Augustine, and recently Kurtz, in Guericke's *Zeitschrift*, 53, have defended this view. Others maintain that he consecrated her to the service of God in the sanctuary; so Clericus, Buddeus, and many others. That the latter view is the correct one, that the sacrifice of Jephthah's daughter must be understood spiritually,—that in consequence of the vow she entered the institution of holy women, which is first mentioned in Ex. xxxviii. 8, then in 1 Sam. ii. 22, finally in Luke ii. 37, where Hanna appears as one who was thus dedicated to the Lord,—is fully proved in the *Beiträge*, Th. 3, S. 127 ff., to which discussion we must refer, as well as to the supplementary section on the institution of holy women in *Egypt and the Books of Moses*. Bertheau and Kurtz have come forward in opposition to this view, without adding any new element to the discussion. Here we can only enter upon the most important arguments in favour of the respective views. The two principal ones which are adduced for bodily sacrifice are the following:—First, the letter of the text forms an unanswerable argument. Luther says: "We

may wish that he had not sacrificed her, but the text is plain." This argument must be quite decisive so long as it is not apprehended that the whole system of sacrifice is a grand allegory. It was necessary for it to give reiterated expression to the spiritual relations which it originally described, as may be proved by numerous passages in the Old and New Testaments: comp., for example, Hos. xiv. 3; Ps. li. 19, cxix. 108; Rom. xii. 1. Again, the bitter sorrow of the father is appealed to. But he had reason enough for this on the other supposition. His daughter would henceforward not be allowed to leave the tabernacle of the covenant, "serving day and night with fasting and prayer," which was just the same to him as if she had been dead. All hope of posterity by her was taken from him. On the other hand, we have the following arguments for the figurative meaning of the oath:—(1.) The offering of human sacrifices is so distinctly opposed to the spirit and the letter of the religion of Jehovah, that in the whole history we do not find a single example of one who was only outwardly acquainted with Jehovah, offering a sacrifice of this kind. In the law, human sacrifices are spoken of as a crime deserving to be cursed, one which can only be met with in connection with complete apostasy from the true God. (2.) If the literal acceptation were the correct one, we might have expected that the monstrous deed, the death of the daughter by the hand of the father, would at least have been intimated, if only by a word. But this is not the case. (3.) If the daughter of Jephthah were devoted to death, we cannot understand why the whole subject of her lament should have been her celibacy, nor how the author can give prominence to this as the hardest and most painful circumstance. The tragic character of the event lies principally in the immediate succession of gain and loss, of exaltation and abasement; in the fact that while the one hand gave to Jephthah, the other took away. In surrendering his daughter to the Lord, he gave at the same time everything else, for she was heiress of the possessions and honours which he had just gained, and these would henceforward lose all meaning for him. By this means Bertheau's objection is set aside: "It is the aim of the narrative to record an immoral, extraordinary event, as may be seen in every word." In our opinion also the event bears that character.

9. With regard to the three judges, of whose deeds we are ignorant, who succeeded Jephthah, there is nothing more to be said. We shall therefore go back to the invasion of the Philistines, which ran parallel with that of the Ammonites, the heaviest and longest of all, and to the high-priesthood of Eli, which came to an end two years after the victory of Jephthah over the Ammonites, and began about twenty years before the Philistine-Ammonitic invasion. It is striking that all at once we meet with a high priest of the race of Ithamar. That he was of this race follows from 1 Chron. xxiv. 3, where it is said that Abimelech, who was descended from Eli, was of the posterity of Ithamar. This is confirmed by Josephus, from what source is uncertain, *Ant. Jud.* i. 5, chap. 12, where he says that after Phinehas, the son of Eleazar, the grandson of Aaron, the high-priestly dignity passed to his son, and from him to his grandson and great-grandson. Then after him the high-priestly dignity passed over from the race of Eleazar to the race of Ithamar, and that too under Eli himself. Moreover, the list of the descendants of Eleazar is given in 1 Chron. vi. 51, without its being expressly stated whether they filled the office of high priest or not. The names are in essential agreement with those of Josephus. Josephus does not give the reason. The question now is, how to reconcile this with Num. xxv. 13, where the dignity of high priest is promised by God to Phinehas the son of Eleazar for ever. The answer may be found in the nature of the divine promises, which generally rest on a condition either expressed or implied: if this be not fulfilled, the promise is null. In such a promise as this, the implied condition is that the descendants walk in the footsteps of their ancestors. We must therefore assume that, when one of the descendants of Eleazar had sinned grievously against God, the high-priestly dignity was taken from this branch and given to Eli, of the tribe of Ithamar. And since the Ithamarites received the promise of continual priesthood under the same condition, it was also taken

from them when they did not fulfil the condition, and given back to the family of Eleazar, in which it remained to the end of the Levitical priesthood, comp. 1 Kings ii. 26, 27, 35; so that there was, properly speaking, only a suspension of the promise, similar to that which the promise of kingship in the family of David suffered by the temporary apostasy of the ten tribes, as well as during the period between Zedekiah and Christ. Only in the interval between Eli and Solomon did the family of Ithamar enjoy the dignity of high-priesthood. That the high-priesthood was not forcibly taken by the family of Ithamar, but became theirs by an unquestionable divine decree, we learn from 1 Sam. ii. 30, where, in the speech of the man of God to Eli, there is a reference to an event respecting which the historical books are quite silent, to a solemn appointment of the family of Ithamar to the high-priesthood by God, and a promise of its perpetual duration, which was doubtless given in the same way as the threat of deposition, by a man of God. This circumstance must put us on our guard against inferring the non-existence of a thing from the fact of its not being found in the narrative, especially in the case of events such as these, which lay beyond the proper sphere of the narrator. For the author of the book of Judges they had no interest; he was occupied solely with the judges. Hence Bertheau is very rash in inferring that in the book of Judges the high priests stepped into the background, and that their activity and importance were very inconsiderable. The same may be said of the author of the books of Samuel, who only goes back to the history as far as the roots of Samuel's existence extended into it. The assumption of a forcible transference, a usurpation, is rendered improbable by the whole personality of Eli, who had not the least desire to be a usurper. That he was the first high priest of the family of Ithamar is confirmed, not only by the express statement of Josephus, but also by chronology. Eli did not attain to the high-priesthood until he reached the age of fifty-eight years. For he was ninety-eight when he died, comp. chap. iv. 15, and he judged Israel for forty years. If the succession had descended in the usual way, the office passing from father to son, Eli would scarcely have been so old when he received the dignity. We seldom find so great an age when the succession is regular. What first attracts our attention is the condition of religion as we find it in the time of Eli. The accounts respecting it in the books of Samuel would appear strange to us, if we had not already found considerable foundation for them in the scattered and casual statements of the book of Judges. As it is, we must regard them as a necessary supplement, as a filling out of that part of the description of the time which the author of the book of Judges, in following his aim, left incomplete. If we collect the scattered notices in the first chapters of the book of Samuel, we find a proof of the assumption of Buddeus which appears paradoxical and incorrect only on superficial consideration: "Religionis non alia hoc tempore ratio fuit, quam sub Mose." "Idemque de cultu numinis externo censendum" is essentially well founded. We shall not enter fully into this subject, but refer to the copious dissertation in the treatise, "The Time of the Judges and of the Pentateuch," in vol. iii. of the *Beiträge*. According to a multitude of data, the tabernacle of the covenant in Shiloh formed the religious centre of the whole nation, where the people assembled annually to celebrate the feast of the passover. By 1 Sam. chap. ii. 18, Samuel was girded with a linen ephod when he served before the Lord. According to the law, linen is the sacred garment of office. From chap. iii. 3 we learn that an event, which happened in the early morning, occurred before the lamp of God had been extinguished. From this it follows that the regulation contained in Ex. xxvii. 20, 21, was still in force, according to which Aaron and his sons were to order the lamp without the vail which is before the testimony. The account of the iniquity of Eli's sons also gives us much information respecting the state of religion at that time. The fact that they dared to indulge in such sin, shows how great the authority of the priests then was. The author presupposes that there was an established law relating to the rights of the priests, according to which their conduct appeared to be illegal. He places the right which they usurped in contrast with the right which had been given to them; comp. chap. ii. 14 with Deut. xviii. 3. In chap. ii. 14 he represents all the Israelites who came to Shiloh as subject to their oppression. But even internally considered, the prevalent idea of the condition of religion in the period of the judges is extremely one-sided. We encounter a beautiful picture of Israelitish piety in Elkana and Hanna. Hanna's song of praise is a ripe fruit of the Spirit of God. Eli, with all his weakness, still remains a proof that the religion of Jehovah had at that time not lost its influence over the heart. We see the most beautiful side of his character in his relation to Samuel. The extraordinary gifts of God were rare at that time, in comparison with the more favoured one in which the author of the books of Samuel wrote. In chap. iii. 1 he says, "And the word of the Lord was precious in those days; there was no open vision." And since the extraordinary gifts stand in close connection with the ordinary, we must conclude that the latter also were sparingly dealt out,—that among the masses there was a great deal of lukewarmness, and even open apostasy. The want of a reformation was urgent. That the extraordinary gifts, however, had not quite disappeared, we learn from the example of the man of God who comes to Eli to upbraid him with his sins, and to announce the divine judgment. And with respect to the ordinary gifts, we are led to the conclusion that there was at that time a not inconsiderable ἐκλογή, not only by the institution of holy women, but also by the custom of the Nazirate, of which we have two contemporaneous examples in Samson and Samuel, and which must therefore have been pretty widely spread. Hence we infer that the spirit of piety was by no means dead, especially since an institution such as that of the Nazarites stands in close connection with the whole national tendency, and can only flourish when more or less supported by it. A few remarks on this institution will not be out of place here. The law respecting the Nazirate is to be found in Num. vi. 6. It seems that the Nazirate did not first originate with this law, but the law only reduced to established rules that which had arisen of itself from spiritual impulse and inclination. The fundamental idea of the Nazirate is, separation from the world with its pleasures, which are so detrimental to consecration, and from its contaminating influences. This is already expressed in the name נזיר, one who lives apart, which also explains all the legally-appointed duties of the Nazirate. First, the letting the hair grow, which, according to the law, was the proper mark of the Nazirate, the form of its outward manifestation. Hence the hair of the Nazarite is termed his נזר. The cutting of the hair belonged to the legal condition of that time; comp. Carpzov, App. p. 153. Whoever let it grow, made an actual declaration that for the time being he withdrew from the world, in order to be able to live for God alone. Again, the total abstinence from all intoxicating drinks, which, out of consideration to the tendency of human nature to free itself partially from burdensome restraint by means of absurd interpretations, was extended also to that which would have been allowable without this consideration, to the enjoyment of fresh grapes, and of everything prepared from grapes. The ascetic character of this ordinance is so plain that it need not be further developed. Finally, under no circumstances might the Nazarite touch a dead person. In Num. vi. 7 we read: "He shall not make himself unclean for his father, or for his mother, for his brother, or for his sister, when they die; because the consecration of his God is upon his head." It was the duty of those who had not taken the vow of the Nazirate to pollute themselves, when death occurred in their family, in attending to the burial. The Nazarite, on the contrary, must consider himself dead to the world: he belongs to God alone; to him we may apply the words, "Let the dead bury their dead." The law speaks only of a temporary Nazirate. The vow was taken for a stated time as an ascetic exercise; and, after the expiration of the self-allotted term, the Nazarite returned to the world which he had outwardly renounced for a time, in order to be able to live in it henceforward without sin. But human nature is such, that pious zeal seeks to increase what is in opposition to it, of which we have many proofs in the history of monasticism. And this tendency is exceptionally strong in times

of great persecution of the Church from within and from
without, such as the period of the judges. Piety then
readily assumes an eccentric character. Here also we find
an analogy in monasticism. We have but to think of
Francis of Assisi. Samuel and Samson were consecrated
to the Lord as Nazarites. While still in the womb,
their mothers abstained from that which was prohibited to.
the Nazarites by law,—a circumstance which has its origin
in the idea that the spiritual relation between mother and
child is just as close as the bodily relation. Not only
in the person of Samuel do we find the Nazirate in close
connection with prophethood, but also in Amos ii. 11, where
the prophet represents it as a great favour shown to Israel,
that the Lord has chosen prophets from their sons, and
Nazarites from their young men. Here the Nazirate appears, like the prophethood, as an institution to which special
dona supernaturalia were attached. We also see that the
command is at the same time a promise: the Nazarite was
not to bear the relation of donor towards God, but the commands laid upon him were only the conditions under which
he was to become a recipient. But we must not overlook the
fact that the Nazirate was only a definite form of consecration to the Lord, that everything prescribed to such an one
comes into consideration only in its symbolical meaning,—
as, for example, the most characteristic mark, allowing the
hair to grow, symbolizing renunciation of the world, since,
without regard to the symbolic meaning, one with cut hair
may serve the Lord with equal uprightness. If this be
apprehended, we shall not conclude, from the example of
a personal union of Nazirate and prophethood in Samuel,
that such regularly took place. The passage in Amos seems
to regard the Nazirate and the prophethood as two different
branches of the same tree. Those who consecrated themselves, or were consecrated to the sanctuary, were certainly
not *all* Nazarites; but rather there were three institutions
(besides that of the holy women) whose members devoted
themselves to the Lord in an extraordinary way, viz. the
Nazirate, the prophethood, and the service of the sanctuary
(which latter form could only occur among the sons of

Levitical families). The circumstance that Samuel united all three in his own person was something very unusual, perhaps the only example of the kind. This was in accordance with his whole personality, which is in every respect comprehensive, concentrating in itself what we find elsewhere only in an isolated form. To go back to the point from which we set out; the continuance of the Nazirate throughout the period of the judges shows that religious life was at that time much less corrupt than is generally supposed; comp. the remarks, *Egypt*, etc., p. 199 ff., where the false view of Bähr is refuted. The same thing applies also to the continuance of the institution of holy women, which is proved by the passage 1 Sam. ii. 22, and by the example of Jephthah's daughter. These holy women performed no external service in the tabernacle of the covenant; their service was rather of a spiritual nature: in complete retirement from the world they applied themselves to spiritual exercises, as we see most clearly by comparing Luke ii. 37 with Ex. xxxviii. 8. Let us now turn from these general remarks on the time of Eli to the separate events which occurred in it. We shall begin just where the narrative begins, with the birth of Samuel. (Respecting his Levitical descent, comp. *Beiträge*, part iii. p. 60 ff., and the introduction to Ps. lxxxix.) In common with Isaac, John the Baptist, and Samson, he was given by God in answer to the prayer of a mother who had long been childless. This circumstance was intended to point out to his parents, to himself, and to the nation, that God had destined him to do great things. The fact that his birth took place against all human hope and expectation, pointed to very special divine co-operation, and was calculated to produce the conviction that God had some other object than to turn the sorrow of a woman into joy. The mother understood the word of the Lord. She perceived that the fact of his having been given by God necessarily involved his consecration to Him. Her perfect conviction of the former she expressed in the name of the child, Samuel, contracted from Shaulmeel. Similar abbreviations of proper names, having no regard to grammar, are current among all nations. As was the prayer, so was the man; and what must have been the prayer of a Hanna! Immediately after Samuel was weaned, he was brought to Shiloh, to the sacred tabernacle. There he was brought up under the eye of the high priest, and was already taught the service of the sanctuary before the time when he was legally entitled to it (according to Num. viii. 24, the Levites were commanded to come and establish themselves in the service of the sanctuary at the age of twenty-five). Eli, the high priest, was a man of true piety, who received Samuel with fatherly love, and certainly did much during his long activity for the foundation of true piety in the nation. He showed himself weak only in not putting a check to the degeneracy of his two sons. In this respect he sinned against God; and the divine displeasure with the rejection of his family was made known to him by a seer. The Scriptures represent him as a warning example of the accountability which rests upon parental weakness; and this example has had more effect than the most explicit commands and exhortations. Samuel grew to be a youth. The special circumstances connected with his birth, the example of his pious parents, residence at the sanctuary, constant occupation in the service of the Lord, the example and instruction of Eli, early awakened in him the pious disposition which distinguished him throughout his whole life. At a time when he slept in the fore-court of the tabernacle of the covenant to be ready for the sacred service, he was first favoured with a divine communication. The divine decree concerning Eli's family was revealed to him. Eli hears it from him, and learns his fate with calm resignation. Now, when Samuel had entered into an immediate relation to God, a relation between him and the nation also began. Being soon favoured with several divine communications, he receives through them the dignity of a prophet, of a mediator between God and the nation. With him prophecy mounted a new step. While the prophets had previously entered powerfully into the history only in solitary decisive instances, *his* prophetic activity was a continuous one. For many successive years he was the spiritual leader of Israel. Again, while the earlier prophets had stood in a more isolated position, his gift was so superior, that its fructifying influence was widely felt, and at the same time it was his direct intention to exercise such an influence. In his old age we find an entirely new sign of the time,—whole bands of prophets, who co-operated with him towards the regeneration of the nation. He soon gained universal confidence (comp. 1 Sam. iii. 20), and prepared the way for that influence over the minds of the people which he afterwards acquired. That which had been foretold with respect to the destruction of the family of Eli was soon partially fulfilled. Oppressed and conquered by the Philistines, who had again become powerful, the Israelites believed themselves certain of victory as soon as they marched against the enemy with the ark of the covenant, though they were stained with sin and with an idolatrous disposition. They based this belief on Num. x. 35, according to which Moses said, when the ark went forward, "Rise up, Lord, and let Thine enemies be scattered; and let them that hate Thee flee before Thee." Their hope deceived them. They were conquered. Eli's sinful sons were slain, and he himself did not survive the sad news. Israel was then first robbed of the sanctuary, typifying the Chaldaic and Roman robberies. But, in comparison with the second and third robberies, this first one bore a mild and transitory character, for at that time the guilt of the people was less. Soon the arrogance of the Philistines was humbled. In their foolish presumption, in accordance with the prevailing idea of the old world, they believed that the God of Israel would be conquered by their idol Dagon,—a figure in the form of a fish, with human head and hands,—and that His holy ark would be brought to their temple in triumph. When the destruction of their idol, which came about without the intervention of human instrumentality, had no effect on them, they were afflicted with grievous plagues and diseases, under circumstances which led them to recognise them as punishments of the wrathful God of Israel. Expositors are at variance with regard to the true nature of this sickness. It is most probable that by עפלים in 1 Sam. v. 6, which means hill-shaped elevations, we should not understand hemorrhoidal pains, but boils, which are a characteristic symptom of the oriental pestilence; comp. Thenius on this passage. We must conclude that it was an infectious disease, from its rapid spread and devastating effect. Made wise by affliction, they sent back the sanctuary which had brought so much trouble on them. Accompanied by the princes of the Philistines to the borders of their territory, the ark arrived at Beth-shemesh. The exulting joy of the inhabitants on its return was changed into sorrow. Of fifty thousand men, seventy died a sudden death. This is the explanation of the difficult passage 1 Sam. vi. 19; comp. Bochart in Clericus, whose objections to Bochart's theory are insignificant. They are removed, not by supplying the preposition מן to the אלף, but by taking it as a concise expression, in which the relation is not expressly denoted,—fifty, a thousand, fifty for every thousand. In opposition to the narrative, some have sought to find a reason for this judgment in a special offence of the inhabitants of Beth-shemesh against the ark of the covenant. But the judgment came upon them only on account of the sin which was common to them with all Israel. By their punishment the Israelites were shown what they had to expect from Jehovah,—that the time of wrath was not past. The author fixes his attention only on the highest cause. A physician would have attributed the misfortune to infection caught by contact with the Philistines. The ark was then taken from Beth-shemesh to Kirjath-jearim in the tribe of Judah, and was thus separated from the sanctuary, which had been transferred by the Philistines from Shiloh to Nob immediately after the ark of the covenant had been stolen, and later, when Saul laid a curse on this city, was removed to Gibeon. The high priest remained with the holy tabernacle. The cause of the separation is plainly shown in the narrative. The ark had proved itself hurtful in a number of cases, last of all in Beth-shemesh. It was made evident that the nation was not yet worthy to receive the perfect fulfilment of the promise, "I will dwell in your midst." They endeavoured to dispose of the ark in the best possible way. It was buried, as it were, at Kirjath-jearim, until the time when

God would bring about its joyful resurrection. No sacrifices were offered before it. From this separation of the sanctuaries, it necessarily followed that there was a freedom with respect to the order of worship which the time of Joshua and the time of the judges had not known. Samuel did not work in direct opposition to this freedom, which continued till the building of Solomon's temple, but himself offered sacrifice in different places. He regarded it as his task to bring about an internal reformation, persuaded that this was the most effectual means to obviate the external destruction of the institutions of worship brought about by God Himself. He looked upon this as a punishment, and thought it his duty to direct his energy, not against the effect, but only against the cause. And the result showed that he was right.

10. We shall now leave Samuel, whose reformatory activity extended over the twenty years from the death of Eli to the decisive victory over the Philistines, laying the only permanent foundation for the external salvation of the nation, and turn to the activity of Samson, which belongs to the same period. The object of his mission is best shown by the triumph of the Philistines after they got him into their power. In chap. xvi. 24 we read: "And when the people saw him, they praised their god: for they said, Our god hath delivered into our hands our enemy, and the destroyer of our country, which slew many of us." If the weakness of Samson afforded a proof of the power of their gods, his strength must have made them painfully conscious of the powerlessness of their gods, and the superiority of the God of Israel. Looked at in this light, the acts of Samson form the intermediate link between that which happened to the Philistines on account of the ark of the covenant and Samuel's final victory over them. It is true that the ark of the covenant was sent back; but the oppression by the Philistines still continued. Their strength at that time was due to what Israel then entirely lacked, to perfect unanimity,—their five small kingdoms and princes acted as one man. Nor was this oppression at an end; for it had not yet accomplished the object for which it had

been sent; its continuance formed the necessary condition of the success of Samuel's efforts for the conversion of the nation. Necessity alone teaches prayer. But before salvation could be fully accomplished, the bold appearance of Samson put a check to the arrogance of the Philistines and to the utter despondency of the Israelites, which must have been as prejudicial to their improvement as a too speedy deliverance. What he, as an individual, accomplished by the power of the Lord, showed sufficiently that the power of the world was not opposed to the people of God like a wall of brass; it was a prophecy of the glorious goal towards which the nation would advance, if it could only rise up again as one man against the many, in the might of the Lord. There seems to be only one objection against this point of view. Samson's whole course of action appears little suited for that of an instrument and a servant of God. But here a distinction must be made between a twofold Samson, the servant of the Lord and the servant of sin. We find the former in chap. xiii.-xv., the latter in chap. xvi. What the first Samson does is not unworthy a servant of the Lord, if we do not set up a false spiritualistic standard. We must not compare him with Samuel, who had received a different calling from God, nor with Luther, who in a spiritual aspect presented a closer affinity with him than any other of the reformers; but with Gustavus Adolphus, or a Christian prince in the Crusades. There is a noble element in Samson, a fund of strong and living faith in God, which is everywhere plainly visible notwithstanding his weaknesses, and shows itself even in his fall. The second Samson became transformed from the servant of God to the slave of a woman; in his struggle against the enemies of the kingdom of God, he forgot the struggle with himself. The author himself clearly sets forth this distinction between the first and the second Samson. It is remarkable that so early as the end of chap. xv. we find the words, "And he judged Israel in the days of the Philistines twenty years," as if his history here came to an end, although it is still continued in the following chapter. It is plainly the author's intention to indicate in this way that the proper career of

Samson was now at an end. The servant of the Lord, the judge over Israel, was now as good as buried,—subsequent history has reference only to his spiritual corpse. In the same way the author's judgment is contained in his account of the fate of the fallen Samson. The eyes by which his heart was led astray are put out. The slave of sin is obliged to perform the most menial services among the Philistines. We could only object to Samson's having been called to the service of the Lord, if the wonderful power with which he was filled as a sign and a wonder to the people, an assurance that in their God they possessed the source of infinite power, had remained unimpaired even after his fall. The narrative shows that the contrary was the case. But was God not to call him because He foresaw his fall? This could only be maintained if God were deficient in means to prove that Samson's sin belonged to himself. But the contrary is apparent. We ought rather to say that God called him just because He foresaw his fall. By his example He intended to show how even the most splendid gifts become useless as soon as the recipient ceases to watch over his own heart. Without that great catastrophe, the power of Samson might appear as peculiarly inherent: now all must acknowledge that it was merely lent to him. The 16th chapter is one of the most edifying portions of Scripture. There are few which form so powerful an exhortation to watchfulness and prayer. If the loss of Samson's strength here seems to be attached to something purely external, the loss of his hair, and thus loses its universal applicability and power of edification, we must not overlook the way in which the loss came about. Taking this into consideration, we perceive that the internal and external loss, the loss of the Spirit of God and the loss of the hair, were interwoven. If Samson had lost his hair by any accident for which he was not to blame, the case would have been different. But the cutting of the hair was only an isolated expression of the impure relation in which he stood. Even rationalistic exegesis must acknowledge this. Studer says: "As from Samson, so likewise did the Spirit of God depart from Saul, when by his disobedience he had violated the contract by which Jehovah had appointed him to be His earthly representative, and had anointed him; thus the Spirit of God was withdrawn from the whole nation when they had broken the covenant of Jehovah, and was afterwards given back to the young Christian Church in a higher sense, as a pledge of reconciliation to God and of restored sonship." This parallel between Samson and the whole nation should be specially considered. It is plain that Samson was a type of the nation; that the fall of the individual has prophetic significance for the mass. It is specially noteworthy that his history fills up the last twenty years of the period of the judges. At the close of a long and important period, God revealed to the nation His whole course of action in the deeds and fortunes of an individual. In this sense it may be said that Samson was the personification of Israel in the period of the judges. Strong in the Lord, and victorious over all his enemies; weak through sin, of which Delilah is the image, and a slave to the weakest of all his enemies: such is the quintessence of Israel's history, as well as of Samson's. His life, which, as Ewald says, resembles a candle that flares up at times, and gives light afar off, but often dies down and goes quite out before its time, is at the same time an actual prophecy of a more satisfactory condition of the people, one more closely corresponding to the ideal, which was first to be imperfectly fulfilled under Samuel and David, and afterwards perfectly in Christ. For in the kingdom of God everything imperfect is a pledge and guarantee of the perfect.

After these general remarks, we may turn to the separate events in Samson's life, especially those which have given rise to doubts and difficulty. And here we shall first draw attention to the fact that the author, in accordance with his aim, conformably to the point of view from which he represents Samson's life, is obliged to give as much prominence as possible to what is extraordinary in the acts, without violation of the truth; so that, taking this tendency into account, we must be allowed to assume intermediate causes and interventions where the author makes no mention of them, because this does not materially affect the thing itself, but only weakens the impression which it is his intention to produce. When, for example, he relates that Samson slew a thousand Philistines with the jawbone of an ass, all attempt to fill out the narrative, by assuming the agency of some other independent power besides that of Samson, must be unconditionally rejected; for if the author had omitted to mention such a circumstance, we could no longer believe him to be reliable, and should have no further reason for endeavouring to prove that the events took place in the ordinary course of nature. On the other hand, if this one main point be only firmly established, we can think of many circumstances which may help us to understand the course of events, without asserting that they happened exactly in that way. It is enough that the author does not by his narrative exclude such circumstances.

Samson's first act was to slay a lion without weapons. This exploit is not the only one of the kind. Ancient and modern writers give many examples. The same thing was done by David and Benaiah. Comp. Arvieux, *Merkwürdig. Nachr.* t. ii. cap. 13; Ludolphi *Hist. Æthiop.* sect. 48; Bochart, *Hieroz.* P. I. iii. cap. 1 *et* 4, and many others. There is one difficulty, however, in the circumstance that Samson afterwards finds a swarm of bees and honey in the carcase of the lion, while it is well known that bees fly from carrion. But the difficulty is removed by the fact that, according to chap. xiv. 8, this discovery was not made until a considerable time after the killing of the lion. The lion could therefore no longer have been carrion at that time. The flesh had either rotted away, or had been eaten by animals; or perhaps the body of the lion had been dried up by the sun, and had become a mummy, so that the bad odour, which bees avoid, had vanished. This frequently happens in that district; comp. Rosenmüller, *Bibl. Alterthumsk.* iv. 2, S. 424. And, moreover, since the *spiritus fortitudinis* was given to Samson only for fighting against the enemies of the covenant-nation, as we are expressly told by the author, this event cannot have its object in itself, but must be regarded as type and prefiguration. The action must be regarded as symbolical, like the cursing of the fig-tree by our Lord. The lion is an image of the power of the world, which rises in terrible opposition to the kingdom of God; comp. Dan. vii. 4. This symbolical meaning extends also to the finding of the bees. Samson himself gives prominence to the general truth which is here contained in the particular, in the riddle which he founds on the circumstance. In this riddle we have the quintessence of the occurrence. In chap. xiv. 14 he says: "Out of the eater came forth meat, and out of the strong came forth sweetness." Words whose sense is thus paraphrased by Brenz: "Qui omnia alia devorat, is præbuit ex se cibum, quem alii devorent, et qui in omnes est trux, crudelis, immanis, is exhibuit de se id, quod valde jucundum, suave et delectabile." The truth of this maxim is confirmed by all time. God not only gives His people victory over their enemies, but also makes all enmity eventually subservient to their blessing and salvation; and the more powerful and terrible the enemy, so much the greater is the salvation. Only let us turn to the period of the judges. What would have become of the covenant-nation if they had had no enemies? Every fruit of righteousness grows upon this tree; all food comes to them from the eaters. Then let us come down to the most recent times. Every enemy has become a blessing to the Church. Looked at in this light, the riddle of Samson is a proverb which cannot be too deeply inculcated, an antidote to the sorrow caused by the devastators of the Church. It is a question of less importance whether Samson followed the laws of riddle; whether the question which he lays down may be called a riddle. It seems that the Philistines could not find the solution. Yet we must remember that the event which took place here was not an unusual one in that district, and that the Philistines, in their guessing, may have found the answer to the riddle given to them,—particularly since the terms "eater" and "strong one" were more applicable to the lion than to anything else, while it was most natural to predicate "sweetness" of honey, just as when sweetness is spoken of among us, our first thought is of sugar. In order to injure the Philistines, Samson caught 300 jackals or foxes, tied them together in pairs, and, furnishing them with firebrands, drove them into the standing corn of the Philistines. Neither is there anything improbable in this, since it is not stated that Samson caught the jackals in one day, nor that he had no assistance from others. For such an enterprise, there are always plenty of helpers to be had. According to the accounts of travellers, jackals are to be found in great abundance in Palestine. They are not timid, but seek men, even following them, and obtruding themselves on them. They run in great flocks, often as many as 200 together, and during the daytime they live in holes in the rocks in equally large numbers. A recent traveller, who was by no means a Samson, killed thirty at once in a cave of this kind. Comp. Oedemann's *Verm. Schriften*, part ii. p. 18 ff.; Rosenmüller, iv. 2, p. 156. It has indeed been maintained that שׁוּעלִים does not mean jackal, but fox. For the jackal the Hebrews have a peculiar name, אִיִּים, screamer; but this particular designation is only poetical, as appears from its appellative meaning, and still more decisively from the fact that it occurs only in poetical books; comp. Ewald, *Song of Solomon*, p. 89. That the species of jackal allied to the fox, and similar to it in form and colour, was included with it under the name שׁוּעל, is probable enough in itself. The unmistakeable origin of the name jackal, which has come to us from the East, from *Shual*, is in favour of this view, and also the interchange of the two species, which is still common in the East, according to the testimony of Niebuhr, *Description of Arabia*, p. 166. שׁוּעל is also applied to the jackal in Ps. lxiii. 11.

Samson is delivered up bound by the Israelites to the Philistines; he breaks his bonds, takes up a new jawbone of an ass, which he finds lying there, and smites a thousand Philistines. The narrative does not employ a word to lead us to suppose that Samson slew the thousand Philistines. There is nothing incredible, or even improbable in the act, if we only consider that he had already become an object of fear and terror to the Philistines by his former deeds, and that the old impressions were not merely revived, but must have been very much strengthened by the bursting of the bonds, which took place before their eyes; and, finally, that they had everything to fear from the 3000 men of Judah who were present, as soon as their cowardice would have time to vanish before Samson's courage. It has been erroneously maintained that, in accordance with the narrative, the fountain from which Samson quenched his burning thirst must have sprung from the jawbone of the ass. That this was not the author's meaning, is plainly shown by the addition, "Wherefore he called the name thereof En-hakkore, which is in Lehi unto this day." The water must rather have sprung up at the place to which Samson had shortly before given the name Lehi, with reference to this event. This is clearly shown by Clericus on Judg. xv. 19; and even expositors like Studer have been forced to give up the theory of the jawbone. Against it, he says, we have (1) the *usus loquendi*; for a tooth-hole in the jawbone of an ass would have been called מכתש הלחי, while אשר בלחי can scarcely mean anything but what belongs to לחי. (2) Even for a miracle, it would be quite too wonderful for a fountain to spring up out of the socket of a tooth, especially since the jawbone was still fresh, and was therefore provided with teeth, in which case the water must have flowed out of the tooth itself. (3) The spring was still in existence at the time of the narrator. And, finally, (4) the analogy of the two streams in the wilderness, Ex. xvii., Num. xx. On the other hand, there is nothing at all to confirm the opinion that the water had its source in the jawbone. The מכתש, properly mortar, like our kettle, a recess, never occurs of a hole or gap in a tooth, but we find it in Zeph. i. 11 as the name of a place; and in Ps. lxxviii. 15, Isa. xlviii. 21, it is used of the fissure in the rock from which Moses brought forth a stream in the wilderness. Moreover, the true interpretation forced itself even upon the Jews, notwithstanding their tendency to seek out absurdities. It is to be found in Josephus and in the Chaldee paraphrast. If Luther had not made an oversight here, there would scarcely be any further necessity for defending it. In the whole history of revelation we find nothing so extravagant, least of all can we expect it in the book of Judges, where, as a rule, everything occurs in so natural a way.

The carrying away of the gate of Gaza certainly shows great, but by no means superhuman, strength. Pliny, in his *Hist. Nat.* 7. 20, tells of a man who bore away 600 pounds. A general lieutenant, in the seven-years' war, lifted up a horse and his rider, together with a large cannon, with great ease. But here also an attempt has been made to invest the narrative with an extravagant character, which in itself it does not possess. It has been maintained that the author makes Samson carry the gate to Hebron, which was about five hours' distance from Gaza. But, on the contrary, it is stated in chap. xvi. 3 that Samson carried the gate to the top of a hill near Hebron, not לפני but על פני. According to Joliffe, p. 285, a small valley extends from Gaza towards the east, and behind it there is a considerable elevation, which is supposed to be the mountain to which Samson carried the gate of the town. Robinson says, book ii. p. 639: "Towards the east the view is cut off by the range of hills which we passed. The highest point is a partially isolated mountain, south-east from the city, at about half an hour's distance." Studer has justly pointed out that the false explanation, recently defended by Winer and Bertheau, would entirely destroy the effect produced by the circumstance that in the morning the inhabitants of Gaza saw the gate of their city on the top of a neighbouring mountain, while they thought that they had shut in the hero with it.

The last act of Samson, the pulling down of the idol-temple of the Philistines, forms a necessary keystone; for without this his weakness would not have appeared in its true light. In his lowest humiliation he repented. The re-growth of his hair was no *titulus sine re;* the consecration which it betokened was an actual thing. Thus the Lord could again employ him as His instrument. But the fall had been so deep that the former relation could not be restored. The Lord required him only for one more deed, and this must involve him, as well as his enemies, in destruction. Henceforward Israel was to be delivered in a more spiritual way. The judgeship was buried with Samson. With respect to the external side of the event, the author has been supposed to have held the untenable view that the burden of a roof which supported 3000 men rested upon two pillars which stood close together. The contrary appears from the fact that in chap. xvi. 29 these two pillars are spoken of as the two middle pillars. The building rested on four side-walls or four rows of columns. The two principal of these, upon which the main weight of the building rested, stood in the middle, close together. Their fall, together with the burden of the great numbers on the roof, entailed the overthrow of the whole building. That there was nothing improbable in this event has been universally acknowledged by architects.

11. We have already remarked that through the whole period in which the acts of Samson gave rise to so much wonder, and were in every mouth, Samuel's reformatory activity continued to work in silence. He used all his influence to bring back the people to the fear of the Lord, and so to freedom; and he found a susceptibility in them. Sorrow had exercised a softening influence on their minds. Above all, he sought to impress the young, to animate them with his own inspiration, and through them to influence wider circles. Finally, in the fortieth year of the oppression by the Philistines, Samuel concluded that everything was sufficiently prepared for the adoption of vigorous measures. At his command the people destroyed all their idols, and in sincere repentance dedicated themselves anew to God. Then, at his command, they assembled at Mizpeh to implore God's help against their enemies. The symbolical act of pouring out water, which occurred there, according to 1 Sam. vii. 6, serves as an expression of their miserable condition, as an exemplification of the words, "I am poured out like water," in Ps. xxii., and is therefore a symbolically expressed κύριε ἐλήισον.

No sooner had the nation turned again to God than He gave them a proof of His love, in order not to try their faith which was still weak. The invading Philistines were smitten by a natural event, which ensued at the entreaty of Samuel, more than by the weapons of the Israelites; their power was broken for a long period, and the cities which they had wrested from the Israelites were retaken. This victory must have served to increase the respect in which Samuel was held, and which he employed solely in the interest of the kingdom of God. He was chosen to be judge during his lifetime, holding office in a different spirit from that of his predecessors. He destroyed all traces of idolatry, and made an annual journey through the country to establish order and administer justice. He dwelt at Ramah, and had an altar there, where he himself performed the service, and thus united in his own person the extraordinary priestly and civil dignity, yet in such a way that he cannot be said to have held the office of high priest. This still existed independently of him, as we learn from 1 Sam. xiv. 3, comp. with 1 Sam. iv. 21. It still continued in the family of Eli. Samuel only performed isolated priestly acts, just as his ordinary civil supremacy was in no way set aside by his office of judge.

12. The establishment of royalty. Samuel had already become old in his vocation, when a twofold cause incited the people to an impatient demand for the establishment of royalty. First, the unseemly behaviour of Samuel's sons, whom he had appointed to assist him in his office of judge; then a war with which they were threatened by the Ammonites, and which they thought themselves incapable of maintaining while their former constitution still continued. The way in which Samuel received the desire of the nation, which was expressed through their legal organs, at first appears strange. His opposition seems to be irreconcilable with Deut. xvii., where directions are given how to act in case the people should desire a king, without a word expressing disapproval of the desire; and still more at variance with those passages in Genesis in which the patriarchs are promised, as a blessing, that kings should proceed from their loins. But the solution of this apparent inconsistency has already been anticipated by former remarks. Samuel's opposition is not directed against kingship in itself, but only against the spirit in which the nation demanded it. In this there was a twofold element of ungodliness. (1.) They did not desire a king instead of a judge *in abstracto,* but a king

instead of Samuel, the judge appointed and gloriously sanctioned by God, as in the time of Moses or Joshua. (2.) The desire of the people for a king was based on the false assumption that God was powerless to help them, and that the reason of their subjection was not their sin, but a defect in their constitution. "The people," says Joh. Müller, "who sought the cause of the evil not in themselves but in the imperfection of their political constitution, chose a king." Comp. the copious examination in *Beitr.*, part iii. p. 246 ff. After Samuel had contended against the perverted mind of the nation, he submitted to the desire, which was in accordance with the will of God, but at the same time he sought to guard against the probable abuse of kingly power, by a document, probably founded on Deut. xvii., in which the conditions were laid down to which an Israelitish king must submit, lest kingship should endanger the supremacy of God; comp. 1 Sam. x. 25.

§ 4.

THE CIVIL CONSTITUTION AT THE TIME OF THE JUDGES.

We have already more than once drawn attention to the fact that the hereditary constitution of the Israelites remained unaltered throughout this period; during it the judicial and executive power was always in the hands of the natural rulers of the people, the heads of families and tribes. Besides the proofs of this already given, we may refer to the transactions of the elders in Gilead with Jephthah, in chap. xi. 6 ff.: the power which is conceded to Jephthah appears as *potestas delegata*, and is so regarded by both parties. The transactions of the elders of the nation with Samuel respecting the establishment of royalty, also show plainly that the office of judge did not interfere with the continuance of the ordinary magistracy. A distinction between this and the former period obtains only in one point, and that of a nature which has nothing to do with the surrender of established institutions, but only with the dissolution of a bond which had always been mainly internal, and was never outwardly established. Owing to the nature of the Israelitish constitution as a nation of tribes, there was necessarily a want of the *centrum unitatis*. In earlier times this want was compensated by the unity of mind, which formed an internal bond of union among the twelve tribes who were outwardly separated, as well as by the free authority exercised by the leading representatives of this tendency, a Moses, a Joshua, and a Phinehas. In the events narrated in the appendix to the book of Judges, we do not find anything of this want. The people rise up as one man. Further on in the period of the judges the only bond which held the tribes together disappeared, and the whole was immediately resolved into its constituent parts. Nowhere do we find a co-operation of the whole nation; nowhere the summoning of a national assembly; nowhere an allied army of all the tribes, nor one commander-in-chief. We meet only with temporary confederacies of separate tribes, such as were called forth by common danger, or by the similar interests of their geographical position. Then the numerous, powerful, and proud tribe of Ephraim, in whose midst was the sanctuary at Shiloh, laid claim to a kind of leadership; and the remaining tribes, with the exception of Judah, which maintained its independence throughout, submitted more or less to this claim. We recognise this claim not only by the reproaches of Ephraim against Gideon in Judg. viii. 1, and their protest against Jephthah in Judg. xii., but even more clearly from Ps. lxxviii., which was composed in the time of David, and which represents it very fully. From it we learn also that this relation was by no means advantageous to the nation. The bad spirit afterwards manifested by Ephraim as the soul of the kingdom of the ten tribes, already characterized them in the time of the judges; and its effect at that time was equally deleterious. But the relation was of a very loose kind, and could not prevent the disunion of the nation. This severance was at once the necessary consequence and punishment of their apostasy from the true *centrum unitatis*, from the Lord. When the nation turned again to the Lord, it was in some measure remedied by the judges whom the Lord raised up. For though none of these succeeded in uniting the whole nation under his command, yet by their means a bond of union was generally established between a few tribes, if only for a time, and thus an end was put to that weakness against the enemy which was the result of separation. We have already shown that the opinion that his activity extended over the whole nation has arisen in a misunderstanding of the remark which the author makes respecting every judge, viz. that he judged Israel. With equal justice we might conclude from the title bishop of the evangelical Church that an evangelical pope was meant. The author does not intend by this remark to point out the special sphere of the activity of the separate judges, but only to draw attention to the fact that the divine benefit was conferred on a part only by virtue of its connection with the whole. The covenant of God, of which the raising up of the judges was an issue, was concluded, not with Dan or Naphtali, but with Israel. If the author had said of the judges that they judged Israel in any other sense than this, he would have directly contradicted himself in the case of Jephthah, of whom he states both that he judged Israel, and that he was merely head over the trans-Jordanic tribes. With respect to the position of the judges, it is generally estimated falsely when they are looked upon as proper judicial personages in our sense, men who were possessed of ordinary judicial power. This error has been occasioned by the assumption that the Hebrew שפט is perfectly synonymous with our *judging*, while in reality it has a much wider signification. The שפט in the book of Judges generally denotes the exercise of authority and superiority. It has undeniably this general meaning at the very beginning with respect to the first judge, Othniel, and therefore is a passage where the author certainly used the word in what he regarded as its true and principal meaning. In chap. iii. 9, 10, we read of Othniel: "The Lord raised up a deliverer to the children of Israel, who delivered them, even Othniel. And the Spirit of the Lord came upon him, and he judged Israel, and went out to war; and the Lord delivered the king of Mesopotamia into his hand." This can have no reference to judging in the usual sense, for the words "and he judged Israel" stand before the giving of the Spirit of the Lord or *gifts* for the conquest of the enemy, and that conquest itself. They can therefore refer only to the authority which Othniel received, by the fact that he was made partaker of the Spirit of God. The history of Samson also necessarily leads to the same idea of the שפט. We read that he judged Israel for twenty years; where there can be no idea whatever of judging in the ordinary sense. Having once obtained a sure foundation in this way, it will certainly appear significant that of no single judge is it expressly stated that he sat in judgment. Only of Deborah do we read, in chap. iv. 5, that the Israelites went up to her for judgment. But she cannot be placed on a level with the judges throughout. She pronounced judgment as a prophetess in matters where no confidence was placed in the decision of the ordinary judicial jurisdiction, and a judgment of God in the proper sense was desired; just as, according to Ex. xviii., the nation, leaving their natural judges, thronged to Moses, to draw justice immediately from its source, and not from the tributary channels, which were so often corrupt. As little does Samuel belong to the ordinary judges: his position was exactly similar to that of Deborah; he was judge in another sense than the judges of the book of Judges. If the mention of judging were wanting only in the case of this or that judge, we might look for the reason in the fact that their activity in the national wars of deliverance was the proper subject of the narrative; but since it is wanting in all, this reason does not suffice. If the judges had really exercised judicial functions, there would at least be some mention of the circumstance, if only a casual one, such as we find in the case of Deborah. Moreover, the author relates much of the judges besides their principal activity. The result is this: the judges had nothing to do with the proper administration of justice. This remained in the hands of the natural rulers of the nation. The judges were men who had gained confidence and authority by what they had done in the strength of the Lord for the deliverance of the nation, and to whom the people were glad to appeal in public and private matters,—in matters of justice, too, in which, however, they acted merely as arbitrators,—and who exercised a guiding influence over them, which, however, was also of a free nature. The only exception was Jephthah, who formally claimed a kind of regency among the trans-Jordanic tribes before he entered into war, and had it confirmed by the natural rulers of the nation.

§ 5.

THE CONDITION OF RELIGION.

In our previous representation of separate historical events, we have anticipated almost all that can be said on this subject, and may therefore be very brief. We have already shown, from a number of facts, how erroneous with respect to worship and religious feeling is the prevalent conception of the period of the judges, according to which it was a time of complete confusion or of rude barbarism. Respecting the worship, we have shown that throughout the whole period of the judges the tabernacle of the covenant formed the religious centre of the nation; that the great feasts, especially the feast of the passover, were then celebrated by the whole nation; that the partial and temporary participation in the heathen worship of Baal and Astarte did it no injury, because this worship was not regarded as antagonistic to the worship of Jehovah by those who practised it; that the Levitical priesthood was universally esteemed and recognised, and worship was performed only in the tabernacle of the covenant. With regard to the second point,—religious feeling,—we saw that, notwithstanding all the corruption which had crept in, there were still many tokens of the continuance of a better spirit, such as the song of Deborah, the prayer of Hanna, personalities like that of Gideon, institutions like that of the Nazirate and consecrated virgins, and many others. Here we shall only draw attention to the fact that we have the most complete representation of the religious and civil condition of the period of the judges in the book of Ruth, "whose historical truth regarding the description of ancient life," Ewald says, "cannot be questioned." We must bear in mind, however, that the events narrated in this book occur at a time in which Israel was purified in the furnace of affliction, and was mightily raised up by the wonderful help of the Lord, so that the picture is nothing but an exact counterpart of the better times of the period of the judges. If a good foundation had not remained even in times of degeneracy, the danger and the deliverance would have passed over without making any deeper impression. We cannot better describe the impression made by this picture than in the words of Roos: "The little book of Ruth stands between the books which treat of war and other things as a most graceful and unparalleled picture of honesty, propriety, wisdom, and uprightness exemplified by different persons in domestic life. This beautiful history contains a representation of every virtue required in the domestic and social life of man. It redounds to the everlasting glory of the God of Israel, that, in the freedom in which His people were living at that time, there was so much chastity, justice, love, and propriety. Who were Naomi, Boaz, Ruth? They were peasants. How charming is their eloquence! How pleasing their friendliness! How fine their manners! What wisdom and judgment they display!" In order to roll this stone out of the way, the credibility of the book of Ruth has been attacked. It has been asserted that the description, with its idyllic colouring, stands in irreconcilable opposition to the book of Judges, and that the preference must be unconditionally given to the latter. But we receive thankfully the candid confession that the book of Ruth is irreconcilable with the prevalent idea. To all unprejudiced persons it forms its own defence against the attack on its credibility. Only come and see! If ever a history bore testimony to its own truthfulness, it is this. In what light we are to regard the alleged inconsistency between this book and the book of Judges will appear from what has already been remarked. In the latter we have pointed out numerous points of contact with respect to the representation of the book of Ruth. We have shown that it was not the intention of the author of the book of Judges to give a complete history, but only to lay stress on a single part,—that it was his object to give special prominence to the *scandala*. Nothing can be more one-sided and narrow than to make the history of a war the measure of the whole religious and moral condition, and to cut away with the knife all that does not at once appear suitable. On the heights above it often snows and freezes, while below in the valleys there is genial sunshine. From this standpoint all the gospels must be regarded as a picture with idyllic colouring, but without any reality. For, in reading the books of Josephus on the Jewish war, we meet with a very different picture. In a time like this we find no footing for a Simeon and a Hannah, for a John the Baptist, for the whole Church of peace which meets us in the New Testament. In reading a description of the Thirty Years' War, with all its horrors, we should not at first expect to find a Paul Gerhard living side by side with a Tilly; and yet his existence cannot be regarded as an isolated case, but is intelligible only on the supposition that he was a member of a whole community. What a contrast there is between the quarrelling of theologians of the seventeenth century and the songs of this period, the most beautiful that we possess! The same time which from one set of sources appears the saddest, when looked at from another point of view seems to be the most glorious of the evangelical Church.

It still remains for us to notice an influential institution which owes its origin to this period, viz. the schools of the prophets. In 1 Sam. x. 5, where they are first mentioned, we find Samuel in connection with them,—a circumstance which has led to the too hasty conclusion that they were founded by him. Yet this view is certainly not far from the truth. For even if the schools of the prophets had begun to form themselves before the time of Samuel, which we have the less reason to doubt since the book of Judges bears adequate testimony to the existence of prophets, and since it lay in the nature of the thing that individuals bound themselves together as closely as possible and joined in a common activity against the spirit of the time, yet we cannot suppose that there was any great extension and formal organization of the institution previous to Samuel, from what is said in 1 Sam. iii. 1 : "And the word of the Lord was precious in those days; there was no open vision." Add to this the sporadic character of the activity of the prophets, which we learn from the book of Judges. Finally, in favour of Samuel's having virtually established the schools of the prophets, we have the fact that after his death we no longer meet with them except in the kingdom of Israel. This circumstance cannot be attributed to lack of information. The fact of our not meeting with them in the kingdom of Judah leads us to infer that they did not exist; and if this were the case, it is impossible to suppose that the schools of the prophets had taken deep root before Samuel. They appear as an institution established by him for a temporary object, and only continued, where necessity demanded it, in the kingdom of Israel, whose relations were in many respects similar to those in Samuel's time, where the prophethood occupied quite another position than in the kingdom of Judah,—not being a mere supplement to the activity of the Levitical priesthood, but possessing the entire responsibility of maintaining the kingdom of God in Israel. The principal passages referring to the schools of the prophets, besides 1 Sam. x. 10, are, 1 Kings xix. 20, 21 ; 2 Kings ii. 5, iv. 38, vi. 1. The designation is an awkward one, liable to cause misunderstanding. No instruction was given in the schools of the prophets: they were regular and organized societies. Taking all these passages together, it becomes evident that the schools of the prophets were in many respects a kind of monkish institution. Those who were educated there had a common dwelling and a common table; the most distinguished of the prophets standing at its head as spiritual fathers. Music was employed as a principal means of edification, and of awakening prophetic inspiration. But what distinguishes the schools of the prophets from the cloisters, or at least from a great number of them, is their thorough practical tendency. They were hearths of spiritual life to

Israel. Their aim was not to encourage a contemplative life, but to rouse the nation to activity: every prophetic disciple was a missionary.

FOURTH SECTION.

FROM THE ESTABLISHMENT OF ROYALTY TO THE DIVISION OF THE KINGDOM.

§ 1.

EVENTS FROM THE ELECTION OF SAUL TILL HIS REJECTION.

Samuel chose a king, apparently as a concession to the impatient demand of the nation, but in reality following the will of God as it had been revealed to him. At the same time he took care that the anthropocracy should not be in opposition to the theocracy, but should serve as a means of realizing it. The choice was made from this point of view. The result was that Samuel did everything to awaken the king who was chosen to a true and earnest fear of God; and when this attempt failed, the family of the chosen was rejected as a warning example to his successors. It was the divine mission of Samuel to see that what was given to the nation for their salvation should not turn to their destruction. He stands forth as the representative of the people no less than of God; for everything that threatened to separate the people from their God undermined their nationality at the same time, the germ of it being a proper attitude towards God. By this relationship Israel had increased from a horde to a nation; and every disturbance of it threatened internal dissolution, which would necessarily be followed by an external one.

Samuel's former activity was an excellent preparation for royalty. He had smoothed the ground for it. The consciousness of religious and civil union was powerfully re-awakened by his means. The unanimity of the people, even as exemplified in their desire for a king, was a result of his activity. An able king had only to reap what he had sown.

In recent times it has been asserted that Samuel was deceived in his choice; that he had afterwards every reason to be dissatisfied with his accidental selection, for nobody could have been less adapted than Saul to represent the king of so oppressed and broken a nation. The subsequent history of Saul may justly be regarded as a proof that the so-called utterances of God, by which the judges and afterwards the prophets give decisions, were often of a subjective nature merely. But this assertion is totally without foundation. What God revealed to Samuel as the task to be absolutely realized by the king who was chosen, "He shall save my people out of the hand of the Philistines," 1 Sam. ix. 16, was actually realized by him; comp. 1 Sam. xiv. 47 ff., where, after the counting up of the nations conquered by Saul, we have the concluding words, "And whithersoever he turned himself, he vexed them." He raised Israel to an external power and importance such as it had not possessed since the time of Joshua. What great gifts Saul possessed in this respect, and how much Israel was indebted to him, we learn best from the lament of David over his death and Jonathan's, 2 Sam. i. 17 ff. Besides this, Saul was zealous in maintaining the letter of the Mosaic law, everywhere introducing discipline and order, and putting an end to that state of things where "every man did that which was right in his own eyes," which is represented in the book of Judges as characteristic of that period. Of this we have many examples,—in the severity of the measures by which he rooted out all kinds of superstition forbidden in the Mosaic law, 1 Sam. xxviii. 9; in the anxious care with which he restrained the violation of the Mosaic regulations respecting the eating of blood, even in the thick of battle, 1 Sam. xiv. 34. It was his honest endeavour to fill the office which our older theologians have assigned to the civil authority, to be *custos tabulæ utriusque* of the law. But Samuel never gives expression to the conviction that he who is chosen will be and remain a servant of the law, truly devoted to the Lord; or to the assurance that this was a part of God's plan: hence we are not justified in attributing it to him. He did what he could to bring about this result. The success of his endeavours, which were frustrated by Saul's hardness of heart,—for he let thorns grow up while the good fruit was choked,—was so little necessary, that their failure was more advantageous to the cause of God. The theocratic principle was more fully developed in the reaction than could have happened had the king been truly pious, so that we may say that Saul was chosen by God, because in His omniscience He foresaw that he would not turn to Him with his whole heart. Saul and David are in necessary connection. On the threshold of royalty God first shows in Saul what the king of Israel is without Him; then in David what the king is with Him. Both are types or representatives. The events which befell them are actual prophecies, which first of all passed into fulfilment in the history of the Israelitish monarchy, and then through the whole history of the world.

Before we turn to isolated events, we must make a remark relative to the character of our source in this period. It is evident that the author of the books of Samuel does not intend to give a complete history of Saul, from the circumstance that he either passes over the most important events in perfect silence, or mentions them very briefly. Thus, for example, we learn nothing of the commencement and origin of the new captivity to the Philistines, in which we here find Israel all at once; Saul's important undertakings against several neighbouring nations are only briefly and summarily mentioned in chap. xiv. 46, 47; we only hear casually of his vigorous measures against superstition; nothing is done for the chronological determination of those separate events which are communicated. Everything leads to the conclusion that the author followed a special aim; that he only gives prominence to certain facts because they were of special importance for sacred history. Hence he gives a full account of the war with the Philistines, because it was a realization of the promise of God that He would deliver His people from the Philistines by Saul; and of the Amalekite war, because Saul's disobedience and perversity were specially manifested in it. The principal aim of the author is to point to these and their melancholy consequences; to show the causes which led to the rejection of Saul and the election of David; and his choice of subjects is explained by the fact that this was the germ of Saul's history, important for all times.

The king chosen belonged to one of the smallest tribes of Israel, the tribe of Benjamin, to the smallest family in this tribe, to an obscure branch of this family, 1 Sam. ix. 21. This happened that he might be the more humble, which was really the case in the beginning, as we learn from the passage just quoted; but the principal object was to show the nation that God's choice was not due to any natural privileges; that He can give greatness to whom He will. Natural greatness might readily have obscured what was to be given by God. In this way each one was led to the true origin of Saul's subsequent greatness.

Before Saul's election he occupied a very low standpoint, intellectually and spiritually. He scarcely knew anything of Samuel, the centre of all higher Israelitish life. His servant speaks to him of Samuel as of one who was unknown, 1 Sam. ix. 6: "Behold now, there is in this city a man of God, and he is an honourable man; all that he saith cometh surely to pass." Nothing moves him to make acquaintance with the celebrated prophet but anxiety respecting his lost asses. If Samuel had acted merely in accordance with human judgment, it could never have occurred to him that such a man was destined to be king. But he is at once absolutely certain of his business, and immediately meets him with an announcement. In the conversation he had with him, 1 Sam. ix. 25, 26, he seeks to stir up a higher life in him; and before leaving he anoints him, *i.e.* he gives him, in the name of God, a symbolical assurance of the bestowment of the gifts of the Spirit, which were necessary to the fulfilment of the office for which he was destined. He then condescends to his weakness, and tells him the principal things that are to befall him in the time to come, — a circumstance from which we perceive the extent of this weakness, how completely Saul had to be drawn out of the rough, how much the divine must manifest itself outwardly, in order that he might be able to recognise it. But the anointing soon developed its power. In 1 Sam. x. 9 we read: "And when he had turned his back to go from Samuel, God gave him another heart." This is no mere figure of speech. We see that there was a decisive change in Saul's life,—that in the parable of the sower he belongs not to the first class, but to the third. On his way he passed through Gibeah, where there was a school of the prophets. A band of the disciples came to meet him, and, having been powerfully stirred up, he was now carried away by their enthusiasm: the Spirit of the Lord came upon him, and he prophesied. What a striking contrast there was between his present condition and his former one, appears from the astonished question of the people, "Is Saul also among the prophets?" They had thought no one less likely to be the subject of higher inspiration than he. But the best answer was given by one of the by-standers: "But who is their father?" thus intimating that the heavenly origin of prophetic inspiration removed what was striking and unintelligible in the contrast between the past and the present, which it certainly had when looked at from a human point of view.

That which had previously happened had reference only to the relation of Saul to God. Even the anointing had no direct reference to the nation, as appears from the circumstance that it was done in secret. Now, after everything has been settled with regard to the higher relation, means are taken to bring about the recognition of the chosen king by the nation. First of all the divine choice is verbally proclaimed in an assembly of the nation called by Samuel at Mizpeh. It is generally supposed that Saul was here chosen by lot. But the mode and manner of proceeding, and the expression in 1 Sam. x. 19–21, are not in favour of this view. The fact that *all* are obliged to appear before the Lord, that the choice is first made among the tribes, then among the families, etc., can properly only serve to heighten the solemnity of the act and to increase attention to it. And it is at variance with ver. 22, "They inquired of the Lord further," which speaks of an appeal to God, which cannot have been made by lot, but must have been made either by the Urim and Thummim, or else through Samuel. If the choice had been made by lot, there would probably have been some allusion in ver. 22 to the difference in the *modus* of asking. Saul's humility appeared on this occasion. He thought himself so little worthy of kinghood, that he hid himself, in order, if possible, to escape the calling made known to him. But this verbal declaration of God was not enough. There must also be an actual one. God's election is not vain and feeble; if it be real, it must prove itself in the gifts and deeds of him who is chosen. The people felt this, even those among them who acknowledged the election with all their heart. Saul himself also felt it. He went quietly home, and continued his former occupation, ploughing with his oxen; comp. 1 Sam. xi. 5. Both the people and Saul waited for the future actual ratification. Until then everything remained as it had been. Samuel was still at the head of affairs. In the assembly at Mizpeh he endeavoured to make the people conscious of the limits put to royalty by the Mosaic law, of the difference which must necessarily exist between kingship in the theocracy and among the heathen. In 1 Sam. x. 25 we read: "And Samuel told the people the manner of the kingdom, and wrote it in a book, and laid it up before the Lord." The "manner of the kingdom" here spoken of is to be distinguished from that which is mentioned in chap. viii., where reference is made to those rights which, alas! are often assumed by kings at the prompting of corrupt human nature; while, on the other hand, we have here to do with those rights which are conceded to them in accordance with the will and word of God. There can be no doubt that Samuel borrowed this "manner of the kingdom" from Deut. xvii.

The actual ratification of the choice of Saul soon followed. A threatened invasion of Nahash, king of the Ammonites, who probably wished to reassert the old claims already made by the descendants of Lot, in the book of Judges, to the country beyond the Jordan, had, according to 1 Sam. xii. 12, first called forth the vehement demand of the nation for a king. In the meantime this invasion actually took place. Nahash attacked the town of Jabesh beyond the Jordan; whose inhabitants in their great need sent messengers to their cis-Jordanic brethren. These came first to Saul, and when he heard their words, "the Spirit of God came upon him." The peasant was suddenly transformed into a valiant hero, who brings help to the oppressed in the power of the Lord, and causes the enemy to fly in wild disorder. Saul's true kingly mind manifests itself after victory. The nation, inspired with enthusiasm for him, demands the death of those who had formerly despised and insulted him. But he replies, "There shall not a man be put to death this day; for to-day the Lord hath wrought salvation in Israel."

The Lord had now set His seal on the election of Saul, and Samuel called the nation to Gilgal, a place hallowed by remembrances from the time of Joshua, that they might recognise this seal. Saul was there solemnly inaugurated as king. The relations into which he now entered are not quite clear to us. Respecting the revenues of the kings we have only scattered statements; comp. Michaelis, *Mos. R.* part i. sec. 59. But we learn from 1 Sam. xvii. 25 that his position was from the beginning truly regal; that he was not dependent only on the presents brought by those who had any business with the king, comp. 1 Sam. xvi. 20, but received regular taxes from all Israel. It is here stated that whoever would kill Goliath would receive, among other things, the exemption of his family from all taxes and imposts.

The appointment of the new king involved Samuel's solemn renunciation of office, so far as it was connected with the sphere of politics. The acknowledgment which the nation made to Samuel on this occasion puts his recent opponents to shame. Samuel provokes this acknowledgment, in order to gain a foundation for the subsequent reproof. He endeavours to make the people conscious that they sinned in desiring a king. But the sin lay partially in the circumstance that they desired a king instead of

Samuel, the judge appointed by God. Above all, it must be established that Samuel invariably proved his divine mission by his deeds. He had foundation enough for the endeavour to make the people conscious of their sin. The kingship they demanded was not an external representation of the kingship of God, but was in direct opposition to it. But the king saw himself in the same light in which he was regarded by the people. Samuel attained his object. The nation were deeply moved by his words, and by the sign which confirmed them,—a storm which he predicted, and which occurred at a time of year when storms were most uncommon in Palestine. And they said unto Samuel, "Pray for thy servants unto the Lord thy God, that we die not; for we have added unto all our sins this evil, to ask us a king." Samuel, however, does not take advantage of this frame of mind to overthrow the kingship, as he must have done in accordance with the recent view of the relation of the kingship to the theocracy and of Samuel's character. He not only formed a just estimate of the subjectively considered sinful character of the demand of the nation, but undoubtedly he knew also that the *vox populi*, objectively considered, was at the same time the *vox dei*. He exhorts the people henceforward to be faithful to the Lord, with their king; and the Lord would then glorify Himself in both.

But we must draw attention to the fact that he only gave up part of his office at Gilgal. Formerly he had united in himself the kingly, priestly, and prophetic office; now he retains only the two latter. In chap. xii. 23 he says: "Moreover, as for me, God forbid that I should sin against the Lord in ceasing to pray for you: but I will teach you the good and the right way." If this be remembered, we shall find no difficulty in the fact that in chap. vii. 15 it is stated, "And Samuel judged Israel all the days of his life." Only we must guard against attributing too narrow and external a meaning to the judging. Every prophet was in a certain sense judge. Samuel judged even the king after he had already resigned his office of judge in a strict sense.

Chap. xiii. 1 begins the history of Saul's reign with the statement of his age on ascending the throne, and the number of years he reigned. But this is of no use to us whatever, owing to its critical inaccuracy. In the statement of his age on ascending the throne, the number is completely wanting; and in the statement of the years that he reigned, it is false, for it is quite impossible that Saul could have reigned only two years. The first important event was a war with the Philistines. They had probably availed themselves of the favourable opportunity when the Ammonites had taken arms against Israel. It is certain that the beginning of hostilities belongs to a time previous to Saul's reign; for in chap. ix. 16 a king is promised by God who should save His people out of the hand of the Philistines. According to chap. x. 5, the Philistines had a garrison at Gibeah, in the midst of the land of Israel, already before Saul was king. We learn that the oppression was very grievous, and extended far over the land, from the circumstance that the people had to do without arms, because, according to chap. xiii. 19, the Philistines had taken away all the smiths. But this measure, and the general intensity of persecution, can only belong to the beginning of Saul's reign, since we find no indication that the Israelites were wanting in weapons in the campaign against the Ammonites. Chap. vii. 13 is also at variance with the supposition that the Israelites were heavily oppressed by the Philistines during the administration of Samuel; for we read here that "the hand of the Lord was against the Philistines all the days of Samuel." It seems as if Saul's accession to the throne, in which the Philistines saw a threatening of danger, incited them to their utmost exertions to extinguish the fire in its very beginning; and at first they appeared to be successful. The author, whose object is only to give prominence to certain events which are important for his aim, suddenly transports us into the midst of these warlike relations between Israel and the Philistines, to a point where the Philistines, with their main forces, had retreated, leaving only a few garrisons in the country. As a precaution against these garrisons, which had perhaps been left in the country in consequence of some treaty, after the principal forces had been disbanded, Saul established a kind of standing army, consisting of 3000 men, which he always retained. A quarrel between this army of observation and the Philistines caused the fire of warfare to break forth again into a clear flame. It is vain to attempt to justify the statement contained in 1 Sam. xiii. 5, that the number of Philistine chariots amounted to 30,000. The nature of the thing, biblical analogies,—Pharaoh, for example, had only 600 chariots in pursuing the Israelites,— the disproportion of the number of riders, who were only 6000,—everything leads to the conclusion that the number is critically corrupt. Some suppose that they had 1000 chariots; the ל belonging to the preceding ישראל being twice written by mistake as the numeral of 30, having given rise to our reading. The most probable supposition is that they had 3000. The number of riders or charioteers agrees best with this. The chariots were generally occupied by two men. On the occasion of this war it first became manifest that Saul's change of heart had been only superficial. Immediately after his anointing, Samuel had enjoined him, by the command of God, to resort to Gilgal, the holy place, in all difficult circumstances of the State. There the prophet would come to him, and, after the presentation of sacrifice, would show him what he should do. Seven days the king was to wait for him, 1 Sam. x. 8. This command was expressly designed to try Saul, to reveal the thoughts of his heart. He did not stand the trial. He certainly went to Gilgal, and waited there almost to the end of the allotted period; but when the seventh day was nearly at an end, and urgent danger, in human estimation, permitted no further delay, he performed the sacrifice without Samuel. The sin did not consist in the circumstance of his offering up sacrifice without being a priest; it is even highly improbable that he did so,—the action is probably attributed to him only because it was done at his command. It lay rather in his disobedience to the divine command, which he himself recognised as such, for he never ventured to question the divine mission of Samuel, even at a time when it would have been his highest interest to do so. Unconditional subjection to the will of the God who had revealed Himself in Israel was the barrier which separated Israelitish kingship from the heathen, and it was necessary to place this distinction clearly before the eyes of the king and the nation at the very beginning, and to punish every violation of it. If mercy had been shown in this case, it would have been the worst possible precedent for all future time, and have put the thing in an utterly false light. If we look merely at the external appearance of the sin, it seems, like the sin of our first parents, to have been very great, yet scarcely so great as to justify the severe judgment of Samuel. But we must remember that Samuel, as a divinely illumined seer, could look into the heart of Saul. He saw not merely the detached fruit, but the tree which had borne it. That he was not deceived, that he did not invade the province of God's judgment, but that God pronounced sentence through him, is shown by the subsequent history of Saul, in which his inner nature revealed itself more clearly: his unbroken heart; his arrogance, which would always be *sui juris*, and refused to submit to a higher authority, still manifested itself more and more plainly. Those who accuse Samuel of severity on the ground of this circumstance, proceed on the false assumption that he possessed no other means of judging of Saul's act than are open to us. But this judgment, when compared with Saul's further development, proves the contrary. Moreover, Samuel does not tell Saul that he is rejected by God as king, but only that the kingdom will not remain in his family. Personal rejection only follows afterwards, when the inner godlessness of Saul, which was covered with the semblance of outward piety, was more plainly revealed. For the present the former relation of Samuel to Saul still continued.

The frivolous oath made by Saul after the overthrow of the Philistines, that whoever should taste any food or drink till the evening should be punished with death, damaged the cause which it was intended to promote; for the nation, deprived of all refreshment, soon tired in pursuit of the enemy; comp. 1 Sam. xiv. 28–30. Yet Saul appears in a far more disadvantageous light even than this oath, in his conduct when his son Jonathan is found to have unwittingly broken the command. Instead of acknowledging what the silence of the Urim and Thummim was intended to indicate, that he had sinned, and humbling himself before God on account of the frivolous use he had made of His name, he lays the blame on Jonathan, and thinks it necessary to kill him, though he had been the author of the victory; but is prevented from carrying out his design by the powerful interference of the people. His hypocritical self-deception, his blind arrogance, goes so far that he would rather lose his son than relinquish aught of his imaginary pre-eminence. But Ewald has no reason in the narrative in 1 Sam. xiv. for making him guilty of having allowed another to die for Jonathan. No example of this kind of substitution ever occurs in Israel.

In Deut. xxv. 19, in the Mosaic law, a command was laid upon the Israelites that when the Lord had given them rest from all their enemies round about, they were to accomplish the curse pronounced on Amalek in Ex. xvii. This condition was now fulfilled by Saul's victories over the neighbouring nations, told in 1 Sam. xiv. 47 ff. He therefore receives, through Samuel, a revelation that the time is now come to accomplish the judgment of divine righteousness on the rejected and radically corrupt race of the Amalekites, whose former offence against Israel is not to be regarded as the sole cause of this judgment, but only as a symptom of their whole state; comp. 1 Sam. xv. 18-33. Saul spared the king of the Amalekites (whose name we do not know—Agag is the *nomen dignitatis* of all Amalekite kings), not from motives of humanity,—otherwise why should he not have spared the children?—but to do honour to the kingly dignity, and thus to himself, and allowed the people to retain the best part of the booty, showing that in so far as he fulfilled the divine commission, he fulfilled it not as such, but only employed it as an occasion for satisfying his own inclination which happened to be in unison with it. If he had remembered to act as the servant of divine righteousness, he would have felt it his first duty to judge the king in whom the bad spirit of the nation culminated; whose sword robbed the women of their children. It was but just, therefore, that the curse should give rise to a new one, which fell upon the unrighteous instrument of its accomplishment. This simple representation of the matter shows the injustice of asserting that Samuel only made use of this opportunity to revenge himself on Saul, who still showed more and more inclination to withdraw from his dictatorial power. With heartfelt sorrow Samuel executed the divine commission. It is true that he was filled with holy wrath on account of Saul's crime, of whose godlessness this act was only a symptom, but he cried to God all night through, hoping to obtain some mitigation of the divine decree; and when this hope proved vain, and he found himself obliged to announce the divine sentence of Saul's rejection, he was moved with such deep sorrow, that he felt it impossible to see him any more; 1 Sam. xv. 35, xvi. 1. We see how completely the single deed was only a symptom of the whole corrupt state, from the behaviour of Saul when Samuel called him to account. How different is the conduct of David after his adultery with Bath-sheba and the numbering of the people! First false and hypocritical excuses: the fault is not his, but the people's; what he withheld from the curse he intended as a sacrifice to God, so that it would have belonged to God in the end. Finally, when he sees that his excuses are of no avail, he coldly admits, "I have sinned." We see how similar in character this confession was to that of Pharaoh, from the request immediately attached to it, that Samuel would honour him before the people. We learn from vers. 17 that the root of his sin was arrogance, for Samuel here contrasts his present with his former position, when he was small in his own eyes. The father's arrogance afterwards descended to his daughter Michal. External service of God served him as a means of making terms with the Lord. This is evident from 1 Sam. xv. 22, 23, where Samuel says to him: "Hath the Lord as great delight in burnt-offerings and sacrifices, as in obeying the voice of the Lord? Behold, to obey is better than sacrifice, and to hearken than the fat of rams," etc. Saul himself acknowledges the justice of the standard by which he is judged. It never occurs to him to denounce the principle which destroyed him, as false. In that which led to his overthrow, he acted against his own conviction. He never doubted the reality of the Lord's supremacy in Israel, that unconditional obedience was due to His commands, or that Samuel was His servant. Those who have recently attempted to justify him at any cost have not considered this. Even from their standpoint he must be condemned. We may regard the theocracy as a delusion, but he shared this delusion. The semblance of injustice to Saul is only attributable to this circumstance, that Samuel's energetic measures against the first manifestations of his evil disposition kept it within certain limits, and hindered it from fully revealing itself. If he could have done as he wished, there would soon have been an end to the supremacy of God in Israel. Rude despotism would have usurped its place. Saul tried to lay a foundation for this despotism by the formation of a standing army. He placed men of his own tribe in the places of command, and sought to bind them to his interest by considerable dotations; comp. his own words in 1 Sam. xxii. 7. Samuel's antagonistic working kept Saul in fear of the principle which he did not love, and thus made the powerful realization of his wishes and tendencies impossible. Since he would not give up his inclinations, he fell into a state of unhappy dualism, which at last brought him to the verge of madness. He was prevented from consistently following out his desires not only by his own indecision, by conscience which was kept alive by Samuel, but also by fear of the nation, whose attention was drawn to his evil designs by the appearance of Samuel, and from the better part of whom he had to expect decided opposition if matters came to the worst. By the determination to reject Saul, we are not to understand that he ceased from that time to be the legal king of Israel. Samuel himself continues to recognise him as such, regarding the anointing of David as possessing only prophetic significance; so also David, whose whole behaviour towards him is guided by the conviction that he is the anointed of the Lord. His rejection involves only this: (1.) That God would henceforward leave him, and withdraw from him the gifts of His Spirit, His counsel through the Urim and Thummim and by His servant Samuel; and (2.) That in a short time the real deposition would be followed by tangible consequences,—the kingly ruins would be destroyed, and the kingdom would not pass to his descendants. Venema gives this interpretation of the divine decree briefly and well in the *Hist. Eccl.* i. p. 407: "Mansit quidem rex legitimus, sed spretus et brevi exscindendus, qui a deo desertus et furiis agitatus subinde nihil præclari amplius gessit, sed continuis se commaculavit facinoribus et reatum suum auxit." Those who would make Samuel instead of Saul a revolutionist, changing the parts, are unable to explain this patient waiting for the time when God Himself would execute His decree. The ἐκλογή followed the prophet. They looked forward with longing to the time when God would fulfil His determination. But no man ventured to do anything to hasten the overthrow of Saul. It is remarkable that he did not venture to do anything against Samuel, even at a time when he hesitated at no other deed of violence. In quiet retirement Samuel still worked for the kingdom of God. So powerful was the impression which his personal eminence exercised even over a hardened mind.

§ 2.

FROM THE REJECTION OF SAUL TO HIS DEATH; OR, SAUL AND DAVID.

This section falls into two subdivisions: the first, David at the court of Saul; the second, David flying before Saul.

1. The rejection of Saul was immediately followed by the anointing of David. The fact that in the ruddy shepherd boy, who was personally unknown to him, Samuel recognised the man after God's own heart, the future greatest one among Israel's kings, shows that he was not left to his own judgment; and this choice not only throws light on

the previous election, but also on the rejection. A separate little book makes us acquainted with the family of David. His ancestors were Boaz and Ruth the Moabitess, God-fearing people, whose beautiful history must undoubtedly have occupied David in his earliest youth. His father Jesse lived in that happy condition which the Psalmist asks in the words, "Give me neither poverty nor riches." The act of anointing was to be kept secret, in order not to provoke the wrath of the king against Samuel and David. Samuel therefore concealed the main object of his going to Bethlehem under a subordinate one,—a circumstance which has been represented as a crime, without any foundation whatever, since the duty of telling the truth by no means includes telling the whole truth. What Samuel says to the elders of Bethlehem in chap. xvi. 4, 5, respecting the object of his coming, gives us some insight into his activity. From it we learn that he often appeared unexpectedly in a place, to reprove unrighteousness and sin. The elders of Bethlehem tremble before him, and ask, "Comest thou peaceably?" We learn also that he held meetings for the worship of God, not only at the sacred places mentioned in 1 Sam. vii. 16, but also here and there in the cities from time to time. At all events there were no witnesses of the anointing except the family of Jesse; and it is not even certain that they were present, since the words "he anointed him in the midst of his brethren," chap. xvi. 13, may mean that he chose him from the number of his brethren. For the object of the anointing it was not necessary that it should be public, since its result with respect to office could only be a thing of the future; the present result was limited to the bestowment of the gifts, the kingly $\chi\alpha\rho\iota\sigma\mu\alpha\tau\alpha$. Not until the anointing had proved itself in existence, was it to be gradually proclaimed. It is self-evident that the words, "The Spirit of the Lord came upon David from that day forward," cannot refer to the kingly $\chi\alpha\rho\iota\sigma\mu\alpha\tau\alpha$ in contrast to the general gifts of the Spirit. The latter must rather be regarded as forming the foundation of the particular. The close connection of the two appears from the words which immediately follow: "But the Spirit of the Lord departed from Saul, and an evil spirit from the Lord troubled him," which cannot possibly have reference merely to the χαρίσματα.

In recent times the rational interpretation of the latter words has been supposed to be that Saul was afflicted with sombre melancholy. The author certainly states this to have been the case, but he says more too,—he points us to the efficient cause of the mysterious condition. It was produced by God; and if we compare the more developed doctrine of the New Testament in this respect, we are led to the conclusion that it was probably a kind of possession, at least at times, and in its highest stage. Chap. xviii. 10 seems especially to point to this view, "And Saul prophesied in the midst of the house," where ecstatic states were attributed to him, analogous to the prophetic, except that they lay at the opposite end. As a punishment for having given himself willingly into the power of the kingdom of darkness, he was also abandoned physically to this power. It is specially analogous when we are told of Mary Magdalene that before her conversion she had seven devils. Then, again, what the Lord says of the man out of whom the unclean spirit first went, but, because he did not watch over himself, goes and takes with him seven other spirits who are still worse than himself, Matt. xii. 43 ff. Those who think that the cause of Saul's dejection lay in the consciousness of his (intellectual) incapacity for government, apart from all else, make him into a completely unhistorical character. If he had been truly changed, he would certainly have made an excellent king.

By a special leading of divine providence, the representative of the good and the representative of the evil principle were soon brought together. It was necessary that David for his education should soon be brought into the circle of those relations in which he was destined to exercise great activity, if further opportunity should offer for distinguishing himself, for displaying the gifts lent to him by God, that the attention of the people might be directed to him; and, what was the main thing, that the good spirit and the evil one should be separated from one another. David was sent to

Saul in the school of sorrow and temptation; and not until he had been well trained in this school was he elevated to the dignity which had been previously promised him by God. It served as part of Saul's punishment that David was brought into proximity with him. It helped to ripen the corruption which was inherent in him, and gave it an opportunity of manifesting itself.

The position of David at the court of Saul was at first very insignificant; for which reason he was not yet an object of suspicion and jealousy. It is true that in chap. xvi. 21 it is stated that David was Saul's armour-bearer; but this does not imply much, since the king had no doubt a considerable number of such armour-bearers or shield-bearers. Joab, a mere general, had ten of them. The proofs that David was held in little estimation are, (1) that before the victory over Goliath he did not remain permanently at the court of Saul, but returned to his father from time to time and tended his flocks, chap. xvii. 15, comp. with chap. xviii. 2; and (2) that when David presented himself to Saul as a champion against Goliath, the latter did not even know his father and his family, although he was probably acquainted with David himself,—so completely was he lost in the multitude.

David's contest with Goliath will only be apprehended in its true light if the latter be regarded as the representative of the world, and David the representative of the church of God. The strength of God triumphed in him over natural strength, the Spirit over the flesh. By this event David's position was essentially altered. The author first records its immediate happy result in chap. xviii. 1–5. It gave rise to the temporary love of Jonathan for David. This friendship is even quoted as a pattern in the New Testament: it rests on the foundation of true religion, and has therefore no parallel in the heathen world. The reason of Jonathan's devotion to David is that he sees in him a living source of faith and love to God, and feels himself elevated by communion with him, placed in an element which he could not reach independently. David was then promoted by Saul to high military dignity, and thus had an opportunity of attracting the attention of the people by his successful undertakings. In vers. 6 ff. we have a far fuller account of the consequences, so sad when looked at from a human point of view, which not merely succeeded to the former, but ran parallel with them. They began already, immediately after the events. It seems that it was the custom in Israel for choruses of women to receive the returning victors. These magnified David above Saul. From that hour Saul regarded him as his enemy; and on the following day, in a paroxysm of his sickness, which was probably called forth by powerful emotion, he made an attempt to kill him. The key to the whole position which Saul henceforward occupied with respect to David lies in the words, "And Saul was afraid of David, because the Lord was with him, and was departed from Saul," chap. xviii. 12. Saul felt himself inwardly forsaken by God, and in this inner abandonment recognised the premonition of his soon-impending outward overthrow. It was this which gave the real sting to the words of Samuel. He looked anxiously and suspiciously about him to see whether he could not find some germinating greatness; and from David's first deed of valour his glance was riveted on him. He guessed that he was the man after God's own heart of whom Samuel had spoken. It frequently forced itself upon him that it would be in vain for him to try to stop his way to the dignity for which God had destined him; on several occasions he found himself constrained to confess this; but indwelling sin constantly impelled him to new strivings against God in David, to try whether by killing David he could not bring the counsels of God to nought. But the secret consciousness of the godlessness and foolishness of his attempt never forsook him. It invalidated all his measures against David; it made his strong and practised arm unsteady when he aimed at him; owing to it he sought to strengthen his wavering irresolution by consulting others, and revealed his intention to his servants and Jonathan, although he knew the tender love of Jonathan to David, and thus gave him an opportunity to warn his friend; comp., for example, chap. xix. 1. This uneasiness of conscience, this inward uncertainty and vacillation of his mortal enemy, was one of the most effective means which God employed for the salvation of David.

After the first attempt at murder, Saul tried to put David out of the way in a less offensive manner, employing him in dangerous warlike expeditions. Even his daughter Michal was obliged to serve as a means to his end, for he offered her to David as a prize. When all this was of no avail, but rather served to bring David nearer his destiny, Saul returned to his direct attempts at murder. At last David was obliged to seek safety in flight, which was accomplished by the cunning of his wife Michal.

David repaired first of all to Samuel to Ramah, to seek comfort and counsel from him, and Samuel took him with him to the dwelling of the prophetic disciples, which was situated in the neighbourhood of the town, as a sacred asylum. Saul sent messengers there to look for him; but these messengers were vanquished by the power of God-given inspiration in the band of prophetic disciples, so that they also were obliged to prophesy against their will, without, however, being prophets. Saul then sets out himself, and the same thing befalls him. The attempt to do away with the proofs afforded by this event for the ecstatic character of the prophetic state, for the power of inspiration, is vain. Saul rends off his clothes, lies naked upon the earth, and prophesies the whole day and night; and we learn that his condition differed from that of the sons of the prophets only in degree, from 1 Sam. xix. 24, "And he stripped off his clothes also, and prophesied." The difference in degree may certainly have been of importance. The fact that inspiration under the Old Testament generally bore a character of violence, had its foundation in the circumstance that the divine principle was not yet sufficiently powerful to penetrate the human completely, and had therefore to be satisfied by overpowering it momentarily. The greatness of the struggle which then arose was in proportion to the degree of estrangement from God. The more violent the symptoms, the lower the state. When a Samuel was concerned, there was no outward manifestation whatever; but when a Saul was in the case, who had to prophesy in the grossest sense against his will, in whom, however, there could not fail to be an inward point of contact, a divine germ, it was accompanied by the most striking phenomena.

David knew, doubtless, that Saul's temporary possession by the Spirit of God could not guarantee him any permanent security, but only an opportunity for flight, because it was a forced state. Of this opportunity he availed himself. But before he formed the resolution of separating himself permanently from Saul, he sought to know his mind, through the intervention of Jonathan, in the way narrated in chap. xx., to ascertain whether his murderous intent was a momentary ebullition, or whether he had formed a definite plan for his destruction. Having ascertained that the latter was the case, he began his wanderings.

2. David in flight. David first turned towards Nob, then the seat of the holy tabernacle. In the beginning of the new epoch of his life it was his desire to make inquiry of God through the Urim and Thummim. We learn that this was the main object of his visit, and that he succeeded in accomplishing it, from chap. xxii. 10–13, although it does not appear from the narrative itself. Probably with the intention of not exposing the high priest Ahimelech to the persecution of Saul, he told him nothing of what had occurred. After having satisfied his first demand, the high priest, at his request, gave him some of the holy bread, since there was no other to be had: it had been taken from the table of the Lord, and was replaced by new. This holy bread, the symbol of the spiritual nourishment which it was the duty of Israel to present to their God and King, of good works, was not to be eaten except by Aaron and his sons in the holy place, Lev. xxiv. 9. Yet that is only to be regarded as the rule which, like all ceremonial laws, was open to exception in certain circumstances, since it was only a veil of the truth, not the truth itself. The saying "necessity knows no law" might be applied to every ceremonial law, but had no application to the moral. It was a duty, for example, to make oneself levitically unclean in a number of cases. The high priest then, at his request, provided David with a weapon, the only thing of the kind

that was to be had in this peaceful place, the sword of Goliath,—everything on the presupposition that David was the servant of Saul, whom he held in high estimation. He then repaired to Gath, to the king of the Philistines. He had hoped to find a good reception there, owing to his separation from Saul; but this hope proved deceitful. The Philistines feared a stratagem; David was in great danger of his life, and only succeeded in escaping by feigning himself mad,—a means so uncertain in itself, that, as David himself acknowledged, comp. Ps. xxxiv. and lvi., the glory of his deliverance belonged to God alone, who blessed this weak means, which was perhaps not quite morally pure. Saul now vented all his wrath on the high priest, of whose conduct he was secretly informed by the meanness of Doeg, a proselyte of the Edomite race. In 1 Sam. xxi. 7 this Doeg is called the "chiefest of the herdmen," though not the most distinguished among them, as we learn from chap. xxii. 7, according to which he was invested with military dignity, but was probably a commander of the troops appointed to protect the royal herds,—the "chiefest (champion and patron) of the herdmen." According to chap. xxii. 9, he was the principal one among the servants of Saul. In consequence of a vow, or a temporarily-undertaken Nazirate, he was in the sanctuary at the time when David came there. He concealed his heathen heart under Israelitish forms. Saul, too, was very scrupulous in such things. The high priest represented his innocence in the most convincing manner; but Saul would not desist from his evil determination, because he felt that all true servants of the Lord were the natural friends of David, and because he hated the religious principle, whose reality he could not deny, and sought to damage it in its servants and instruments, and to revenge himself on it. But this occurrence shows in a remarkable way how much he was bound by the religious principle, notwithstanding his aversion to it. Saul slays eighty-five priests in Nob, besides everything in the city that had breath,—women, children, and even cattle. There can be no doubt that this course of action has reference to the law respecting the curse which was to fall upon an Israelitish city which should serve other gods, Deut. xiii. 13 ff. Saul puts the alleged *crimen læsæ majestatis* on a level with idolatry; he extends what has been said by God even to His visible representatives, not without reason, comp. Ex. xxii. 28, according to which cursing the prince is equivalent to cursing God, who has impressed His image on the king, if (1) the crime were really established, and (2) if Saul had laid claim to his position on the ground of having fulfilled his duties. But since, like a hypocrite, he made the word of God an excuse for his deeds of horror, and at the same time recognised the theocracy when it answered his purposes, he gave it full scope wherein it appeared to him destructive. For David the incident must have been a painful one, because by his conduct he had aroused Saul's suspicion of the high priest, though without any evil intention. But it had one happy result for him. A son of Ahimelech, Abiathar, escaped with the ephod and came to him; from which time he was his companion in wanderings, a new sign of Saul's rejection and his own election. The two recognised means of inquiring of the Lord, through the prophets, and through the Urim and Thummim, were now taken from Saul by his own fault. David was henceforward accompanied, not only by a representative of the priesthood, but also by a prophet, Gad, and stood in close connection with the head of the prophets, Samuel. The event is also of importance, in so far as it shows us how numerous and important the priests were at that time. In a single town we find eighty-five priests, and they are held in such high estimation, that not one of all Saul's Israelitish servants ventures at his command to lay a hand on them. Only Doeg, who still retained an Edomitish heart notwithstanding his outward turning to God, had courage to do it. It was doubtless in consequence of this event, whose memory is perpetuated by David in the 52d Psalm, that the holy tabernacle was transferred from Nob to Gideon, where we afterwards find it. It could not remain in Nob; for, according to Deut. i., a cursed city was to be made an eternal heap of ruins.

After having happily escaped danger from the Philistines, David repaired to the cave of Adullam, in the tribe of Judah. There he sang the 57th Psalm, whose motto, "Destroy not," represents his mental attitude throughout this whole period. There he was joined not only by his family, whose life Saul had endangered, but "every one that was in distress, and every one that was in debt, and every one that was discontented," gathered themselves unto him as to their leader, chap. xxii. 2. But we learn better what kind of people they were from the psalm which David composed at the time than from this often misunderstood description. See Ps. lvii., where they are represented as the צדיקים, the ענוים, the יראי יהוה, the ישרי לב. In Saul's later days justice and righteousness were very little regarded. In chap. xxii. 7 he boasts that he has given fields and vineyards to all his Benjamite servants and accomplices; and what he gave to them he must have taken away from others. The creatures of the king were at liberty to do whatever they pleased; he was the centre about which all that was evil assembled, the soul of the עדת מרעים. Those who had lost their possessions and property through these, assembled round David as the bearer of the good principle. Among others, Gad the prophet belonged to them; comp. chap. xxii. 5. There was also a number of brave warriors among them, who soon formed an army of heroes under the guidance of David. He had no intention of leading them to battle against Saul. He organized them into a kind of free band, which he led against the predatory neighbours of Israel whenever an opportunity occurred. In this way he worked into the hands of the king himself, and formed the germ of an army for his own kingdom, with which he afterwards raised Israel to an importance scarcely before anticipated. With this band David went from place to place, partly from regard to his own safety, and partly to assist others who were in danger. First he took them to a place called Mizpeh Moab, a fortified town on the borders of the Moabites; but, at the direction of the prophet Gad, soon returned to the land of Judah. With his band he saved Keilah, a town which was besieged by an army of the Philistines. Saul was told that David was come to Keilah; and what he says on this occasion is characteristic of him: "God hath delivered him into my hand; for he is shut in, by entering into a town that hath gates and bars," chap. xxiii. 7. In every circumstance that seems to favour his criminal intent, like a hypocrite, he sees a sign from God, an actual assurance of divine aid. David flies to the wilderness of Ziph, and, being betrayed by the Ziphites, is in great danger of his life. He is saved, however, by the circumstance that Saul is obliged to make a hasty retreat on hearing of an invasion by the Philistines. Ps. liv. is devoted to the memory of this event.

In the wilderness of En-gedi, whither David now resorted, and where Saul went to look for him with his 3000 men, the standing army which he had formed immediately on his accession to the throne, David was led into great temptation. Unsought, an opportunity was given him of slaying his mortal enemy. To many of his companions the opportunity even seemed to contain a divine command to this effect. There were many specious arguments to justify such an act: David chosen by God; Saul rejected; the murderer of so many servants of the Lord, the oppressor of the just, David's persecutor, thirsting for his blood;—arguments so plausible, that many scholars—for example, Clericus —have maintained that David would have been justified in killing Saul. David himself does not seem to have been quite free from the temptation to do it. The words, "And it came to pass afterward, that David's heart smote him (*i.e.* his conscience pricked him) because he had cut off Saul's skirt," chap. xxiv. 5, are only intelligible on the supposition that on cutting off Saul's skirt David's thoughts were not directed only to the use which he afterwards made of it, at least in the beginning, but that his object was rather to prove the goodness of his thoughts at the first weak beginning he made to carry them into effect. But his better self soon awoke; all impure thoughts fled; his eye became clear; with horror he put the temptation from him. He himself gives the cause of this dread in ver. 6: "Seeing he is the anointed of the Lord." Saul had indeed no longer the gifts, but he had still the privileges of a king; God had reserved to Himself the right to deprive him of the latter.

Well knowing that Saul's momentary better impulses gave him no security, David repaired with his men to the wilderness of Paran after the death of Samuel, which occurred about this time. This wilderness is not, as Thenius supposes, on the borders of Egypt, but is the south-eastern part of Arabia Petræa; and here David was almost close to the southern boundary of Judah. In the incident which occurred with Nabal, who had his flocks on Mount Carmel,—not the well-known mountain, but one on the southern borders of Judah,—David sinned grievously, for he took an oath to revenge the injury done to him by Nabal (very characteristically called כלבו, "cor suum sequens, sui arbitrii homo," in ver. 3) on his whole house. It needed, however, but a small excitement of his better self from without, and he repented, recognising the greatness of his danger, and thanking and praising God for having kept him from self-revenge and murder. On this occasion, therefore, we learn both his weakness and his strength, his old man and his new. We see how much he needed purification, but at the same time also that he was susceptible of it— that together with the dross there was noble metal. Events such as these give us the key to the heavy sorrows with which God afflicted David, showing us how necessary they were, and form the theodicy with respect to them.

A second treason of the Ziphites, and a persecution by Saul to which it gave rise, gave David further opportunity to prove his magnanimity towards his enemy, and the vitality of his piety, on which alone it rested. In David's address to Saul, who was deeply moved at the time, these words are specially remarkable: "If the Lord have stirred thee up against me, let Him accept an offering (*i.e.* let him seek to propitiate His wrath by sacrifice, not as *opus operatum*, but as an expression of a corresponding state of mind, and therefore by true repentance: offerings represent good works, and their presentation μετάνοια; comp. *Beiträge* iii. p. 649 ff.); but if they be the children of men, cursed be they before the Lord, for they have driven me out this day (David was just about to leave the land) from abiding in the inheritance of the Lord, saying, Go, serve other gods."

Both suppositions were true: God had stirred up Saul, and men had done it,—the latter as His instruments, which did not, however, by any means justify them. It was part of Saul's punishment that he was constrained to persecute David, and in so doing he suffered more than David,— consuming hatred, fear, the perpetual consciousness of the fruitlessness of all his measures,—all this was perfect torture to him. Doubtless he would willingly have been freed from it, but there was only one way in which he could obtain this freedom, viz. by true repentance; and this way he refused to take. Because he would not desist from sin in general, he could not become free from this special form of sin. This was his fate. David's piety is seen in the fact that he characterizes it as the greatest sorrow inflicted on him by his enemies that they obliged him to leave the land of the Lord and go out into the heathen world, depriving him of the blessing of religious communion, of which he felt all the importance. On this occasion Saul is again obliged to bear witness against himself: "Blessed be thou, my son David: thou shalt both do great things, and also shalt still prevail." David does not distrust his momentary sincerity, but he knows too well that Saul was not his own master not to perceive that it would have been tempting God to have trusted himself to him on the basis of a transient emotion. He knew that this very emotion must serve to prepare the way for a stronger outbreak of Saul's hatred; and hence, despairing of escaping the persecution of Saul any longer in the land of Israel, he repairs immediately after this event to the land of the Philistines, probably after having first assured himself that now, when the relation between Saul and David had become universally known, their king Achish was differently disposed towards him from what he had formerly been. Older theologians have attached great blame to David for leaving the land of Israel. He had received the command of God through the prophet Gad to remain in Judah. He showed want of faith in not believing that God could save him in his fatherland. These arguments are not decisive. For this command of God had reference only to a certain time; and it is scarcely appropriate to speak of want of faith, since

David had not yet received a definite promise that God would protect him in the land of Israel. Hence he might have believed that he was tempting God by remaining there. Indeed, we see from the following history that he was exposed to great temptation in the land of the Philistines, to which he partially succumbed, and may therefore doubt whether he would not have done better by remaining in his fatherland, when the external dangers were greater, but the internal less.

We cannot blame him, because, when the king of the Philistines had appointed him the deserted little town Ziklag as a residence for himself and his band, he made expeditions from it against Canaanitish races and the Amalekites. Neither are we justified in at once accusing him of cruelty for his conduct towards the conquered. This accusation would have had some foundation if he had been actuated merely by the prudential motives given in chap. xxvii. 11. But this was certainly not the case. The principal reason is rather to be sought in the Mosaic law, which declares these races to be under the curse. But it is impossible to justify the equivocation by which David tried to make the king of the Philistines believe that he was in the habit of making inroads with his band on the territory of his own people, in order by this means to gain his confidence more and more, and thus to establish a secure footing in his country; whereas it is noticeable that those peoples upon whom David really made war were not friends, but enemies of the king, as nearly all those were who had anything to lose. This is evident at least with respect to the Amalekites, chap. xxx. 16.

Such dishonesty attained its object; but by the very fact that it did so, it brought punishment with it. The confidence of the king of the Philistines was so great, that he proposed to David to accompany him with his people in a new campaign which he was about to undertake against Israel. This proposition must have placed him in a position of the greatest embarrassment. He could not take arms against his own people without incurring grievous sin; and a refusal, which he had made impossible by his former assertion, would have been ruinous to him and his people. In this embarrassment he formed a rash determination. He declared himself ready to go with the king, while in his heart he thought, Time will bring help; hoping that if he escaped the momentary danger, God would save him from that which lay farther away. And this actually came to pass in a way which must have filled his heart with the most profound gratitude. The Philistine princes, over whom the king only exercised a kind of supremacy, did not share his confidence in David, and obliged him to dismiss him with his men. Thus he was at liberty to return to Ziklag. New trouble awaited him there, but because he "encouraged himself in the Lord his God," chap. xxx. 6, this trouble also was soon turned into joy. The Amalekites, taking advantage of his absence, had fallen upon Ziklag, and had carried away wife and child and property. But, under the visible assistance of God, whom he interrogated by the Urim and Thummim—Abiathar the high priest, with the ephod, was still with him, comp. chap. xxx. 7—he overtook the enemy, contrary to all human expectation, defeated them, and took all their booty from them, besides a great deal of other property, of which, with the wisdom which characterized him, he gave a part in presents to the elders of the neighbouring cities of Judah, always keeping his glance fixed on the goal pointed out to him by the Lord. In the great embarrassment into which David was brought by the Amalekites many have seen, not without apparent foundation, a punishment for his precipitate determination to join the Philistines, and his consenting to fight against his own people. But because he erred only from weakness in an urgent and perilous situation, in which it is so exceedingly difficult always to do right, the revelation of divine justice must at the same time give occasion for the revelation of divine love.

In the time between David's dismissal from the army of the Philistines and his victory over the Amalekites, the accomplishment of the divine decree of rejection fell upon Saul, as described in chap. xxviii. The king's heart is filled with fear of the Philistines. It was not want of physical courage,—he was a valiant hero,—it was the consciousness that God had rejected him, which gave rise to this fear. He felt that his hour was come. In despair he turned to God, and sought comfort and counsel from Him; but all the sources of divine revelation were closed to him. The high priest, with the Urim and Thummim, had been obliged to fly before him from the land of the Lord. God spoke to him through none of His prophets; and even for internal promptings he waited in vain. These were only given to those whose hearts were sincerely attached to the Lord; and he was not willing to surrender his heart to the Lord even yet, —he would rather die in despair. What was denied him in a legitimate way by his own fault, he seeks in despair to obtain in an illegal way. In Deut. xviii. the prohibition of all wizards and necromancers was based upon the fact that God would give His people counsel and comfort in difficult cases by legitimate means, viz. by the prophets. From this event we see clearly how necessary it was that this command should be founded upon the promise. In a better time, when Saul had still free access to God in a lawful way, he himself had purged the land from all wizards and necromancers, in fulfilment of the determinations of the law, and had forbidden all practices of this kind under penalty of death, the punishment established by law, Lev. xx. 6; comp. 1 Sam. xxviii. 9, from which it appears that "he had cut off" is not to be limited to mere banishment. Now when the right means were taken from him, he himself sought these miserable substitutes. Respecting the incident between him and the woman of Endor three leading views have to be considered:—(1.) Many suppose that Samuel did really appear to Saul. So, for example, Jesus Sirach, who represents the appearance of Samuel as his last act, chap. xlvi. 23, and whose opinion is certainly not to be regarded as an individual, but a national one; Justin, *dial. c. Tryph.* p. 333; Origen on 1 Kings (Sam.), 28; Ambrose, Augustine, and others. (2.) Others maintain that the whole thing was a deception on the part of the woman; so Anton v. Dale, Balth. Bekker, Thomasius,—plainly suspicious names, notorious persons; comp. the proofs in Deyling, *Observ.* ii. p. 196. (3.) Finally, some maintain that an evil spirit assumed the form of Samuel. This latter view was the prevailing one among the Lutheran theologians. It is defended by Buddeus, p. 311 ff., Deyling, and Pfeiffer, *Dub. vex.* p. 379, who adduces the advocates of it in great numbers. Of these views the first is in harmony with the narrative. For, (1.) The author says, in ver. 14, that Saul " perceived," not fancied, that it was Samuel; and in ver. 15 he says, " And Samuel said to Saul; " while the paraphrase of the defenders of the other views, " Dixit personatus ille Samuel," only shows how the author would have spoken if he had been of their opinion. (2.) The words which are put into the mouth of the apparition are fully worthy of a Samuel, and are quite unsuitable for an evil spirit. (3.) The appearing one foretells things which no human acuteness could have foreseen,—the defeat of Israel, which was to take place on the following day, and the death of Saul and his sons,—a circumstance which tells strongly against the second opinion. The arguments which have been brought forward against the only view which has any foundation in the text may easily be set aside. (1.) This view, it is said, is at variance with God's goodness and providence, which could not suffer the rest of one who had fallen asleep in Him to be disturbed by evil spirits in the service of godless men. But we have only to suppose that the power of these spirits is limited to those who have died in their sins, a part of whose punishment it is that they should be subject to such power, but that in this case God effected what the adjuration in itself would not have been in a position to do. (2.) Samuel's appearance would have been a hazardous confirmation of necromancy. But in all Holy Scripture the warning against such things is never based on the fact that they have no reality, but rather that they are an abomination to God. The statement that Saul himself in his better days had cut off all sorcerers from the land, is a sufficiently plain condemnation of the king's act on the part of the author. It is impossible for this event to inspire any one with an inclination for necromancy. Saul was punished by the appearance of Samuel. His violation of God's law had truly awful consequences. (3.) The pretended Samuel says to Saul, "To-morrow shalt thou and thy sons be with me." This was a lie, since Saul belonged to hell, Samuel to heaven. But under the Old Testament one and the same *Scheol* received both the pious and the godless, though to different destinies. It would only be possible to oppose the view that Samuel was also in *Scheol*, by fully identifying *Scheol* with hell. The account of Saul's death in 1 Sam. xxxi. must be supplemented by 2 Sam. i. To escape falling into the power of the Philistines, Saul falls upon his sword, chap. xxxi. 4; and when he fell down for dead, his armour-bearer did the same thing, ver. 5. But Saul's wound was not immediately fatal, because the armour paralyzed the force of the thrust. He came to himself again, and begged an Amalekite who was passing to put an end to his life, which he did, 2 Sam. i. 9, 10,—a remarkable dispensation. As the curse on Amalek was accomplished by Saul, so that on Saul was accomplished by Amalek. It has been frequently maintained that the Amalekite, who had been received among Israel, only lied in stating that he had had part in Saul's death, in hope of reward. But this view is certainly false. If such had been the case, the author would at least have given some indication of it. The diadem of Saul, which the Amalekite brings to David, puts the seal of credibility to his declaration. The king's corpse, which was insulted by the Philistines, was stolen by the inhabitants of Jabesh in Gilead at night, with danger to themselves, for they remembered with noble gratitude the assistance which he had formerly given them against the Ammonites. At variance with the usual Israelitish custom, they burnt him, probably lest the Philistines, hearing what had happened, should make it a point of honour to recover the corpse, and that at great risk to themselves. Thus they prevented all further insult to the corpse.

§ 3.

DAVID AND ISH-BOSHETH.

David's behaviour after Saul's death; the lively sorrow to which he gave expression; the punishment which he inflicts on the Amalekite who had laid presumptuous hands on the anointed of the Lord—for although it was done at Saul's own desire, yet this desire itself was presumption; and the message which he sends to the inhabitants of Jabesh,—have been frequently attributed to political reasons. David's conduct is indeed such as to win all hearts; but this is only to be regarded as the blessing which invariably attends a noble course of action. To act nobly is always the best policy. The uprightness of his heart and the sincerity of his feelings cannot for a moment be doubted by those who read his lament over Saul and Jonathan with an unprejudiced mind. Pretended sorrow could never speak thus.

David left the land of the Philistines, and repaired to Hebron, where he was at once recognised as king by his own tribe, the tribe of Judah. The same circumstance which made it easy for this tribe to recognise the divine choice, made it difficult to the other tribes, who were by no means ignorant of it, as appears from the confessions of Jonathan and Saul, of Abner, comp. 2 Sam. iii. 9, and even of the elders of the tribes, chap. v. 2. The jealousy which had already existed for a long time between these tribes and Judah, and which at last led to the separation of the kingdom, made it somewhat difficult for them to come to the determination to submit to a Judaic king. Yet the divine influence which drove them to David would probably have triumphed over the human feeling which kept them at a distance from him, had not a man of imposing personality, Abner, made himself the representative of the interests of Saul's weak son, Ish-bosheth, and given a handle to the evil disposition of the ten tribes. Thus David reigned in Hebron over Judah; Ish-bosheth at Mahanaim over the remaining tribes. It makes a difficulty that the length of Ish-bosheth's reign seems to be limited to two years in chap. ii. 10. For, (1) according to chap. iii. 1, a tedious war was carried on between Judah and Israel; and (2) according to chap. ii. 11, and chap. v. 5, David reigned seven years and six months at Hebron over Judah alone. But Ish-bosheth's reign lasted as long as David was king merely over Judah. If David reigned seven years over Judah, Ish-bosheth must also have reigned seven years over Israel. We must therefore, with Thenius, regard ver. 11 as an interpolation, and connect the words, "and reigned two years," immediately with ver. 12, equivalent to "he had reigned two years when Abner went." Ewald has here committed himself to views which are quite untenable. In David's conduct towards Ish-bosheth his fear of God shows itself in a very beautiful way. God called him to be king over all Israel; he had the courage and power to make good his claims; but nevertheless he waited in perfect quietness. During the whole seven years there was only one small fight, and this occurred in the absence of David, and was provoked by Abner. What God had destined for him, David would not have until God gave it to him. "Hitherto God had led and guided him; God had caused the throne to be vacant, and had made him what he was; God would provide for him in the future also. He would have everything from God."

His confidence in God did not disappoint him. The sole support of Ish-bosheth's kingdom, viz. Abner, was offended by the weak king; and now, when it suited his inclination, he acknowledged the divine right of David, and made every exertion to vindicate it in Israel. It seems that Ish-bosheth himself, after Abner had openly and resolutely told him that he must henceforward work for David, perceiving that it would be impossible for him to maintain his power, had given his consent to the negotiations which Abner carried on with David, after he had gained the favour of the elders in Israel. We are led to this conclusion, (1) by the fact that Ish-bosheth sends back to David his former wife Michal, whom Saul had taken from him and married to another; and (2) by the remark, in chap. iv. 1, that Ish-bosheth despaired when he heard of the death of Abner, which can scarcely be explained if Abner be regarded as a rebel and traitor, but is quite intelligible on the supposition that Ish-bosheth hoped to obtain an honourable satisfaction by his mediation. Abner was murdered by the ambitious Joab. The ostensible reason for this act was revenge for his brother, who had been slain by Abner,—a bad reason, for he was slain in battle, and no blame attached to Abner; but the secret reason was Joab's fear lest Abner should be placed on a level with him, or even be exalted above him. This matter gave the deepest pain to David,—the more, since it was to be expected that he would be accused of secret participation in the deed which he detested. But he was obliged to be content with a loud and public expression of his pain and horror, since he was so little established on the throne, that Joab was too powerful to be visited with the rigour of the law. The words in which he calls to God for revenge have often been regarded as an expression of exaggerated passion : " I and my kingdom are guiltless before the Lord for ever from the blood of Abner the son of Ner: let it rest on the head of Joab, and on all his father's house; and let there not fail from the house of Joab one that hath an issue, or that is a leper, or that leaneth on a staff, or that falleth on the sword, or that lacketh bread." Chap. iii. 28, 29. But David here wishes nothing more than what the law predicts; and it can never be sinful to wish God to do what, in accordance with His will, He must do. The extension of the curse to the descendants clearly refers to the threatenings of the law; and in both cases the offensive character disappears, if we only remember that whoever by true repentance freed himself from connection with the guilt was also exempted from participation in the punishment. Soon afterwards, Ish-bosheth was slain by two of his servants, whose crime David punished with death, instead of granting the expected reward. Notwithstanding David's perfect innocence of the deaths of Abner and Ish-bosheth, and the moral detestation of them which he felt and expressed, certain malicious persons, judging him by themselves, did not hesitate to accuse him of having a share in these deeds. We see this from the example of Shimei, who calls David a man of blood on account of them. The prevailing view, however, must have been a different one, otherwise the elders of Israel would not unanimously have chosen David to be king after the death of Ish-bosheth.

§ 4.

DAVID KING OVER ISRAEL.

David's first undertaking, after he had become king over all Israel at the age of thirty-seven years, was the conquest of Jerusalem. Hebron was well adapted for the capital of Judah, but not for the capital of the whole country. Jerusalem was admirably fitted for it: its firm fortress had remained invincible to the Israelites in Joshua's time, and throughout the whole period of the judges. It was also very well adapted for the capital, because it lay immediately on the borders of Judah, and formed a part of the territory of this tribe; and yet it was not in Judah, but in Benjamin, so that the claims of Judah and the remaining tribes were alike satisfied. David enlarged and beautified the city. Saul had in reality been nothing more than commander-in-chief; David wished to be king in the full sense of the word; and for a well-ordered state, a large place of residence is indispensably necessary. From this time Jerusalem formed the focus of Israel's spiritual life; connection with the principal town bound the separate tribes more closely together. Hiram, king of Tyre, sent experienced artisans for the erection of a magnificent citadel. David took more wives than before, making undue concession to the corrupt oriental custom according to which a full seraglio belonged to the royal position; he raised a body-guard, the Cherethites and the Pelethites, distinct from the heroes so often mentioned who formed the nucleus of his warlike power. The body-guard did not go to battle as a rule. He appointed such officers as were necessary for the enlarged and well-ordered state. The highest among these are reckoned up in 2 Sam. viii. 15. Joab was commander-in-chief; Benaiah commanded the body-guard; Jehoshaphat filled the highest civil office, as מזכיר; Zeruiah was a kind of state secretary; the sons of David were priests, *i.e.* mediators between him and the nation, chief about the king, as it is explained in 1 Chron. xviii. 17. They held the highest offices in the state, and formed a medium of access to the king and of intercourse between him and the nation.

With envy and fear the surrounding nations saw the close consolidation and increasing prosperity of Israel, and David found himself obliged to undertake a series of wars, in which he was invariably the aggrieved party. We shall here briefly enumerate them in succession. The Philistines made a beginning. Hearing that David, who had already become so dangerous to them as the servant of Saul, was king over all Israel, they thought it necessary to crush his power, which threatened to destroy them, in the germ; but were conquered by David in two battles. In a third campaign he penetrated into their own land, and, according to 2 Sam. viii. 1, "took Metheg-ammah out of the hand of the Philistines," *i.e.* he wrested from them the capital which ruled the country. In the parallel passage, 1 Chron. xviii. 1, we read that he took Gath, which was at that time the principal city of the Philistines, and her daughters, *i.e.* the dependent towns. Then followed the siege and subjection of the Moabites, 2 Sam. viii. 2; a war which must have been provoked by very cruel conduct on their part towards the Israelites as follows from the hard treatment to which David subjected the conquered, probably, however, only the warriors. In judging this and similar measures of David, we must take care not to apply the standard of our own times. We learn from his behaviour towards the Ammonites, in 2 Sam. x. 2, how willingly he would have lived in peace and friendship with the surrounding nations; and his conduct with respect to the Canaanitish remnant of the inhabitants of Jerusalem shows that he exercised mildness where it was judicious. According to 2 Sam. xxiv., Araunah dwells among the Israelites as a wealthy and respected landowner; Uriah the Hittite is among the heroes of David. But, as a rule, clemency towards the surrounding nations would have been the greatest severity to Israel. These nations were for the most part rapacious hordes, always intent on satisfying their desire for booty and their ardent hatred to Israel. It was necessary to employ energetic measures against them having the semblance of cruelty, and to meet like with like vigorously, in order to procure rest for Israel; scope for their inner development which was so necessary. We learn how needful it was that an example should be made of them, from the experience of some centuries in the period of the judges. It was appointed by God to David as one of the great tasks of his life, to take energetic measures in this case. What Florus says, t. 3, c. 4, applies here: "Nec aliter cruentissimi hostium, quam suis moribus domiti, quippe in captivos igne ferroque sævitum est." The subjection of the Moabites caused great anxiety to the king of Zobah, between the Euphrates and Orontes, north-east of Damascus, who had the kings of Mesopotamia as vassals, according to 2 Sam. x. 16, 19. He thought it necessary to offer temporary resistance to a power which seemed to endanger his supremacy beyond the river. But David conquered him, and at the same time also the king of Damascene Syria, who came to his assistance. The land of the latter was occupied and made tributary, and the conquest secured by the establishment of garrisons; comp. chap. viii. 3–8. The Edomites also, who had taken advantage of this war to make incursions into the land, and whom fortune had greatly favoured in the beginning, comp. 1 Kings xi. 15, Ps. xliv. and Ps. lx., were conquered and made subject. Then followed war against the Ammonites, which, like all David's wars, was provoked by the shameful treatment of his ambassadors. Notwithstanding the powerful Aramæan allies of the Ammonites, who made this war the most dangerous of all that David had to undertake, they were conquered and punished according to strict martial law; comp. chap. x. 18, a passage which some have tried in vain to soften by explaining away. Nor must we forget that it was the Ammonites who wished to put out the eyes of a nation who submitted to them, 1 Sam. xi. 2, and who ripped up the women with child in Gilead, Amos i. 13. After the close of this war, a great thanksgiving festival was appointed, and Ps. lxviii. was sung on the occasion. This psalm bears the character of a concluding one. That war was the last important foreign one of David, and from the circumstances it was easy for him to perceive that it would be so. The name Solomon, which he gave to the son who was born soon afterwards, shows that he now regarded peace as secured for a long time. Thus all the surrounding nations were humiliated, and Israel stood in power and importance formerly unheard of. The idea expressed by Balaam, that the people of God should triumph with irresistible power over all the surrounding nations, was now fulfilled in its fullest extent, because the nation and the king more nearly answered to the idea of the people of God than had ever been the case before. All the countries east of the valley of the Jordan, from the Elanitic Gulf to the shore of the Euphrates in the extreme north, were subdued,—all at once Israel had become the great power in Western Asia. It has been very foolishly maintained that this position was quite different from that which had been assigned to Israel in the law. But the prophecies of Balaam suffice to prove the contrary. The standpoint of the law is not so limited that it placed itself in opposition to the natural, historical development. In it the Israelites are enjoined to warfare,—stout warfare against their enemies,—and they did nothing further than follow this command. History and prophecy everywhere regard this position as the blessing of God.

We have here combined the wars of David in one sketch, and must now treat of an event which belongs to a time previous to most of them, to the time immediately after the first two victories over the Philistines. David recognised how important it was that Jerusalem should be not merely the civil but the religious capital of the nation; and, besides, it was the fervent wish of his heart to have the sanctuary as near as possible. In consequence of the capture of the ark of the covenant by the Philistines at the end of the period of the judges, the ark of the covenant and the holy tabernacle were then separated from one another, the first being at Kirjath-jearim, the other at Gibeon. David made a beginning by bringing the ark of the covenant to Jerusalem. This was the easiest to do, since no worship was connected with it, and no local interests were attached to the possession of it. He therefore wished to bring the ark of the covenant in solemn procession to Jerusalem; but here he committed the mistake of letting it be driven, instead of having it carried by the Levites as was enjoined by the Mosaic law. This gave occasion for the sin of Uzzah, the waggon-driver, who took hold of the ark in an irreverent way; and in the punishment of his sin David also was involved. From the severity here displayed, he thought himself justified in concluding that the time of resurrection for the ark of the covenant had not yet come; that God would not yet dwell among His people. The ark was therefore set down on the way, in the house of Obed-edom, a Levite, not far from Jerusalem. But David's longing desire soon reasserted itself. A special blessing seemed to rest upon the house of Obed-edom from the time the ark of the covenant was with him, and thus the king perceived that the severity which he had experienced had been a consequence of his own indiscretion. The ark of the covenant was now brought to Jerusalem in safety. On this occasion David's piety was strikingly manifested; and his light is enhanced by the shadow of Michal, the representative of the house of Saul. His humility is so great, that he completely lays aside the kingly attire, and enters the solemn procession in the simple dress of the Levites. 2 Sam. chap. vi. 21, 22, gives us special insight into his heart, where he addresses the proud Michal, among others, in the words, "I will yet be more vile than this, and will be base in mine own sight: and of the maid-servants which thou hast spoken of, of them shall I be had in honour." Several psalms were composed by David for this occasion, especially Ps. xxiii., "The Lord is my shepherd," and Ps. xxiv. The expression of perfect trust in God in Ps. xxiii. he follows by a representation of the moral demands which God makes on His people, lest hypocrites should take to themselves what did not belong to them. Then follow Ps. xiv. and xv., which stand in a similar relation to one another. David erected a new tent for the ark of the covenant. Already he occupied himself with the idea of building a permanent temple to the Lord, nor would he neglect the interests and attachments connected with the sanctuary at Gibeon in favour of a state which was simply provisional. Public worship was now performed in this Davidic tent, no less than in the Mosaic one at Gibeon, comp. 1 Chron. xvi. 37 ff.; and hence it was necessary to inaugurate two high priests, Abiathar, who remained at Jerusalem with David, and Zadok, who was sent to Gibeon to the Mosaic tent, ver. 39 ff. And just because David fully recognised the provisional with regard to the sanctuaries, he made no attempt to limit the freedom which had arisen in this respect since the capture of the ark of the covenant by the Philistines. He allowed everything to remain as it was, regarding the complete re-organization of this relation as only appropriate to the time of the existence of a permanent temple. But from the beginning and onward, the sanctuary at Jerusalem remained in the background. The psalms of the Davidic time have nothing whatever to do with the tabernacle of the testimony in Gibeon, that shell without a kernel. Wherever the sanctuary of the Lord is mentioned in them, the reference is to that in Zion, to which everything that was present in Israel of higher life turned with love, while only idle custom formed a link of attachment to the sanctuary at Gibeon. This is the only important point in which the condition of religion in the Davidic period is not conformable to the Mosaic legislation, far less than in the period of the judges. In other respects the Mosaic law was observed, even to the smallest details. We learn, for example, from chap. xi. 2, 4, that the laws respecting purification were in force; and in chap. xii. 6 we find a most remarkable reference to a very special Mosaic law, and one which bears an accidental character. David passes judgment on the rich man who had taken away the poor man's sheep in the parable of Nathan, after he had declared him to be guilty of death, and at the same time states that he would willingly have subjected him to far more severe punishment if it had been in his power, as fourfold compensation. According to Ex. xxi. 37 (xxii. 1), when a man had stolen an ox, he was to restore five; if a sheep, four. In connection with David's provision for the sanctuary are his efforts for the organization of the priestly and Levitical constitution. He divided the priests and Levites into twenty-four classes, who had each to perform the service for a week in succession. Sacred music was raised to a completely new step of development by David in conjunction with his three distinguished minstrels, Asaph, Heman, and Jeduthun. A company of 4000 Levites was devoted to it, the germ being formed by a select body of singers composed of members of the families of the three minstrels, which continued without interruption to the time of the return from captivity. This advance of sacred music, whose beginnings are coeval with the sanctuary of the Lord, had its foundation in the advance of sacred poetry, which was due to David. He was the true author of psalmody, with which we shall occupy ourselves more closely in the introduction to the Psalms.

We have already remarked that the arrangements made by David with respect to the ark of the covenant were only provisional. His real intention was to erect a permanent temple. This thought lay very near. The sanctuary, which had formerly been portable, was properly adapted to the condition of the nation only during the march through the wilderness. The dwelling of God in a tabernacle presupposes the dwelling of the nation in tabernacles. Only from the fact that the whole constitution during the period of the judges was provisional, can we understand how it was that the idea of erecting a permanent sanctuary was not conceived and carried out during that time. Now, when Israel was consolidated, circumstances seemed to present the most urgent demand for the building of a temple; and David recognised the demand with joy, and was anxious to carry it out as soon as possible. Nathan the prophet, to whom he disclosed his plan, judging from the standpoint of ordinary consciousness, gave his full consent at first, but was immediately afterwards taught by a divine revelation that the building of a temple by David himself did not lie in God's plan. Ewald's attempt to attribute to him the view that a temple was by no means necessary is quite absurd. Nathan's first answer is correct in the main, only it is more closely defined and modified. David is to build the house, not personally, however, but in his seed. Yet, as a reward for his zeal, God will build David a house of eternal duration.

This revelation is an epoch-making one for his inner life. It brought an entirely new element into his consciousness, which, as the Psalms show, moved him powerfully. He received the promise of the perpetual supremacy of his tribe, of the establishment of his kingdom amid the changing of all earthly things. How deeply David was affected by this promise we learn from his prayer of thanksgiving in chap. vii. 18 ff. It has reference, not to the Messiah originally, but to an ideal person of the race of David; indirectly it contained an assurance that it would find its final fulfilment in the Messiah, since the eternity of a purely human kingdom is inconceivable. David saw this more and more clearly when he compared the promise with the Messianic idea which had been handed down from the fathers, and finally attained to perfect certainty by the further inner disclosures attached to this fundamental promise, with which he was occupied day and night. Ps. ii. and Ps. cx. afford special proof that such spiritual disclosures were really given him. The Messianic hope, which had experienced no further development since Gen. xlix., now acquired much greater fulness and life. It had a substratum for further development, hallowed by God Himself, in the kingdom which was already in existence, and especially in David's personality and fortunes. The answer to the question why David was not allowed to build the temple himself, is given in 1 Chron. xxviii. 3, comp. chap. xxii. 8. He had fought great battles and shed much blood. The reason is symbolical. War, however necessary it may be under certain circumstances for the kingdom of God, is only something accidental, the result of human corruption. The true nature of the kingdom of God is peace. The Lord appears to the Church as the Prince of peace already in Isa. ix. 5. According to Luke ix. 56, the Son of man came not to destroy men's souls, but to save them. In order to bring this view of the nature and task of the Church to mind, the temple, the symbol of the Church, could not be built by the warrior David, but only by Solomon the peaceful, the man of rest, 1 Chron. xxii. 9.

The long-continued fortune which David had enjoyed was

now followed by a chain of misfortunes; and between these two experiences there lies an event which shows us how necessary it was that he should thus suffer affliction, and at the same time throws light on his long-continued former sorrows, viz. his adultery with Bath-sheba. It occurs soon after the last of the recorded successful wars, that against the Ammonites, who were no longer able to maintain themselves in the open field, and the conquest of whose principal town, Rabbah, David had left to his general Joab. This single act can only be regarded as an expression of his whole disposition of mind. Fortune in itself is difficult to bear, but especially fortune in war. The heart far too readily becomes unruly, and is even drawn into fellowship with the evil which has been subdued. We here see in a remarkable way how one sin begets another. The means which David took to extricate himself from the complications in which his adultery had involved him appeared well chosen; but there was one thing he had not taken into consideration, that he could not here, as in former embarrassments, confidently expect the assistance of God. It was God's design that David's sin should be fully manifested, for only in this way was perfect cure possible, and therefore He suffered the means to fail. Thus the king saw no other mode of extrication, and took the life of one of his thirty heroes, of Uriah. How Joab must have rejoiced when David sank down to his own level! Doubtless he had never executed any commission with so much pleasure. The melancholy state of David's soul continued for a considerable time, for it was not until after the birth of Bath-sheba's son that Nathan stepped forward reprovingly. His task was not to gain a confession, but only to facilitate it. He was appointed by God to await the time of the internal crisis in David. Calvin, on Ps. li., has excellently depicted the character of this state. We are not to conceive of him as one who had quite fallen, nor as one spiritually dead, but as sick unto death. It is certain that he had not quite lost all desire after God, that he had not entirely given up prayer; doubtless there were still many fruits of faith perceptible in him, but his soul was checked in its flight towards

God, a curse rested upon him, which made solitary communion with the Divine Being for any length of time intolerable, and moved him to seek distractions in order to escape the torment of conscience, and keep it from attaining to full life. In passing judgment on his sin, it ought never to be forgotten that he was a member of the old covenant, and that the same means of grace which we have were not at his command. His weakness cannot therefore serve as a palliation of our own; but his repentance is rather placed before us as a pattern. Let whoever is inclined to throw a stone at him first prove himself whether in this respect he is superior, or even equal with him. The plain and simple confession, "I have sinned against God," is a great thing, if we remember how rich the corrupt human heart is in the discovery of excuses and apparent justifications, and that the king was assailed by one of his subjects with hard, unsparing rebuke. The narrative in the books of Samuel tells us scarcely anything of the greatness and difficulty of the repentance of David, nor of the length of time before he could fully appropriate the assurance of the forgiveness of his sins which he received through the prophets; but it is apparent from Ps. xxxii., li., which have reference to this. As a circumstance which aggravated David's sin, it is stated in chap. xii. 14 that he made the enemies of the Lord to blaspheme. This observation gives us a deep insight into the whole position of David. In him the good principle had attained to supremacy, the godless party had seen this with terror; and now they mocked piety in its representative, who, because he held this position, ought to have kept watch over his heart the more carefully, and afterwards made use of the first opportunity which presented itself to throw off the burdensome yoke. The great success which attended Absalom's conspiracy is scarcely intelligible except from this position of David. At the first glance it may appear strange that everything with which he was threatened as a punishment for his sin,—the entrance of the sword into his house to avenge the death of Uriah; the shame of his wives, as a punishment for his having allowed himself to lust after the wife of his neighbour; and, finally, the death of the child begotten in sin,—all these did actually take place, although he had found forgiveness. But in general the forgiveness of sins has only this result: punishment is changed into fatherly chastisement, the rod into the correction of love. Outwardly the consequences of sin remain the same, only their internal character is changed. If it were otherwise, the forgiveness of sins might too readily be attributed to caprice.

The death of the child was the beginning. Then followed the murder of his son Amnon by Absalom, whose sister he had dishonoured,—a deed by which David was reminded in in the most heartrending way, of the lust which had led him to commit adultery with Bath-sheba. Still greater evil was caused by the weakness which he showed in giving full pardon, at the instigation of the impure Joab, to Absalom, who had fled, and allowing him to return. This and many other things lead to the inference that David showed weak indulgence towards his children, and shut his eyes to their sins. But his own psalms, viz. iii., iv., lxiii., and xlii., xliii., lxxxvi., which the sons of Korah then sang out of his soul, show how David strengthened himself in God during that trying time of his life. At a later period, a new sin brought heavy affliction. This was the numbering of the people, 2 Sam. xxiv. and 1 Chron. xxi. In 2 Sam. xxiv. the event is placed at the end of his life, and, on internal grounds also, it can only belong to an advanced period of it. The numbering, which required nearly a year, could only be undertaken in a time of rest from the enemies round about, and the victory already gained over these enemies formed the ground of temptation to which David succumbed. By the favour of God, the children of Israel were raised to supremacy in the south-west of Asia. In the striving of the human heart after more, it occurred to them to extend the limits still farther by their own hand. We cannot suppose that this happened in the very last days of David, when death was constantly before his eyes. At such a time men do not undertake these far-seeing plans.

In what did his sin consist? There can be no doubt

that the numbering was a military one, a kind of muster. It was proposed in the assembly of chief officers, and was carried out by Joab, the commander-in-chief, in conjunction with them. All the souls were not counted, but only "valiant men that drew the sword." To facilitate the numbering, a camp was set up; this is expressly mentioned at the place where the numbering began, and we may assume that it was the same at the other places. The length of time occupied by the numbering, almost a year, shows that it was a difficult and complicated business; and its military character is apparent from the circumstance that Joab waited as long as possible before extending the measure to Benjamin, lest he should provoke the rebellious disposition of that tribe, who could not forget the supremacy they had enjoyed under Saul. But we cannot attribute any *direct* military object to the measure. That it was first intended only as a means of ascertaining the number of men capable of bearing arms, is shown by 2 Sam. xxiv. 2, where "that I may know the number of the people" is given as the object; and also by the fact that, in consequence of the divine judgment, the number of males was not recorded in the annals of the kingdom, 1 Chron. xxvii. 24. This must therefore have been the original object. But warlike thoughts certainly stand in the background; if we fail to see this, we lose the key to the whole transaction, and the divine judgment is incomprehensible. David feeds his heart on the great numbers, on the thought of what his successors on the throne would be able to attain with such power. From its first origin, Israel was called to the supremacy of the world. Already in the blessing of Moses (Deut. xxxiii. 29) this assurance was given to Israel: "Thine enemies shall be found liars unto thee; and thou shalt tread upon their high places." David now thought that he could rise step by step to such elevation without the help of God, who had provided for the beginning. The records should bear witness to all time that he had laid a solid foundation for this great work of the future.

Had his preception been clear, he would not have disregarded the special hint contained in the law respecting the danger connected with the numbering of the people. In Ex. xxx. 11 f. it is ordained that on the numbering of the people every Israelite should bring a ransom, "that there be no plague among them, when thou numberest them." By the ransom offered to God they would be released, as it were, from the death incurred by their proud arrogance. It reminded them of the danger of forgetting human weakness, so imminent where an individual feels himself the member of a large whole. The important lesson for all time is this, that even the smallest feeling of national pride is sin against God, and, unless there be a powerful reaction, calls down the judgments of God. With this feeling even the Romans presented offerings of atonement at their census.

In 2 Sam. xxiv. the narrative is introduced with the words, "The anger of the Lord was kindled against Israel." The punishment falls upon the people, and on David only in so far as he made the sorrows of the nation his own. From this we see that the guilt belonged chiefly to the nation,—that they had infected the humble heart of the king with their own arrogance, which had been called forth by their success. The same thing appears from the fact that, when the punishment begins, he seeks the guilt in himself alone, and tries to excuse the nation.

In 1 Chron. xxi. 1, the determination to number the people is attributed to the influence of Satan on the mind of David, and, in 2 Sam. xxiv., to the influence of God. But we learn that this is not intended to exonerate him and the nation from participation in the guilt, from the fact that the punishment, which presupposed guilt, was accomplished on David and on the nation; and from the universal teaching of Scripture, which invariably attributes the first origin of sin to man, as James says, "Let no man say when he is tempted, I am tempted of God;" "Resist the devil, and he will flee from you;" and finally and specially, from Ps. xxx., which has reference to this event. Here David himself describes the state of his mind, which offered a point of contact for the temptation, and gave rise to it: "And in my prosperity I said, I shall never be moved. Lord, by Thy favour Thou hast made my mountain (*i. e.* my kingdom) to stand strong: Thou didst hide Thy face, and I was troubled." According to this, confidence was the melancholy root of sin, both in David and the nation. Soft indolence, says Calvin, had taken possession of his mind, so that he had no inclination for prayer, nor any dependence on the mercy of God, but trusted too much to his past fortune. Where this corrupt disposition is found in the soul, God's influence, making use of Satan as its instrument, leads the corrupt germ to its development, rousing to action that which slumbers in the soul, in order to bring about the retributive judgment in which man, if otherwise well-intentioned, learns fully to recognise his sinful condition, and is moved to repentance. The question is not of simple permission on the part of God, but of a real action, and that of a nature which each one may still perceive in his own tendencies. Whoever once yields to his sinful disposition, is infallibly involved in the sinful deed which leads to retributive judgment, however much he may strive against it.

Even before the punishment, and still more decisively after it had begun, David's better disposition reasserted itself, and the mercy of God, to which he had turned with humble supplication, checked the course of justice. The punishment had already begun its course in the metropolis, where some deaths had occurred, 1 Chron. xxi. 15. On hearing of these deaths, David's conscience was fully awakened; it had been powerfully affected even before the beginning of the judgment, immediately after the numbering was accomplished. The awakened conscience opened his spiritual eye, that he saw the angel of the Lord in his house, "by the threshing-place of Araunah the Jebusite," 2 Sam. xxiv. 16, "standing between the earth and the heaven, having a drawn sword in his hand stretched out over Jerusalem," 1 Chron. xxi. 16. As in 2 Kings vi. 17 the source of seeing the heavenly powers was in Elisha, and by his mediation the eyes of his servant were opened, so here the flight of David's mind communicated itself to the elders of his retinue, whom he had collected about him; and, after he had repaired to the place where he saw the vision, was revealed even to the sons of Araunah.

The event is also of importance in so far as it gave occasion for the determination of the site of the future temple. The Lord forgave David on condition that he would build an altar on the place where He had appeared; and at the dedication He hallowed it by fire from heaven, 1 Chron. xxi. 26. By this means He made an actual declaration that this should henceforward be the place of His worship; and the king followed the declaration. Even at this time the place was made the national sanctuary, and was called the house of God, Ps. xxx. 1; 1 Chron. xxii. 1: for David foresaw that the form would soon be superadded to the essence, and already perceived in the spirit the building which was to be completed by his son, and for which he made preparations with great zeal; comp. 1 Chron. xxii. 2 ff. It is very remarkable that the pardoning mercy of God towards His own people, which David extols in Ps. xxx., on the basis of this event, was virtually characterized as its spiritual foundation, even before the laying of the external foundation of the temple.

David's last words form the keystone of his life, his prophetic legacy, 2 Sam. xxiii., to which the cycle of psalms, Ps. cxxxviii.-cxlv., must be regarded as supplementary. "No prince," says Ewald, "can end his life with more blessed divine rest, and a clearer, more certain glance into the future." He accompanies his own through the history, and offers them the anchor of salvation in the storms which, from his own life-experience, he knew that they had to encounter. He points to the fulness of salvation which the dominion of the righteous ruler will bring with it, after the affliction has been endured, and to the corruption which will then overtake the opposing evil.

§ 5.

THE LIFE OF SOLOMON.

Solomon, a son of David and Bath-sheba,—according to 1 Chron. xxii. 9, thus named by a command of God, given to David through Nathan before his birth,—the peaceful, in contrast to the warlike David, brought up under the supervision of the prophet Nathan, ascended the throne before he was 18 years of age. This happened half a year before the death of his father, in consequence of the machinations of one of his brothers, Adonijah. Solomon was not indeed the first-born; but the king had the right of naming as his successor the son whom he regarded as most capable. David's choice had long fallen upon Solomon, and had received the divine sanction through the sentence of the prophet Nathan; he was therefore universally known as heir to the throne. Nevertheless Adonijah, disregarding the divine and the human right of Solomon, made an attempt to gain the supremacy. David, warned by Bathsheba and Nathan, caused Solomon to be publicly proclaimed king, and to be anointed by the high priest Zadok and the prophet Nathan. When this became known, the adherents of Adonijah dispersed.

Solomon began his reign under the most favourable circumstances. Foreign enemies had been conquered by David, and every land from the Mediterranean to the Euphrates did homage to him. At the time of David's death, Israel alone numbered about six million souls, 1,300,000 " valiant men that drew the sword;" comp. Michaelis on 2 Sam. xxiv. 9. The Philistines, formerly an object of special terror to the Israelites, had lost their independence. Neither was there anything more to be feared from the cruel, rapacious Amalekites. Their power was first broken by Saul, and then by David completely and finally, so that they totally disappear from the history. The possession of the mountainous district of Idumea, whose inhabitants were famous for their valour, was secured by garrisons. The land of the Moabites offered great advantages by its rich flocks, of which a considerable number was given as tribute; comp. 2 Kings iii. 4. The warlike Ammonites, who had pressed the Israelites so hard during the period of the judges, were held in subjection by the circumstance that the Israelites had possession of the fortress Rabbah in the centre of the land. All the conquered nations were tributary, and paid heavy taxes; they were so completely subdued by David, and the military power of the

Israelites was in so good a condition, that it was impossible for them to think of rebelling. Only in the interest of an arbitary interpretation of Ps. ii. has Ewald imagined a universal rising of the conquered nations at the time of Solomon's accession to the throne. Internally there was a well-ordered constitution. But, what was the principal thing, true fear of God prevailed throughout the land. Solomon himself, educated by Nathan, was resolved in this respect to tread in his father's footsteps. In 1 Kings iii. 3 we read: "And Solomon loved the Lord, walking in the statutes of David his father;" and the supplementary clause, "Only he sacrificed and burnt incense in high places," is not intended as a limitation of this praise, but only points to the fact that in the beginning of his reign, owing to the fault of the relations, the Mosaic law respecting the unity of the sanctuary could not be carried out. It was no fault of his, but only a misfortune, which it was part of his task to remove. Until this was possible, Solomon presented his offerings partly before the ark of the covenant in Jerusalem, and partly in the holy tent at Gibeon. 1 Kings iii. 4-15 gives us a glance into the mind of the king at the time when he began his reign. He appointed a great religious feast of thanksgiving to be held at Gibeon, which was celebrated with great splendour and expense. Here he had a dream, which bears testimony to his pious disposition, and served to foster it. God appears to him in the dream, and says, "Ask what I shall give thee." Solomon has only one wish, a request for a wise and pious heart, and God promises to grant it, and to give him also what he had not asked, just because he had not asked it, viz. riches and honour. Solomon was endowed with the greatest gifts. Those who suppose that his far-famed wisdom was an external possession, something acquired, are ignorant of what they say. The Proverbs sufficiently show what fulness of original spirit there was in him; and in them we also possess an absolutely certain testimony how the gift of wisdom under the sanctifying influences of divine grace became in him the $\chi\acute{\alpha}\rho\iota\sigma\mu\alpha$, thus refuting those who, in opposition to the additional testimony of the historical books, apply to Solomon in general what can only be said of him in his old age, and refuse to recognise his apostasy, believing that he was never sincerely devoted to the Lord.

These critics appeal, in the first place, to those acts of cold severity which characterized his very first measures. But these acts appear in another light if we look at the matter in an unprejudiced way. He had promised his brother Adonijah that he should be perfectly safe if he would remain quiet. This condition was not fulfilled. The latter thought of a means of acquiring a kind of right to the throne, and believed that he had found it in an alliance with Abishag the Shunamite, familiar in the history of David. Adonijah sought to gain his object by stratagems, and even succeeded in inducing the innocent Bath-sheba to intercede for him with Solomon. But Solomon saw through him, and sentenced him to death, as a punishment for his high treason. If we consider that Adonijah did not stand alone, but was supported by the two most powerful and influential men of the state, Abiathar the high priest, and Joab the commander-in-chief; that the question was not one of dealing with an ambitious thought, but with a concerted and mature scheme of rebellion, comp. 1 Kings ii. 22; if we take into consideration the weakness of the kingdom, and the unutterable misery which David had brought upon himself and the whole nation by his ill-timed indulgence towards Absalom, with whom Adonijah may the more readily be compared, since he too is to be regarded as the representative of the godless principle, the centre of the godless party,—we shall certainly be more cautious in our judgment. Solomon deposed Abiathar the high priest, who also deserved death, and banished him to his own possessions, remembering that he had been his father's companion in affliction. In his place he appointed Zadok, with whom the line of Eleazar again attained to the high-priesthood. Abiathar's sin served to hasten the fulfilment of the prophetic judgment on the house of Eli, to which he belonged. In passing sentence of death on Joab and Shimei, Solomon only followed a charge of David's. In the "fatal oblivion into which the old traitor had fallen," we cannot fail to recognise the hand of God which led him on to punishment. But it is true that, with all Solomon's sincere piety, he was yet deficient in the deeper life-experiences of his father, that he had not yet attained to an experimental knowledge of the depth of sin, to profound humility, or to a life of fear and trembling. Here was the point where the tempter might find admittance, and where he afterwards really did find it.

Solomon was endowed with rich gifts, and did what he could to improve them. All that was worth knowing interested him. His knowledge of nature extended to all the kingdoms of creation, and the products of every country; comp. 1 Kings v. 13. He gave special attention to the study of man. His manifold observation and experience he expressed in maxims, of which, according to 1 Kings v. 12, he composed three thousand, and of which only some have been preserved in Proverbs, such as had a moral-religious tendency, and were written under the special guidance of the Spirit of God. The fame of Solomon's genius and knowledge must have spread with a rapidity in proportion to the rarity of such a phenomenon at that time. Strangers thronged from foreign lands to learn to know the wise king, and to admire his institutions and appointments; comp. 1 Kings iv. 34. Even the queen of Sheba or Yemen, in Arabia Felix, thought nothing of the trouble of the long journey, that she might be convinced of the truth of what she had heard. She is mentioned not only in the sacred historical books, but also in the traditions of other orientals; comp. Herbelot, *Biblioth. Or.* v. Balkis; Iliob L. h. A. t. II. c. 3. All these accounts, however, are dependent on the biblical narrative, and have therefore no historical importance whatever. The contest respecting them between the Arabs and the Ethiopians must be determined decidedly in favour of the former. שבא always belongs to Arabia. The designation βασίλισσα νότου in Matt. xii. 42, Luke xi. 31, also leads to Arabia. With a large retinue and many presents she appeared at Jerusalem, perhaps about the twentieth year of Solomon's reign, as we learn from the fact that she found all the large buildings already completed; comp. 1 Kings x. 4, 5. She made herself acquainted with all the appointments of Solomon, tried his acuteness by propounding difficult riddles, and her admiration was unbounded.

Solomon proved his love for art by the erection of great buildings. He built himself a castle to reside in, and another palace was erected for his wife. He then made important arrangements for the security of the kingdom. Jerusalem was newly fortified. He established a series of new fortresses on the borders of the country, especially toward Damascus, which had raised itself to a new independent power during his reign; comp. 1 Kings xi. 23-25. In chap. vii. 4 of the Song of Solomon, the proud watch-tower toward Damascus serves as a symbol of the greatness of Israel. The ruins of this castle on the Lebanon are probably still in existence; comp. Thenius on 1 Kings ix. 19. By the trade which he first created, Solomon opened new resources to himself and the nation. Outward circumstances favoured this enterprise. Palestine, as it then was, was better situated for trade than almost any country. It lay in the centre of the then known world. Its situation on the Mediterranean Sea gave it all the advantages possessed by the Phenicians, and in its proximity to Egypt it had an advantage over them. Moreover, David already possessed Idumea, which was situated on the Red Sea, and the two harbours, Ezion-geber and Elath. But Solomon could have profited very little by all these advantages, owing to his people's ignorance of the arts of shipbuilding and navigation, and their inexperience in trade, if he had not entered into an alliance with the Phenicians. He concluded a treaty with the king of Tyre, which was equally advantageous for both parties. For on the one side the territory of the Phenicians was very limited. It consisted of a small stretch of land, about twenty-five miles in length, and perhaps nowhere more than four to five miles in breadth. Hence they were unable to maintain any great number of soldiers, and, moreover, the spirit of trade had crushed all disposition for war. In the piracy which was then prevalent, however, it was impossible for them to dispense with a military guard. Hence it must have been most desirable that they should be able to man their ships with Israelites, who had been brought up as warriors under David's rule. On the other hand, the harbours Ezion-geber and Elath would by this means be opened to the Phenicians, and an opportunity be given to them to extend their trade over the Red Sea, and even beyond it. It is probable that the Israelites as well as the Tyrians took no inland produce with them. Owing to the great population of the country, the export could not be very considerable. The superfluous wheat and oil were probably consumed by the Phenicians alone; comp. 1 Kings v. 11. It is more probable that they bought up the products of one land, and then disposed of them again with profit in another, thus carrying on a kind of barter. This view is confirmed by the long duration of the sea-voyages. Solomon carried on trade on his own account. The ships went partly from Solomon's harbours on the Red Sea, partly from the Phenician harbours in the Mediterranean. From the former the Israelites sent out their own vessels, which, however, were doubtless built by the Phenicians, and were under the direction of Phenician pilots, to the famous gold district Ophir,— according to Gen. x. 29, undoubtedly in Arabia, but with vague geographical limits, so that it probably includes India also; comp. the discussions on Ophir by Lassen, *Indian Archæology*, i. p. 538 ff. The voyage generally occupied three years, probably because they went from country to country, and bartered the products of the one against the products of the other. The navigation from the harbours of the Mediterranean Sea, on the other hand, was undertaken by Phenician ships. Besides this, Solomon carried on a very profitable trade in horses with Egypt. For a long time this land had reared the best horses, and was specially adapted for this object owing to its large and excellent pasturage. It must have been an easy matter for Solomon to monopolize the trade in Egyptian horses, and to provide all his neighbours with them. For all other purchasers, —Syrians and Arabs, for example,—were obliged to pass through Palestine, which Solomon could easily prevent; comp. Michaelis on the oldest history of horse-breeding, appendix to the third part of the *Mosaic Laws*.

By this trade great riches were brought to Jerusalem.

Gold and silver, every article of luxury, the most costly spices and kinds of wood, accumulated there. Jerusalem gained quite the appearance of the capital of a great oriental kingdom. But the enterprise had also a specious side. It brought the Israelites into contact with the most vicious nation of antiquity; and the danger was the greater, because in their high culture the evil was clothed in a garment of light. The constant intercourse tended first of all to beget a religious tolerance, such as was incompatible with the exclusive character of the religion of Jehovah; and from this it was easy to pass over to participation in the sinful worship of idols. Luxury endangered the old simplicity and severity of morals, and readily produced an aversion to the Mosaic law, which demanded such austerity; while it fostered an inclination for the religion of the idolatrous nations, in which a man might follow his own desires under the semblance of piety. But these consequences are not so necessarily connected with the thing, that Solomon was to blame for entering into such universal mercantile relations. It would be just as reasonable to reproach the present Government for favouring railways, which also bring so many new temptations with them. That the promotion of trade is contrary to the Mosaic law is a false theory advanced by Joh. Dav. Michaelis, and is carried to extremes by Bertheau. When Moses founded the state mainly upon agriculture, he had regard to the relations of his time, which presented no facilities for trade. In the blessing of Jacob in Gen. xlix. 13, Zebulun is characterized as happy in being so favourably situated for trade, and this is attributed to the blessing of God. The same thing occurs still more emphatically with respect to Zebulun and Issachar in the blessing of Moses, Deut. xxxiii. 18, 19.

The nation was very happy under Solomon. In 1 Kings iv. 25 we read: "And Judah and Israel dwelt safely, every man under his vine and under his fig-tree, all the days of Solomon." "Judah and Israel were many, as the sand which is by the sea in multitude, eating and drinking, and making merry." Not until nearly the end of his reign do we find a change taking place. The nation complained of heavy taxation and despotic rule; comp. 1 Kings xii. 1-4. The erection of such huge buildings and the splendour of the court required immense means. In his old age Solomon fell into idolatry. Many, indeed—among others, Justi in his *Miscellaneous Essays*, i. pp. 88-145—have endeavoured to show how improbable it was that Solomon should really have fallen into idolatry. But where we have definite historical testimony, probabilities are of no account. Not only is it said in 1 Kings xi. 4 that "his wives turned away his heart after other gods," but also in ver. 5, that he "went after Ashtoreth the goddess of the Zidonians." And we learn that the expression "to go after idols" really points to idolatry, from Deut. xi. 28, xxviii. 14, and especially from 1 Kings xviii. 18, comp. with chap. xvi. 31. In 1 Kings xi. 33 it is definitely affirmed that Solomon, and the nation led by his example, worshipped idols. Thus it came to pass that in the country which was consecrated to the worship of the true God, the same abominations of idolatry were practised on account of which the land had been wrested from its former inhabitants. For more than 300 years the evil seed which had been scattered by Solomon bore evil fruit. The altars on the high places were first destroyed by Josiah. And in proportion as the nation was irreligious, it was corrupt and immoral. The less worthy the king proved himself of the dignity of God's representative, the more the nation lost their respect for him, which rested only upon his relation to the invisible Ruler; the more were they inclined to rebellion, which was scarcely kept in check till the death of Solomon. But the apostasy of Solomon is not to be regarded as complete. In 1 Kings xi. 4 it is expressly stated, "And his heart was not perfect with the Lord his God, as was the heart of David his father." Neither are we to suppose that he gave himself up to polytheism in that rude form in which it obtained among the surrounding idolatrous nations. He adhered firmly to the unity of the divine essence. The words, "Behold, the heaven, and the heaven of heavens, cannot contain Thee," in 1 Kings viii. 27, to which he gave utterance in his prayer on the consecration of the temple, and which bear remarkable testimony to the depth of his knowledge of God, were still his motto, even in the time of his apostasy. Having a clear consciousness of the glory of the one divine nature, he regarded it as a narrow conception to confine the revelation of this nature to Israel alone. In Jehovah he recognised the most perfect manifestation of this nature, and at the same time that which was specially intended for Israel. Jehovah was therefore the principal object of his adoration. But he thought it necessary to recognise imperfect and lower manifestations of the Divine Being in the idols of the neighbouring nations, and regarded it as the task of an enlightened and large-hearted piety to express this recognition in a palpable way, by the establishment of subsidiary worships for these idols, of whose unreality he was the less able to persuade himself, since he saw the power which faith in them exercised over the minds of his heathen wives.

While recognising the incompleteness of the apostasy, we cannot fail to see that already in the earlier life of Solomon there was a predisposition to this apostasy, although we must repeat that the testimony of Holy Scripture is decidedly averse to making no distinction between the earlier and the later Solomon. We find this predisposition in the fact that from the beginning of his reign (his union with the daughter of the Egyptian king belongs to this period), in choosing his wives, he paid no regard to religion. This shows that from the beginning he had no deep consciousness of the sharp antagonism between the religion of Jehovah and heathenism, due to the definitely exclusive character of the former. Other accusations which have been brought against Solomon previous to his fall seem to us to be totally unfounded. Thus when it is assumed that the providing of many horses is in opposition to the law respecting the king in Deut. xviii. If this were the case, it would still be forbidden; for the reason given, "that his heart be not lifted up," is not peculiarly Israelitish, but applicable to human nature in general. The command is evidently not externally binding, but is only to be regarded as drawing attention to the dangers connected with the maintenance of a splendid court. Whoever, recognising these dangers, kept watch over his heart that it should not be lifted up, might do externally whatever was demanded by altered circumstances.

Solomon's apostasy was followed by a series of divine punishments. While he was still on the throne, Idumea began to throw off its allegiance, under the guidance of a certain Hadad, a descendant of the old Idumean kings who had been deposed by David, who had married a daughter of the king of Egypt, and was supported by him. Another successful opponent, Rezon, took Damascus from him, and all Damascene Syria, and became the founder of a kingdom which afterwards proved very destructive to the Israelites. A still heavier punishment was to fall upon Solomon in his descendants. It was made known to him by a prophet that the greater part of his kingdom would be wrested from his son. Preparation was made for the fulfilment of this threat even in Solomon's lifetime.

It is generally supposed that Solomon repented before his end, and completely renounced the worship of idols. But this opinion is based only on the assumption, which is decidedly erroneous, that Solomon was the author of Ecclesiastes, which is regarded as bearing testimony to and proving his conversion, although the book nowhere expressly speaks of Solomon having repented, as many have asserted, nor even of his having fallen. Nor do the historical books contain the slightest indication of a later conversion of Solomon, and it is at variance with the passage, 2 Kings xxiii. 13, according to which the idolatrous worship instituted by Solomon continued long after his death. The first fruit of his conversion would have been to destroy the scandals which he had established.

Solomon died after having reigned for forty years. Unquestionably the most important event of his reign was the building of the temple. He found great treasures, which David had already collected for this purpose, as well as drawings and models. David, who was not allowed to build the temple himself, had at least tried to prepare everything for it. But Solomon was determined to build a temple which should far surpass the highest ideal of his father.

With this object he entered into an alliance with the king of Tyre, with whom his father had already been on friendly terms. This alliance was most advantageous to him. By this means he obtained the best material, cedar wood; for king Hiram was possessor of the western part of Lebanon, on which the cedars grow. It also enabled him to procure workmen and artisans. We learn that the Tyrians had very skilful artisans even at that time, and that Hiram was acquainted with and promoted the art of building, not merely from the accounts of Scripture, but also from those fragments of Dius and Menander which have been preserved by Josephus. After these preparations a beginning was made by procuring materials. Notwithstanding the immense number of work-people, this occupied so much time, that it was not until the fourth year that the building could be begun. David had already fixed upon Mount Moriah as the site of the temple. Without doubt the proximate cause for the choice of this place was the divine vision which had there been vouchsafed to him; comp. 2 Sam. xxiv. 1 ff., 1 Chron. xxi. 28, xxii. 1. But this vision was only a renewal of the remembrance of a former one, a strengthening of the demand already made, to choose this place. On Mount Moriah Abraham had confirmed his election by the highest proof of his faith: here the angel of the Lord had appeared to him and had renewed the promise. When the building of the temple was completed after seven years, the feast of dedication was celebrated with great splendour, in an assembly of the princes of the tribes and the heads of the families, and amid a great multitude of people. The ark of the covenant was brought from the tabernacle on Zion to the temple-mountain Moriah, and God's mercy was sought by sacrifice, and songs, and prayers. The solemnity made a happy impression on the nation. Sacrifice on the heights, which had formerly been tolerated, was now entirely abandoned. It is true that Bertheau infers the contrary from 2 Kings xxiii. 22, according to which the feast of the passover in Solomon's time was not kept as enjoined by the Mosaic law, the whole nation being assembled at the sanctuary. But this passage only makes a general reference to the time of the kings, in which, for the most part, it was impossible to realize the Mosaic determination owing to the separation of the kingdom. The short time in which the Mosaic law was fully carried out is left out of sight.

The arrangement of the temple has been discussed by Keil, *The Temple of Solomon*, Dorpat, 1839, and best by Bähr, 1848. The patriotic fancy of Josephus and the Rabbis satisfied itself in embellishing and exaggerating it; and they have been only too closely followed by Christian scholars until the latter half of the past century, when some have gone to the opposite extreme. Voltaire declared that, in all antiquity, he could remember no building, no temple of any nation, so small as the temple of Solomon. Joh. Dav. Michaelis thought that his house at Göttingen was larger than the admired temple of the God of Israel at Jerusalem. The truth is, that the temple itself, which was not, like our churches, intended to accommodate a congregation, but only to conceal the holy vessels and to give space for the performance of certain sacred acts, was of no very great extent; but the whole erection, including the fore-courts, was of an imposing size.

The temple was nothing more than an enlarged and immoveable tabernacle of the covenant, and was characterized by the same threefold division. First came the fore-court of the people, which was surrounded by a wall containing porches for shelter in bad weather, and was entered by gates fastened with brass. This fore-court of the people led to the higher or inner or priests' fore-court, which was separated from the outer one by three rows of freestone and a row of cedar beams. In this court there were large brass pedestals on wheels, five on the right side, and five on the left side, with large basins on them, intended for the washing of the meat-offerings; then the brazen sea, a basin ten cubits in diameter and five cubits high, resting on twelve brass wheels, for the purification of the priests; finally, the large brass altar for burnt-offerings, twenty cubits in length and breadth, and ten cubits in height. Next to the court of the priests came the temple itself. First of all there was a porch or court containing two large brass pillars, with artistically wrought chapiters. In breadth it was equal to the sacred court, and was ten cubits long. Leading from it into the temple-house was a door five cubits wide, with double wings of cypress wood overlaid with gold, and ornamented with carving of cherubs, palms, and open flowers. This was 60 cubits long, 20 wide, and 30 high: 20 cubits were set apart for the holy of holies, being separated by a cedar wall, with folding doors, and a curtain behind it. The walls of the temple were of hewn stone, and were wainscoted inside with cedar wood, ornamented with carving of palms and cherubim. Inside, the holy and the holy of holies were inlaid with thin gold plates. The floor was of cypress wood, the roof of cedar beams. In the sanctuary, besides the golden altar of incense before the entrance to the holy of holies, there were ten golden candlesticks and the table of shew-bread. Outside, round about the holy and the holy of holies, there was an accessory building which enclosed the temple on three sides, so that only the porch in front remained open. This building consisted of three stories, each five cubits in height, with simple chambers or sacristies. The temple, with the porch and the surrounding building, occupied a space of about 90 cubits in length and 46 cubits in breadth. The priests' fore-court was probably about 200 cubits long, and nearly 100 cubits wide; the outer court was 300 cubits long, and of equal width.

With regard to the symbolical meaning of the temple and its vessels, all that we said before respecting the tabernacle of testimony is applicable to it, for the distinction between them is only a material, and not a theological one. The only symbol peculiar to the temple is to be found in the palms and the flower and fruit ornaments, which, together with the cherubim, the representation of the living creation, revealed the God of Israel as the Lord of nature.

The building of the temple had most important results. We learn how powerfully it promoted religious public spirit, from the fact that Jeroboam despaired of the success of his attempted division of the citizens, unless he could put a stop to the annual feast-journeys to the temple. For those who feared God among the ten tribes, the temple continued to be a magnet which drew them to Jerusalem. The greater the temptations to idolatry in the time of the kings, the more important it was that a centre of Jehovah-worship should be given to the nation in the temple, with its glorious service; otherwise idolatry would certainly have made much more rapid progress.

Solomon's reign was important not only for the building of the temple, but also because it gave birth to a new branch of sacred literature, viz. the creation of proverbs, which, with its predominant objective mode of view, could only flourish in a time of rest and peace, while times of battle and of excited feeling were favourable to sacred lyrics. Finally, because it gave a new substratum for the Messianic idea. Just as David's reign quickened the hopes in the Messiah as the mighty victor over all the enemies of the kingdom of God, as we find from Ps. ii. and cx., which are founded on the relations of the Davidic time, so Solomon's reign afforded a glance into the government of the Prince of peace, a name which is used by Isaiah in chap. ix. 5 with plain reference to Solomon. We see from Ps. lxxii. and xlv. how all that God granted in this respect under Solomon, was, even at that time, regarded as a prophecy of that which He would do far more gloriously in the future. This is still more clearly shown in the Song of Solomon, in which he extols his antitype under the name of the heavenly Solomon. Care was taken that the present should not afford perfect satisfaction, but should only awaken a more intense longing after the true and heavenly Prince of peace. In close connection with a high state of national prosperity, we perceive the beginning of a cancerous growth which incessantly eats away, destroying the nation's fear of God, the condition of their salvation, and hence this salvation itself. We are taught that the peace given by a merely human ruler bears in itself the germ of decay; bringing temptations which an inferior anointed of the Lord cannot give power to overcome. The result of the whole brilliant period was a Kyrie Eleison, and the prayer, "Oh that Thou wouldst rend the heavens and come down!"

FIFTH SECTION.

FROM THE DIVISION OF THE KINGDOM TO THE BABYLONISH CAPTIVITY.

§ 1.

REHOBOAM AND JEROBOAM.

The punishment with which Solomon had been threatened was fulfilled soon after his death. And if these punishments fell upon the people also, they had the less cause to complain, since they had taken part in the apostasy of Solomon; they, not less than he, had succumbed to the temptations incident to a long time of peace. We see how low they had fallen under the reign of Solomon, from the fact that Jeroboam could venture to introduce the worship of calves without finding universal opposition. The states which show themselves so zealous in a political aspect, here show perfect indifference. The opposition is not national, but only proceeds from a small, God-fearing community. The punishment was a heavy one. Not only were their best powers diffused by the separation of the kingdom, but they were destroyed in bloody internal wars. The subjugation of Israel was now an easy matter for the great rising Asiatic world-empires: the weakness of the Israelites increased with the power of their enemies. It lay in the plan of the divine providence to abandon them to oppression, to lead them to repentance through the school of misery. The separation of the two kingdoms also in a great measure involved the loss of the other acquisitions which had been made under the reign of David and Solomon, of prosperity and higher culture. But the loss was accompanied by gain. The faith of the elect grew strong in the struggle with despair, which was so powerfully called forth by the visible. Opposition to the ever-increasing corruption enhanced the zeal of the pious, and developed their gifts. Among the better, the

Messianic hope became more and more a central-point. Necessity drew them to the future Redeemer. The wonderful deliverances vouchsafed to the people when they cried to God in urgent need, such as those under Jehoshaphat and under Hezekiah, called forth a mighty working of the Spirit among the whole nation. The separation of the kingdom surrendered the ground which had given birth to the prophethood, so important for the Church at all times. And the long series of psalms characteristic of the struggle of despair with faith, in which the Church of all times has one of its noblest treasures, would never have existed had it not been for the disorder called forth by the separation of the kingdoms, which gave the death-blow to the greatness of Israel. The object of the prediction of the separation of the kingdom made by the prophet Ahijah, was that it might not be attributed to accident, but that the co-operation of a divine causality might be recognised, and that by this acknowledgment the attainment of its object might be promoted. The supremacy could not be quite taken away from the family of David, as it was from so many rulers in the later kingdom of Israel. This would have been inconsistent with the promise given to David in 2 Sam. vii., which demanded even more. According to it, the separation of the kingdom could only be temporary, for it promised the tribe of David the supremacy over Israel, though pointing to the interruptions due to sin. Hence the prophet Ahijah only declared the temporary separation. "I will for this afflict the seed of David," says the Lord in 1 Kings xi. 39, "but not for ever,"—a saying which has found its perfect fulfilment in Christ.

We have now considered the separation of the kingdom in so far as it was the result of a divine causality. But this mode of consideration must be regarded as quite distinct from a merely human one. From the latter standpoint the separation appears as a result of the battle of sin against sin.

Solomon was succeeded by Rehoboam, who was at once recognised as king by the tribe of Judah. But the ten tribes assembled in their delegates at Sichem, under the mere pretext of making him king there, having the secret intention of dethroning him. This intention already appeared from the choice of the place of assembling. Sichem was the principal city of the tribe of Ephraim. They thought they could act more freely there than at Jerusalem, where Solomon had been made king. Jeroboam, the type of all modern demagogues, was active in the matter from the beginning. Apparently they desired nothing further than a lightening of the burdens which Solomon had laid upon the nation; and there seems to have been justice in this demand. Solomon, who was never a man of the people as his father had been, had oppressed the nation toward the end of his reign by his excessive expenditure and his despotic rule. Rehoboam might therefore readily have promised to lighten their burdens, the more so since those who made the demand were not an assembled mob, but the legal representatives of the nation. We have already seen that kingly power among the Israelites was not absolute even in a political aspect,—that the king was restrained not only by the law of God, and by the ordinary and extraordinary servants, the priests and the prophets, who had been appointed for its administration, but also by the states, whose origin dated from the beginning of the nation, which were older than the kingdom, which had been first called into existence by them, and whose rights he had as little power to trample upon as they on his. Hence the answer which the king gave by the advice of his imprudent friends is most strongly to be condemned, especially on account of the mocking, disagreeable way in which it was put. "My little finger," he said, "shall be thicker than my father's loins. My father chastised you with whips, but I will chastise you with scorpions." It is generally supposed that scorpions here mean scourges; but the usual meaning of the word is quite applicable here. Scorpions, the evil, poisonous reptile, are an image of the most severe measures. In these words we hear no "king by the grace of God," who, conscious of the similar origin of his rights and his duties, is equally mindful of both, but an overbearing despot, who imagines he can easily become master of the people by the help of his warriors. This does not, however, by any means justify the conduct of the people. First of all, we must bear in mind that their demand was in all probability nothing more than a pretext; that they would have deserted Rehoboam even if he had redressed their grievances, or if there had been no well-founded grievances. This resolution was only the culminating point of the jealousy of the ten tribes against Judah, a feeling which had long been in existence, especially among the tribe of Ephraim, which had succeeded in acquiring ascendency over the remaining tribes. The two tribes Judah and Joseph (Ephraim and Manasseh were looked upon as one tribe) were the most numerous among all. Moreover, both had no inconsiderable claims. Judah had already been brilliantly distinguished in the blessing of Jacob; Moses had given him the first place in the camp of the Israelites; in Canaan he had received exceptionally large territory. Ephraim, already preferred before his brother by Jacob and Moses, Gen. xlviii. 19, 20, Deut. xxxiii. 17, and always appearing as the representative of the whole tribe of Joseph, was proud of the pre-eminence of his ancestor, called a prince over his brethren in the blessing of Jacob, proud that Joshua had sprung from his midst, proud of the distinction of having possessed the tabernacle of the covenant at Shiloh for so many years, proud of the leadership which he had maintained during the whole period of the judges; comp. his reproaches against Gideon in Judg. viii. 1, and his rising against Jephthah in Judg. xii., also the 78th Psalm, which shows clearly that during the whole period of the judges Ephraim had been in possession of a certain pre-eminence. Pride on account of real or imaginary superiority could not fail soon to awaken jealousy between the two tribes. This was plainly seen after the death of Saul. To avoid being subject to the Judaite David, Ephraim and the remaining nine tribes, which he had succeeded in reducing to a kind of dependence, probably on the pretext that the disproportionate power of Judah demanded a strong counter-influence, joined Ish-bosheth without regard to the will of God, which had been revealed by Samuel, and confirmed by the destruction of Saul and of his sons, who were not capable of reigning. David's personal qualities finally gained the victory over this jealousy. Internal differences were swallowed up by the prospect of external power. David was voluntarily acknowledged king by the ten tribes also. But the fire still smouldered in the ashes, and David's wisdom, which led him to choose his residence and the seat of the sanctuary without the tribe of Judah, did not avail to extinguish it. The success of Absalom's revolt is certainly mainly attributable to the jealousy of Ephraim: the tribe which had refused allegiance to David hoped to derive advantage in the general confusion. This was immediately followed by the revolt of Sheba, to whom all Israel deserted, while the tribe of Judah remained true to its king. The 78th Psalm, composed by the Davidic Asaph, is highly instructive with respect to these relations. The object of the whole psalm is to meet the danger of refusing to submit to the divine decree by which the prerogative of the tribe of Ephraim was transferred to the tribe of Judah, of regarding as usurpation that which contained a divine judgment, and rising up against the sanctuary in Zion, and against the supremacy of David and of his tribe. It shows plainly that the spirit of rebellion among the ten tribes, and especially in Ephraim, existed as early as David's time. But under David and Solomon participation in the national fame of Israel founded by these great kings formed an antidote to the jealousy of Ephraim, by which means its energy was broken, just as the Republicans in France remained quiet during the brilliant period of Napoleon. But after Solomon's death it broke forth into clear flame, and the consequence of disregarding the true warning of Samuel was the deplorable separation of the kingdom, which dealt the Israelitish nation a mortal wound. This must be attributed not only to the jealousy of Ephraim, but also in some measure to the deep-rooted hatred of Benjamin towards Judah, who could never forgive the loss of the kingdom. We see how great this hatred was, from the conduct of the Benjamite Shimei on Absalom's revolt, from the rebellion of Sheba, himself a Benjamite, and from the circumstance that Benjamin was the only tribe that was not numbered, doubtless because Joab feared to awaken its rebellious disposition. But even granting that the Israelites had represented their grievances with honest intent, yet they would have had no right to rebel when they found no hearing. Some, indeed, such as Michaelis, have affirmed the contrary. The ten tribes were under no obligation to accept the king of the tribe of Judah. For seven years David had been king over Judah alone, before he had been chosen and appointed king by the remaining tribes, who in the meantime had a king of the house of Saul. But this assertion is based on a completely false view. The kingdom was never an elective one: until now God had always reserved to Himself the right of appointing the king; the states had nothing to do but to acknowledge His choice. Their omission to do this for the seven years succeeding the death of Saul was their first sin, and cannot serve as a justification of a second. God had called David and all his race to the throne; hence the apostasy was directed against Him until He gave the people permission to choose a new ruler. It is true, indeed, that this revelation of God's will had been contained in the announcement made by the prophet Ahijah to Jeroboam during Solomon's reign. But this does not by any means justify Jeroboam and the nation, even if the announcement did really contain a summons to action, and was not rather a prediction of the future, whose accomplishment Jeroboam and the nation should quietly have left to the Lord, without trying to bring it about by their own sin. Their conduct shows that they had little regard to this announcement of God's, which was entitled to some consideration, even if misunderstood, as the spring of their actions. Their motives appear to be purely carnal, without the smallest trace of a higher spirit. But the announcement of Ahijah, still totally misapprehended by Ewald, cannot be otherwise regarded than as the promise of kingship to David through Samuel, and David's conduct shows us how the ten tribes ought to have acted.

The answer of Rehoboam was very welcome to the ten tribes, as his experienced counsellors had foreseen, according to 1 Kings xii. 7. A soft answer would have placed them in an embarrassing position, by obliging them to reveal their disposition to rebel. They declared their desertion from the house of David, and broke up the assembly. Rehoboam now became aware of his imprudence, and sent Adoram, one of his servants, to pacify them. This too would have been successful if the people had really sought nothing further than an alleviation of their burdens; but since this was not the case, it only served to increase their rage, the more so because the king had been imprudent enough to choose as his ambassador a hated commissioner of taxes. The nation stoned Adoram, in order to make the breach irreparable. Rehoboam now fled in haste to Jerusalem. There he made preparation for war against Israel, but gave up his preparations as soon as the prophet Shemaiah, in the name of the Lord, forbade him to make war, revealing that the continuance of the separation was the will of the Lord. This obedience shows that he still retained more pious disposition than the wretched Jeroboam. Thus the kingdom was divided into two unequal parts. Besides the tribe of Judah, Rehoboam had supremacy over the children of Israel who dwelt in the cities of Judah, according to 1 Kings xii. 17. By the former representation, these included the Simeonites and a part of the tribe of Benjamin, viz. Jerusalem and its nearest Benjamitic environs, those immediately dependent on the capital. It is generally supposed that the whole tribe of Benjamin remained true to the Davidic kingship; but it has been shown in my commentary on Ps. lxxx. that this view is wholly untenable. Only one tribe, therefore, remained to the royal house of David; for Simeon, which had been incorporated with Judah, no longer existed as a tribe at the time of the separation of the kingdom. This Judaic kingdom lasted for four centuries, the length of time which elapsed from the separation of the kingdom to the Chaldaic destruction. Of the foreign conquests, the royal house of Judah still retained the lands of the Philistines and the Idumeans, which bordered on the tribe of Judah. But the former seem to have emancipated themselves very early. Ewald conjectures that they took advantage of the Egyptian invasion under Rehoboam. Then Judah was joined by the whole tribe of Levi. Levi was bound to the sanctuary, and could not recognise the intended innovations of Jeroboam without the grossest apostasy. From the beginning Jeroboam had assumed the most insolent manner towards this tribe, because he despaired of winning it permanently to his cause. Thus the kingdom of Judah was at least in some measure on a par with Israel. Israel, indeed, had all the tributary lands in the east as far as the Euphrates; but under existing circumstances this was a most precarious possession, and was in fact soon lost.

Jeroboam was the representative of the evil spirit which animated the tribe of Ephraim even during the time of the judges, as we learn from Ps. lxxviii., and in the time of his leadership exercised as injurious an influence on the whole of the nation, as afterwards upon Israel. He sought to retain by carnal means the kingdom which had been won by carnal means. In 1 Kings xii. 26 we read: "And Jeroboam said in his heart, Now shall the kingdom return to the house of David." In 1 Kings xi. 38 the Lord had promised him that He would give the throne to him and to his family if he would walk in His ways. But this promise made no impression on him, because he had no faith. His evil conscience kept him in continual fear. He was particularly suspicious when Jerusalem remained as before the seat of the sanctuary for the ten tribes also. Looked at merely from the standpoint of human wisdom, there was great foundation for this suspicion. The religious union which was maintained by the yearly pilgrimages to Jerusalem might readily awaken a desire for the restoration of civil union, and it would be a matter of great difficulty to stifle the old allegiance to the royal house of David, which was enveloped in special glory by the circumstance that it resided at the seat of the sanctuary, if it still received new and powerful incentive. If Jeroboam had been a truly pious king, he would have confidently left it to God to ward off these evil consequences; but he showed by his conduct that he was utterly godless, and regarded religion only as a means for his own ends. Religious separation would make the political breach irreparable. If *sacra communia* no longer existed, the striving after civil unity would of necessity cease also. Under the pretext that the pilgrimage to Jerusalem was too burdensome to the nation, owing to the great distance, he set up two golden calves,—the one at Dan, the northern limit of the kingdom, the other at Bethel, the southern limit,—and tried to deprive the thing of its offensive character by appealing to the example of Aaron, who had established a similar worship immediately after the exodus out of Egypt. We learn that Jeroboam appealed to the example of Aaron, from the complete agreement of his words with those of Aaron in Ex. xxxii. 4 : " These be thy gods, O Israel, which brought thee up out of the land of Egypt." The calf-worship which he established was not, however, mere dead imitation, but had also a new root. We are led to this inference by what is said in 1 Kings xii. 2 with reference to Jeroboam's sojourn in Egypt,—" for he was fled from the presence of king Solomon,"—and also by the twofold number of the calves, and the fact of their being set up in different places. Two sacred bulls, the Apis at Memphis, and the Mnevis at Heliopolis, were worshipped by all Egypt. The worship of one of the two, of Mnevis probably, first began in the interval between Moses and Jeroboam. The erection of a new sanctuary in itself would have been a crime, even if the worship had been conducted in perfect accordance with the directions of the law. We see how deeply this was recognised in early times, by the dealings with the two and a half tribes, in the book of Joshua. But the establishment of this worship was a far greater crime. There can be no doubt that Jeroboam was actuated by a desire to destroy the inner unity, after the outer religious unity had been removed by the establishment of new places to worship God, and thus to form an indestructible barrier between Judah and Israel. It was impossible for the Judaites to regard the Israelitish worship except with horror. Complete idolatry was by no means intended, just as little as in the wilderness and in the image-worship of Micah. The calves were only intended as a symbolization of Jehovah. Hence throughout the books of the Kings the sin of Jeroboam is distinguished from idolatry proper, and represented as comparatively less : thus, for example, in 1 Kings xvi. 31–33 ; 2 Kings iii. 2, 3, x. 30, 31. In the minor prophets also a distinction is made between the worship of calves and the worship of Baal, however strongly the former might be denounced; comp. Michaelis, *Mos. Recht*, S. 245. The passage, 1 Kings xiv. 9, where the prophet Ahijah says to Jeroboam, "Thou hast gone and made thee other gods," only points out that the crime of worshipping Jehovah under the image of a bull was of the same nature as idolatry, just as the Lord had previously characterized the licentious glance as adultery, without meaning to assert that it was completely identical with it. But the worship of images was also most strictly prohibited in the law, and was characterized in the Decalogue as a kind of idolatry. The way in which it was punished in the wilderness shows what a grievous crime it was in the sight of the Lord. To those who are not acquainted with human nature, it seems incomprehensible, at the first glance, how Jeroboam could have influenced the ten tribes to commit such an abomination. It seems that it must have been impossible for him to find any plausible pretext. But experience suffices to show what incredible ingenuity man possesses in perverting the clearest statements of Scripture, when they are in opposition to his desires. We do not know what distinctions Jeroboam invented in order to show that the Mosaic law was not applicable to this case. We learn from 1 Kings xii. 28 that he did really try to make his conduct appear consistent with the law. Probably he argued that the people had now become mature, so that the prohibition which had been intended for their childhood was no longer applicable. This innovation of Jeroboam's had the most disastrous consequences. The chosen symbolization of Jehovah necessarily gave rise to low ideas of Him. His ethical attributes—that which distinguishes the God of Israel most markedly from the idols of the heathen—were by this means thrown completely into the background, only the aspect of power is made prominent. And, moreover, the prohibition of the worship of images in the Pentateuch was as definite and clear as possible. And since the people had allowed themselves to interpret the law against their better knowledge and conscience in so important a case, they naturally did the same thing in other matters, whenever the corrupt desire of their hearts suggested it. Every conscious unfaithfulness, if cherished and excused, inevitably leads to complete ruin in the community, no less than in the individual. The introduction of image-worship offered a loophole to heathenism, through which it could not be prevented entering. A second means which Jeroboam employed for the destruction of religious unity was this,—he robbed the Levites of the dignity which had been bestowed on them by Moses, and had been so gloriously ratified by the miracle of the budding rod and the destruction of the company of the rebels, and even drove them completely from the land: comp. 2 Chron. xi. 13–17; 1 Kings xii. 31, xiii. 33. If the Levites had continued to be the common servants of the sanctuary in the two kingdoms, there would always have been an element of union between them. And even if it had been possible to gain over some of the Levites in the beginning to the interest of the innovations, yet the spirit of tribe and of position was too powerful to allow this intrusion to have any permanence. The deposition of the Levites, which was apparently justified by the opposition of the tribe to the changes made by the king,—an opposition which must have been very welcome,— gave him an opportunity of attaching a number of individuals to his own interest. He chose new priests from the midst of the nation. From these, whose dignity had no divine foundation, but rose and fell with the political government, he could expect no opposition to his attempt to constitute himself spiritual ruler and chief exponent of the law: comp. 1 Kings xii. 32 ff., according to which he himself offered up sacrifice and incense and ordained the priests; Amos vii. 13, where the high priest Amaziah calls the sanctuary at Bethel the "King's Chapel." It was of course necessary for the king to vindicate this position, otherwise an end would soon have been put to his innovations: they could only be maintained by the same power which had first called them into life. The worship of calves was first established at Dan, and then at Bethel; the feast of tabernacles was celebrated in both places, in the latter in the presence of Jeroboam, but not as it ought to have been done in accordance with the law, on the fifteenth day of the seventh month, but of the eighth month. Perhaps he availed himself of the pretext that the feast of tabernacles was at the same time a feast of thanksgiving for fruit and vintage, but in some northern districts of the ten tribes these did not come to an end until after the legal term. His true object was nothing else than to destroy the religious unity between Judah and Israel. Hence the time had now come for the Lord to assert His sovereignty over Israel, unless the godless king were to persevere in his evil course. The way in which this happened is narrated in 1 Kings xiii. We take for granted a knowledge of the contents of this chapter. Jeroboam, in his carnal wisdom, had not thought of the strongest link which bound the people to the Lord and to one another, viz. the prophethood, which offered a more powerful and effectual resistance to the abuse of religion in the service of a self-seeking, political interest, than the priesthood would have done. He soon found to his cost that he had erred in his calculation. A prophet from the kingdom of Judah, who had come to Bethel at the command of the Lord, while Jeroboam was officiating in his assumed character of high priest, prophesied, with a precision adapted to existing circumstances, that at a future time a king of Judah would destroy the altar and slay the high priests,—a prophecy which was only fulfilled 350 years afterwards by Josiah, the pious king, who destroyed the altar of Jeroboam at Bethel, having special regard to the prediction of the prophet, whose grave the people of the city pointed out to him, and recognised what happened as the fulfilment of the well-known prophecy. A doubly remarkable event, the rending of the altar and the stiffening of the arm of the king, which had been threateningly raised against the prophet, together with the healing of it at his request, confirmed his divine mission, and strengthened the impression on the people, who were assembled in great numbers. If we take our standpoint on the sphere of revelation, events such as these must necessarily have occurred according to idea and analogy. This object was still more definitely attained by the subsequent fate of the prophet himself. The Lord had given him a command neither to eat nor drink by the way,

nor to return by the same way. This command was given
out of consideration to the weakness of the prophet. It was
to be anticipated that the king, in order to do away with the
injurious impression which the prophecy had made on the
nation, would try by every means in his power to gain over
the prophet to his side. Hence a long stay exposed him to
great temptation, and, if he persisted in it, to great danger;
if he were to choose another way, he would not be so readily
found by the king's messengers. He resisted the entice-
ments of Jeroboam; but when the tempter assailed him
in a more disguised form, he succumbed. The instrument
of his seduction, the old prophet from Bethel, is a very
remarkable man in a psychological aspect. In ancient
times it has been contested whether he was a true or a
false prophet. The truth lies between the two extremes.
He was originally a true prophet of the true God, but
sinned by keeping silence respecting the innovations of
Jeroboam. He was not, however, quite hardened. This
is shown by the same history which forms a monument of
his apostasy. When he heard of the prediction and the
deeds of the Judaic prophet, he was seized with deep shame
on account of his fall; and the struggle to conceal from himself his own disgrace and to appease the torments of his
conscience explains why he urged the prophet so strongly
to go home with him. He sought to vindicate his honour,
as it were, to himself and to others, by proving that a true
prophet would have fellowship with him. The fact that to
gain this object he employed such disgraceful means—the
false pretext of a revelation received from God—shows how
strong the stings of conscience were, so that he felt it necessary to purchase at any price what seemed to promise him
some measure of rest. The assertion of those who look upon
the old man simply as a false prophet, that it was pure
wickedness which prompted him to lead the Judaic prophet
to transgress the divine command, is inconsistent with the
narrative throughout. The Judaic prophet pays no heed to
his proposal until he feigns a divine revelation. Hence
Michaelis designates his transgression as comparatively innocent, but very erroneously. He was firmly persuaded that

the revelation which had been given to him was divine, which was not the case with respect to the other. He would therefore not have yielded to the entreaty if his inclination had not led him to believe in the truth of that which was least authenticated. His punishment, though quite just, would not indeed have been so severe, if it had not been intended to furnish a striking example of the severity with which God avenges the neglect of His commands, and at the same time to confirm his divine mission. God also so ordered the circumstances of the punishment, that it could not be regarded as the work of accident, and effected the salvation of both prophets. He who by a false prophecy had seduced the Judaic prophet, was compelled to announce the judgment that was to follow, overpowered, like Balaam, by the Spirit of God. The circumstance that the lion, contrary to his nature, left the corpse and the ass uninjured, must have excited universal astonishment. The old prophet must have been deeply moved by the knowledge that by his guilt, another, far more innocent than he, should have died so terrible a death. That the matter really did exercise a salutary influence upon him, appears from chap. xiii. 21, 32, where he expresses the strongest faith in the fulfilment of the promise with respect to Josiah, as well as from ver. 33, where, in strong contrast to the salutary impression produced on the prophet, we have a representation of the obduracy of Jeroboam. Josiah held the grave of the Judaic prophet in great honour, as that of a holy man.

Jeroboam persisted in his obduracy, and soon received another divine warning. The prophets of the true God must have been an abomination to him, for they were sworn opponents of his image-worship. Nevertheless, on the sickness of his son Abijah, anxiety impelled him to send his wife to one of these prophets, Ahijah. But lest this sending should be regarded as a public recognition of the divine calling of the prophet, and should therefore bring shame upon him, she was to disguise herself as a woman in humble life, and to take with her such small presents as were in keeping with this station. With the inconsistency always found in combination with unbelief, Jeroboam trusted that the prophet, in consequence of his age, was almost blind. But the Lord revealed to Ahijah what his bodily eye could not see. Immediately on the entrance of the queen he announced the complete rejection and destruction of the house of Jeroboam on account of his grievous sins, and at the same time predicted the heavy misfortunes which would come upon Israel, until their final carrying away into captivity beyond the Euphrates. And that there might be no doubt regarding the truth of his announcement, he made a prophecy with respect to the immediate future: the son of the king should die immediately on the return of the mother. He only of the posterity of Jeroboam should receive a solemn burial, because he was found to be good before God in comparison with the remainder of the house of Jeroboam. The boy must have distinguished himself from the remaining children of the rejected Jeroboam by a pious disposition. Jeroboam was so hardened, that even the accurate fulfilment of this prediction was powerless to move him. With respect to the other events which befell him, and his actions, the author refers us to the more systematically chronicled records of Israel, because they were not suitable for his object, which was to write sacred history. We remark further, that Jeroboam raised Tirzah to be the capital of his kingdom, without paying any regard to the established claims of Sichem. He was perhaps led to do this by the Song of Solomon vi. 4. It is quite in keeping with his politics, which invariably sought to find substitutes for the privileges enjoyed by the kingdom of Judah,—setting Bethel, for example, in opposition to Jerusalem, and the calves which had been consecrated by the example of Aaron in opposition to the ark of the covenant,—that he should choose for his residence a town which had been so honourably named by Solomon in connection with Jerusalem, and had been characterized as enjoying equal privileges.

Turning now to the kingdom of Judah, we see clearly that it was much more favourably situated. We here find the temple at Jerusalem as the one place of the pure worship of Jehovah, in opposition to the impure worship at Dan and Bethel, as well as many other sacred places, among which Gilgal and Beer-sheba, situated in the kingdom of Judah, were very much resorted to. The class of the priests and Levites, strengthened in their natural dependence on the law by their banishment from the kingdom of the ten tribes, formed a strong bulwark against the entrance of godlessness. Since the Mosaic separation between the ecclesiastical and the civil sphere had been maintained in the kingdom of Judah, the prophethood had greater scope. The dynasty of David, resting upon divine right, and surrounded by venerable memories, which guaranteed even to its weaker members the recognition and love of the people, continued to form the central point of the nation, and secured its quiet development; while in Israel no dynasty succeeded in establishing itself, revolution succeeded to revolution, the people were distracted by the bloody party struggles, and a rude military despotism prevailed. Even the heritage of higher culture and civilisation which had been gained under Solomon passed over to Judah. Memories of the time of David continually reacted against intruding corruption, and gave powerful assistance to the reformations by which they were set aside, never allowing the heathen tendency, which had been advancing ever since the last days of Solomon, to acquire permanent supremacy.

Of Rehoboam the history tells comparatively less than of Jeroboam. The fact that chap. xiv. 21 represents Rehoboam as having been forty-one years of age when he ascended the throne has given rise to suspicion. Grotius, Clericus, and Michaelis have maintained that we must undoubtedly regard this as a critical error. The following are the reasons which they adduce:—According to this, Rehoboam must have been born a year before Solomon began to reign. But at this time he was still very young. This argument is not decisive. Solomon was eighteen years of age when he began to reign, and in this respect we must not judge the East by the West; and the argument that on Rehoboam's accession to the throne he is described as young, and as having grown up with the young counsellors, has no weight. There is certainly a youthful character about the answer which Rehoboam gives to the ten tribes; but, if not generally, yet very frequently, judgment fails to come with years. It must be conceded that a critical emendation, without the authority of manuscripts, is more admissible in a statement of numbers than elsewhere. But in this case the accuracy of the account is confirmed by the fact that we find the same thing in 2 Chron. xii. 13. Rehoboam's first care was to erect fortresses on the frontier towards Israel; comp. 1 Chron. vi. 5 ff. In the first three years of his reign the condition of the nation in a religious, and hence also in a political aspect, was pretty flourishing, as we are expressly told in Chronicles. All the priests and Levites had repaired to the kingdom of Judah; and a great number of God-fearing laymen, who abhorred the worship of calves, preferred to leave their fatherland rather than give up the freedom of sacrificing to the true God in the place which He had commanded. By this means the kingdom of Judah not only received a considerable accession to external power, but was also greatly strengthened internally. Opposition towards the corrupt spirit which prevailed in the kingdom of Israel at first roused nation and king to active zeal for the law of the Lord. But here also it was shown that religious movements, when connected with political struggles, have no lasting character; already, after the expiration of three years, Rehoboam turned aside from the good course which he had first trodden. His example exercised a most injurious influence on the nation, though a considerable ἐκλογή still remained. Idolatry, even in its most detestable forms, prevailed also in the kingdom of Judah, not, however, as a part of the fundamental constitution, but as an abuse opposed to it. This indeed went so far, that even the shameless worshippers of the god of love, who were consecrated to abandon themselves for money, קדשים, were tolerated. Here the crime was immediately followed by punishment. Already, in the fifth year of Rehoboam, Judah was attacked by Shishak king of Egypt, whether at the instigation of Jeroboam, as Ewald suspects, or not, we cannot be certain. If this had been the case, there would probably have been some indication of it in the sources. The separation of the kingdoms was sufficient reason in itself. With envy and apprehension Egypt had seen a powerful Israelitish kingdom rise up in its neighbourhood; it was natural at once to take advantage of its weakness. On the approach of the hostile army, the prophet Shemaiah earnestly upbraids the terrified king and nation for their sins, which have called forth this judgment; and when they accepted this punishment in a repentant spirit, he announced the mitigation of the divine judgment. The city surrendered to Shishak; but he contented himself with carrying away the treasures of the king and of the temple. The account of this Egyptian invasion has received remarkable confirmation from recent discoveries in Egypt. In the first court of the great palace at Karnak has been found the gigantic figure of a king described by the name "Shishonk, the beloved of Ammon." It is evident that this is Shishonk, from the circumstance that among the conquered nations there is one with a beard and of unmistakeably Jewish physiognomy, who bears the name Judah Hamalek, or Melk, the kingdom of Judah. In Manetho, Lesonchis, the first king of the twenty-second dynasty of the Bubasti: Rosellini, 1, 2, p. 79; Champollion, *Pr.* p. 66; Wilkinson, 1, p. 136. Yet the repentance of Rehoboam was not thorough. 1 Kings xiv. 30, where we read, "And there was war between Rehoboam and Jeroboam all their days," has reference only to the hostile feeling which manifested itself in individual disputes, in contrast to the alliances afterwards existing between various kings of Judah and Israel. There was no open war between them.

§ 2.

ABIJAM AND ASA IN THE KINGDOM OF JUDAH. NADAB, BAASHA, ELAH, ZIMRI, OMRI, AND AHAB IN THE KINGDOM OF ISRAEL.

Rehoboam was succeeded on the throne by his son Abijah or Abijam, who was contemporary with Jeroboam, who reigned, however, only three years. His history is very briefly given in the books of Kings, but more fully in

Chronicles. In 1 Kings xv. 2, his mother is said to have been a daughter of Absalom. According to the chronology, she cannot possibly have been his daughter in the true sense; but it was not unusual to pass by the obscure parents, and speak of the grandsons and granddaughters as sons and daughters of their grand-parents, or even of their great-grand-parents. Absalom left no son, but only a daughter, Tamar, 2 Sam. xviii. 18, xiv. 27. Maachah must have been her daughter. This is expressly corroborated by Chronicles. In 2 Chron. xi. 20, according to the same mode of speech employed in the books of the Kings, the mother of Abijah is called "Maachah, the daughter of Absalom." On the other hand, in chap. xiii. 2 she is more accurately described as "Michaiah, the daughter of Uriel of Gibeah." This Uriel had married the daughter of Absalom. Abijah, like Rehoboam, was not wholly devoted to the Lord. Yet, from 1 Kings xv. 3, where we read, " And his heart was not perfect with the Lord his God," we infer that he was not utterly godless; probably he had not polluted himself with the worship of idols, but was lukewarm in promoting the fear of God and in ejecting idolatry. The same thing also appears from the severity with which he rejected the illegal worship introduced by Jeroboam, which presupposes that he had at least in some measure a good conscience; and again, from ver. 15, according to which he made valuable presents to the temple, to compensate for that which had been stolen by the king of Egypt. Under Abijah war broke out openly against Israel. In 1 Kings xv. 6, it is merely stated, " There was war between Rehoboam and Jeroboam all the days of his life." The words "between Rehoboam and Jeroboam" have made unnecessary difficulty here. Rehoboam is named instead of Abijah, because the war waged by the son was merely a continuation of that which had been begun by the father, for whom it was carried on, as it were.

Abijah was succeeded by his better son Asa, who had begun his reign by the destruction of all idolatry. In the commencement of his reign, his grandmother Maachah, who had inherited the bad spirit of her father Absalom, had considerable influence, which is explained by the circumstance that Asa must have been still very young when his father died. But when she made use of her power for the strengthening of idolatry, it was taken from her by Asa, and an image which she had dedicated to the Phenician goddess Astarte was publicly destroyed. מִפְלֶצֶת, which occurs only in 1 Kings xv. 13, is most probably explained by *horriculum*, *horrendum idolum*, פלצות, frequently in the sense of horror. But notwithstanding all his zeal, Asa was not able to destroy the altars on the heights which had been consecrated to Jehovah in various parts of Judea, in opposition to the law respecting the unity of the sanctuary. Those who possessed one of these sanctuaries in their midst would not relinquish the freedom of offering up sacrifices in these places, which were hallowed by past events, and Asa was obliged to content himself with the knowledge that he had at least completely exterminated idolatry. The reason why it was so difficult to do away with the custom of sacrificing on the heights, was because it assumed the disguise of piety. The former hostile relation towards Israel still continued, for the kingdom of Israel was not yet recognised by Judah; whence we read in 1 Kings xv. 16, " And there was war between Asa and Baasha king of Israel all their days." But in the first ten years of Asa it was not open warfare, and during this period the land enjoyed perfect peace; comp. 2 Chron. xiv. 1. He employed this time in making reformations, and in building fortresses. From the tenth to the fifteenth year of his reign Asa seems to have been involved only in struggles which were of little importance, and are therefore not mentioned in the historical books. The first great war against the Cushite king Zerah, which is not mentioned at all in the books of the Kings, but is fully narrated in Chronicles, was already at an end in his fifteenth year, but cannot have lasted long, since it was determined by a battle. The Cushites dwelt partly in Southern Arabia, partly in Africa, which lay opposite to it. But here the reference can only be to the African Cushites, for we find no trace elsewhere of the Arabian Cushites having been a conquered nation. And what is quite decisive is the fact that, according to chap. xvii. 8, there were also Libyans in the army of Zerah. The enemy must therefore have come out of Egypt, which is corroborated by the circumstance that, according to chap. xiv. 14, in their flight they took the way across Gerar, which lies on the usual route from Canaan to Egypt. Champollion, *Précis*, p. 257, ed. ii., has supposed that the Cushite Zerah was the Egyptian king Osorkon, in Manetho and on the monuments. In favour of this view, we have, (1) the fact that they lived at the same time. From the fifth year of Rehoboam to the defeat of Zerah there are thirty years; and the time occupied by the reigns of the two first Pharaohs of this dynasty, Lesonchis (*i.e.* Shishak) and Osorkon, amounts to thirty-six years, according to all the compilers of Manetho. (2) The similarity of name. The three first consonants of Osorkon reappear in the זרח. But Rosellini, 1, 2, p. 87 ff., has brought forward the following arguments in opposition to this view: (1) The omission of the *n*, which forms an essential part of the name Osorkon. (2) Zerah is called an Ethiopian, and not Pharaoh, nor king of Egypt, which occurs of Shishak and all the kings of Egypt. But these arguments are by no means to be regarded as decisive. Zerah had a twofold position, as Ethiopian monarch, and as king of Egypt. It is natural that in Egyptian sources the latter should be made prominent, while the biblical narrative should take his principal position into account. Asa gained a brilliant victory over this powerful king, and Israel was now left in peace for a considerable time, until Josiah, for the Egyptians were fully occupied with themselves. The returning king was received by the prophet Azariah with an earnest discourse, in which he drew his attention to the fact that the victory was only a result of his faithfulness towards God, and urgently exhorted him and the nation to continue in it, predicting that the future would bring a time of heavy affliction for the whole nation, in which it would not only be robbed of its worship, but would be totally deprived of every manifestation of God in its midst,—a prophecy which was first realized in the prelude to the time of the Chaldean exile, and completely fulfilled after the Romish destruction. This formed a powerful incentive to employ the time of grace, and thus to ward off the threatened misfortune. This discourse increased the zeal of the king. He called a general assembly of the nation to Jerusalem, and there solemnly renewed the covenant with the Lord. The whole nation was seized with lively enthusiasm. Many God-fearing people of the kingdom of the ten tribes emigrated to the kingdom of Judah. This invariably happened when pious kings reigned in Judah, and when, in consequence, the Lord made Himself known to the tribe by the deliverance which He granted it. For Judah this was a great blessing: the best powers of Israel flowed thither. But for Israel it was ruinous,—it became more and more a mass without salt.

Open warfare afterwards broke out with the kingdom of Israel. In 2 Chron. xv. 9, xvi. 1, we read that there was no war until the thirty-fifth year of the reign of Asa; but in the thirty-sixth, Baasha undertook a campaign against Judah. Here the difficulty arises, that, according to 1 Kings xvi. 8, Baasha died in the thirty-sixth year of Asa. There are only two alternatives. Either the date in Chronicles must be critically corrupt, or the *terminus a quo* of the thirty-six years is not the beginning of the reign of Asa, but the separation of the kingdom; so that Asa, like Rehoboam, is not to be regarded as an individual, but as the representative of the kingdom of Judah, in the thirty-sixth year of the line represented by Asa. According to the latter view, the thirty-sixth year coincides with the fifteenth of Asa, and the war against Israel must have begun in the same year in which the war with the Cushites came to an end. This latter becomes probable by assuming an original union of the two wars, which may be demonstrated. According to 2 Chron. xv. 9, many Israelites went over to the kingdom of Judah in consequence of the victory over the Cushites. But, according to 2 Chron. xvi. 1 and 1 Kings xv. 17, this very circumstance gave rise to the war with Israel. Baasha resented these emigrations. He feared that, unless he could succeed in putting a complete stop to all intercourse with the kingdom of Judah, his subjects would all eventually return to the king of Judah, who seemed to be specially favoured by God. He therefore determined to fortify the city of Ramah, which was two hours' journey from Jerusalem, situated on an elevation, and commanding the way to Judah, and thus to cut off the passage. If this work were successfully accomplished, it was probably his intention to invade the kingdom of Judah. With this object in view, he had concluded an alliance with Benhadad, king of the Damascene Syrian kingdom, which had arisen in Solomon's time, comp. 1 Kings xv. 19; and from 2 Chron. xvi. 7 we learn that Benhadad's troops were actually advancing. Asa thought he could only escape the danger by endeavouring to bring over the king of Syria to his side. With this object he sent him the treasure of the temple, which had been newly replaced by himself and his father. The plan succeeded. The king of Syria invaded Israel instead of Judah, and took several towns situated in the neighbourhood of the Sea of Gennesareth. Baasha was obliged to abandon the fortification of Ramah, and to hasten to the protection of the northern parts of his kingdom. But on this occasion Asa sinned from want of faith, and his sin was held up to him by the prophet Hanani, just as King Ahaz was afterwards reproved by Isaiah for seeking help from the king of Assyria against Israel and Syria. The king was not absolutely forbidden to make any alliance. Here, however, the question was not so much of an alliance as of subjection, which, though it might be temporarily advantageous, would be most prejudicial as a permanent thing. Asa would have seen this if he had not been blinded by fear; and this fear was the less excusable, because he had shortly before so definitely experienced God's power and will to help, in far greater danger, on the attack of the Cushites. If he had looked at the matter with an unprejudiced eye, he could not have regarded the Syrians as the instrument appointed by God for his salvation. Unless looked at in this way, all use of human means is sinful, because it proceeds from want of faith. Not to use those natural means which are permitted is to tempt God; to use those which are not permitted is to blaspheme Him, since it shows a want of confidence in His will and power to help.

That the king was really deeply moved by the censure of the prophet, he made evident by his conduct towards him. He threw him into prison. He is also accused of injustice towards others then in the nation, probably towards such as ventured to express disapproval of his conduct towards the prophet. Towards the close of his life the king was afflicted by a disease in his feet. The fact that he is reproved for having sought the help of physicians, and not of God, does not apply to the use of physicians in general, but to their use apart from God. These weaknesses of the otherwise pious Asa are only noticed in the books of Chronicles, and are not mentioned at all in the books of the Kings, which little accords with the partial predilection for the kingdom of Judah and its kings attributed to the Chronicles by rationalistic criticism. The king was interred in a grave which he himself had caused to be excavated, and a great number of fragrant things were burnt to do him honour. The view upheld by many—for example, by Michaelis in the note on 2 Chron. xvi. 14, and in the treatise *De combustione et humatione mortuorum ap. Hebr.*, in the first part of his *Syntagma Commentt.* p. 225 ff.—that the body of the king itself was burnt, is quite opposed to the sense of the passage in Chronicles which we have quoted, as Geier has amply proved, *De Luctu Hebræorum*, chap. 6. Asa lived to see that with the rise of the house of Omri matters assumed a more peaceful aspect between the kingdom of the ten tribes and the kingdom of Judah. On the whole, the long reign of Asa must be regarded as an actual advance towards a better state of things. But in his son Jehoshaphat the principles by which he had been guided assumed a purer and more definite form.

We now pass over from the kingdom of Judah to the kingdom of Israel. When Jeroboam died, in the second year of Asa, he was succeeded on the throne by his equally godless son Nadab. Under him the divine judgment, with which the house of Jeroboam had been threatened, passed speedily into fulfilment. In the third year of Asa, Nadab with a large army besieged the city Gibbethon, which is mentioned in Josh. xix. 44 as belonging to the inheritance of the tribe of Dan. The city was at that time in the power of the Philistines, and the object of Nadab's expedition was to take it from them again. During the siege, Baasha formed a conspiracy against him and slew him. Having thus gained the throne, he murdered the whole family of Jeroboam. Thus sin was punished by sin, which was again to be punished by other sin; for we are afterwards expressly told by the author of the books of the Kings that Baasha was not justified by the fact that what he did was in accordance with the divine decree. In the history of the kingdom of Israel we may learn how it fares with a kingdom which has no share in the favour of God, and how this is the heaviest scourge which can be laid upon a nation. The kingdom was founded by apostasy from the Davidic dynasty, which had been chosen by God, and this circumstance rested upon it as a continual curse. The right of kings belonged to Ephraim by human appointment, and consequently it could not violate the feelings of any when dissatisfaction with the royal race was followed by human deposition. Here there was no check to ambitious passion. Whoever found himself in possession of the same means as his predecessor, thought himself therefore justified in pursuing the same course of action. Thus dynasty succeeded dynasty, king after king was murdered. In the bloody battles thus occasioned, the nation became more and more unruly: sometimes there were interregna, and occasionally complete anarchy. By these internal wars external power was more and more broken. No regent could stop this source of evil; he would have had to give up his existence. Baasha showed himself just as godless as Jeroboam. For this reason the prophet Jehu was sent to him to announce the complete destruction of his house. The Lord upbraids him with his ingratitude; for though He had raised him from the dust and made him a prince, he had yet heaped sin upon sin. The thought is this: If God had treated him as he deserved, He would at once have allowed him to reap the reward of his revolt against his king, and of his selfish barbarity towards the king's family. But because He forbore to do this,—because He allowed him to assume the sovereignty,—he was under the greater obligation to be led by the leniency of God to repentance for that which was past, and not by continued sin to perpetuate the remembrance of the former, and to call down punishment for it on his house. In 1 Kings xvi. 7 we find the fact that he slew the house of Jeroboam, his son and the other members, represented as a concomitant cause of the sentence of destruction on the house of Baasha pronounced through Jehu. At the same time this throws light on the revolt of Jeroboam. It is clear that it was not in the least justified by the circumstance that the separation of the two kingdoms was decreed by God. It throws light also on the acts of the subsequent murder of the king. Existing authorities will always be sacred in the eyes of him who fears God. If their power have been won by evil means, and be applied to sinful purposes, he will quietly wait until God destroy them. To this end God employs the ungodly as His instruments, and then again destroys them by the ungodly. This is the prevailing view of Scripture. The Assyrians and Chaldeans, for example, appear in the prophets as the scourge of God, as His servants, His instruments, by which He punishes the sins of His people and of others. Nevertheless they in their turn are abandoned to destruction on account of that which they have done against the covenant-nation and against others. This view of Scripture opens up a grand insight into the disposition of divine providence and the exercise of the divine government of the world. Baasha's son Elah began to reign in the twenty-sixth year of Asa, but already in the second year he lost his throne in the very same way in which it had been won by his father. (The statement in 1 Kings xvi. 8, that he reigned for two years, is proximate.) The siege of Gibbethon was probably raised on account of the murder of Nadab. The new king Baasha was more importantly occupied in strengthening his government internally. His son renewed the siege, but while his army lay before the city, he was slain at a banquet by Zimri, one of his generals, who then slew all his family. Zimri, however, was not allowed to reign for so long a period as Jeroboam and Baasha. The army were not satisfied with his accession to the throne. They made Omri, their general, king, and at their head he marched towards the royal residence Tirzah. When Zimri saw that the besieged city could not hold out, he burnt himself with the royal palace—a second Sardanapalus. Zimri's death did not yet secure to Omri the peaceful possession of the throne. A part of the nation joined Tibni, the opposition king. For several years Tibni reigned as well as Omri, but with less power, for Omri had the army on his side. After the death of Tibni—it is uncertain whether this took place in a natural way or not—Omri finally attained to sole sovereignty in the thirty-first year of Asa, according to 1 Kings xvi. 23. The struggle with Tibni had lasted for four years, from the twenty-seventh to the thirty-first year of Asa. Altogether the reign of Omri lasted not quite twelve years, from the twenty-seventh year of Asa to the thirty-eighth. In the first six years he had his residence at Tirzah, like the former kings. Afterwards he founded the city of Samaria, and built a citadel there. Samaria, situated on a mountain which forms a prominence in a fruitful plain, remained the royal residence to the end of the kingdom, for two hundred years. But Bethel continued to be the religious capital of the kingdom, though not in the same sense as Jerusalem for Judah. The kingdom of Israel had a multitude of places for offering up sacrifice. Omri sought peace without, that he might be able to establish his house firmly within. He kept on friendly terms with the kingdom of Judah, and the other members of his house remained true to his policy in this respect. He had to buy peace with Damascene Syria by some sacrifices. He gave up a few towns to the Syrians, and allowed them the right of making streets in Samaria, 1 Kings xx. 34, *i.e.* to have a quarter of their own in it, where they might freely exercise their religion and have their own jurisdiction. But while it cannot be denied that Omri was wise in his policy, his religious influence was throughout destructive. He surpassed his predecessors in ungodliness, but was himself surpassed by his son Ahab, whose reign is very remarkable on account of the activity of Elijah, which belonged to this period. Formerly the worship of the Lord, though under images, had been the legal religion: idolatry proper was only practised by a few individuals, and that not in conscious opposition to the service of the Lord, but in syncretic blindness along with it (comp. what we have already said on this subject in the history of Solomon). Even the most depraved kings had not persecuted the prophets of the true God, however openly they had been opposed by them. Under Ahab the evil reached its highest pitch. The king himself was a servant of the Phenician gods, of Baal and Ashtaroth, personifications of the masculine and the feminine principles in nature, of its begetting and birth-giving power; comp. Münter, *The Religion of the Carthaginians*, pp. 6 and 62, and Movers, *Phenicians*, i. p. 188 ff., according to whom Baal was the begetting, sustaining, and destroying power in nature, and at the same time the god of the sun, while Ashtaroth was the goddess of the moon. The prophets, who could not keep silence respecting this abomination, suffered bloody persecution. The people for the most part united the worship of images with idolatry, if they did not quite give themselves up to the latter. But even at that time apostasy, which is at all times so loath to unveil itself completely, did not come forward in distinct opposition to the service of the Lord and to the Mosaic law. On the contrary, the servants of Baal, with Ahab at their head, maintained the identity of Baal and Jehovah; and the persecution was not directed against the servants of Jehovah in general, but only against those among them who bore powerful witness against the union of the irreconcilable, loudly maintaining that Jehovah identified with Baal was no longer Jehovah. The proposition, which Elijah from his standpoint expresses thus: whether Jehovah be God or Baal? was understood by the servants of Baal from their standpoint thus: whether Jehovah-Baal be God, or Jehovah in His exclusiveness? That this is the correct view is most clearly shown from 1 Kings xviii. 21: "How long halt ye between two opinions?" (properly, *super duabus opinionibus*)—how long do ye hesitate undecided between two opinions? "If the Lord be God, follow Him: but if Baal, then follow him." This plainly presupposes that in the view of the nation the heterogeneous religious elements had flowed together into one. This syncretism would indeed appear incomprehensible, if we did not recognise the influence which inclination exercises upon judgment, and call to mind the analogies offered by our own time, which is also zealously endeavouring to amalgamate the God of Scripture and the God of the spirit of the age, notwithstanding their infinite diversity,—even doing honour to the term "Mediation-Theology," so weak in itself. The worship of Baal and Astarte is the most horrible known to all antiquity: human sacrifices were everywhere common to it, comp. Münter, p. 17 ff.; the unchastity practised in the temples of Astarte in her honour is notorious to all antiquity, comp. Münter, p. 79 ff., Movers, *The Religion of the Phenicians*, p. 689 ff. The fearful moral effects of this religion generally are described by Münter in a special section, p. 150 ff. Syncretism was in many respects worse than open opposition. He who identified Jehovah and Baal had the former only in name. Moreover, the servants of Baal-Jehovah still continued to rely upon the promises of Jehovah and His covenant, and to presume upon their external service, and therefore upon their sin itself, and were consequently strengthened in their false security. The union of the king with Jezebel, a daughter of the Phenician king Ethbaal, gave occasion for this change for the worse. Her energetic wickedness won absolute influence over Ahab's effeminate weakness. Here we find a remarkable conformity between sacred and profane history. According to a fragment from the Syrian year-books in Josephus, viii. chap. 7, translated into Greek by Menander, Ithobalos was king of Tyre during the reign of Ahab. We find this by a comparison of the years there given with those in Scripture from Solomon to Ahab. The name Ithobalos signifies, with Baal, one connected with Baal. By this comparison, Ithobalos was born in the second year of the separation of the kingdom, and was therefore fifty-six years of age when Ahab came to the throne, and might therefore very well have been his father-in-law. Compare the copious calculation in Joh. Dav. Michaelis in the remarks on the books of the Kings. The fact that Ethbaal, or, with the Greek termination, Ithobalos, is spoken of in the books of the Kings as king of the Sidonians, while in Menander he appears as the king of Tyre, forms only an apparent difference. Sidon was the oldest, and had previously been the most powerful city of the Phenicians, to which the others were in a certain sense subordinate, and hence the name of the Sidonians was transferred to the Phenicians generally, and even clung to them long after Tyre had taken the place of Sidon; comp. Gesenius on Isa. xxiii. 4, 12. At that time Sidon, as well as the other cities of Phenicia, stood in a certain relation of dependence towards Tyre, so that Ethbaal was also king of the Sidonians in the narrower sense. This appears from another fragment of Menander to be noticed afterwards, in which it is related that Sidon and the other Phenician cities, tired of the Tyrian oppression, combined with Shalmaneser against them. It is remarkable also that by Menander's account, Ithobalos, formerly high priest, had made his way to the throne by regicide. In Jezebel we find the same union of zeal for idolatry with the spirit of murder, which we can suppose must have characterized the former high priest. Moreover, her fanaticism and her spirit of persecution exactly correspond with the character of the Phenician-Carthaginian religion, of which their union forms the characteristic feature, in distinction from most other religions of antiquity; comp. Münter, p. 157 ff., and with regard to the dependence of the Israelitish worship of Baal on the Phenicians, comp. Movers, *The Phenicians*, i. p. 178 ff. Ahab built a chief temple of Baal in Samaria, with a large pillar giving a representation of it, and several smaller pillars. We find no mention of a temple of Astarte. A sacred grove, עשרה, was dedicated to her. Four hundred and fifty prophets of Baal and 400 prophets of Astarte were placed in opposition to the prophets of the true God, as the spiritual representatives of the religion of this world; comp. 1 Kings xvi. 31 ff., xviii. 19; 2 Kings iii. 2, x. 25–27. There can be no doubt that those who had till then acted as calf-prophets now willingly appeared as prophets of this new form of worldly religion. Corruptibility is an essential characteristic of the false prophethood. It invariably lent itself to the ruling power, in order to gain advantage from it. This, therefore, was just the time for the appearance of a man with the ardour of Elijah, if the last traces of the supremacy of God were not to disappear from the kingdom of Israel. The great question of the existence or non-existence of the true religion in Israel was pending; a last attempt was made to save a sinking nation from the abyss. And if we powerfully realize this state of things,—if we consider how palpable it was necessary for the manifestations of the divine omnipotence to be, in order to make any impression on the deeply sunk nation and its depraved king, how mighty the consolations for the prophet himself, since all things visible were so entirely opposed to him,—we must acknowledge that everything extraordinary in his life appears quite natural. The wonderful can occasion the less surprise, since the prophet himself is the greatest wonder. A character such as this,—an iron will, a lightning glance, a voice of thunder, and at the same time showing mildness and friendliness where it was possible for him to display these qualities, as in relation to the widow of Sarepta, the kingdom of God his only thought, God's honour his only passion,—such a character defies all natural explanation, especially in such surroundings. An expression peculiar to Elijah is the calling upon Jehovah " before whom he stood," whom he served, whose word he was obliged to follow even if it brought him into conflict with the whole world, and cost him his life.

We must consider also that the position of the prophets in the kingdom of Israel was essentially different from their position in the kingdom of Judah, and was far more difficult. Their relation to the priests was completely hostile. Because the prophethood had no support and foundation in a hierarchy venerable for its antiquity, and hallowed by divine signs and wonders, it was necessary that it should be far more powerfully supported from above, and ·far more palpably legitimized. With respect to the origin, culture, and earlier fortunes of Elijah, history is silent. It first brings him before us charged with an important mission to Ahab, which presupposes that he had already held the prophetic office for a considerable time. From 1 Kings xvii. 1, where he is said to have been of the inhabitants of Gilead, some have concluded that Elijah was not a born Israelite, but rather a proselyte from heathendom, who had settled in the country beyond the Jordan, perhaps with his immediate ancestors. But this conclusion is too hasty. In the passage adduced, Elijah is called the Tishbite of the inhabitants of Gilead. He was from Tishbah in Gilead, where, however, he possessed no civil rights, but dwelt as one who had no home. His forefathers had emigrated thither from another part of the Israelitish territory. This assumption is less remote than that of his heathen origin, of which there is no indication whatever. That God will not be mocked with impunity, Ahab first learned in a way involving comparatively little personal suffering. We have already seen that Joshua laid a curse on the rebuilding of Jericho. There can be no doubt that this was universally known; and until this time no one had ventured to think of rebuilding the city, fearing lest he should bring down the curse upon himself. Ahab may have treated this fear as childish superstition. Undoubtedly it was at his command that Hiel undertook the work, which promised great advantage from the position of the place. The prophecy was literally fulfilled: all the sons of Hiel died before the work was concluded. But this made no impression on Ahab, who may have ascribed it to accident. It was necessary, therefore, that a judgment should come upon him which should touch him more sharply,—one which could not be attributed to accident, since it followed immediately upon the prediction of Elijah. Elijah appeared suddenly before the king. His address is only given in part. Doubtless he either now preceded the announcement of punishment by a severe exhortation to repentance, as the prophets were always accustomed to do, or else he had previously done so. The punishment was to consist in a great drought, followed by a famine. Formerly the divine judgments had touched the kings alone, now king and nation were to be punished alike. The threat is an individualizing of Deut. xi. 16, 17: "Take heed to yourselves, that your heart be not deceived, and ye turn aside, and serve other gods, and worship them; and then the Lord's wrath be kindled against you, and He shut up the heaven, that there be no rain, and that the land

yield not her fruit." The prophet does not say how long
the punishment is to last. This would have weakened the
influence of the threat. It it probable that the king paid
little regard to the discourse of the prophet, whom he looked
upon as a fanatic; hence he allowed him to depart without
injury. The question now was, how to deliver the prophet
from the power of Ahab. If that which was predicted should
come to pass, Ahab, in accordance with his idolatrous superstition, could only think that the prophet had brought about
the public calamity by a magic power exercised over his
God, such as his priests pretended to be able to exercise.
This was necessarily connected with the idea that by the
same magic power, by incantation and spells, he could also
cause it to cease, and Ahab would naturally make every
exertion to oblige him to do this. And in event of the
prophet refusing,—and he could not do otherwise even if he
wished, since he had only foretold the plague at the command
of God, and had not produced it, although it happened in
consequence of his prayer, according to Jas. v. 17, — his
life, so valuable for the kingdom of God, would be exposed
to the greatest danger. For this reason Elijah repaired to
the most inaccessible hiding-place which the land offered
him, to the brook Cherith, not otherwise known, supposed
by some to be identical with the נחל הקנה, the river Kanah,
Josh. xvi. 8, xvii. 9, comp. Reland, i. p. 293; according to
Robinson, part ii. p. 533, the present Wady Kelt, in the
neighbourhood of Jericho. Ewald and Thenius are wrong
in urging the objection that, according to 1 Kings xvii. 3,
the brook Cherith flowed on the east of the Jordan, rather
eastwards from Samaria towards the Jordan. Elijah probably dwelt in a rocky cave of the thickly-wooded mountain
through which the torrent flows. No man was to know his
abode, otherwise he could not have escaped the zealous search
instituted by the king, who even sent messengers into all the
neighbouring countries. His maintenance must therefore
be provided for by extraordinary measures. The way
in which this happened seems so incredible to many, that
they regard the most absurd hypotheses as preferable. These
have already in ancient times been excellently refuted by

Bochart, *Hieroz.* part ii. B. 2, chap. 14, and by Reland, *l.c.* ii. p. 913 ff. Taking into consideration the whole position of Elijah at the time, there is more probability in favour of an extraordinary course of things than of an ordinary: there can be no question of a miracle here. The natural side of the matter appears to be this, that the ravens, allured by the water of the brook Cherith, there consumed the booty that they had gained in inhabited lands. After the lapse of a year, with the increasing drought the brook Cherith dried up. Elijah now received a command from the Lord to repair to Zarephath in the land of the Sidonians; for the אשר לצידן, 1 Kings xvii. 9, must be explained thus, and not "which belongeth to Sidon." There He had commanded a widow to provide for him. It required strong faith to follow this command. Already the king had sought him in every land, and now he was to repair to the very place of the godless father of the godless Jezebel. Elijah rose up without hesitation. Zarephath is Sarepta, a town on the Mediterranean between Tyre and Sidon, now Zarphan or Zarphend. The drought and the famine had extended even to those districts, as appears not only from this history itself, but also from a fragment from the Phenician year-books which we shall quote later on. Elijah finds the widow immediately before the gate of the city. By a divine revelation he becomes aware that he is not mistaken in the person. His address to her is intended to give her an opportunity of revealing her faith in the God of Israel, and thus justifying the divine choice. She was indeed a heathen by birth, which is confirmed by Luke iv. 25, 26; but the knowledge of the true God had come to her from the neighbouring Israel, which now itself renounced this knowledge in so disgraceful a way, and she had received it with joy. Her oath by the God of Israel shows this; and still more the fact that, believing the promise of God given to her through Elijah that He would sustain her, she prepared for the prophet the little food that she still had in store. She must already have had something in her mind, otherwise she would not have been so impressed by the divinity of the prophet as to renounce that which was certain for what to human understanding was uncertain. Elijah now took up his abode with the woman. He had no cause to fear betrayal, even if he had fully revealed himself to her, which is doubtful; for the widow reverenced him as a benefactor sent to her by God. He occupied the most retired part of the house, the upper chamber. It is certain that Elijah must have done everything to further the widow in her knowledge of salvation, and soon he found an opportunity of affording her faith an extraordinary confirmation. The son of the widow died. At the prayer of the prophet the boy was restored to his mother. This whole event bears a symbolical character, which is made specially manifest by its New Testament antitype. Christ, persecuted by the Jews, goes into the country of Tyre and Sidon, and there rewards the faith of the Canaanitish woman, in order to prefigure the future transference of the kingdom of God to the Gentiles.

When, in accordance with the divine decree, the drought was to come to an end, Elijah received the command to repair to Ahab. According to 1 Kings xviii. 1, this happened after the lapse of a long time, in the third year. Here the *terminus a quo* is the sojourn of Elijah at Sarepta; and if we also reckon the year which he spent at the brook Cherith, according to chap. xvii. 7, or even a longer or a shorter space of time, since the expression made use of in this passage is not quite definite, we get a period of three to four years for the whole duration of the drought, quite in harmony with the account in Luke iv. 25, Jas. v. 17, that at the time of Ahab it rained not on the earth for the space of three years and six months. A notice of the event has been preserved even in heathen history. In Josephus, viii. 13. 2, Menander says: "Under him (Ithobalos) there was no rain from October in one year to October in the following year; but at his prayer there was frequent lightning." The only essential difference here is, that the time of the famine lasted only for a year. But it is not therefore necessary to assume a mistake in the Tyrian accounts, for it is possible that there may still have been occasional rain in Phenicia when complete drought had already overtaken Israel, since Phenicia lay nearer to the Mediterranean Sea, from which Palestine gets nearly all its rain; comp. 1 Kings xviii. 43. The other variation—the statement that the rain came at the entreaty of the former idolatrous priest Ithobalos—may readily be recognised as a distortion due to jealousy. We have abundant proof of the fabrications and patriotic fancies of the Tyrians, even in the few fragments which have come down to us from them. For example, it is somewhat analogous when they represent Solomon as having engaged in a contest respecting the solution of riddles with Hiram, by whom, with the help of another wise Tyrian, he was conquered, and to whom he was obliged to pay an immense sum. Just as they there invested their own king with the honour belonging to Solomon, so here they give him the honour which was due to Elijah. It is remarkable, however, that even in this account the drought appears as an extraordinary event, and the rain as a consequence of the hearing of prayer.

On his way to the king, Elijah meets Obadiah, a pious officer, who was travelling through a part of the country, by the king's order, for the purpose of inquiring whether food were not to be had somewhere, while the king had taken the opposite direction with the same object in view. In the bloody persecutions of Jezebel, this man had concealed and supported 100 prophets, principally disciples and servants of the prophets, but by no means only such, who received important revelations respecting the future—a thing which happened to comparatively few. These 100 prophets again call our attention to the difference between the Judaic and Israelitish prophethood. In Judah, where the activity of the prophets was merely supplementary, we never find the prophethood in such masses. In consequence of this, the false prophethood also appears far more powerful in the kingdom of Israel than in the kingdom of Judah. The vehement character of the defence of the religion of Jehovah called forth also a vehement character of opposition towards it. The hundreds of prophets of the true God are opposed by hundreds of prophets of calves, comp. 1 Kings xxii., and at the time when the spirit of the world completely stripped off its veil, and openly professed the religion of the world, by hundreds of prophets of Baal and Astarte, who cannot be confounded with the priests of these deities, but whose existence rather presupposes that of the true prophethood. In Judah we find everywhere priests of Baal alone. Obadiah had already incurred the hatred of the queen and the suspicion of the king by his protection of the prophets. Hence, when Elijah commissions him to inform Ahab of his presence, he first begs to be spared this errand, lest the Spirit of the Lord should again suddenly carry him away, in which case the whole wrath of Ahab, on account of his deceived hopes, would be directed against *him*, and he would naturally be suspected of having a secret understanding with Elijah, with the intention of making sport of the king. It seems that there had already been similar cases of a sudden disappearance in the history of Elijah, otherwise it would be impossible to understand this fear on the part of Obadiah; comp. 2 Kings ii. 16. Elijah sets him at rest by an assurance confirmed with an oath, and he executes the commission. On receiving news of the reappearance of Elijah, Ahab immediately hastens to meet him. At first he tries to impress him by a severe address, but soon perceives that nothing is to be gained in this way; for Elijah with reckless candour casts back on him the reproach of having been the originator of the misfortune that had come upon Israel,—an accusation which Ahab had made against Elijah on the presupposition that he had caused the drought by the magic exercise of his power over God. Elijah offers to prove the truth of his assertion that Ahab's idolatry was the cause of the whole misfortune, in a visible way, and for this purpose desires that the king shall collect the (450) prophets of Baal and the (400) prophets of Astarte on Mount Carmel. The latter were fed from the table of Jezebel, the daughter of the high priest of Astarte. Although the king accepted the proposition of Elijah, and commanded all the prophets to assemble on Mount Carmel, it appears that the latter, guessing what was impending, were able to evade the royal decree by the assistance of the queen. At all events the prophets of Baal only are mentioned in what follows.

Mount Carmel is a large and wide plateau, with fresh springs, hanging over the sea in the form of a promontory, covered with fragrant herbs on the summit, and offering an extensive sea-view. Where its base touches the sea, the brook Kishon falls into the famous Bay of Acre or Ptolemy, which flows from Mount Tabor through the mineral district of Esdraelon. The situation of the place, which made it even in later times one of the principal seats of the heathen worship of nature (comp. Movers, p. 670), was calculated to strengthen the impression of the act which Elijah was determined to undertake. On the appointed day, a great multitude of people, together with the priests of Baal, assembled on Mount Carmel. To the people Elijah first directed his address; for his object was to work upon them rather than upon the weak king, on whom he could scarcely expect to make any lasting impression, on account of the influence which the ungodly Jezebel had over him. The prophet addresses the people in these words: "How long halt ye between two opinions? If the Lord be God, follow Him: but if Baal, then follow him." In this way he upbraids the people for their foolishness in striving to reconcile the irreconcilable. The religion of Jehovah was exclusive in its character; it must therefore either be entirely rejected, or the true God must be worshipped solely and exclusively. The people felt the force of the alternative: of Jehovah-Baal there was nothing to be said,—either Jehovah or Baal. But they did not know for whom to decide. It was time, therefore, that the great question, which was constantly reappearing in other forms, should be decided in a palpable way, —whether the Lord was God, or Baal, the god whom the world had invented in the interest of its own inclinations. We invariably find such a decision wherever, under the old covenant, the true God came into conflict with idols. It was the case in Egypt; in the time of the Assyrian invasion; in Babylonia, when the true God seemed to have lost His cause against the idols, by the destruction of His people. Under the Old Testament, in accordance with its whole character, it happened in a more visible and palpable way. Even under the New Testament it constantly recurs, but in a more refined and spiritual form. There we read: He wieldeth His power in secret. The priests of Baal could not do otherwise than accept the proposal of Elijah, with whom we take it for granted they were acquainted. The people had received it with enthusiasm: its fairness was the more evident, since Elijah as an individual was opposed to so great a mass. A refusal would have had the same consequences as inability to fulfil the stipulated condition. They doubtless supposed that Elijah would be just as little able to do what was prescribed as they, and thus the matter would remain undecided. No doubt also there were many among them who, being deceived and fanatics, expected that Baal would do what was demanded. When midday was already past, and it was not apparent that they had been heard, according to chap. xviii. 26 they leaped upon the altar. This is an ironical description of the dances customary in the worship of Baal, which were of an enthusiastic kind, as the whole delineation shows (especially ver. 29). Then, being mocked by Elijah with holy irony, they cut themselves with knives and lancets, as was customary in all enthusiastic worships, by the testimony of the ancients. In this way the orgiastic feasts of Cybele and of the Syrian goddess were celebrated, when, amid the beating of drums and the playing of flutes, and the moving in wild dances, they scourged each other till the blood came, and even, in the excess of their madness, laid violent hands on themselves before the eyes of the people, and unmanned themselves; comp. Creuzer, ii. p. 61 ff., and especially Movers, p. 681 ff. In the description of the whirling bands of Cenadi, principally after Apuleius, we there read: "A discordant howling opened the scene. Then they flew wildly about, the head sunk down towards the earth, so that the loosened hair dragged through the dirt. They begin by biting their arms, and finally cut themselves with the two-edged swords that they are accustomed to wear. Then follows a new scene. One of them, surpassing all the rest in madness, begins to prophesy, amid sighs and groans; he publicly accuses himself of the sins that he has committed, and will now punish them by chastisement of the flesh: he takes the knotty scourge, beats his back cruelly, and cuts himself with swords till the blood drops down from the mutilated body." At last, when all was in vain, Elijah began his preparations, at the time when it was customary to offer the evening sacrifice in the temple at Jerusalem. There had been an altar to the true God on Mount Carmel, and here pious Israelites had been in the habit of sacrificing, after the institution of calf-worship. In erecting this or other altars, they had not sinned. If their minds were only directed towards the sanctuary in Jerusalem, the sin of violating the Mosaic law respecting the unity of the sanctuary belonged not to them, but only to the rulers of the people who had placed them in this difficulty. But Ahab had destroyed this altar, together with all those which were exclusively dedicated to Jehovah. Elijah in his haste repaired it. Chap. xviii. 34 is remarkable: "And he took twelve stones, according to the number of the tribes of the sons of Jacob, unto whom the word of the Lord came, saying, Israel shall be thy name." This was a virtual declaration on the part of Elijah that he did not acknowledge the rightfulness of the actually existing religious separation of the two kingdoms, but looked upon it as a result of sin, and regarded all the tribes together as still forming one covenant-nation. On this occasion the author points out the injustice of the ten tribes in appropriating to themselves alone the name of Israel, since this name, having been given by God to the ancestor of all the tribes, belonged equally to all. The form of decision chosen by Elijah has reference to Lev. ix., where Aaron after his consecration offers up sacrifice, first for himself, then for the people. The glory of the Lord appears, ver. 24: "And there came a fire out from before the Lord, and consumed upon the altar the burnt-offering and the fat: which when all the people saw, they shouted, and fell on their faces." The circumstances were now the same, only still more urgent. There the first solemn sanction of the worship of Jehovah; here the renewal of it, in opposition to the worship of Baal. In what God had done on the former occasion, therefore, Elijah justly saw a promise of what He would now do. In dressing the sacrifice, Elijah closely followed the injunctions which had been given in Leviticus with respect to the offering up of bulls. His object in surrounding the whole altar with water was to avoid all suspicion of deception. The idolatrous priests had attained to great excellence in these arts. They were able to kindle the wood by fire which they concealed in the hollows of the altars. Although the number of attentive observers was too great to allow such a deception to be practised in this case, yet they would probably have been shameless enough to accuse Elijah of it, if it had not been absolutely impossible for them to attribute a fire which consumed such a quantity of water to natural causes.

The prayer of Elijah, "Hear me, O Lord, hear me; that this people may know that Thou art the Lord God, and that Thou hast turned their heart back again," shows the point of view from which we must regard not only the miracle that immediately follows, but also everything miraculous in the life of Elijah and Elisha. The avowal of this aim excludes all opposition against the truth of the events narrated, except that which proceeds from the standpoint of a complete denial of revelation. The miracle, the consumption of the sacrifice by a flash of lightning from a clear atmosphere, attained its object. The people fell down worshipping, with the confession, "The Lord, He is the God; the Lord, He is the God." The priests of Baal were then seized by the people, at the command of Elijah, taken down to the brook Kishon, and there slain. This proceeding must be judged by Deut. xiii. 15, 16, xvii. 5, where it is made a sacred duty on the part of the people to punish the seducers with death. We have already shown that these injunctions bear a special Old Testament character. With regard to the priests of Baal, there were indeed special aggravating circumstances which might have called upon the civil government to carry out the punishment of death even under the New Testament, as, for example, the heads of the Anabaptists in Münster were justly punished with death. The priests of Baal had not been content with a religious freedom already quite irreconcilable with the Old Testament economy: at their instigation Jezebel had slain the servants of the true God; by her instrumentality the blood of the prophets had been poured out in streams. It was their intention to exterminate them even to the last man; comp. 1 Kings xviii. 4, 13, 22, xix. 10, 14; 2 Kings ix. 7. It has been asked whether Elijah did not on this occasion overstep the limits of his office, and encroach on the office of the government, to whom alone the sword has been entrusted by God. But this doubt is removed, by the remark that the prophet had received an extraordinary divine commission for the fulfilment of that which the disloyal king had not fulfilled, but countenanced by his silence. The fear that a similar special commission might be assumed by every fanatic has no foundation whatever. Such a one must first of all legitimize himself by an unquestionable divine wonder.

The more boldly Elijah had opposed the king when the honour of God was at stake, the more humbly he behaved towards him when this had been vindicated. The whole occurrence had lasted from morning till evening. In eager expectation of the event, neither king nor people had eaten anything. Elijah invites the king to go up the mountain again, and there in all confidence to eat and drink; for since the cause of the curse was destroyed, this too would soon have an end. Already in the prophetic spirit he heard great clouds of rain disburden themselves. While the king contentedly follows his proposal, the prophet goes to a very different occupation. In an attitude of humble supplication he casts himself down on Carmel before the Lord, entreating Him to fulfil His promise and to accomplish His work. And when he sees the faintest beginning of fulfilment, when a small cloud arises from the Mediterranean Sea, he sends to the king and tells him to make preparation for his departure, lest he should be overtaken by the rain,—a mark of attention which, together with what follows, ought to have taught Ahab to love the servant of the Lord, whom he had previously only learned to fear. Elijah was so strengthened by the power of love, that, notwithstanding the immense exertions he had already undergone, he was able to keep pace with the horses of the king, and accompanied him to his residence. Just as he had assumed superiority over the king as the servant of God, so by this action he testified his deep submission as his subject, and thus sought to strengthen the impression made on the heart of the king, and to arm him against the powerful temptations of his wife, who made his weakness subservient to ungodliness. Such self-abasement presupposed the most profound humility; so distinct a separation between the personal unworthiness of the king and the dignity bestowed on him by God called for a wisdom such as the Spirit of God alone could impart.

Just as the previous history shows us the prophet in his divine power, so the following reveals him in his human weakness. God subjected him to a severe temptation, lest he should be lifted up on account of the great divine revelations and powers which had been given to him, and at the same time to guard against any carnal admixture in the pure divine zeal; but He also comforted him when he was on the point of giving way, and raised him up after he had made him deeply conscious of his own weakness. What we here see in the leadings of Elijah constantly recurs in the way which God takes with all His distinguished servants and instruments: we find it, for example, in the life-history of a Paul and a Luther. The whole narrative has the deepest internal character of truth. The higher the divine power, the more necessary and therefore the deeper are always the humiliations on account of the depravity of human nature. The king tells Jezebel of all that has happened. As soon as he returned to her vicinity, he was unable to divest himself of her accustomed yoke. The queen fell into an impotent rage. On account of the people, and probably also from fear of the king, she dared not venture at once to sacrifice Elijah to her revenge. We learn that the event had made a powerful impression, from the fact that from this time without intermission the prophets again exercise free activity in the kingdom of Israel, and that Ahab does not venture to punish the prophet Micah, by whom he believes himself deeply offended, except by imprisonment; and again from the circumstance that from this time idolatry totally disappears from the kingdom of Israel, while the worship of calves, with which the Israelitish prophets Hosea and Amos have so much to do, again steps distinctly into the foreground. But the rage of the queen is so great that she cannot refrain from at least giving expression to the threat which she is still too weak to carry out: she sends word to Elijah that he must die on the morrow. The determination of so near a time is probably due to her passion. But nevertheless Elijah has reason to fear the worst, since the queen, even if she dared not act openly, had still so many secret means at her command. Hence he was warned by the passionate imprudence of the queen, and fled אל נפשו, 1 Kings xix. 3, *ad salvandam animam suam.* He repaired first of all to Beer-sheba, at the extreme south of the kingdom of Judah. There he left his servant behind him, and set out on his journey into the Arabian desert. It is not quite certain what his object was,—whether he only resorted to the barren wilderness because he felt himself not secure even in the kingdom of Judah, owing to the friendly relations then existing between it and the kingdom of Israel; or whether it was his intention from the beginning to undertake a pilgrimage to Mount Sinai, in order to strengthen himself there by the lively remembrance of the great events of former time. The latter is the more probable hypothesis from what follows. But the divine object is more certain than the human object of Elijah. To him we may apply Matt. iv. 1: ἀνήχθη εἰς τὴν ἔρημον ὑπὸ τοῦ Πνεύματος, πειρασθῆναι ὑπὸ τοῦ διαβόλου. Where Israel had been tempted, he also was to be tempted. After Elijah had ended the first day of his journey in the wilderness, the temptation reached its greatest height. He was already old; the immense exertions of the previous days had made great demands on his strength; his mind was filled with deep sorrow, since even the greatest manifestations of divine omnipotence appeared to have been so utterly fruitless. Everything seemed dark, even that which the Lord had actually done by his means; and the small remnant of true piety which still existed in the kingdom of Israel escaped his glance. He began secretly to murmur against God, because He did not, by the judgments of His omnipotence, destroy that which could not be improved. The waste desert offered nothing for the refreshment of his bodily weakness. He threw himself down under a broom-tree (not under a juniper), and besought God to let him die. "The broom," says Robinson, chap. i. 336, "is the largest and most noticeable shrub in the wilderness, frequently found in the beds of rivers and in valleys, where travellers seek places of encampment where they may sit and sleep, protected against the wind and the sun." But soon the Lord began to glorify Himself in the weakness of Elijah. Already he received preliminary consolation, but the definitive was given on Sinai. Exhausted by excess of grief, he fell into a deep sleep. On awaking, he found miraculous strengthening food. And the angel of the Lord said unto him, "Arise and eat; because the journey is too great for thee." "And he arose, and did eat and drink, and went in the strength of that meat forty days and forty nights unto Horeb the mount of God." Many think that during this time Elijah ate what nourishment the wilderness afforded; and this opinion is not irreconcilable with the letter, which only says that this meat, which corresponds to the manna, strengthened him miraculously, so that he was able to bear the long journey. Mount Sinai was about forty German miles distant from Beer-sheba; according to Deut. i. 2, there are only eleven days' journey from Sinai to Kadesh-barnea. If, therefore, the divine object had only been that he should reach this place, he would not have required a period of forty days. But it was appointed by divine decree that he should spend exactly forty days in this journey, to make it manifest to himself and to all others that the prophecy contained in the forty years' guidance of Israel through the wilderness, of a similar guidance for all the servants of the Lord, was realized in him. The external agreement pointed to the internal. The germ, the temptation, is common to both. Arrived on Sinai, Elijah repairs to the cave in which Moses had once taken refuge when the Lord was about to reveal His glory to him; comp. Ex. xxxiii. 22. The promise which that appearance contained for him, and which he held up to God by the fact of choosing the place where it was given, was fulfilled in him. The word of the Lord came to him and said unto him, "What doest thou here, Elijah?" The object of this address was to lead Elijah to give expression to that state of mind on which the subsequent leadings of God were intended to operate. The answer of Elijah shows that he was not completely at rest, that he was not yet filled again with faith. It challenges God to punish the rejected, secretly reproaching Him for His long delay; it bears testimony to the most dismal view of things, for Elijah believes that he is the only remaining servant of God. All that happens has reference to this state of feeling. The object is to remove it, to free the servant of God from his weakness, and, after he has been sufficiently humiliated, to raise him up again. This is done first of all by a symbolical appearance, the interpretation of which is to be found in the words uttered, as in all similar cases,—a truth which is overlooked in the prevailing and evidently false exposition continually to be met with in sermons. Storm, earthquake, fire, in which the Lord with His grace is not manifest, are an image of the trials sent to all the people of the Lord and to His individual servants; the quiet stillness which follows them is an image of the καιροὶ ἀναψύξεως ἀπὸ προσώπου τοῦ Κυρίου, Acts iii. 19, bringing purification and sifting. By the verbal revelation of God which follows, this general comfort is individualized, and the despair of the prophet met by a definite allusion to the previous leadings of God; the persons also are named who are to bring about the results in which God is to reveal Himself as King of Israel. The first place among these is occupied by Elisha, who is pointed out to the prophet, who feared lest the kingdom of Israel should die with him, as his servant and successor, and whom he consequently called immediately on his return from the wilderness. Elijah is commanded to repair to the wilderness of Damascus, in the neighbourhood of the kingdom of Israel, until a convenient time; here he was safe from the revenge of Jezebel, and was at the same time near the scene of his activity. Then he is to appoint Hazael king over Syria, Jehu king over Israel, and Elisha (descended from Abel-meholah on Mount Gilboa, between Sichem and Bethsean in the half-tribe of Manasseh) as his successor, *i.e.* to announce to them in God's name that they are appointed to this dignity. He that escaped the sword of Hazael was to be slain by Jehu, and he who escaped the sword of Jehu was to be slain by Elisha. These men are to be the instruments by which God will accomplish His judgments on the obdurate: Jehu and Hazael by the sword, the former exterminating the family of Ahab, and the latter grievously oppressing Israel; Elisha by his word, which, being given by the Lord, must inevitably be fulfilled, and bring down the judgments of God on the sinners. Of these three commissions Elijah himself executed only one, the naming of Elisha as his successor. The other two were reserved for Elisha, upon whom his spirit rested, and whose prophetic activity can only be regarded as a continuation of that of Elijah. The Lord goes on to add, that in the impending judgments He will spare the seven thousand who have remained faithful to Him. This was at the same time humiliating and consolatory for Elijah: humiliating, in so far as it revealed to him his want of faith; for, looking only at the visible, he had failed to perceive the hidden workings of the Spirit of God: consolatory, because it showed him that his former activity had not been in vain, and also that his future activity would not be in vain, since the Lord would not yet repudiate His people; and at the same time, also, because it afforded him a proof of the particular providence of God, who knows His own by number and by name.

Elijah now set out from Sinai, and journeyed to the place where Elisha, a rich farmer, probably already known to him, resided. He met him on the field ploughing with one of his team of oxen, while the remaining eleven were led by his servants before him; or, according to another interpretation, when he had just ploughed his twelve acres of land, and was working on the twelfth and last. But the former interpretation is to be preferred. This circumstance is made prominent, because the lower calling was a type and prefiguration of the higher. The twelve yoke of oxen represent the twelve tribes. Elisha is not to be prophet for the ten tribes alone, but for all Israel. His activity in a part is to pass over to the whole. For five and fifty years he was to work on this stony spiritual field. Elijah threw his mantle upon him, the distinctive dress of the prophet, and Elisha at once understood the significance of this symbolical act. Resolved to follow him, he only asks permission to say farewell to his parents. Elijah answers, "Go back again: for what have I done to thee?" equivalent to, Remember that the call comes not from me, but from the Lord, and that thou incurrest grave responsibility in delaying to follow Him. There is a reference to this event in the words of our Lord: "No man, having put his hand to the plough, and looking back, is fit for the kingdom of God." Elisha therefore followed him, when he had first sacrificed the yoke of oxen with which he himself had been ploughing, and had made his neighbours a feast of the animals that remained, cooking them with the woodwork of the plough and the yoke. This was intended to signify that he renounced his former calling for ever.

The narrative of the war of Israel with Ben-hadad, king of Damascene Syria, shows that the former miraculous manifestation had not been quite without fruit. We find the prophets of the true God again in full public activity at Samaria. The king obeys their commands, and does not venture to do them any injury, although they proclaim the divine word in all severity, and announce his impending overthrow. It shows us how the Lord can vindicate His honour against all those who despise His name; how He gives the victory to the nation that is called after His name, lest the heathen, inferring His weakness from that of His people, should triumph over Him; and, at the same time, how He does not leave unpunished the transgressions of those who ought to be His servants. The name of the hostile king, the son of Hadad, the idol of Damascus, is less a proper name than a royal title; this explains its frequent occurrence. Ben-hadad had entered the kingdom of Israel with all his forces, and had advanced unchecked to Samaria, to which he laid siege. The boundaries of the Damascene kingdom had been greatly extended by him. He had succeeded in conquering all the surrounding smaller states; and their thirty-two kings, who were now his dependents, accompanied him with their people. By the bad reign of Ahab the power of the kingdom of Israel had been very much deteriorated. Ahab therefore thought he could only find safety in submission. Ben-hadad sent messengers to him with the words, "Thy silver and thy gold is mine; thy wives also and thy children, even thy goodliest, are mine." Ahab understood this as if he demanded nothing more from him than from the other kings who were subject to him, viz. the recognition of his supremacy, so that in future he would hold in fee from Ben-hadad what he had formerly possessed independently. Ben-hadad had certainly so worded the message as to allow this interpretation, intending afterwards to keep the king to his word. Ahab was deceived, and consented; and now Ben-hadad came forward with his real meaning. He demanded the actual surrender of Ahab, with his possessions and those of his subjects, with wife and child, that he might carry them away, as the Assyrians and Babylonians afterwards did. Ahab was the more embarrassed owing to his former imprudent concession; for if he now took it back, he would appear in a certain sense faithless to his word, and Ahab would thus acquire a sort of advantage over him. In this perplexity he turned to the elders or states of the people, who had fled from the whole country into the besieged capital. At their advice, he told Ben-hadad that he would fulfil the proposed conditions only according to *his* interpretation, and not in the sense given to them in the second message. Ben-hadad was greatly enraged by what he considered the impotent defiance of Ahab, and sent him word that, since he would not have peace under these conditions, he, with his immense army, would leave not a grain of dust in Samaria. Ahab answered, "Let not him that girdeth on his harness boast himself as he that putteth it off;" equivalent to, "It is impossible to sell the skin of a lion before it is caught." The king, who was feasting with his subordinates when he received this answer, at once gave command to prepare for an assault. Now when extremity had reached its greatest height, the help of the Lord, if vouchsafed, must necessarily have a powerful effect on the people, if not on Ahab. A prophet of the Lord appeared before Ahab, and in His name foretold victory over the immense army of the Syrians, adding as a reason, "And thou shalt know that I am the Lord." The king is commanded not to await the assault of the enemy, but to make a sally. The servants of the princes of the provinces were to go first. The heads of the city had fled to Samaria. These were accustomed to choose out for their servants, as a kind of body-guard, the largest, strongest, and bravest men. Ahab himself was to command the troops. Necessity had called forth a glimmering of faith; for if he had regarded the matter with merely human understanding, without any confidence in the Lord, he would not have ventured to expose himself to danger at the head of so small an army. The divine promise passed into fulfilment. The Syrians were totally defeated. The human causes which, under the guidance of God, helped towards the accomplishment of this end were, the confidence of Ben-hadad, which despised all precaution; his drunkenness, and that of his leaders; and, above all, as we see from what follows, the cowardice of the tributary kings, each of whom was anxious to spare his own people, and therefore fled whenever the small band of the Israelites turned in his direction. In the following year, however, the Syrians, to do away with this disgrace, undertook another expedition against Israel. The Syrians themselves did not presume to doubt that their defeat was due to the efficacy of the God of Israel. But, in accordance with their heathen ideas of divine things, they inferred nothing more from this than that the God of Israel had supremacy over their idols in mountainous districts, for this was the character of the whole country in which He was worshipped, and Samaria, its capital, was situated on a mountain; but the plains, they thought, were the proper territory of their deities, since Damascus lay on a plain. Expositors have collected a number of passages from heathen authors in which similar ideas are to be found. They resolved, therefore, only to engage in battle on the plain. Thus foundation was once more given for a divine determination. Moreover, on account of the reasons already given, the army was not commanded by the subordinate kings as before, but by royal generals. "The children of Israel," we read, "pitched before them like two little flocks of kids." Probably the Israelites had taken up their position on two adjoining heights; hence they are compared with two small flocks of kids pasturing on the slopes of the mountains. Ahab was encouraged by the announcement of the prophet that the Lord would give him the victory, as a proof that He was the true, absolute, omnipotent God. The Syrians indeed suffered a great defeat. The remnant fled to Aphek, now Fik, between Tiberias and Damascus. Probably one part of them took up their position, while another, covered by their guns, took refuge under the walls of this city. But suddenly the wall fell down — not by an actual miracle; Thenius suspects that it was undermined — and buried a number of the Syrians. Those who escaped with their life were scattered. But the Syrians were not all slain, as many have supposed; we see this clearly from 1 Kings xx. 30. In mortal terror, Ben-hadad fled from one hiding-place in the city to another. In all humility his servants repaired to Ahab to beg for his life. Ahab was moved by impure motives to grant their request at once. It flattered his vanity to be so imploringly besought by his former arrogant opponent, and to be able to show magnanimity; in recognising the inviolability of the person of another king, he believed he was doing honour to his own royal dignity. All reasons to the contrary prevailed nothing against this determination. He did not stop to consider that clemency towards the faithless and cruel enemy of his nation was the greatest severity; and what is still more, he paid no regard to the command of God which he had received through the same prophet who had promised him the victory, as we learn from what follows. Peace was concluded, on condition that the king of Syria would deliver up the cities which had been taken from the kingdom of Israel by his father, and allow the citizens of the kingdom of Israel a quarter of their own in his capital Damascus, in which they might live under their own laws,—a privilege which the Syrians had formerly enjoyed in Samaria. A prophet received the commission to punish the king on account of his disobedience and his ingratitude. Following the example of Nathan in 2 Sam. xii., he tries to draw from the king a confession of his own guilt, and allows him to pronounce judgment on himself. He got another prophet to wound him, and came before the king disguised with blood and ashes. He told the king a feigned story. In battle against the Syrians a warrior had given a prisoner into his charge, under a threat of severe punishment if he should escape by his fault. This had happened, and the warrior had wounded him. The king declares that he deserved the fate which had befallen him, which was just what the prophet wished. He now made himself known to him, and announced that, because he had spared the king, destruction would overtake him and his people.

Then follows the narrative of Ahab's robbery of the vineyard, in which his character betrays itself most openly. It is a remarkable proof of the shallowness of the Pelagian judgment, that in rationalistic times every possible attempt was made to excuse this king. Michaelis, for example, maintains that he was a very good man, but, as is generally the case with those whose heart is too good, made a bad king. Thenius, too, argues in the same way. As if weakness, such as we find in a remarkable degree in Ahab, were not just as much the result of guilty unbelief as carnal and positive vice; as if the form in which the depravity found expression were not due to mere difference of temperament, and other causes without the sphere of responsibility. The king was in his summer residence at Jezreel. He wished to enlarge his garden by the addition of the adjoining vineyard of Naboth, and believed that Naboth would accede to his proposal the more readily, since he himself, as we learn in the course of the narrative, had his actual residence not at Jezreel, but in another city, chap. xxi. 8,—probably in Samaria, for Elijah prophesies to Ahab that in the same place where dogs had licked the blood of Naboth they would lick his blood also. But the latter happened in Samaria. Naboth refused to give up his field to the king,—not from stubbornness, as many have supposed, but from a religious motive. The Israelites were forbidden in the law to sell their inheritance, in order to keep alive the remembrance that they held their land as a loan from God; comp. Lev. xxv. 23, Num. xxxvi. 8. Only in case of the most extreme poverty was it allowed, and even then only until the year of jubilee. The whole history becomes intelligible solely by means of this key. Naboth might have made a very advantageous bargain; but he thought it would be a religious crime to consent to it. This presupposes that the Mosaic law had very deep roots in Israel. Ahab, accustomed to have all his wishes gratified, was greatly enraged by the answer of Naboth. It was not so much his kindly disposition as his weakness which would not allow him to employ force. When the ungodly Jezebel offered to undertake the responsibility, he gave her his seal, with absolute power to use every means; and from his knowledge of her character he could have no difficulty in conjecturing of what nature these means would be. His only reason for not taking anything more to do with the matter was, that he might be able to satisfy his conscience, which was at any rate not quite so hardened as hers, with the empty excuse that he had not expected her to act in this way. Jezebel sought to attain her object by the most indirect means. The letter of the law, which Naboth had in his favour, stands in opposition to her despotic mind like a wall of brass, which cannot be broken through, but must be circumvented. Her whole conduct is regulated by the purpose of gaining her end within the limits of the Mosaic law, even by means of the law. Under the authority of the king, she wrote to the chief men in Samaria. She accused Naboth of the crime of high treason, which was at the same time a crime against God, because the king was honoured as bearing the image of God. The accusation is based specially on Ex. xxii. 28: "Thou shalt not revile the gods, nor curse the ruler of thy people;" equivalent to, "Thou shalt not curse thy prince;" for every crime against a visible representative of God in His kingdom is a crime against God. When it serves her detestable ends, the ungodly Jezebel speaks good theocratic language. She carries her hypocrisy so far as to command the appointment of a fast-day, as was the custom when the whole country or any single place had been polluted by great crime. Then, after the fast had roused the nation to the greatest horror of the crime, an assembly was to be called, in which Naboth was to be set on high and accused by two witnesses, in accordance with the prescription of the Mosaic law respecting condemnation, comp. Num. xxxv. 30, Deut. xvii. 6, 7; but these witnesses had been corrupted by Jezebel.

When we find them termed bad men in the writing of Jezebel herself, we must unhesitatingly attribute this designation to the author. Instead of "two men, sons of Belial," there probably stood "two men, such a one, and such a one;" for otherwise we should have to assume that Jezebel openly betrayed her infamy, and that the whole magistracy, notwithstanding the clearest, so to speak, official conviction of Naboth's innocence, condemned him to death out of disgraceful complaisance,—both hypotheses equally improbable. The plan succeeded. Naboth was stoned, together with all his family, as we infer from 2 Kings ix. 26. The punishment to be inflicted on him who blasphemed the king was not determined by law. But if it were established that to curse the king was equivalent to cursing God, the ordinances in Deut. xiii. 11 and xvii. 5 appeared applicable, according to which those who gave themselves up to idolatry were to be punished with death, and that by stoning. Ahab learned that Naboth was dead, and, taking good care not to inquire into the circumstances, he joyfully took possession of the vineyard. The property of those who were condemned on account of idolatry, under which the crime of Naboth had been classed, fell to the crown. But his joy in the new possession was very much embittered when suddenly Elijah entered the vineyard,—a representative of his slumbering conscience,—sent by the Lord, and greeted him with the double accusation of murder and of robbery. The terror with which his appearance inspired the king is revealed in the cry of anguish, "Hast thou found me, O mine enemy?" in which the term "mine enemy" betrays the ·hypocrite, who seeks to justify himself, and to attribute the censure and threat of the prophet to personal enmity, though against his conscience, as his anguish shows. It is not this, the prophet answers, but the sin which has bound thee in its fetters, that is the cause of my unwelcome coming. The prophet then foretells not only his violent death, which he had already announced on his entrance, but also the complete extermination of his family and the fearful end of Jezebel. Ahab shows all the signs of a repentance which was indeed sincere for the moment, as the consequent softening of the punishment shows, but, as we learn from his subsequent history, was not thorough. The prophet now declares that the Lord will not accomplish the total destruction of his family until the days of his son. That which had been decreed with respect to himself, and which had been foretold by another prophet even before this time, remained unaltered.

In the third year after the former battle with the Syrians, Ahab entered into an alliance with Jehoshaphat, king of Judah, for the purpose of making war on them. Occasion was given by their violation of the conditions of peace. Ramoth, a free Levitical city in the tribe of Gad, had not been delivered up by the Syrians. A number of the prophets with one voice foretold success to Ahab. All these were prophets who approved of calf-worship. Idolatry proper had almost entirely disappeared from the kingdom of Israel since that great catastrophe. No prophet of Baal here appears. The prophecies of the followers of the false worship are suspicious to Jehoshaphat. He inquires if there be no prophet who adheres to the worship of the true God as prescribed in the law. Elijah had gone back again to his concealment in the wilderness. The king therefore names Micaiah, the son of Imlah, but at the same time declares his hatred towards him, because he prophesies no good but only evil concerning him. Many have suspected that Micaiah is the same who had received the king with unwelcome tidings after the last war with the Syrians. At all events, the king must already have learned to know him from this side on some definite occasion; for we must infer from his command to lead him back to prison, 1 Kings xxii. 26, that he was then in prison. It is generally regarded as a piece of childish absurdity on the part of the king to be angry with Micaiah because he prophesies only evil, and of the messenger to beg him to prophesy good. But the matter has a deeper foundation in the heathen ideas of prophecy with which Ahab was infected. We have already seen that he ascribed to the prophets a magic power over the Deity, and hence regarded Elijah as the author of the drought which he had foretold. His anger had its root in this error. Jehoshaphat tries to express his fear to Ahab, and Micaiah is brought. In the meantime the prophets of the calves did their best, by words, gesticulations, and symbolical acts, to convince the two kings of the truth of their announcement and the divine character of their mission, and thus to do away with the evil impression of the prophecy of Micaiah, which might possibly bear a different character. A certain Zedekiah especially distinguished himself. He made himself horns of iron, and said, "Thus saith the Lord, With these shalt thou push the Syrians until thou have consumed them." We here see plainly how the prophets of the calves concealed their ungodliness under the semblance of piety. The symbolical act is plainly an embodiment of the image in Deut. xxxiii. 17, where we read of Joseph, "His horns are like the horns of unicorns: with them he shall push the people," etc. This brilliant promise, specially referring to the posterity of Joseph, was the foundation on which the false prophets took up their position, while they overlooked only the one circumstance, that the promise was conditional, and that the condition was not present. Everywhere we find this marked distinction between false and true prophecy, that the former announced salvation without repentance, gospel without law, and thus destroyed the ethical character of the religion of Jehovah. When Micaiah arrives, he finds the calf-prophets all assembled *in corpore* before the two kings, and still in full occupation. The ironical answer with which he first met the question of Jehoshaphat respecting the issue of the war was in keeping with the ridiculous spectacle. The meaning which his expression and countenance led the king to infer, although the words themselves foretold success, he soon reveals in the dry words: "I saw all Israel scattered upon the hills, as sheep that have not a shepherd," 1 Kings xxii. 17. The prophet in a vision sees the Israelites under the image of a flock robbed of their shepherd, which represents the death of the king. The foundation is formed by Num. xxvii. 16, 17, where Moses beseeches the Lord "that the congregation of the Lord be not as sheep that have no shepherd." Here, because Israel was no longer Israel, there came to pass what Moses had designated as incompatible with the existence of the covenant-nation. For this he censures the false prophets in another vision. The mistaking of the symbolical clothing has here given rise to much misunderstanding. In ancient times it was the common idea that *Satan* was meant by the spirit who offered to deceive Ahab by putting false prophecies into the mouths of the prophets of the calves. But this idea is untenable, on account of the article in הרוח; for there is no proof whatever that הרוח, the spirit, was ever employed as a kind of *nomen proprium* of Satan. By the spirit we ought rather to understand personified prophecy, prophecy taken as a whole, without regard to the distinction between true and false prophecy. This at least is contained in the passage,—an assumption that the false prophets as well as the true were subject to an influence external to their nature; and the exposition of many recent commentators, who limit the meaning of the whole vision to the prediction that Ahab, led away by false prophets, should be unfortunate, is plainly nugatory, and throwing away a part of the kernel with the shell. The existence of a spirit influencing the false prophets is also assumed elsewhere, as in Zech. xiii. 2; and in the teaching of the New Testament, appearing most prominently in the parable of the tares among the wheat, and again in the Apocalypse, xvi. 13, according to which three unclean spirits like frogs come out of the mouth of the dragon, represents the spirit of the world, which fills the minds of the ungodly,—the antithesis of the Holy Spirit. Our narrative points to the fact that this spirit of the world is no less subject to the disposition of God than the Holy Ghost. It forms part of the judgment on the ungodly, that they are suffered to be led astray by false prophets, against whom God could easily protect them if He would. Zedekiah is bold enough to mock Micaiah by word and action. The prophet tells him that he will learn the truth of his prediction in the day when he shall go from one chamber to another to hide himself. This prophecy was undoubtedly fulfilled, after the prophecy of Micaiah with respect to the issue of the battle had been accomplished. According to the Mosaic law, those prophets whose prophecies the result proved to be false were punished with death. Micaiah was led back to prison at the command of Ahab, there to be fed with the bread and water of affliction, *i.e.* to have this for his daily food (comp. Ps. xlii., "My tears have been my meat day and night"), until the king would return in peace. It was his intention then to slay him; he did not venture to do it now, because he could find no just pretext. The only two were these: if a prophet prophesied in the name of a false god, or if his prophecies were not fulfilled. He might, however, imprison him with an appearance of justice, in order that he might not escape if the result should prove his prophecy to have been false, as Ahab presupposed; comp. the similar treatment of Jeremiah, Jer. xxxvii. 15, 16, and chap. xxvi. Micaiah, though conscious of his good cause, has no objection to make to this conduct. "If thou return at all in peace," he says, "the Lord hath not spoken by me." Referring to Deut. xviii. 20–22, he declares himself perfectly willing to submit to the prescribed punishment, if his prophecy be disproved by the result. He probably foresaw that his later release would place the victory of the true God in the clearer light, and with this object appeals to the whole nation as witnesses, in words which the later canonical Micah has placed at the head of his prophecies, drawing attention to the oneness of spirit which characterized him and his older namesake. Both kings now went up to Ramoth in Gilead. Ahab had learned through his spies that the king of Syria had given orders to single him out in battle; for Ben-hadad had no stronger wish than to have him in his power, either dead or alive, to wash out the disgrace he had suffered three years before. Ahab therefore disguised himself. Jehoshaphat, on the contrary, went to battle in his royal dress, and was in the greatest danger of his life, because the Syrians mistook him for the king of Israel. A cry to which he gave utterance in his extremity, probably intended to summon his people, was the means of his deliverance in the hand of the Lord. The Syrians became aware of their error, and ceased to press so violently in that direction. The precaution of Ahab, on the other hand, failed to protect him against the destiny which God had appointed him. Those who sought him were not able to find him, but the source gives prominence to the fact that he was discovered by an arrow shot at a venture into the whole mass by a common Syrian. Mortally wounded, he wished to be carried out of the battle; but either the charioteer was unable to obey his command because the press was too great, or Ahab himself reversed his determination, lest by his absence the battle, which raged more and more violently, should be lost. So he bled, and died. The battle remained indecisive. But when the death of the king was known, the Israelitish army turned homewards. Ahab was brought to Samaria, and there buried. When his chariot was washed in the pool, the dogs licked up his blood. The chariot was washed by harlots. So great was the curse which rested upon him, that no respectable persons would undertake the task, which thousands would willingly have done for a pious king, blessed by God and beloved by his people. It was therefore necessary to employ the most despicable persons to do it for wages.

§ 3.

JEHOSHAPHAT.

We must now go back to the history of Jehoshaphat, Ahab's contemporary in the kingdom of Judah, the successor of Asa,—to those events which occurred during the reign of Ahab, but were not interwoven with the history of Israel, and have therefore not yet been mentioned. While the author of the books of the Kings, i. 22, only gives a few brief notices, the author of Chronicles, ii. 17 ff., draws from the common source at greater length. Jehoshaphat zealously strives to walk in the way of the Lord. For this reason the kingdom of Judah was flourishing and powerful at the same time when the kingdom of Israel sank down completely. The love of his subjects was so great, that by rich voluntary contributions, in addition to the ordinary taxes, they placed him in a position to pay those debts which had probably been incurred by his father in his wars. Jehoshaphat's zeal increased when he found that the Lord blessed all his undertakings. The dwellers in the country had succeeded in concealing some idolatrous altars and groves from the search made by Asa, or in restoring them after they had been overthrown. Jehoshaphat destroyed this last residue of idolatry. But he also did what was still more advantageous: he sent Levites through the whole land, with authority to instruct the people in the law, and to reform everything according to the direction of the law. It was this which gave the first foundation for the visitation of the churches. In order to give greater authority to these spiritual members, he appointed them to several of the highest state offices. The commission always carried with them the book of the law, as the rule by which the visitation was held and reform undertaken. One result of the flourishing state of the kingdom is to be found in the circumstance that the Philistines, who had been made tributary by David, but had neglected the payment of the tribute under the former weak governments, now voluntarily returned to their allegiance. Some Arabian nationalities also, who had probably been subdued by David, and had continued to pay tribute to Solomon, comp. 1 Kings x. 15, sent presents in order to propitiate the powerful king. Jehoshaphat tried to strengthen his military power by organizing a kind of militia, to which all belonged who were able to bear arms, in addition to the standing army which occupied the fortresses. Yet Jehoshaphat was not free from error. One of these was the close connection into which he entered with King Ahab. He saw how injurious the former enmity between Judah and Israel had been to both kingdoms, and this knowledge led him to the other extreme. He sought to consolidate the union by an alliance of Athaliah, the daughter of Ahab and Jezebel, with his son Jehoram. In spite of the warning of Micaiah, he accompanied Ahab in his campaign against the Syrians. The Lord had patience with his weakness, and allowed him to escape with his life, but at the same time administered a sharp rebuke on his return to Jerusalem, through the prophet Jehu. This was in every respect deserved. Jehoshaphat acted wisely in striving to put an end to the war with Israel, but he was greatly to blame for entering into close alliance and friendship with an enemy of God, and being on familiar terms with him; for giving his son a wife who had had so bad an example in her parents, and who, as the result showed, was fully worthy of them; and for joining himself with the ungodly Ahab in common undertakings, although he ought to have known that they must necessarily end in failure. He showed that at times a false wisdom outweighed higher considerations. Yet the way in which he accepted the censure proved that he had erred only from weakness. He redoubled his zeal for the spread of the true fear of God, and for the establishment of a settled administration of justice, which seems to have been very inferior in earlier times. He represented to the judges the loftiness of their calling, since they were destined under Israel to administer justice as the instruments of God. The way in which he did this testifies to the depth and force of his spiritual life, and shows that he formed a true estimate of his own position in its distinction from that of the heathen kings. He set up a supreme court of judicature at Jerusalem, half composed of civil and half of spiritual members, whose business it was to administer justice to the inhabitants of Jerusalem, and to receive appeals from the inferior tribunals throughout the whole land. Formerly, it seems, the final appeal had been to the king in person. Here also he had regard to the highest aim of the theocratic administration of justice. The judges were to instruct the parties respecting right and wrong from the word of God, and by this means to prevent the crime which led to sentence of punishment. This court of justice had a spiritual president for the settlement of spiritual affairs, and a temporal one for temporal affairs.

A great danger which soon afterwards threatened the kingdom of Judah was only intended to strengthen the nation and king in their pious disposition, by the glorious deliverance vouchsafed. Jehoshaphat received news of the approach of a large hostile army, which had already occupied Engedi on the western shore of the Dead Sea. In 2 Chron. xx. 1, they are characterized as the Moabites, Ammonites, and מהעמונים. This can only mean "nations living at a distance from the Ammonites," beyond them. Besides the Ammonites and Moabites, who are expressly named in Ps. lxxxiii. as the instigators, there were great swarms of the inhabitants of Western Arabia in the army, whom the author does not designate more exactly, because they had no common *nomen proprium*. In 2 Chron. xx. 2 they are spoken of as a great multitude from beyond the sea on this side Syria, *i.e.* from the district east of the country which is bounded on the north by Syria, on the south by the Dead Sea, and therefore from Western Arabia, whose hordes invariably made Palestine the object of their predatory incursions. This therefore exactly corresponds to the expression, beyond the Ammonites. In all probability the matter stands thus. Instigated by the Moabites and Ammonites, a movement arose among the tribes of the wilderness similar to that at the time of the migration of the nations. They wished to exchange their waste dwelling with the fruitful Palestine. They attempted what they afterwards finally accomplished in the middle ages, while the Arabs of the wilderness continued to overrun Palestinian Syria, till at last they had dislodged almost all the older inhabitants. For it is evident that the reference here is not merely to passing strife and robbery, from the fact that in 2 Chron. xx. 11 Jehoshaphat expressly says, "The enemy come to cast us out of the possession which Thou hast given us to inherit." According to Ps. lxxxiii. 5, the enemy intended nothing less than to do to Israel what Israel had formerly done to the Canaanites. Moreover, the immense booty which the Israelites made shows that the enemy had gone out with bag and baggage. The sons of the wilderness now turned to the country of the Ammonites, by whom they had been stirred up. In them, as well as in a portion of the Edomites, they found willing allies. Respecting their further march Robinson observes, part ii. p. 446: "Without doubt they travelled south of the Dead Sea to Engedi, by the same route, as it appears, which is now taken by the Arabs in their predatory excursions along the shore as far as Ain Idy, then up the pass, and so northwards to below Thekoa." "The way," he says, p. 485, "which we took to-day is the great Arabian street through the wilderness, the Dead Sea, by which the Arabs of the south-west, and those who come round from the east by the southern end of the sea, are able to penetrate far north without the tribes or villages which lie farther west knowing anything of their movements." The consideration that in this way alone they could get rid of their troublesome guests without injury to themselves, must in itself have been a strong inducement to the Edomites to join the movement; but how much more the hope of enriching themselves by the overthrow of their hereditary enemy, for whom they could have been no match by themselves, and the prospect of being safe from them in the future, and receiving a portion of their land! Probably the object of the enemy in going so far south, instead of entering by the pass on the Jordan, as the Israelites had done, was to conceal the aim of their expedition. This explains why Jehoshaphat heard nothing of it until the enemy had already occupied Engedi. Josephus thinks that they passed through the Dead Sea at Engedi, for there are places which can be waded through, so that even now the Arabs wade through with their camels. But it is more probable that the enemy travelled as far as the southern extremity of the sea, then suddenly turned and entered Palestine from the south-east; for the sea is only wadeable in the south, and although this ford very much shortens the way from the east to Judea, it is but little used, since the march through the brine is very difficult for naked feet. But if wading through the sea present difficulties even to individuals, it is the less probable that the heavily laden army of the enemy should have purchased the small shortening of the march at such a price. Moreover, we learn from what follows that some of the Edomites had joined the enemy, which seems to presuppose that they had touched their land also. Jehoshaphat was indeed in great dismay at the beginning, but he sought help where it was to be found. He appointed a fast-day, that by true repentance the nation might remove the only cause which could deprive them of divine assistance. He then besought the help of the Lord in a solemn public prayer, and received the promise of it through

Jahaziel, of the sons of Asaph, probably the author of the eighty-third psalm, in which the help of the Lord is entreated in that danger. Firmly trusting in the promise, he marched at the head of his people towards Tekoa, a city to the south-east of Jerusalem, where the wilderness of Judah begins, through which the enemy must march against Jerusalem. Jehoshaphat's faith was so strong, that he made the Levites go before the army in their sacred garments, singing psalms of praise and thanksgiving, placing equal value on the help which was promised and on that which had already been vouchsafed. The enemy were swept away by bloody discord, which arose among them before the eyes of the Israelites without any intervention on their part. This very concise narrative has recently been quite misinterpreted by Ewald and Bertheau (Com. on Chron.), who make the מארבים in ver. 22 a kind of evil spirits sent forth by God against the enemy. The following is the explanation: Only a part of the Idumeans had joined the enemy, the rest thinking it more advisable to remain true to the king of Judah, to whom they were tributary,—the revolt of the Idumeans under Solomon had not quite destroyed their relation of dependence,—and when opportunity offered, to attack the enemy, whose spoil promised greater satisfaction to their rapacity, and by whom they probably feared to be attacked even in their dwellings after they would be in possession of Palestine. The Idumeans might have been joined also by rapacious swarms of tribes from Waste and Stony Arabia. They concealed themselves in the mountains which surrounded the Dead Sea. The sound of the singing told them of the approach of the Israelites, and gave them the signal of attack. But since the Judeans did not at once fall upon the enemy, as they had expected, it would have been easy for the latter to slay the troops who were so few in comparison with themselves. But now the enemy turned their arms against each other. Because the assailants were mainly composed of Idumeans, the rest began to suspect that the Idumeans associated with themselves had only entered into the alliance for purposes of treachery, and had an understanding with their opponents. They therefore fell upon them and slew them.

And suspicion soon extended still further. Each nation believed that the others had joined it merely for treachery sake and only awaited the attack of the Judeans to carry out its plan. Thus a general slaughter ensued, and those who remained took to flight, leaving all their possessions, because the attack of Judah was momentarily expected. When the Judeans, therefore, reached an elevation commanding a view of the wilderness, they saw the remarkable spectacle of a camp destitute of enemies, and covered with corpses and rich spoil. After having taken possession of the latter, they held a great thanksgiving feast, first in the neighbourhood of the battle-field, and then at Jerusalem. On the former solemn occasion Psalm xlvii. was sung; on the latter, Psalm xlviii. The place where the first thanksgiving was held, the valley of blessing or praise, has been discovered by recent travellers, Robinson and others, in a wadi and a place called Bereikut, in the vicinity of the ancient Tekoa; comp. Ritter, part xv. p. 635. Little more is told of the subsequent life of Jehoshaphat, to which we pass on at once by way of sketch, although the narrative extends into the following section. By the event last narrated, the Idumeans were again completely subject to Jehoshaphat. In 1 Kings xxii. 47, we read that they had no independent king, but only a deputy. This observation, as well as the whole subsequent narrative, presupposes an event such as that which has been related, an event by which the Idumeans were again placed in the same relation to the kingdom of Judah into which they had been brought by David. Hence the important harbour Ezion-geber on the Ælanitic gulf of the Red Sea, the present Assium, which had formerly been at the command of Solomon, was now again in the hands of Jehoshaphat; comp. Burckhardt, part ii. p. 831. He would not leave this advantage unused, and entered into an agreement with Ahaziah, king of Israel, to build a merchant fleet. One part of the fleet was to leave the Ælanitic Gulf for Ophir, another was destined for Tartessus. The latter was not intended to circumnavigate Africa, as Michaelis assumes, but was to be transported across the small neck of land which separates the Heroopolitan arm of the Arabian Gulf from the

Mediterranean Sea, the isthmus of Suez,—an attempt which was afterwards made with more numerous and doubtless with larger ships; comp. the compilations in Vitringa on Isa. i. p. 84, Keil on the Hiram-Solomonic voyage to Ophir and Tarshish, Dorpat, 1834, p. 8 ff. But immediately on leaving the harbour the fleet was destroyed by a storm. The harbour of Ezion-geber is full of rocks, and was afterwards quite abandoned on account of the frequent shipwrecks. Ahaziah tried to persuade Jehoshaphat to build a new fleet. But Jehoshaphat, warned by a prophet, would not, by union with an ungodly king, expose himself a second time to the misfortune which must inevitably befall such undertakings, and gave up his design of renewing the Solomonic trade. The short notices of the commercial enterprises of Jehoshaphat in 1 Kings xxii. 48, and 2 Chron. xx. 36 ff., contain many difficulties, on which comp. Keil, p. 21 ff., whose solution, however, seems to be incorrect. Notwithstanding all his zeal, Jehoshaphat was unable to do away with the practice of worshipping the true God on the heights, owing to the stubbornness of the people, which clothed itself in a pious garment, but all traces of idolatrous worship were happily destroyed. He died, after having reigned for twenty-five years, including the years of the co-regency of his son Jehoram. He was guilty of grievous error in taking Athaliah the daughter of Ahab as a wife for his son. By this means he helped towards the destruction of that which it had been the highest aim of his life to build up.

§ 4.

AHAZIAH IN THE KINGDOM OF ISRAEL.

Ahaziah ascended the throne in the beginning of the seventeenth year of Jehoshaphat, and reigned until the end of the eighteenth. He closely resembled his father. Soon after the death of the latter, the Moabites, who had been subject from the time of David, fell away from the kingdom of Israel, to which they had been annexed on the separation of the kingdom; comp. 2 Kings i. 1. In all probability this happened on the occasion of their union with the Arab tribes, which belongs to the very same period. For, according to Chronicles, it happened after the death of Ahab, and before the common building of the fleet. Thus there is no single event more fully narrated in Chronicles to which there are not references in the books of the Kings. In the second year of his reign the king met with a dangerous accident. He was leaning on the lattice-work of the gallery on his flat roof, when it gave way and he fell down; but this misfortune failed to make any impression on him. He sent to the Philistine idol Baal-zebub to ask whether he would recover from his illness. It is generally supposed that this god is honoured as having possessed the power of protection against flies, which gave rise to his name. It has been argued that even the Greeks have their Ζεὺς ἀπόμυιος, their *Hercules locustorius*, their Ἀπόλλων μυόκτονος. But these examples would only be analogous, if it could be proved that a god was worshipped by a whole city or a whole district with sole reference to benefits so comparatively small. The correct idea is rather that Baal-zebub is a contemptuous transformation of the true name of the idol. Of this falsification of names not a few examples might be quoted; comp. the compilations in part ii. of the *Beiträge*, p. 26. The proper name of the idol was Baal-zebul, under which name it also appears in the New Testament, *dominus habitationis*. זבל, *habitatio*, stands for heaven, God's throne and habitation, so that Baal-zebul is synonymous with the Phenician Baal, Baalsamen, *dominus cœlorum*. By the change of one letter the Israelites altered the alleged king of heaven into what he really was,—a fly-king, a king with no real authority. Elijah was commissioned to reprove the king for his wickedness. He suddenly stepped forth from his concealment to meet the messengers of the king, and commanded them not to continue their journey to Ekron, but to return to the king and to tell him that his death was irrevocably decreed. The king at once conjectured from whom the message came, and his conjecture was changed to certainty when the messengers described the outward appearance of the prophet, dressed in a hairy garment with a leathern girdle about his loins. But his designs of revenge were frustrated in the manner fully narrated in the source. The outward *habitus* of Elijah, as described on this occasion, had a symbolical meaning,—it was a *sermo propheticus realis*. The hairy garment is always the garb of repentance. The preacher of repentance appeared as repentance personified. In that which he did he set an example to the nation; comp. 1 Kings xxi. 27, where Ahab imitates the repentance which the prophet exemplifies: " And it came to pass, when Ahab heard those words, that he rent his clothes, and put sackcloth upon his flesh, and fasted." John the Baptist afterwards borrowed this *habitus* from Elijah, as an indication of the idea which he possessed in common with him. Ahaziah, like Ahab, believes that Elijah, as his personal enemy, not only foretells, but also effects the threatened misfortune. He wishes to bring him into his power, for the purpose of either compelling him to avert the misfortune, or, if unable to do this, at least to revenge himself on him. With this object he sends out a captain, as ungodly as himself, with his troop, to seize the prophet. This captain, fearing lest the prophet should escape while he was ascending the mountain, sought by stratagem to induce him to give himself up voluntarily. The most certain means to accomplish this end seemed to be to gain his favour by a feigned recognition of his prophetic dignity. Hence he addresses him: "Thou man of God, the king hath said, Come down." But Elijah sees into his unbelieving heart. Thou shalt soon learn that I am in reality what thou termest me in thy hypocrisy. A flash of lightning slew the captain and his host. Ahaziah, after the usual manner of scepticism, attributed the misfortune to accident. He sent a second captain, who was no better than his predecessor, and failed to take warning from his example. He too was overtaken by righteous judgment. The king then sent a third captain with his troop. It seems, however, that the second misfortune had softened him in some measure, so that he no longer thought of laying hands on the prophet, but only wished to speak with him, that by gentleness he might perhaps induce him to alter his determination, and designedly chose a pious captain, hoping through him to attain his object more easily. The justice of Elijah's former conduct, which the Lord in Luke ix. 55 does not blame, but only characterizes as inappropriate to the new covenant, is plainly shown in the whole manner of his behaviour towards this captain. He goes back with him to the king, and simply repeats what he had said to his messengers. His sentence was speedily fulfilled. The king died, and because he had no son, his brother Jehoram succeeded to the throne. The statement in 2 Kings i. 17, that this happened in the second year of Jehoram the son of Jehoshaphat, presupposes that Jehoshaphat had taken his son Jehoram as co-regent in the seventeenth year of his reign; for, according to chap. iii. 1, Jehoram began to reign over Israel in the eighteenth year of Jehoshaphat. Soon after the death of Ahaziah, Elijah was miraculously taken away from this life,—an event which was destined to seal his whole life of activity, to impart strength of faith to his successor Elisha, and to the whole remaining ἐκλογή in Israel, who had gathered about him as their head. The narrative of this event in the books of the Kings has verbal reference to Gen. v. 24, and in this way draws attention to the fact that the miracle with respect to Enoch was repeated in Elijah. In general most of the miracles of Elijah and Elisha are prefigured in the Mosaic history,—for example, the fire from heaven which kindles the offering and consumes those who are refractory; the dividing of the water of the Jordan; the healing of the bitter spring, etc. The object of this conformity is to point to the fact that the God of Israel is still the same, the ancient God still living; that Elijah and Elisha stand towards Him in the same relation as His anointed servants of former time; that the cause which they served was equally the cause of the Lord; that the community which they represented was the continuation of the original community of the Lord. Just as the miracles of Elijah and Elisha are connected with those in the Mosaic history, so to these are attached the miracles of the New Testament, where the object is to show the connection between this and the Old Testament, to represent the New not as being in antithesis to the Old, but as its fulfilment. This connection between the miracles of Scripture must be postulated if we take the Scripture standpoint, and is far from throwing doubt on its historical truth. We are the less justified in coming to such a conclusion, since the dependence is everywhere associated with independence, the later miracles never appearing as simple reproduction. Elijah knew by a divine revelation what would befall him; it was also made known to Elisha, but without the knowledge of Elijah. The latter made several attempts to free himself from Elisha, his companion. His extreme modesty would fain have dispensed with all witnesses to his glorification. But Elisha steadily refused; he would enjoy his beloved master to the last moment of his sojourn upon the earth. Elijah repaired beforehand to the place where his activity had borne the most joyous fruits, the seat of the prophetic schools of Bethel and Jericho. It seems that in the former place Elijah had established a seminary of the Holy Spirit, in order by powerful measures to check the corruption which had gone out from this city over all Israel, viz. the false worship of God, and to influence the numbers who made pilgrimages thither. Elijah wished to make a few final arrangements in these places, and to exhort the prophetic schools as his spiritual sons. He thought that they would know nothing of that which was impending; but the Lord had revealed it to some among them, or to their heads. If the event were to have its intended effect, it must be known to many of the faithful with unerring certainty. Elijah's ascension happened not for his own sake, but for the sake of those who were left behind. So far as he alone was concerned, we see no reason why he should not have have gone the way of all flesh. The prophetic disciples told Elisha what they knew, and he exhorted them to silence. He was too well acquainted with the mind of his master not to know his strong aversion to all display. From Jericho Elijah and Elisha took their way towards the Jordan. Fifty disciples of the prophets accompanied them part of the way. While these remained standing at a short distance from the Jordan, Elijah parted the waters of the Jordan by the power of the Lord, so that he and his companion passed over dry-shod. When they had reached the farther shore, Elijah permitted Elisha to make a last request, persuaded that the Lord would grant it at his petition. " I pray thee," Elisha asks, "let a double portion of thy spirit be upon me." Many have understood this request as if Elisha had demanded a double measure of the spirit possessed by Elijah. But the words themselves do not admit of this interpretation. The ברוחך, "of thy spirit," shows that Elisha only asked for a portion of the spirit which rested upon Elijah; otherwise the request would have been too bold, and its fulfilment, though promised by Elijah, could not be historically proved. Elisha appears throughout as subordinate to Elijah, only carrying on his work, and standing towards him in the same relation as Isaac to Abraham, Joshua to Moses, Timothy to Paul, Bugenhagen and Jonas to Luther. Elijah, and not he, appears in the transfiguration with Moses the head, as the second representative of the old covenant, as the coryphæus of the whole prophethood. It is more correct to suppose that Elisha requests Elijah to grant him a double portion of his spirit, that he would appoint him his spiritual heir, with an allusion to the law, according to which a double portion of the inheritance fell to the lot of the first-born, Deut. xxi. 17. The very request that he would leave him his spirit points to a spiritual relation of dependence on the part of Elisha towards Elijah, and proves that the former was far from laying claim to a higher position than his master's. This narrative also throws light upon the former, where a task is given to Elijah which is only accomplished by Elisha; perhaps also upon a later narrative, in which, after the death of Elijah, mention is made of a scriptural prophecy respecting it. Elijah associated the granting of the request with a visible sign: if he should be a witness of his ascension. He did this in order to help the weakness of Elisha. In the troubles incident to his divine calling, he could comfort himself with this assurance: As certainly as I saw my master ascend to heaven, so certainly am I divinely called to be his successor. Even if I fail to perceive in myself the requisite gifts, yet I must possess them. The ascension took place with accompanying phenomena which presented to Elisha the appearance of fiery horses and chariot. The connection of these phenomena with the cherubim is based on an utterly false view of the latter. When Elisha sees his master disappear, he cries out, "My father, my father! the chariot of Israel, and the horsemen thereof." Elijah had been the pillar of the Israelitish nation, its support in temporal and spiritual need. Chariot and riders typified the greatest power of the states then in existence: with chariots and riders Aram had prevailed against Israel. In token of his sorrow, Elisha rent his garments. He then set out to return to the country on this side of the Jordan, to enter upon his calling. Having reached the Jordan, he commanded its waters to divide, saying, "Where is the Lord God of Elijah, He Himself?" The words אף הוא have here given much difficulty to expositors, and have been subjected to false interpretation from the earliest times. The simplest explanation is this: and He, equivalent to He Himself. Elisha expresses his firm confidence that the God of Elijah, the same who had proved Himself so powerful through him and in him, He Himself, and no other deity less powerful and gracious, would also hear his request as Elijah's successor. From the fact that this request was granted, it is evident that it was not a tempting of God, but rather a suggestion of the Holy Spirit Himself. The object of the granting of the request was not only to assure Elisha himself of his calling and to strengthen his faith, but still more to attest his appointment as the successor of Elijah to the prophetic schools, and indirectly to the nation. This appears from the explicit observation of the author, 2 Kings ii. 15: "And when the sons of the prophets saw him, they said, The spirit of Elijah doth rest on Elisha. And they came to meet him, and bowed themselves to the ground before him." The whole contents of 2 Kings chaps. i. and ii. show that by the efficacy of Elijah the prophets in the kingdom of Israel had received a certain organization, and that a certain distinction of rank obtained among them, proportionate to the difference in the divine gift,—not, however, as among the priests, an external distinction resting upon carnal birth, but an internal one resting upon spiritual birth. After Elisha had now by a doubly remarkable event been legitimized by God as the successor of Elijah, he was recognised as the head of the whole institute. The second miracle performed by Elisha, the healing of the water at Jericho, must be looked at from the same point of view. This place, situated in a region like Paradise, was deficient in wholesome drinking water. Among other evils, the waters gave rise to premature births,—a property which still characterizes many of the mineral springs in Germany. Mineral water abounds in the vicinity of the Dead Sea, and for this reason cannot be drunk by those who are pregnant. Elisha sent for salt in a new dish, and shook it into the waters. Of course the salt could not of itself produce the effect which was intended, and which was actually realized. The act was symbolical. Salt was in olden times the symbol of purification and healing. Just as salt seasons what has no taste, so the power of God would have a salutary effect on the water. The use of the new dish also belonged to the symbol. The power of spiritual salt is weakened when mixed with impurities. The prophetic disciples at Jericho, though not doubting that Elijah had been taken away by the Lord,—for they themselves had been witnesses,—were yet unable to reconcile themselves to the belief that his body had been taken away from the earth for ever. They thought it probable that the Lord had taken his soul to Himself in heaven, but that after this had happened, his body must have fallen again somewhere upon the earth ; they wished, therefore, to search for it to pay it the last honours. Elisha tried to dissuade them from their purpose, but finally yielded to their request, that they might be convinced of the futility of the attempt. Fifty men now set out in all directions to seek the corpse. The fruitlessness of this zealous searching served to confirm the truth of the ascension of Elijah in its whole extent, and to exclude all possibility of doubt. This is the object of the author in narrating the event. From Jericho Elisha turned to Bethel. Here also, in the place of the illegal worship, it was necessary that his divine mission should be ratified. The boys who mocked him there were the ungodly children of ungodly parents, who scoffed at the prophet as such, and in him therefore scoffed at God. The baldness of the prophet, the result not of age, but of excessive intellectual labour, was only a vehicle, and not the actual ground of their mockery. The punishment which befell them was not the satisfaction of a carnal desire for revenge on the part of the prophet, but a righteous divine judgment, intended to serve as a warning to others who were like-minded, and was especially necessary in this place. It was a settlement of the dispute between the adherents of the calf-worship and those who worshipped the God of Israel according to His word. For the mockery of the boys is only to be regarded as an isolated expression of the bitter feeling of the former towards the latter.

§ 5.

JORAM IN THE KINGDOM OF ISRAEL AND IN THE KINGDOM OF JUDAH.

Ahaziah, as we have already stated, was succeeded by his brother Jehoram, who reigned for twelve years. He renounced the service of idols; but calf-worship was so closely bound up with the national interests of Israel, that he had not courage to abolish it. While in the beginning he paid little heed to the prophets of the true God, they afterwards by their deeds, especially those of Elisha, acquired great authority over him,—without his experiencing a true change of heart, however. His first care was to regain his ascendency over the Moabites, who had revolted immediately after the death of Ahab, and had refused to pay the heavy tribute obtained from their large flocks, which found rich pasture partly on their own land, and partly in the neighbouring Waste and Stony Arabia. With this object in view, Jehoram besought King Jehoshaphat for his assistance, who promised it the more readily, since by this means he had an opportunity of punishing the Moabites for the invasion of his land which they had made shortly before, in conjunction with the tribes of the wilderness. Notwithstanding the great extremity in which the kings at first found themselves, the war came to a prosperous ending. There were two ways of invading the country of the Moabites,—either from the northern boundary, passing the Jordan in the neighbourhood of Jericho, and then crossing the Arnon; or the allied army might advance to the southern end of the Dead Sea, and then reach the southern territory of the Moabites through the northern part of the Edomite mountain-district. The king of Israel left the choice to the king of Judah, because the latter way, which led through his territory, could only be undertaken with his permission. The king of Judah decided in its favour. It was attended with such great hardships and dangers, that the Moabites probably thought themselves secure on this side, where Mount Seir seemed to form a boundary-wall insurmountable to a whole army; and might therefore be surprised the more easily. In this way, too, it would be easier to collect the auxiliary troops of the king of the Edomites, who was tributary to Judah. When, in 1 Kings xxii. 47, we read that there was no king in Edom at the time of Jehoshaphat, the meaning, as we see from the context, is that there was no independent king, in distinction from a vassal. But notwithstanding the apparent wisdom of the plan, it brought the army into the greatest danger. It was necessary for them to traverse the mountain-pass formed by the Wadi Hössa, which hastens from the west to the east towards the Dead Sea, the natural boundary on the side of Arabia Petræa, probably the same way which was formerly taken by Naomi when she left the land of the Moabites and returned to her home in Bethlehem, which was followed by the Crusaders when they journeyed from the Valley of Salt, Seyon, to Syria Sobal, and was afterwards taken by Seetzen on his way from Moab, past the Dead Sea, to Jerusalem. The kings had probably calculated that the Wadi Hössa would afford them a sufficient supply of water; but in this hope they were deceived. The brook had been dried up by long-continued drought. Their position was desperate; the fainting army was in hourly expectation that the Moabites would come down on them from the northern mountains. In this extremity the difference of disposition between the king of Judah and the king of Israel betrays itself in a remarkable way. Jehoram is quite in despair: he thinks he sees certain destruction before him, because he knows that he has deserved the punishment of the Lord. Jehoshaphat has a better conscience, although it is not quite pure, since his connection with the king of Israel, which he had probably regarded as allowable because Jehoram was not an idolater like his predecessor, might now appear to him in another light. He refuses to give up hope, and inquires whether there is not a prophet of the Lord in the place. Elisha was in the camp, or in its vicinity,—a circumstance only explicable on the supposition that he had received a revelation from the Lord to the effect that He would want him there. For the embarrassment in which the king was involved immediately when he began his reign, was intended as a means in the hand of the Lord to procure authority and perfect freedom for His prophets in the exercise of their calling, under this new reign. The kings, humiliated by misfortune, repair to Elisha in person. Elisha at first gives the king of Israel an evasive answer, referring him to his calf-prophets. He knew that this was the time, if ever, when punishment would make a salutary impression on the king. Jehoram is deeply humbled by sorrow. He begs Elisha not to repel him in this way, now when the Lord has brought such heavy misfortune upon him and his allies, but, if possible, to show him the way out of his embarrassment. Elisha perceives that the repentance of the king is merely superficial, and therefore seeks to move him still more deeply, by declaring that he will only interest himself in the matter for the sake of the pious Jehoshaphat. He now sends for a minstrel, and by a stringed instrument is brought into the frame of mind necessary to the reception of the Spirit of God. Where the Spirit was to speak, it was requisite first to wrap one's own life in silence, and to fill the soul with utter rest and stillness. Perhaps Elisha felt the greater need of such a preparation, because he had been agitated by his conference with the king of Israel. But it is unnecessary to assume this to have been the case, since music appears even elsewhere as the ordinary means employed by the prophets for the suppression of self-consciousness. The prophet now prophesies that they will soon not only receive an abundant supply of water, but will completely conquer the Moabites. The natural means employed by God for the fulfilment of the former prophecy was doubtless as follows: Violent showers of rain, or a kind of waterspout, fell in the Edomitic mountains. The water ran in streams through the bed of the dried-up torrent on which the allied armies were encamped, to the Dead Sea. Thus the army received water without having seen a rain-cloud. Because the mountain-torrent, which had its origin in a sudden shower of rain, would necessarily soon subside, and the former need recur, therefore the army, at the command of Elisha, had made ditches in the bed of the torrent itself, and round about it, in which the water was retained. By divine decree the water did not come until the day after these preparations were already ended, and just at the time when the morning sacrifice was offered in the temple at Jerusalem, in order at the same time to serve for a confirmation of the legal worship. In many miraculous manifestations of God, prominence is given to the fact that they happened just at the time when His mercy was entreated by sacrifice and prayer in the sanctuary appointed by Him. In the meantime the Moabites with all their forces had repaired to their southern border, and had occupied the mountainous district north of the wadi. In all probability the water had taken a reddish hue from the red ground over which it flowed. According to Burckhardt, the mountains there are composed principally of sandstone. The illusion was strengthened by the rays of the rising sun, which were refracted in it. The Moabites, with their accurate knowledge of the district, knew that the wadi was dried up. Hence it was difficult for them to think that it was water which they saw shimmering down in the distance. The recollection of the way in which the former campaign had been thwarted by mutual destruction was still fresh in their memories. They knew the former hostile relation, and the natural jealousy existing between Israel and Judah; they knew that the Edomites were less voluntary than compelled allies of the Judaites. Thus the idea suggested itself to some, that what they saw was blood, and that their enemies had destroyed one another. The mass of the people assumed the truth of what they wished, without waiting to prove it. Eager for booty, they left their secure position in the mountain, and fell upon the hostile camp. In the valley the superior force gained an easy victory over them. Their whole land was now conquered and laid waste, as Elisha had foretold, though without approving of the cruelties then perpetrated, which, however, cannot be judged according to our more recent martial law and the code of nations. The king had thrown himself, with a part of his troops, into the fortress Kir-hareseth. This was the most important fortress in the country. It appears in Isa. chap. xvi. 7 under this name, and in chap. xv. 1 under the name קיר מואב, the walls of Moab. It was situated on a very high and steep mountain-rock in the neighbourhood of Zared, and commanded a view over the Dead Sea, and across to Jerusalem. In the twelfth century the ruined fortress was rebuilt, and played an important part under the name of Karak; comp. Gesenius on Isa. xv. 1, xvi. 7. This fortress was besieged by the allied armies, and the slingers did great damage to the garrison. Yet it was only by starving out the garrison that they could hope to occupy the fortress, unless, like Saladin, who besieged this fortress in the middle ages, they had sling machines which were included among the slingers. Machines of this kind appear in the history of Uzziah in 2 Chron. xxvi. 15. The Moabitish king, reduced to the last extremity, made an attempt with seven hundred men to cut his way through the enemy, choosing the side occupied by the Idumeans, because he expected less resistance in this quarter. When his attempt failed, he offered up his own son on the wall to his god Chemosh. His object was to make an impression on the minds of his enemies,—to fill them with fear of the divine revenge on account of their unmerciful conduct. That in cases of extreme need the heathen sought to propitiate the wrath of their idols by human sacrifices, is proved by not a few examples. Even in a much more enlightened age, the Tyrians, when besieged by Alexander, were on the point of resorting to it at the advice of the Carthaginians. This deed of horror was revolting to the heart of the pious Jehoshaphat, and perhaps also to the Idumeans. Their anger was kindled against the Israelites, because they had given occasion for this crime by their want of compassion in reducing the besieged to the utmost extremity. The king of Israel was obliged to yield to their decidedly expressed wish to raise the siege, and the allied armies departed homewards with the booty from the country which they had laid waste. It redounds to the honour of the covenant-nation that, from fear of God, they forbore to carry matters to extremes; and it is in vain for Ewald to represent as superstition what was the result of deep and living piety.

The miraculous deeds of Elisha narrated in chap. iv. of the second book of Kings find their vindication in the fact that in the kingdom of Israel the Levites had not a legally recognised position as the servants of God, as was the case in Judah; hence the prophethood had far greater importance in the latter. Moreover, the miracles performed by some among them who were specially gifted, served as an authorization of the whole class, which was the more needed, because they stood not in transitory opposition to individual ungodly kings, but in permanent hostility towards the state-religion, which was closely connected with the state. The fact that, notwithstanding these miraculous manifestations of God, the people as a whole were so little improved that the Lord was obliged to visit them with the punishment of the captivity, is a strong argument for their necessity. We shall first of all make a few observations on the history of the Shunammite. Shunem was a town of the tribe of Issachar, through which Elisha passed on his journey from his usual abode on Mount Carmel to Samaria, where, as we learn from ver. 13, he was held in high estimation, and had unbounded influence with the king and his highest officers,—an influence which he carefully made use of for the establishment of good or the destruction of evil. In visiting the prophetic schools at Bethel, Gilgal, and Jericho, which were subject to his supervision, Elisha was obliged to touch at Shunem also. In these journeys he was entertained by a rich pious Shunammite with eager hospitality, based on his relation to the Lord. As a reward, her marriage, which had formerly been childless, was blessed at the prayer of the prophet. The death of the child was intended to reveal the faith of the woman and the power of the Lord. The former shows itself in the answer which she sent to her husband. He was still in the field with his men, at some distance, it appears, from the city, and knew nothing of the death of the child. The woman sends, asking for a servant to accompany her to the prophet,—a message which causes some anxiety to the husband, who inquires, "Wherefore wilt thou go to him to-day? It is neither new moon nor sabbath." He was accustomed to his wife's visiting the prophet on holy days. From this passage it follows that on these days a small number of the faithful were in the habit of assembling about the prophets, to be taught and edified by them. But now, on an ordinary day, the husband has a presentiment of something unusual. In the kingdom of Judah we find no example of this kind of regular teaching on the part of the prophets. The history of Jehoshaphat shows that this duty devolved on the priests and Levites. The woman, without telling him the object of her journey, sets his mind at rest with the assurance that nothing evil has occurred. She was firmly convinced that the prophet would raise her dead child to life again. Hence she resolves not to trouble her husband, whose faith is weak, with news of a calamity which, persuaded by the eye of faith, she regards as no longer in existence. Her faith is still more fully shown in her address to the prophet himself. She has no doubt whatever that he can come to her assistance if he will; and from his own promise she shows him that he must be willing to do so. He had promised her a son, as a reward for the love and faith which she had shown him. A child who dies again so soon, she maintains, is no reward, but a punishment. From the way in which Elisha treats the dead child, it seems as if the Lord had suffered him to retain a faint germ of life, which was ripened by the power imparted to Elisha. But the event must by no means be removed from the sphere of the miraculous. Gehazi finds no sign whatever of life in the child, and in chap. viii. 5 the event is expressly characterized as a miracle. The similar miracle of Elijah was undoubtedly greater, because it had no point of contact in natural causes. After this event Elisha left his customary abode on Mount Carmel and went to Gilgal, where he had last been with Elijah. There he remained for a long time, and inspected the greatly frequented schools of the prophets, whose members, the sons of the prophets, must invariably be regarded not as pupils, but as subordinate teachers,—as those who, under the supervision of their head, were responsible for the spiritual nourishment of the people. A famine there gave him an opportunity of proving the divine nature of his authority in a twofold way before the eyes of the sons of the prophets, and also of ratifying the position of the servants of God in the kingdom of Israel in the face of the calf-prophets. A disciple of the prophets had gone out into the field to look for all kinds of herbs as vegetables for the whole community. These disciples dwelt together in a kind of convent, and the arrangements among them seem to have been more like those of a cloister than the earlier evangelical theologians, from false polemic interest against the Romish Church, would concede, though not so much so as this Church asserted. The fruit of a climbing plant attracted the attention of the youth, who had more experience in divine things than in household matters, since, owing to its great size, it promised great gain. It was a kind of wild gourd—the coloquintida. The fruit, about the size of a fist, and covered with a white skin of the nature of leather, has a soft, spongy juice, which has the bitterest and most horrible taste. It is called the devil's apple. Taken frequently, it produces violent sickness, and finally causes death. The youth gathered as much of this plant as he could carry; and those who provided for the common kitchen were no better skilled in natural science than he: it was only by tasting it that they gained experience. Elisha remedied the evil by a means which in itself could not have had this effect. Another incident occurred in the same place. According to the law, the first-fruits of corn, wine, and oil were to be given to the priests; also some of the first bread baked of fresh corn,—the amount of the present being left to the will of the giver; comp. Deut. xviii. 4, 5, Num. xviii. 13. But because the priests were banished from the kingdom of Israel, those who feared God, finding it impossible to fulfil the law according to the letter, sought to fulfil it in spirit. While there can be no doubt that the great mass of the people transferred to the calf-priests what had been appointed for the Levitical priests, the God-fearing brought their first-fruits to the extraordinary representatives of the priests appointed by God,—the prophets and their disciples. In the time of the famine there came, among others, a man from Baal-shalisha,—a place otherwise unknown,—bringing twenty loaves of bread to the prophetic school at Gilgal. Besides this, on the foundation of Lev. ii. 14, xxiii. 14, he brought a bag full of carmel,— a word of uncertain meaning,—according to some, "green ears." These are roasted by fire in the East, and then eaten, which is the case in Egypt, as modern travellers attest. Elisha commands that this food be given to the famishing disciples of the prophets to eat. "What! should I set this before an hundred men?" his servant replies. The school of the prophets had greatly increased, owing to the presence of Elisha. Twenty loaves were a small thing for a hundred men; for Eastern loaves are only the size of a plate and the thickness of a finger; comp. Korte's *Travels*, p. 458. But Elisha foretells in faith that all shall be satisfied, and a remnant be left over. His word was fulfilled,—a prefiguration of the similar but far greater miracle of Christ. In both narratives, and also in that of the lost axe, which has erroneously been regarded as an actual miracle, (the extraordinary part of the thing was, that the prophet should have hit the handle of the axe at the first stroke of the stick, thus raising the iron with the wood), the life of the disciples of the prophets appears as one of great poverty,—as a life of renunciation and want,—and we can well conceive that it was necessary for God to reveal Himself to them in a very powerful way, if they were to give up all earthly things for His sake.

With reference to the healing of Naaman the Syrian, related in 2 Kings v., we have only a few remarks to make. We there have the story of the cure of the leprosy of Naaman the Syrian captain, who had acquired great influence with the king of Syria, owing to the skilful discharge of his office. He was indeed afflicted with leprosy, but had nevertheless retained his post, for the laws of separation on account of leprosy were not so strict among the Syrians as in Israel. By an Israelitish prisoner who dwelt in his house, his attention was directed to Elisha as the only one who was in a position to free him from his most irksome malady. The king probably thought that the prophets were subject to the king of Israel, just as his own venal idolatrous priests were subservient to him. To specify more definitely the way in which the cure was to be effected, was beneath his dignity, he thought. Hence Joram thought that the object in demanding from him what he was not in a position to render, was nothing less than to find a pretext for war. His unbelief made him forget the power of the Lord, which, as he himself had already experienced, was able to effect that which was impossible to man. He was greatly perplexed. Owing to these circumstances, under the guidance of God the healing of the Syrian produced a powerful impression not only on Naaman and his countrymen, but also on the king of Israel himself and his people, making them conscious of the infinite distance which separated their God from the dead idols of the heathen, and constraining them to worship him with grateful hearts. Elisha sends word to the king to send the Syrian to him, that he may know that there is a prophet in Israel. These words give the highest object of the miraculous cure. In every case when the heathen either mocked the true God, or sought His aid, He revealed His power. In this respect the character of God remains the same throughout all centuries, as a proof that He is a true historical God, and not the mere invention of fancy. Elisha does not suffer Naaman to come into his presence, but tells him through his servant what he is to do. Many have attributed this conduct to false motives. It was undoubtedly intended to humiliate the Syrian, who prided himself on his dignity, and could not yet have understood the humility of Elisha; while asserting his dignity as a servant of the true God, Elisha at the same time pointed him to the reverence due to God on his part also. The means which Elisha prescribes to Naaman for his bodily cure, form an excellent representation of those which true religion affords for spiritual purification. They are as simple as possible, dispensing with all appearance of inherent power, that the divine power may be the more strikingly manifested. Naaman's first words give us a true picture of the mind of the natural man. The means which the prophet prescribes to Naaman are too simple for him: he himself has scarcely any part in them; and the prophet will not even be present on their application. Thus so far all human instrumentality is excluded; and yet the natural man still places his hope on it, and in his heart ascribes to it the greatest part of the result, though confessing with his mouth that he expects everything from God alone. The observation of Naaman's servant is quite true: had the prophet told him to do some great thing, he would have done it at once. We here see the origin of the opposition of the natural man to the doctrine of the atonement. "Wash and be clean," is just as incomprehensible and offensive to the natural man in a spiritual aspect as it is here in a corporeal aspect. Yet Naaman at last follows the command of the prophet, and at once experiences the rich blessing which follows his obedience. He now wishes to give Elisha the rich presents which he had brought with him for this purpose. But Elisha refuses them, which seems strange at the first glance. We have many other examples showing that the prophets did receive presents; it even appears that the schools of the prophets were entirely supported by free-will offerings. But there can be no doubt that these gifts were only taken from those to whom the prophets stood in a pastoral relation. The prophet could accept nothing from the stranger without weakening the effect of that which had happened, on the still unstable mind of Naaman, and on his countrymen. At the same time, Naaman's further conversation with the prophet shows that he did not stop at the gift, as is generally the case, but raised himself to the giver, in whom, by an illumination from God Himself, he recognised not one deity among many, endowed with special power, in accordance with the polytheistic notion, but the only true God; but this new light had not yet expelled all darkness of perception and will. He wishes to take a few loads of earth from Canaan, for the purpose of building an altar with it, where he might sacrifice to the true God. An element of superstition, though innocent, is here unmistakeable. Naaman goes on to say that on one point he must ask the forbearance of the Lord. When accompanying the king in his official capacity to the temple of the idol Rimmon, he cannot avoid bowing down with him before this idol. Many—for example, Buddeus—have endeavoured to set aside this inconvenient sense by a forced interpretation. Others, as Michaelis, maintain that Naaman was obliged to bow down, not to worship the idol, but from respect to the king, who was most grossly insulted if any one remained standing beside him while he was prostrate on the ground. But this latter argument plainly proves nothing. It might indeed be Naaman's duty to bow down with the king as long as he retained his office; but why could he not give up his office for the sake of God? He is in some measure excused, though not justified, on the supposition that he zealously and assiduously made known his faith in the one true God, and his complete renunciation of all idols, so that at least the greater number of those who saw him bow down knew that he did it only for the sake of the king, and not for the sake of the idols. In this case his taking part in the ceremonies could only in an imperfect sense be called the profession of a cause which he despised in his heart. Elisha's conduct on this occasion is remarkable. He dismisses Naaman with the words, "Go in peace." By many these words have erroneously been regarded as conceding the points referred to by Naaman, not only that just mentioned, but also his desire to take away earth from the holy land for the building of an altar for the Lord in Syria. The words are only the customary formula of departure, here spoken with emphasis and with their original meaning, and certainly show that on the whole Naaman was in the right way, and that his attitude of heart pleased the prophet. The prophet designedly refrains from entering into the two points. With respect to the former, Naaman had not asked his permission, nor made the matter dependent on his decision. He had absolutely stated that the Lord must pardon him in this matter, since it could not be otherwise. Elisha had too much wisdom not to see that by insisting on the discontinuance of these outward acts he might have done more harm than good, perhaps even have destroyed the work which had been begun; the refusal of the presents shows that there is no question except of a faith still future. He therefore left him to the guidance of the Lord, who alone was able to lead him on in spirit, but took care not to utter a single word in justification of his weakness. The favour extended to the heathen was followed by another remarkable prefiguration of the future,— the punishment of a member of the covenant-nation, and that of one who, by virtue of his constant intercourse with the prophet, stood in a near relation to God. Gehazi, the servant of Elisha, who held the same relation towards his master as Elisha had formerly held towards Elijah, both carnally and spiritually, as the history of the Shunammite shows, was led away by avarice to hasten after Naaman, and, under a false pretext, in the name of Elisha, to ask a portion of the possessions which his master had rejected. Avarice here truly showed itself to be the root of all evil. It led him into falsehood,—first towards Naaman, and then towards his own master. It stifled all higher considerations; for if he had yielded to these, he would have hesitated to destroy the work of God, so far as it lay in his power. Naaman's faith clung to the instrument which God had employed as a means of calling it forth. But what must he think of this instrument, when he, who had shown himself so disinterested in his presence, now sent after him, and on a suspicious pretext yet demanded his reward? The punishment which fell upon Gehazi was not simply just, it was necessary for the sake of the cause. The news of it must soon spread abroad in every direction, and would reach even Naaman. The leprosy with which Gehazi was afflicted was a far heavier calamity for him than it had been for Naaman. For the latter, it was only of the same nature as any other sickness. It was evident that among the Syrians no ignominy was attached to leprosy, from the circumstance that Naaman held his high dignity afterwards as well as before, continuing to live in the society of his wife and children, and visiting the temple of the god Rimmon. It was quite different with leprosy in Israel. By the law, it was appointed to be a type of sin, and the leper was treated as the actual sin, being thrust out from society. And the fact that leprosy was by law an image of sin, explains why the punishment of leprosy was inflicted on Gehazi. The image of sin is best adapted to reflect it: the sinner before God is in this way revealed as a sinner before man, before whom he must bear the image of sin. This punishment was the more appropriate in this case, since Gehazi had played the hypocrite, concealing his sin under the semblance of piety. God now made it manifest before the eyes of all the world.

After a short interruption, the war with the Syrians began again. Elisha had here another opportunity of convincing the king and the nation of the deity of the Lord, and of the divinity of his own mission. The magnanimity shown to the captive Syrians, and at the same time the divine co-operation so apparent in the matter, induced Ben-hadad, the Syrian king, to suspend hostilities for a time. Soon, however, these motives lost their power. Ben-hadad again invaded Israel with a large army, and besieged Samaria. But palpable punishment was destined to overtake nation and king, because all their previous experience had failed to bring forth in them the true fruits of repentance; they had contented themselves with mere admiration of the divine power and external obedience to the prophets, and had not felt themselves constrained to seek help in their spiritual need, which is the object of all temporal aid. The famine reached its greatest height in the city. Even kinds of food which were forbidden in the law, and were unclean according to it, could only be had for a high price. An ass's head was sold for eighty pieces of silver, and a small measure of dove's dung for five pieces of silver. The latter designation ought perhaps to be taken figuratively, as the name of a coarse kind of food unknown to us, similar to that which bears the same name among the Arabs; comp. Bochart, *Hieroz.* ii. 1. 1, chap. 7. Ewald and Thenius, indeed, hold to the literal meaning. "If the excrement of snipe can be eaten as a luxury," the latter remarks, "necessity might readily permit the use of dove's dung." Experience alone can decide, and the defenders of this view ought to have made the experiment. Scenes of horror occurred such as Moses had foretold as a divine judgment on the transgressors of the law, Deut. xxviii. 53 ff., and were afterwards repeated when Jerusalem was besieged by the Chaldeans, comp. Lam. iv. 10, and again by the Romans. But when the need was greatest, divine help appeared.

Not long afterwards, Elisha repaired to Damascus, or to the neighbourhood of this town. Notwithstanding the importance of the services which Elisha had rendered to Jehoram, no lasting impression had been made on prince and people. Jehoram, though not personally attached to heathendom, yet suffered it to pursue its course, and his mother Jezebel retained great influence; comp. 2 Kings x. 13, ix. 30. It was God's design soon to make a reckoning with nation and king. Elijah had been commanded by God to anoint Hazael, a chief servant of the king of Syria, as king over Damascus, *i.e.* to declare solemnly that by divine decree he was appointed to this dignity. Elijah had left the carrying out of this command to Elisha, who now received the divine instructions that the time for it was come. This interference in the affairs of a foreign country by a prophet who was only designed to be active among his own people, seems strange at the first glance. But the strangeness disappears on closer consideration. It becomes evident that the interference of the prophet stands in the closest relation to the kingdom of Israel. Hazael was destined to be a fearful instrument for the accomplishment of the divine revenge on Israel. If these judgments were to attain their object,—if they were to lead the nation to repentance,—it was necessary that they should be recognised as such, and should not be regarded as accidental effects of the sin of the human instrument. This mode of consideration was excluded by the fact that the divine decree of the exaltation of Hazael to the Syrian throne was pronounced by the prophet: all that happened by his instrumentality must now appear as foreordained by God. The sorrows which He inflicted upon Israel formed an argument not against, but in favour of His deity. We have already seen that the proclamation of such a divine decree does not justify the human deed, which is condemned by the law of God; and even Hazael did not on this account acquire the smallest right to murder his lord and king. It is a different thing when the Lord commands something to be done by His prophets, and when he simply makes known that it will happen. At that very time Ben-hadad lay sick. He had already had opportunity enough to learn to know the prophet as such; hence he no sooner heard of his arrival than he sent a messenger to him —by God's dispensation Hazael himself—to ask whether he would recover. The rich presents destined for the prophet, in accordance with the custom of the East, were borne by a multitude of beasts of burden quite disproportionate to their magnitude, in order to make them appear still greater than they were in reality. According to another view, the words "forty camels' burden" only indicate the value of what was sent,—the quantity of corn carried by a camel being taken as the measure. The answer of Elisha has given rise to many discussions. In 2 Kings viii. 10 we find two different readings. The reading of the text is, "Go, say unto him, Thou canst not recover: howbeit the Lord hath showed me that he shall surely die." The marginal reading is, "Go, say unto him, Thou shalt live." Instead of the לא, "not," of the text, the margin has לו, "to him." If the reading of the text be taken as correct, no difficulty exists. Moreover, this alone has external authority in its favour. The marginal readings are only conjectures *ex ingenio*; the textual readings so strongly confirm what is in the MS., that the Masoretes did not venture to insert their "emendations" or deteriorations in the text. The marginal reading presents this difficulty: it makes the prophet charge Hazael with a lie,— a supposition which we cannot accept. The way in which the marginal reading originated is easily explained. It was thought that the prophet must necessarily have charged Hazael with the same message which he delivered to the king. Elisha then makes known to Hazael his future dignity, and at the same time with deep sorrow foretells the misery which he will bring upon Israel. Hazael feigns astonishment, in order not to betray himself, though he had no doubt conceived the plan long before, and prepared everything for its accomplishment. By his lying declaration he makes Ben-hadad glad with the certain prospect of recovery.

On the very day following he carried out his murderous intent, in such a way that the corpse of the king showed no external marks of violence or injury. He dipped the net, or perhaps a cloth (the meaning of the expression is uncertain), which is used in the East during sleep as a protection against mosquitoes and other insects, in water, so that no fresh air could penetrate it, and spread it over the sleeping king, so that he was suffocated.

We must now give a brief summary of the parallel history of the kings of Judah, because it is closely connected with that of Israel. In 2 Kings viii. 16 we read that Jehoram became king over Judah in the fifth year of Joram of Israel. This does not imply, as the verse itself shows, that Jehoshaphat was then already dead. He lived for two years afterwards. But he then transferred the greater part of the government to Jehoram, whom, according to chap. i. 17, he had taken as co-regent several years before. In the acts of Jehoram we soon perceive the injurious effects of the union of Ahab with the Phenician Jezebel, whose equally infamous daughter Athaliah had been married by Jehoram. The Mosaic prohibition against marrying heathen wives, which is still binding in spirit on the Church of God, here receives its justification. Michaelis says very justly: "In this respect Tyrian, Israelitish, and Jewish history coincide. The spirit which then possessed Tyre, together with much misfortune, was brought into Israelitish history by marriage. The king of Tyre contemporary with Jehoram is Pygmalion, who murdered the husband of his sister Dido, merely to gain possession of his treasures. So also, according to 2 Chron. xxi., after the death of Jehoshaphat, Jehoram slew all his brothers, for no other reason, as it appears, than to have the treasures which his father had bequeathed to them. As idolatry had formerly been openly introduced into Israel at the instigation of Jezebel, so it was now in Judah at the instigation of Athaliah." Here also apostasy was followed by divine judgments. The first of these was the revolt of the Idumeans, whose king had previously been a vassal of the Jewish kings. Faithfulness towards the Lord was the principle of the Israelitish nationality; the necessary consequence of the apostasy was weakness within and feebleness without. In God alone lay the strength of Israel. Soon afterwards Jehoram received a prediction of still heavier misfortune by a writing in the hand of Elijah. This appears strange at the first glance, since Elijah had already been dead for some time. Among the various attempts which have been made to solve this problem, some of which are absurd enough, two only deserve notice. According to one of these, the thing which was accomplished by Elisha is here attributed to Elijah. This explanation loses the forced character which it bears at first sight, when we take into consideration what has already been said respecting Elisha's relation of dependence towards Elijah, whose spirit was bestowed upon him. But there is another view which has still greater probability in its favour. According to 1 Kings xix., Elijah had foreseen the elevation of Jehu to the throne of Israel, and the impending destruction by his instrumentality of the family of Ahab; also the accession of Hazael to the throne, and the heavy misfortunes inflicted on the Israelitish kingdom through him. If in this case the future were revealed to him, the greatest of all the prophets of the old covenant, why might it not also have been revealed to him that Jehoram, who came to the throne about four years after his death, and already before it had allied himself with the infamous Athaliah, would draw down upon himself the judgments of the Lord by grievous sin? This prophecy, which he had written down and given to Elisha, was at the proper time sent by the latter to the king of Judah, and was soon afterwards fulfilled. The Philistines, in alliance with Arab Bedouins, entered the land and fell upon the camp of the Judaites, where Joram was with his wives and children and a part of his treasures. All his sons, with the exception of the youngest, Jehoahaz, or, by transposition, Azariah, were slain. This was retribution for what he had done to his brothers. Jehoram himself died in the eighth year of his reign of a dreadful disease. The angry people would not suffer him to be buried in the royal sepulchre. The solemnities usual on the burial of kings were omitted. His son Ahaziah ascended the throne at the age of twenty-two years; comp. 2 Kings viii. 26. It is plainly a mistake of the copyist when 2 Chron. xxii. 2 represents him as forty-two years of age, since it is stated immediately before that his father died at forty years of age. He was completely under the influence of his ungodly mother Athaliah. An important crisis took place at this time. In both kingdoms heathenism, favoured by royalty, threatened to supplant the true religion. It is a striking example of divine retribution, that since Ahaziah had taken part in the crime of the family of Ahab, with which he had so closely allied himself, so too he was involved in their destruction, after having reigned for one year. This was brought about by Jehu, the captain of the host, who slew the king of Israel, Jezebel, and all the house of Ahab, and afterwards the king of Judah, who was on a visit to the king of Israel, together with a whole company of princes of the royal house of Judah whom he encountered on their way to the Israelitish court. Various judgments have been passed on this act of Jehu's. The following is the correct view: The family of Ahab had wickedly sought to destroy the foundation of the kingdom of God in Israel; they had not only continued the worship of calves, but had also introduced idolatry; from 2 Kings chap. x. we see that in the latter days of Jehoram the service of Baal, which had been suppressed for a time by Elijah, now reasserted itself in the kingdom of Israel with all its horrors. They had persecuted and slain the prophets and other servants of the true God. For this, by the law of retribution, destruction was to overtake them, otherwise the threats of Moses in Deut. xxviii., and in so many other passages, would have been falsified. But if any one had undertaken to destroy the house of Ahab with his own hand, however well-merited the destruction may have been, yet he who had been the cause of it would have incurred grievous sin, and have been an object of the divine wrath. Here, however, the case was very different. Two prophets, who proved their divine mission in a way excluding all doubt and all abuse of their example, had pronounced the divine sentence of punishment on the house of Ahab, and empowered Jehu to execute it. This was done in order that the punishment might be openly manifested as such,—that every one might recognise in Jehu only a servant of divine righteousness, and in that which befell the family of Ahab a prophecy of their own fate if they would incur similar guilt. If Jehu's act, however, were to be perfectly just, it was not sufficient that it should be in external harmony with the divine command, it was necessary that internally also he should be guided by no other motive, that he should not be influenced by human ambition and cruelty. This was nevertheless the case. The honour of God served him for a veil.

We go on to remark that the condition of Israel, which left the pious mind in a state of dissatisfaction, called forth peculiar separatistic phenomena. Among these are the Rechabites mentioned in 2 Kings x. 15–23, and in Jer. xxxv. Their founder was Jonathan the son of Rechab, contemporary with Jehu, and associated with him against the worship of Baal. They strictly refrained from all participation in civil and ecclesiastical fellowship, led a solitary life in the wilderness, and for food limited themselves to its productions. From the Nazarites, whose continuance in the ten tribes appears from Amos ii. 11 ff., they borrowed the principle of total abstinence from wine and all intoxicating drinks. In them Christian asceticism has an Old Testament type. We see from Jeremiah that it still continued in the time of the Babylonian exile.

§ 6.

JEHU, JEHOAHAZ, JEHOASH, JEROBOAM II., AND ZECHA-
RIAH,—THE FIVE KINGS OF THE DYNASTY OF JEHU,
—IN THE KINGDOM OF ISRAEL.—JOASH, AMAZIAH,
UZZIAH, IN THE KINGDOM OF JUDAH.

One of Jehu's first acts after he came to the throne was one of murder, perpetrated on the servants of Baal. With respect to this deed the same thing holds good that we have already said regarding the acts by which Jehu made his way to the throne. Objectively considered, it was just, for by the law idolatry was punishable with death. But we are led to form a different judgment when we examine into the subjective motives of Jehu, even apart from the unjustifiable stratagem. These motives seem to have been almost exclusively selfish. The servants of Baal were by every interest attached to the house of Ahab. By their destruction Jehu hoped to bring over to his side the far more numerous party of the adherents to the worship which had formerly been legally introduced into the kingdom of Israel. This view is based not solely on the universally reprehensible character of Jehu, but also specially on the circumstance that he allowed the continuance of calf-worship. This shows that he used religion only as a means to his end. If his zeal had been truly pious, he would have destroyed the illegal calf-worship. But he feared by this means to break down the wall of separation between the kingdom of Israel and the kingdom of Judah, and at the same time to make enemies of the followers of calf-worship. As a punishment for this reprehensible frame of mind, it was foretold that his family would retain the throne only to the fourth member, and even during his lifetime the kingdom of Israel was very much oppressed and weakened by the Syrians under Hazael. He died, after having reigned for a period of twenty-eight years. When the wicked Athaliah received news of the death of her son Ahaziah, in the kingdom of Judah, her ambition, which amounted almost to madness, led her to slay the royal princes and take possession of the government. Yet Jehosheba, a

sister of Ahaziah, probably by another mother, married to
the high priest Jehoiada, had succeeded in keeping Joash,
a very young son of Ahaziah, from her murderous hands,
and concealed him in an apartment adjoining the temple.
After Athaliah had ruled over the kingdom for six years,
Joash, the lawful heir to the throne, whom the people followed
with enthusiasm, with whose preservation the fulfilment
of the promise made to David was associated, was raised to
supreme authority. "The party inclined to heathenism,"
Ewald remarks, "which had been formed in Jerusalem
during the short supremacy of the two former kings, may
have supported Athaliah, as well as the faithful followers of
the house of Omri who might fly to her in Jerusalem when
persecuted in the kingdom of the ten tribes. But in the
kingdom of Judah, since the days of Asa and Jehoshaphat,
the attachment to the old religion had become too powerful,
and the love to David's house could not long be suppressed.
The foreign element which had been introduced by Jehoshaphat's
close connection with the house of Omri, was thrust
out." Joash was seven years of age when he ascended the
throne, and remained for a considerable time under the influence
of the high priest Jehoiada, even after he was grown
up, and, while this priest lived, proved himself a God-fearing
ruler. He showed great zeal in the restoration of the
temple, which, according to 2 Chron. xxiv. 7, had not only
been neglected, but intentionally destroyed. After the death
of Jehoiada a great change took place. It became apparent
that the piety of the king had been without independent
basis,—that he had only followed Jehoiada. To the worldly-
minded higher nobility the supremacy of the priesthood, as
it may be called, had always been an abomination. Yet
while Jehoiada lived they had not ventured to make any
revolt; but after his death, according to 2 Chron. xxiv. 17,
they had turned to the king with a request that he would
remove the prohibitions against idolatry and proclaim universal
freedom of religion. The king yielded, and soon the
disorder which had existed under Ahaziah and Athaliah
again prevailed. As invariably happened in time of need,
the Lord raised up prophets, who reproved the people

for their sin, and announced the punishments which threatened them. By the commandment of Joash, Zechariah, the most prominent among them, the son of his fatherly teacher Jehoiada, was slain, because the king's conscience testified too loudly to the truth of his censure. While dying, he continued to predict the closely-impending judgments The instrument of their accomplishment was the army of the Syrian Hazael, which inflicted a severe defeat on the stronger Judaite army,—Joash being slain by some of his own servants, after having reigned for forty years. His son Amaziah succeeded to the throne. In the kingdom of Israel, in the twenty-third year of Joash king of Judah, Jehoahaz ascended the throne. Of him little is related of any consequence. During his reign the Syrians brought the kingdom to the brink of the abyss. But its allotted time had not yet run out. The weak beginnings of repentance in king and nation were followed by deliverance.

After having reigned for seven years, Jehoahaz was succeeded by his son Joash, under whom Elisha died at an advanced age. The news of the mortal illness of the prophet deeply affected the king, though not at other times piously disposed. He thought he must now necessarily succumb to the dangers which threatened him on the part of the Syrians, who were again making preparations for war. The Lord graciously accepted even this weak beginning of faith, and comforted the king by a favourable promise given through the prophet. The prophet connected this promise with a symbolical action. The king was to shoot an arrow from the window towards the direction of the Syrian kingdom. This arrow, the prophet says, is a symbol of the complete destruction which thou shalt bring upon the Syrians. He then tells the king to take the remaining arrows and shoot them into the earth. The king complies, but ceases after having shot three arrows. By this means he betrayed his want of faith, or rather the weakness of his faith. He knew from what had gone before that the shooting of an arrow signified a victory over the Syrians. Hence he could have had no other reason for ceasing so soon, than doubt as to whether the Lord could do more than what was already promised. Three victories over so mighty an army strike him as something so great, that he scarcely believes the Lord sufficiently powerful to grant it. With justice, therefore, the prophet is angry; with justice he accuses him of having deprived himself of complete victory over the Syrian kingdom by the want of faith which betrayed itself in this outward act. King and people—the people are not to be regarded as in opposition to the king, but as represented in him—thus saw how faith was the only means of salvation, want of faith the sole cause of their misfortune. The promise of Elisha with respect to the Syrians was accurately fulfilled. Thrice conquered, they were obliged to restore the cities which they had wrested from the Israelites under the former reign.

In the kingdom of Judah Amaziah appeared at first in a favourable light. His first care was to put to death the murderers of his father. In 2 Kings xiv. 6 it is expressly stated that he spared their children on account of the law. At that time, therefore, the word of God had more influence over him than the oriental custom, the result of carnal disposition, arising on the one hand from a spirit of revenge, and on the other from timidity. Afterwards, however, he was guilty of great crimes, in consequence of which the judgments of the Lord overtook him and his people. He began a war against the Idumeans, who, as already related, had revolted under Joram, without his having been successful in reducing them to subjection again. The Idumeans sustained a great defeat in the Valley of Salt, at the extreme end of the Dead Sea, and the victorious army of Judah succeeded in penetrating to their capital, Sela or Petra. This battle very much weakened the power of the Idumeans, and it was long before they recovered themselves. From Amos ii. 1-3, it seems to follow that the king of the Idumeans lost his life on this occasion, his corpse becoming an object of revenge for the Moabites, on account of the former participation of the Edomite in the Moabite expedition. Incidentally, however, this war led to the fall of Amaziah. He had captured several Edomite idols, and to these, it is related in Chronicles, he paid divine honour. This is explained on the assumption that he was infected by heathen ideas. Doubtless he looked upon Jehovah as the supreme God, and could not do otherwise, since he had just experienced His superiority over the Edomite idols. Nevertheless he regarded the latter as having a real existence, and thought that by showing honour to them as well as Jehovah, he would bring them over to his side, and thus best prevent their rendering assistance to their oppressed people, and making it more difficult for him to keep them to their allegiance. It was therefore sheer unbelief which prompted this mode of action; and, being blamed for it by a prophet, he threatened him with death. The prophet declared that the Lord would punish him, and the prediction was speedily fulfilled. The victory over the Idumeans had in every respect exercised a most injurious influence on the king, who was not sufficiently strong in spirit to be able to bear good fortune. It had led him to indulge in foolish arrogance and pride. On an empty pretext, he declared war against Joash the king of Israel, who had become very powerful through his conquest over the Syrians. Joash warned him in vain. He then anticipated him, and made war in the territory of Judah. At Bethshemesh the Judaites suffered a great defeat. Jerusalem was taken, the treasures of the king and of the temple were carried away, and a portion of the wall broken down, in order to give free access to the Israelites. Joash died soon afterwards; Amaziah survived him for fifteen years. It seems, however, that the angry people dethroned him immediately after the taking of Jerusalem, in consequence of which he was obliged to flee to Lachish, a city of Judah. The government was then carried on in the name of his son Uzziah; and Amaziah, making a final attempt to recover it, was slain. In favour of this we have 2 Chron. xxv. 27, where we read that from the time when Amaziah turned away from following the Lord, they made a conspiracy against him in Jerusalem; so also 2 Kings xiv. 19.

In the books of the Kings the successor of Amaziah is called Azariah; but in Chronicles, Isaiah, and Zechariah he appears under the name of Uzziah. This is explicable from the circumstance that the names of oriental kings were more *appellativa* than *propria*, and hence others, having the same meaning, were frequently substituted for them. Under the long reign of Uzziah (he was sixteen years of age when he came to the throne, and reigned for twenty-five years), the kingdom of Judah rose to great prosperity and power,—a consequence of the pious disposition of the king. But the nation was not able to bear its prosperity, and sank into luxury and immorality, though there still remained a considerable number who feared God in spirit and in truth. Externally the fear of God prevailed almost universally under Uzziah. This God-fearing community attached itself to the prophets, who continued to come forward more and more powerfully and numerously from the time of Uzziah, as the great divine judgments in the kingdom of Judah approached nearer to their consummation. Uzziah was under the spiritual guidance of the prophet Zechariah; but when Zechariah died, and he was thus left to himself, he was unable to bear his prosperity. Not satisfied with the kingly dignity, arrogance led him to aspire to the priestly dignity also. This could only happen by means of a gross violation of the Mosaic constitution. And when the king was guilty of this, he was smitten with the punishment of leprosy. He now lost his own dignity, as a retribution for having striven after that which did not belong to him. For, being a leper, he could not associate with any one, but was obliged to dwell in a house apart; hence he could not carry on the government, which fell to his son Jotham, who held it in the name of his father. What makes the reign of Uzziah specially remarkable, is the fact that the first beginnings of prophetic authorship belong to it,—a circumstance which is by no means accidental, but is due to the fact that from this period prophetic prediction found richer material. We shall readily be convinced of this, if we consider the subjects with which prophecy occupies itself in Isaiah: for example, Isaiah appeared in the latter days of Uzziah; as early predecessors he had the three prophets, Hosea, Amos, and Jonah, in the kingdom of the ten tribes, and also Joel and Obadiah, the two prophets of Judah.

The kingdom of Israel was destined to rise once more to

brilliant supremacy, then to sink down for ever. Jeroboam II., the son of Joash, enlarged it to the same extent which it had had at the time of the separation under Jeroboam I. But with the death of Jeroboam the kingdom of Israel advanced towards destruction with rapid strides. Under his long reign, which was not characterized by a spirit of piety, immorality and apostasy from the Lord prevailed more and more. Bloody internal dissensions prepared the way for ruin, which was finally accomplished by the Assyrians. Ewald says: "The germs of internal dissolution and destruction, which lay hid in the kingdom from its foundation, broke forth the more rapidly and unchecked owing to the long period of undisturbed prosperity; and the rising supremacy of the Assyrians found it the more easy to destroy a kingdom which from the begining had possessed no healthy life." The death of Jeroboam, which took place after a reign of forty-two years, was followed by an interregnum of twelve years. Finally, his son Zechariah was established on the throne by his adherents; but, after a wicked reign of six months, he was slain by Shallum, and thus the prophecy was fulfilled that the family of Jehu should occupy the throne only to the fourth member. God had taken care that the nation should know the interpretation of its fate. The predictions of the two prophets,—viz. Amos, who was sent out of Judah into the kingdom of the ten tribes under Jeroboam, but was soon driven thence, and Hosea, who appeared towards the close of the reign of Jeroboam, and preached almost to the end of the kingdom of the ten tribes,—pointed unmistakeably to the perverted foundations of this kingdom, rebuked its apostasy, and announced the impending judgments—the fall of the house of Jehu, and the complete overthrow of the kingdom of the ten tribes.

§ 7.

HISTORY OF THE KINGDOM OF ISRAEL TO THE TIME OF ITS COMPLETE DISSOLUTION.

Shallum maintained the throne, to which he had made

his way by murder, only for a month. He was slain by Menahem, a general, who usurped the reins of government. Under his reign the Assyrians first marched into the Israelitish kingdom, and the king was obliged to buy them off by a heavy tribute. Our first historical knowledge of the Assyrians dates from this period, when they begin to enter into Israelitish history. There can be no doubt that a powerful Assyrian kingdom existed in very early times. This is equally confirmed by biblical, Egyptian, and Greek accounts. With regard to the first, according to Gen. ii. 14, the Euphrates flows "towards the east of Assyria." This presupposes that at the time of its composition an Assyrian monarchy was already in existence; for it is impossible to predicate of Assyria in the narrower sense that it lay west of the Euphrates. Moreover, the Assyrians appear in Balaam's last prophecy as one of the most important peoples of Asia, who should extend their conquests in the future as far as the Mediterranean Sea. On the Egyptian monuments the Assyrians, under the name Shari, appear as already engaged in war with the Egyptians, under the reign of the great Raamses, so that even at that early time they must have possessed that tendency towards the west which afterwards brought them into violent and lengthened conflict with the Egyptians. The Greek accounts, notwithstanding their prevailing unhistorical character, yet lead to the conclusion that a primitive Assyrian kingdom did exist. But not only is this older Assyrian kingdom little known in history, but it seems also that in the post-Mosaic time it had lost much of its importance. In the time of which we now treat, the Assyrian kingdom received a new impulse. Favoured by the wars of the Syrians, Israelites, and Judaites among themselves, it succeeded in gaining supremacy over western Asia. This it maintained, yet without being able to swallow up Judea altogether, till it was supplanted by the Chaldeans, who founded a new world-empire, making Babylon, which had till then been subject to the Assyrians, their capital. The motive which led the Assyrians and Chaldeans to turn their eyes constantly to Israel and Judah, is shown by the following words of Schlosser, *Universal*

Historical Survey of the History of the Old World, part i. p. 213 : "From this time Palestine became the battle-field of the two powers, who marched against each other from the Euphrates and Tigris, and from the Nile, with immense armies. Whoever had occupied Palestine was certain of his retreat, for all marches necessarily led through it." The following is the order of the Assyrian kings mentioned in Scripture : Pul, to whom Menahem was tributary, 773 B.C.; Tiglath-pileser, about 740; Shalmaneser, about 720 ; Sennacherib, about 714 ; and Asarhaddon. Sargon also is frequently put between Tiglath-pileser and Shalmaneser, on the authority of Isa. xx. 1. But an examination of Assyrian monuments has led to the conclusion that this Sargon was identical with Shalmaneser. He here appears under the name Sargina, and the same acts are attributed to him which Holy Scripture attributes to Shalmaneser; comp. Niebuhr, *The History of Assyria and Babylonia*, p. 160. " The reign of Sargina," he says, "whom the Jews called Shalmaneser, was very brilliant, and under him the kingdom of Nineveh stood on the highest summit of its power after its restoration and before its fall." We meet with the same king in Hos. x. 14 under the abbreviated name Shalman.

After a reign of ten years, in the fiftieth year of Azariah, Menahem was succeeded by his son Pekahiah, who was slain, however, after having reigned for two years, by one of his captains, Pekah the son of Remaliah. Pekah reigned for a period of twenty years. Of his alliance with Rezin, the Syrian king, we shall speak hereafter. One consequence of this alliance was the carrying away captive by the Assyrians of a portion of the two and a half tribes beyond the Jordan. Ahaz had appealed to the Assyrians for help, and in the same campaign they conquered Damascus also. This was only the prelude to the total destruction of the Israelitish kingdom. Pekah was slain by Hoshea, the last king of Israel, who reigned for nine years. Hoshea, though otherwise comparatively worthless, at least distinguished himself above his predecessors by the circumstance that he gave his subjects freedom to make pilgrimages to Jerusalem. He was made tributary by Shalmaneser, but sought to throw off his dependence by entering into a treaty with the king of Egypt, the natural enemy of the Assyrian, as afterwards of the Babylonian kingdom. This gave rise to a new expedition on the part of Shalmaneser, in which Samaria was conquered after a siege of three years. The Assyrians now followed the universal policy by which Asiatic conquerors sought to render themselves secure in the possession of conquered territory. They led away all the Israelites of whom they could gain possession into exile in Assyria and the countries subject to them. The pain which Judah felt on the captivity of the ten tribes found its expression in Ps. lxxvii. and lxxx., psalms which bear remarkable witness to the catholic spirit which has at all times pervaded the Church of God. Probably the king of Assyria intended from the beginning to people the country by a new colony, and it is uncertain what caused the execution of this project to be deferred until the reign of Asarhaddon, his second successor. In the interval, the Israelites who had concealed themselves in forests and caves, or had fled to neighbouring countries, reassembled and occupied the unappropriated land, whose desolation and depopulation occasioned a great increase of beasts of prey in it. It was not until Asarhaddon colonized the country from Babylonia, Syria, and other lands, on which occasion, in all probability, the remnant of the old inhabitants were also led away captive, that the Israelitish kingdom entirely ceased to exist. Asarhaddon is the Israelitish name of the king; in Ezra iv. 10 the Aramæan colonists call him by another name, Asnapper, which, however, makes no difficulty, since the oriental kings had several names or titles. At first the new heathen colonists established their idolatry in the land, but soon resolved to worship Jehovah also, the former God of the country, as one among many; and at a later period they entirely abandoned the worship of idols, but without ever being able altogether to renounce their heathen nature. These heathen colonists, covered with a thin Israelitish varnish, are either called *Cuthites*, after the former dwelling-place of some of their number—Cutha was a town in the vicinity of Babylon—or *Samaritans*, after their later habitation. Between them and the Judaites there was irreconcilable enmity, because the Judaites neither would nor could allow their claim to an independent part in the kingdom of God.

§ 8.

JUDEA UNDER JOTHAM, AHAZ, HEZEKIAH.

With regard to Jotham's reign there is little to be said. In it the conditions were in every respect the same as they had been under Uzziah. After having reigned for sixteen years, Jotham was succeeded by Ahaz, the worst among all the rulers of the kingdom of Judah. He combined the worship of Jehovah with idolatry, and was so fanatical in the latter, that he offered up one of his sons to Moloch. In all probability Ahaz perpetrated this horror when he was placed in the utmost extremity by the expedition of the Syrians and Israelites. Rezin king of Syria, and Pekah king of Israel, had already, in the latter days of Jotham, entered into an alliance against Judah; but it was only in the first years of the reign of Ahaz that they began to carry out their plan, which was destined to serve as a just judgment on this king. He thought he could only prevent the destruction of the whole kingdom by seeking help from the Assyrians, to whom accordingly he sent great presents. Isaiah, who directed him to the Lord as the sole helper, and warned him against alliance with the Assyrians, found no hearing. He had to repent his unbelief bitterly. He sustained a great defeat from Rezin and Pekah. Probably the retreat of these kings was caused by fear of Tiglath-pileser king of Assyria, who had promised to come to the assistance of Ahaz, and did really advance with his army a short time afterwards, occupying Damascus, the capital of Syria, and leading away captive a considerable number of the inhabitants of the kingdom of the ten tribes. But Ahaz was obliged to purchase this help at a great sacrifice. Even at that time he was heavily oppressed by the Assyrians, comp.

2 Chron. xxviii. 20; and under his successor Hezekiah the dependent relation of the country towards Assyria brought heavy misfortune upon it, for its bulwarks against Assyria, Syria, and Israel, had been broken down by the fault of Ahaz.

After a reign of sixteen years, Ahaz was succeeded by his pious son Hezekiah, who made it his first care to remove the abominations of idolatry and to re-establish a worship in accordance with the Mosaic law. His reformation is very fully described in the books of the Chronicles. The faith of the king at once brought salvation to him and his people. His victory over the Philistines is but a small thing in comparison with the help which the Lord vouchsafed him at the time when the nation was most grievously oppressed by the Assyrians, after the counsels of the ungodly nobles who had sought help from Egypt, unknown to the prophet Isaiah and contrary to his advice, had by the result been shown to be utterly worthless. The Egyptian cavalry, they had hoped, would offer effectual opposition to the dreaded Assyrian cavalry. The assumption that the overthrow of the Assyrians before Jerusalem was caused by a ravaging pestilential disease sent upon them by the Lord, probably owes its origin to the account of the dangerous illness which fell upon Hezekiah after the retreat of the Assyrians. A distorted tradition of the event is to be found in Herodot. ii. p. 141, drawn from the account of Egyptian priests. Here also the defeat of the Assyrian army appears as a most remarkable occurrence, and as having taken place in one night, owing to divine agency. The fact that it is attributed to the Egyptian idols and not to the true God forms no essential difference. This does not alter the fact itself, but only the judgment with respect to its causes. The transference of the event to Pelusium also owes its origin to Egyptian vanity. It is characteristic that it remained at the frontier town. When Egyptian tradition relates how field-mice ate the arrows, bow-strings, and shield-straps of the Assyrian forces in one night, we must undoubtedly understand this symbolically,—the mouse being an image of secret destruction. The king of Assyria now returned home in hasty flight. Here he was afterwards slain by two of his sons,—a statement which has received confirmation from a fragment of Berosus in the Armenian Chronicle of Eusebius, i. pp. 42, 43. Niebuhr says, p. 170: "For those who, notwithstanding the deadness of our day, still retain capacity for the vivid contemplation of the past by means of the simple and few words of the old narratives, there is nothing more striking than the Old Testament description, how Sennacherib, in all the arrogance of the conqueror, in the delusion of supernatural endowments, was dashed to the ground by a sudden stroke direct from the hand of God. It is a judgment such as that which took place in Moscow, but more sudden, and hence more fearful. And in fact there are few greater turning-points in history. From this time the supremacy of the Shemites draws ever nearer and nearer to its end."

The sign of the retrograde movement of the shadow, which was given to Hezekiah through Isaiah, caused so much excitement, that, according to 2 Chron. xxxii. 31, an embassy of Babylonians, who occupied themselves with astronomic and kindred investigations, was sent to the king in order to ascertain the true nature of the phenomenon. In addition to this and its other avowed object, the embassy was sent to congratulate the king on his recovery. Probably it had also another hidden motive. The Babylonian monarchy was not independent at that time; the king of Babylon was only a subordinate king appointed by the Assyrians. It is not improbable that the then king of Babylon, taking advantage of the great defeat of the Assyrian army before Jerusalem, had either already revolted from Assyria, or was about to do so, and the embassy was designed to invite the king to enter into an alliance against the common enemy, as well as to make observation of his resources. This conjecture, already previously made, is raised almost to certainty by the Armenian Chronicle of Eusebius. According to a fragment of Berosus to be found there, i. pp. 42, 43, the Assyrian vice-king Merodach-Baladan revolted at Babylon, but was slain after having reigned for six months; whereupon his successor returned to the old relation towards Assyria, until a later period, when the rebellion was renewed under more favourable circumstances, and Babylon took the place of Nineveh in the Asiatic supremacy. Niebuhr's remarks on the mutual relation of Assyria and Babylon, p. 146, are very important for the understanding of many Old Testament passages, especially for the prophecies of Isaiah, in which Babylon, with its Chaldeans, appears as successor to Assyria in the dominion of the world: "Among the nations to whom the ruling people belonged, Assyria was by no means the most important or the oldest. It was the inhabitants of Shinar, the Babylonians, that were so. The Ninevites had gained ascendency over them by bravery and good fortune; and the older race, who possessed the centre of religion, the greatest wealth of the land, the origin of history, was obliged to submit to the younger. We see how galling the Babylonians felt this disgrace from their repeated attempts to revolt. It is very probable that the Babylonians under Nineveh's supremacy may have had an independence which must, according to our political ideas, be called very great. It is not impossible that there was a kind of twin-relationship between the Ninevites and Babylonians, the Babylonians having a sort of participation in the government. This does not, however, exclude a state of oppression." Supplementary to Isaiah's account respecting an embassy from Babylon to Judea, we have Ezek. xxiii. 14-18, a passage of great historical importance. In a historical survey of the political fickleness and idolatry of Israel, he there states that attempts had been made by Judah to enter into an alliance with the Chaldeans at a time when the Assyrian power was still in existence, and therefore before the embassy of Merodach-Baladan, Judah taking the initiative in every respect. The pictures on the walls mentioned in this passage are doubtless traditional representations of the Chaldeans as a proudly aspiring power, who might perhaps be able to afford help against the old oppressor Assyria.

This embassy prepared a temptation for Hezekiah to which he succumbed. He was not so well able to bear fortune as misfortune. The proposition of the Babylonians flattered his vanity. He wished to show that he was worthy

of such a proposal, that he was an ally not to be despised.
Triumphantly he showed the ambassadors all his treasures;
and where his treasure was, at that moment his heart was also.
Instead of giving the honour to the Lord, he placed a carnal
confidence in his human resources, which might so easily
and quickly be taken from him by the same hand which had
bestowed them. A union of his power with the Babylonian,
he thought, would render both invincible to the Assyrians.
The greater the mercies which had formerly been granted
to him, the more he deserved the censure of Isaiah. His
enthusiasm for the Babylonians must have cooled very considerably, when the prophet told him that all these treasures,
the object of his vain joy, and even the royal family, would
at a future time be carried away captive into that land, and
by those in whom in his blindness he now placed a sinful
confidence. That this remarkable prediction, with which
the other prophecies of Isaiah respecting the Babylonish
captivity are connected, and which is also announced by his
contemporary Micah, had a natural foundation in the present,
upon which it rested, appears from the fact of the revolt of
the Babylonian vice-king, which, though fruitless at the
moment, shows us a rising greatness in opposition to a
decaying one. The answer of the king shows recognition
of his sin, and a mind in harmony with the leadings of God.
The subsequent life of Hezekiah, who reigned altogether
twenty-nine years, fifteen after his illness, which occurred
at the close of the fourteenth year, is passed over in silence
in the historical books, doubtless because it passed quietly
and without any very remarkable events. What most of all
distinguishes the reign of Hezekiah is that it forms the culminating point of the activity of Isaiah, who, moved by the
threatening aspect of the power of the world, drew the picture of the future Redeemer with a clearness and completeness previously unheard of, making it the centre of the
spiritual life of the elect in Israel.

§ 9.

FROM MANASSEH TO THE CAPTIVITY.

Hezekiah was succeeded by his very dissimilar son Manasseh, who was twelve years of age when he ascended the throne, and reigned altogether fifty-five years. He abandoned himself to every kind of idolatry, and his example exercised a most injurious influence on the nation. He instituted bloody persecutions against the prophets, who were loud in their censure of the apostasy and announced the punishment of the impending captivity. The history of Manasseh in the books of the kings closes with these accounts. Chronicles here contains additions which are of special importance. Manasseh was taken prisoner without the walls of Jerusalem by the Assyrian king Asarhaddon, and carried away to Babylon, which was then still under Assyrian rule. This probably happened in the same campaign in which Asarhaddon drove out the remnant of the Israelites and placed new colonists in the kingdom of the ten tribes. The misfortune of the king had no further influence upon the state. In accordance with the prophecy of Nahum, of which the danger then threatening from Asshur formed the starting-point, the city and temple remained uninjured. Misfortune had a good effect on the king. He repented, and became truly changed. After a time he was set at liberty, and again came to the throne. The nearer circumstances connected with this release are unknown to us.

Manasseh was succeeded by his son Amon, who resembled his father in his earlier period, when he was addicted to idolatry. After having reigned only two years, he was slain by conspirators, who again met with the destruction they deserved at the hands of the people. The kingly dignity now passed to Josiah, his son, who was only eight years of age, of whom we read in 2 Kings xxxiii. 25, "And like unto him was there no king before him, that turned to the Lord with all his heart, and with all his soul, and with all his might, according to all the law of Moses." Prominence is given in Scripture to the eighth, twelfth, and eighteenth years of Josiah's reign as important for his development and activity. In the eighth year of his reign, and therefore in the sixteenth year of his age, he began to seek the God of his father David; comp. 2 Chron. xxxiv. 3. In the twelfth year he began his reformation. In the eighteenth year the finding of the temple copy of the law gave new impulse to his zeal. Ewald very unjustly reproaches him for being no friend to religious freedom in a modern sense. His proceedings against idolatry rested altogether upon the law of God. The reformation of Josiah, however, was the less able to restrain the course of divine judgment for any length of time, since the nation had for the most part only submitted to it reluctantly and from fear, not having experienced any fundamental internal reformation. The beginning of these judgments, a presage of their full approach, was the early death of Josiah himself. Humanly speaking, it was caused by the expedition of Pharaoh-nechoh, the mighty Egyptian king, against Nabopolassar, the king of the Chaldees. Ewald's view, incautiously adopted by Niebuhr, that the expedition was at first directed against the Assyrians, and that it was only during it that the new power of the Babylonians rose up, is based merely on a false interpretation of the passage 2 Kings xxiii. 29, where the king of Babylon is called the king of Assyria, because he ruled over the same district. The Chaldees were the original inhabitants of Babylon, and were not transplanted thither at a later period by the Assyrians. Against the latter view compare Delitzsch on Habakkuk, p. 21; it rests only on a misunderstanding of the passage Isa. xxiii. 13. These Chaldees, after having destroyed Nineveh in conjunction with the Medes, under Josiah (compare the discussions in Delitzsch, p. 18, on the period of these events), had taken the place of the Assyrians in the Asiatic supremacy, and had likewise inherited from them the enmity against Egypt. The Egyptian king believed he could stifle in its infancy the power which threatened danger to his supremacy. First of all he marched towards Charchemish or Circesium, on the Euphrates. It was not his intention to make war on the kingdom of Judah. It even appears that, in order to avoid touching it, he had not taken the nearest route from Egypt to Syria by land, but had transported his army in ships to Akko or Ptolemais, which must have been an easy matter, judging from Herodotus' account of the size of his fleet. Only on this assumption can we understand how the battle between the Egyptians and Judaites should have occurred at Megiddon, a town situated farther north than the kingdom of Judah, in the vicinity of Mount Carmel and the Bay of Akko. In all probability Josiah had hastened thither with his army on hearing of the intended landing of the Egyptians. Not trusting their assurances, he feared that instead of going to Syria they would first of all proceed to Jerusalem, and that their only object was to make sure of it. This suspicion, which was probably unfounded, proved the cause of his fall. He was slain in battle. Herodotus also mentions this engagement from Egyptian sources, betraying no knowledge of the fact that it was the Chaldees against whom the expedition of Pharaoh-nechoh was properly directed, and that he was soon afterwards conquered by them in the great battle at Circesium,—an omission due to the circumstance that his informants were Egyptian priests, who were silent respecting all that was offensive to their national vanity. When he calls the place of battle Magdalon, this is probably a perversion of Megiddon, where, according to Zech. xii. 11 also, the battle occurred, and may have arisen by confounding the true place with Magdolon, an Egyptian town on the Arabian Gulf. A place called Megdel, not far from Akko, which Ewald suggests, is too obscure. Cadytis is undoubtedly Jerusalem, called by the Jews קדושה, the holy city, a name which it still bears among the Arabs. This view has, however, been contested by Hitzig in a special treatise and in his Early History of the Philistines, as well as by Ewald and others, but has been proved by Niebuhr in his treatise on the Armenian Chronicle of Eusebius, by Bähr on Herodotus, and others. Gaza never appears under this name. The death of the king caused great sorrow in Jerusalem. The mourning for Josiah was employed as a designation of the deepest grief even after the time of the captivity, as appears from Zechariah. Jeremiah, the first half of whose activity falls in the reign of Josiah, composed a lament on him. From this time Judah advanced with rapid strides to its destruction, which was accelerated by the ever-increasing corruption of the people, who were deaf to all exhortation and blind to all threatening signs. Pharaoh-nechoh, after having taken Jerusalem, either himself or by a detachment of his army, continued his way to the Euphrates. He seems at first not to have troubled himself as to which of the sons of Josiah should succeed to their father's throne. Two sons of Josiah contended for supremacy,—Eliakim, the eldest in years, and Jehoahaz, who laid claim to the right of the first-born because he was the eldest son of that wife of Josiah who had held the first rank. The latter was raised to the throne by the nation. Eliakim now turned to the king of Egypt, whom he brought over to his side, probably by the promise of a large tribute. Necho summoned Jehoahaz to his camp at Riblah in the land of Hamath, and there put him in chains, afterwards carrying him away into Egypt. He raised Eliakim to the throne, after having changed his former name into Jehoiakim, which has the same meaning. This was very generally done by oriental conquerors, as a sign of their supremacy. For the first three years of his reign the ungodly Jehoiakim remained under Egyptian dominion. Towards the end of the third year, according to Dan. i. 1, with which Berosus fully coincides, the great expedition of Nebuchadnezzar against the Egyptians began. He had been taken as co-regent by his father Nabopolassar, who had become weak from old age. The decisive battle at Circesium, in which Pharaoh-nechoh was totally defeated, occurred in the fourth year. The Chaldee conqueror now pursued his way unchecked. After subduing Syria and Phenicia, both under Egyptian supremacy, he advanced to Jerusalem and took the city. Nebuchadnezzar's first intention was to carry Jehoiakim away into Babylon, but he spared him, and contented himself with carrying away a number of prisoners, most of whom were of high rank, and among whom were Daniel and his companions. He also carried away many of the vessels of the temple. He then continued his march to Egypt; but on reaching its borders, received news of the death of his father, and returned home in haste. This was the first of the many deportations to Babylon. For three years Jehoiakim paid the tribute imposed upon him. In his seventh year, or the beginning of his eighth, he rebelled, trusting to Egyptian power. Nebuchadnezzar deferred his revenge until a more convenient time, which only presented itself in the eleventh year of Jehoiakim. Jerusalem was then taken by a Chaldee army, and the king slain, as a just judgment for his neglect of all the warnings and rebukes of the prophets who had been raised up by the Lord, especially of Jeremiah, who is the main prophetic figure of this whole period.

Jehoiachin, or Jeconiah, the son of Jehoiakim, now succeeded to the throne. He soon, however, made himself suspicious to the Chaldees; probably they thought that he had a leaning to the Egyptian side. Three months after his accession to the throne, a new Chaldean army appeared before Jerusalem. The king voluntarily surrendered, and was carried captive to Babylon, where he was set at liberty, after thirty-seven years, by Evil-merodach, the son of Nebuchadnezzar. With Jehoiachin the germ of the nation was led away captive. This is the first great deportation, in which, among others, Ezekiel was carried away captive, and from which he dates his chronology. As Jehoiachin's successor, Nebuchadnezzar appointed Zedekiah, his father's brother, the third son of Josiah. From the prophecies of Jeremiah, we infer that he was not so bad as Jehoiakim, but excessively weak, and therefore under the influence of evil counsellors, who at last succeeded in leading him, in violation of his oath, to revolt against the Chaldees, disregarding the urgent warnings of Jeremiah, and foolishly trusting in Egypt. This led to the city being besieged by the Chaldees; and, after an obstinate defence, it was conquered and laid waste, together with the temple, the national independence of the nation being utterly destroyed. With the exception of a few unimportant individuals, the whole nation was carried away captive to Babylon, 390 years after the separation of the kingdom.

SIXTH SECTION.

JEWISH HISTORY FROM THE CAPTIVITY TO THE DESTRUCTION OF JERUSALEM.

§ 1.

THE BABYLONISH CAPTIVITY.

The first point is to determine the chronological relations of this period, so important for Israel, where we must necessarily enter into a discussion of a somewhat dry nature. The duration of the period is prophetically given as seventy years by Jeremiah, in two passages: chap. xxv. 11, "And this whole land shall be a desolation, and an astonishment; and these nations shall serve the king of Babylon seventy years;" and chap. xxix. 10. The same number of years is historically attributed to the period by those who lived after its expiration, 2 Chron. xxxvi. 21, Ezra i. 1; compare with these Zech. i. 12 and Dan. ix. 2.

Respecting the terminating point of these seventy years there can be no doubt. The first year of Cyrus forms their natural boundary, when the Israelites, after the fall of the Chaldean supremacy, were dismissed to their home. But the point at which they began is not so clearly defined. Yet it too may be ascertained with certainty. For this object we have only to consider the first of the two passages from Jeremiah already quoted. In chap. xxv. 1, the prophecy begins with the words: "The word that came to Jeremiah concerning all the people of Judah, in the fourth year of Jehoiakim the son of Josiah king of Judah, that was the first year of Nebuchadrezzar king of Babylon." And when a seventy years' servitude is threatened in the 11th verse of this prophecy, which is not without reason so accurately defined as to chronology, the terminus *a quo* can only be placed in that year in which the prophecy was uttered, viz. the fourth year of Jehoiakim. Moreover, the whole contents of the chapter are in harmony with this view. They show that the beginning of the threatened catastrophe was immediately impending, that the threatened misfortune was already at hand. The prophet holds a great reckoning with the nation. He reproaches them for having given no hearing to the summons to repentance which he had already given them for so many years, and declares that the divine long-suffering is now at an end, that those who would not hear must now feel, now when in the place of Josiah, the last pious king, the throne was occupied by a king after the people's own heart.

With this result obtained from the first passage of Jeremiah, the second is not at variance, as has been supposed. This prophecy, uttered already in the middle of the period, and addressed to the Jewish exiles, in which also the length of the period of the humiliation of the people of God is fixed at seventy years, does not give a new terminus *a quo*, to be sought in the time of the composition of the prophecy, but contains a statement, with express reference to the former well-known prophecy, that the appointed number of years must, in accordance with the unalterable divine decree, first run their course before there could be any thought of a return of the exiles; thus showing how foolish it was to listen to those false prophets, who, pointing to a great anti-Chaldaic coalition then forming under the guidance of Egypt, flattered the exiles with vain hopes of a speedy return, agitating their minds, and bringing them into external danger, but what was still worse, leading them away from the task to which they had now been set, viz. with true repentance to seek reconciliation with the Lord. In chap. xxix. 10 we read : " For thus saith the Lord, That after seventy years be accomplished at Babylon (*i.e.* when Babylon shall have had dominion over you for seventy years, when the Babylonian captivity will have lasted for seventy years) I will visit you, and perform my good word toward you, in causing you to return to this place." The expression "my good word" shows that the prophet here refers to something definite already known, the former announcement that the Babylonish captivity would last for seventy years, but only for seventy years, and that judgment would then be fulfilled on the oppressor; comp. chap. xxv. 12-26.

We are led to the same result, to place the beginning of the seventy years in the fourth year of Jehoiakim, if we consider what is spoken of as constituting this beginning, and then, turning to the history, look at the time when it occurs. In chap. xxv. 11 we read: "And these nations shall serve the king of Babylon seventy years." We must therefore look for the beginning of the seventy years in that period, since Judah with the surrounding nations was already subject to the Chaldees, before the time when the temple was destroyed and the whole nation carried into captivity, which did not happen until eighteen years afterwards. But the servitude of Judah and the surrounding nations began in the fourth year of Jehoiakim. In this year the Egyptians were conquered by Nebuchadnezzar in the great battle at Charchemish, and, in consequence of this victory, Phenicia, Judea, and Syria came into the power of the Babylonians. Berosus tells us this explicitly in the third book of the Chaldee history in Josephus, *Ant.* x. 11, 1, classing the Jews among those nations from which Nebuchadnezzar carried away captives into Babylon, even naming them first. The same expedition is spoken of in 2 Kings xxiv. 1, 2 Chron. xxxvi. 6; and Jeremiah alludes to it in chap. xxv., when in this prophecy, uttered in the fourth year of Jehoiakim, he considers the Babylonish servitude to be close at hand. The day of fasting and repentance, which, according to Jer. xxxvi. 9, was held in the fifth year of Jehoiakim, in the ninth month, was probably the anniversary of the day of the occupation by the Chaldees. Finally, it is expressly stated in Dan. i. 1, that in the third year of Jehoiakim, Nebuchadnezzar entered upon the campaign in which Jerusalem was taken.

The result already obtained is also confirmed by the fact that the seventy years exactly coincide, if we take the fourth year of Jehoiakim as the starting-point,—a circumstance which serves at the same time to refute those who maintain that the number seventy in Jeremiah expresses only an indefinite time, an assumption which is already sufficiently refuted by the fact that those who lived after the restoration fix the servitude at seventy years, declaring the prophecy of Jeremiah to have been literally fulfilled. These passages we have already quoted. According to Berosus, Nebuchadnezzar reigned forty-three years. But this is the number of the years in which he was sole occupant of the throne; while the first year of Nebuchadnezzar mentioned in Jeremiah, coinciding with the fourth year of Jehoiakim, is the first year of his co-regency with his father, who stands in the background from an Israelitish point of view, because Israel had to do only with the son. Nebuchadnezzar only became sole monarch in the beginning of the sixth year of Jehoiakim, so that we get forty-four years for Nebuchadnezzar. To these we add two years for Nebuchadnezzar's son Evil-merodach, four years for Neriglossar, nine months or one year for Laborosoarchad, seventeen years for Nabonned, and two years for Darius the Mede,—altogether exactly seventy years.

From the facts given, it follows that it is not quite accurate to speak of a seventy years' *exile*, although not absolutely wrong, since a deportation did take place already at this first occupation, though very inconsiderable so far as numbers were concerned. Daniel and his companions were carried away captive at that time. Accurately speaking, the exile, so far as we understand by it the removal of the whole nation from their former dwellings, did not begin until eighteen years later, seven of which belong to Jehoiakim and eleven to Zedekiah. It was not until this time that the city and temple were destroyed. Hence it is better to speak of a seventy years' servitude to Babylon, following the example of the Scriptures themselves. Ewald's assertion (*History of Israel*, iii. 2, p. 83), that in 2 Chron. xxxvi. 21 the seventy years of Jeremiah refer to the time of the destruction of Jerusalem, "as long as she lay desolate she kept sabbath, to fulfil threescore and ten years," until the seventy years of the Babylonish servitude were at an end, is incorrect. This is the only explanation suited to the context.

With respect to the Chaldee rulers during this period, Berosus names Nebuchadnezzar and Evil-merodach as the two first: Josephus, *c. Ap.* 1, 20. The latter, a son of Nebuchadnezzar, was slain, he says, in the second year of his reign, by Neriglossar, his sister's husband, on account of the disgraceful and wanton abuse which he made of his power,—a statement for the truth of which we have no trifling guarantee in the fact that the name of the king appears also in the Bible. It is evident that his proper name was only Merodach, and that Evil, fool, is only a later nickname. Berosus then goes on to relate that the son of Neriglossar, Laborosoarchad, only maintained the throne, to which he succeeded while still a boy, for nine months, and was slain by his friends. The conspirators then placed Nabonned, the Babylonian, one of their number, on the throne. In the seventeenth year of the reign of this king Babylon was taken by the Persians under Cyrus.

Of Nebuchadnezzar Niebuhr says, in his *History of Assyria and Babylon*, " He was one of the most powerful princes that Asia has ever seen, and raised the kingdom of Babylon to a might and a splendour such as it had not had since the mythical ages." The book of Daniel gives important information with respect to this king; and what it says respecting his frenzy and the royal edict published after his recovery, has been confirmed by the decipherment of the cuneiform inscriptions, in so far as we learn from them that the great kings in Asia were accustomed to tell their own history to their subjects and to the after-world on public monuments of this kind. That Nebuchadnezzar invaded Egypt in the latter years of his reign, in harmony with the prophecies of Jeremiah, in chap. xliv. 30, xlvi. 25 ff., and of Ezekiel, in chap. xxix. 17-20, is shown by the statements of Abydenus in Eusebius in the *Præp. Evang.* ix. 41, and of Syncellus, who relates that the Chaldees only left Egypt from fear of an earthquake. Not one of the three last-named Chaldean kings appears in Scripture under this name. Neriglossar and Laborosoarchad are nowhere mentioned in it, but Nabonned is undoubtedly the Belshazzar of the book of Daniel. Niebuhr has made it probable that the name Belshazzar was not the proper name, but a mere honorary title, " such," he says, " as was given to Daniel also, with a slight difference in form." In vain some have sought in ancient times to identify Belshazzar with Darius the Mede; while in modern times Hävernick and others have asserted his identity with Evil-merodach. One single argument suffices to overthrow all such attempts, and to establish the identity of Belshazzar and Nabonned, viz. this, that the death of Belshazzar and the division of his kingdom among the Medes and Persians are immediately connected in Dan. v. 28 ff., which can only be explained on the assumption that Belshazzar, like Nabonned, was the last Chaldee monarch. Evil-merodach's death was in no way connected with the division of the kingdom. The arguments which have been brought against the identity of Belshazzar and Nabonned have but little weight. When it is asserted that, according to the book of Daniel, Belshazzar was the son of Nebuchadnezzar (*i.e.* his descendant; he was his grandson by Evil-merodach), and that, on the other hand, according to Berosus, Nabonned was not of the royal family at all, Berosus is made to say what in fact his narrative does not contain. True, he does not say that Nabonned was of royal blood, but neither does he say the contrary. If he did so, we should have a strong reason for rejecting his narrative. The passages, Jer. xxvii. 7, where Israel is made subject to Nebuchadnezzar, to his son, and his son's son, and 2 Chron. xxxvi. 20, " They were servants to him and his sons, until the reign of the kingdom of Persia," necessarily demand that during the exile there should have been another direct descendant of Nebuchadnezzar on the throne besides Evil-merodach. But Neriglossar was Nebuchadnezzar's son-in-law, and Laborosoarchad was the son of Neriglossar. Hence the reference can only be to Nabonned, which is the more probable, since it is presupposed that the Chaldean supremacy came to an end under a son of Nebuchadnezzar. Nor must we leave out of consideration the fact that Herodotus also represents the last king of Babylon, whom he calls Labynet, as a son of Nebuchadnezzar. Again, it is *à priori* most natural and probable that Nabonned took possession of the throne as the representative of the rights of the male succession, in opposition to the female. It is neither probable, nor does it correspond to the historical relations in the ancient Asiatic kingdoms, that, as one in the midst of the nation, he should have put forth his hand to the throne with success.

The condition of the Israelites in exile was from an external point of view quite tolerable. The Judaites were by no means slaves of the Chaldees, as appears from the fact that they were set at liberty by Cyrus with so little hesitation. Certain districts were made over to them, from which they probably paid a moderate tribute. Compulsory service, such as their ancestors had performed in Egypt, was not required of them. They stood in exactly the same position as the heathen colonists whom Asarhaddon had planted in the kingdom of the ten tribes. Evil-merodach did not treat the Jews with his usual severity and cruelty. Immediately on his accession to the throne, he released King Jehoiachin or Jeconiah from his bonds, and gave him the first place among all the subordinate kings, together with a liberal maintenance; comp. 2 Kings xxv. 27 ff., Jer. lii. 31 ff. In Ps. cvi. 46, the Lord is extolled because He made Israel to be pitied of those who had carried them away captive; and Ps. cxxxvii. also leads us to infer that the former bitter hatred against Judah was replaced by a better feeling after they had been led away into captivity. We are not even justified in supposing that the civil independence of the Judaites was quite destroyed. The elders of the people— their chiefs and judges—are mentioned in many passages of Ezekiel; and the ease with which the people are organized, when Cyrus grants them permission to return, is only explicable on the assumption that the foundations of an organization still remained, even during the exile. This was the case even in Egypt, where the Israelites had lived in very different and much harder relations. It is certain that many individuals attained to considerable prosperity. Opportunities of becoming rich were probably more numerous than in Palestine.

Nevertheless we cannot maintain, as some have recently done, "that the position of the Israelites during their exile was not so oppressive as is generally supposed," if by the Israelites we understand not those who were merely accidentally and externally allied to this race, those of whom the Apocalypse says, in chap. ii. 9, οἱ λέγοντες Ἰουδαίους εἶναι ἑαυτοὺς καὶ οὐκ εἰσίν,—these might be satisfied with the flesh-pots of Babylon, just as they had longed after Egypt in the wilderness,—but rather those to whom the Lord in John i. 48 applies the term ἀληθῶς 'Ισραηλῖται, whom St. Paul in Rom. ii. 29 speaks of as τοὺς ἐν τῷ κρυπτῷ 'Ιουδαίους with the περιτομὴ καρδίας, those who were animated by the principle which formed the true national essence of Israel, viz. faith in the God of Israel. It is a lowering of humanity to make man's material welfare the sole measure of his happiness. Even a faithful dog is not satisfied with abundant food, when separated from his master. The position of a true Israelite in exile was very trying; his legitimate frame of mind was deeply sorrowful, even if he were not wanting in prosperity. We must not, however, forget that most of those who were carried away captive had lost all their possessions, and it must have been very difficult for them to gain even small means. Let us remember that the exile was not simply a *misfortune*, it was punishment,—chastisement for the sins of the people, which the Lord had already declared through Moses, which had been threatened for centuries by the prophets. When the time was now fulfilled, it fell on the heart of the people with hundredfold weight; they were burdened with a deep and oppressive sense of guilt. They dared not look up to God,—He appeared as their enemy; and if they often succeeded in rising up to take hold of the forgiveness of sins and the promise, of which we have an elevating example in the ninth chapter of Daniel, yet they invariably sank back again; their glance always reverted to themselves by reason of their sinfulness and the consequent wrath of God, as long as the consequences of this wrath rested upon them. And the intention was that it should be so. The sorrows of repentance were to be deeply and permanently felt by the Israelites, that they might be radically changed. They were not intended to derive comfort so easily. This is why the punishment was so hard, and the exile of so long duration. The people only received so much mercy and comfort as to keep them from despair, but at the same time the continuance of the punishment guarded against that frivolity which had made the former lighter visitations fruitless. If any one will fully realize the mind of the Israelites in this respect, the depth and intensity of their repentance, let him read the prayer of penitence offered up by Daniel in chap. ix. in the name of the people, also the 106th psalm, which may be regarded as the lyrical echo of this prophetic passage, with which it is in striking harmony. It is from beginning to end mainly a confession of sin. It also refers to the divine mercy which had formerly been the salvation of Israel notwithstanding their sin, and would now again deliver them. It is always a great misfortune for a people to be driven from their ancestral home, and robbed of their national independence and honour. But this misfortune affected Israel much more severely than is generally the case. Canaan was to them more than a fatherland in the ordinary sense,—it was the holy land of the Lord, the land which they had received as a pledge of His grace, and had lost in consequence of His displeasure. They had not merely ceased to exist as a nation, but at the same time had ceased to exist as the people of God. The height of their shame was that they could now with justice be asked the question, Where is now thy God? They had lost that which had been their greatest ornament, their privilege over all the nations of the earth. They went about with the feeling that they were marked with a brand. One great cause of sorrow was the loss of the temple. All true worship was by the law connected with the national sanctuary, no offering might be presented in any other place. Thus the nation was deprived of its lovely feasts and the beautiful services of the Lord. The house where they had dwelt with the Lord (in a spiritual sense) was broken down, and they wandered about without shelter. (Already in the law the sanctuary is called the tent of assembly, where the Lord dwells together with His people.) Joy in the Lord, and with it all other joy, had departed. This sorrow is very graphically depicted in Ps. cxxxvii.: "By the rivers of Babylon, there we sat down; yea, we wept, when we remembered Zion. We hanged our harps upon the willows in the midst thereof. For there they that carried us away captive required of us a song; and they that wasted us required of us mirth, saying, Sing us one of the songs of Zion. (But we said,) How shall we sing the Lord's song in a strange land? If I forget thee, O Jerusalem, let my right hand forget her cunning. If I do not remember thee, let my tongue cleave to the roof of my mouth; if I prefer not Jerusalem above my chief joy." The children of Israel sit by the rivers of Babylon, because they regard it as the image and symbol of their rivers of tears. The harp comes into consideration as an accompaniment of joyful song. Out of Zion this must be dumb, because there alone the nation rejoiced in the presence of its God, and this joy is the condition of all other joy. The request of the conquerors, that Israel should sing a joyful song, such as were customary in Zion, especially on occasion of feasts, proceeds from the wish that they should forget the old and true Zion, and in imagination build up a new one in Babylon, that they might feel at home in the land of their banishment. Israel puts back this desire with a firm hand. To sing joyfully and to rejoice in the strange land would be shameful forgetfulness of Zion, and would deserve that the misused tongue should lose the power to sing, the misused hand the power to play. How deep a sorrow it was to the faithful among Israel to be surrounded on all sides by heathen impurity,—external impurity and the internal which it represented,—is shown in a vivid manner by Ezekiel, chap. iv. 12-15; and in chap. xxxvi. 20 he shows how painfully the nation was burdened with the consciousness that by their sins they had made God a subject of mockery and scorn among the heathen, who inferred the weakness of the God from the misery of His people.

To these causes of sorrow we may add much hard treatment on the part of the oppressors. Actual religious persecution was far from the mind of the Chaldees; but yet we learn from Dan. iii. that toleration had its limits, when opposed by the inflexible exclusiveness of the religion of Jehovah, to which the heathen consciousness could not at all reconcile itself; for the world tolerates only the world, and there were cases in which the choice had to be made between martyrdom and a denial of the God of Israel. But the Israelites had far more to suffer from mockery and wantonness, which they were often obliged to provoke by the duty laid upon them of bearing testimony against the heathen, than from actual persecution. Belshazzar, according to Dan. v., went so far that he boldly desecrated the vessels of the sanctuary. This mockery, which went side by side with the kinder treatment represented in Ps. cxxxvii., was the more felt because it was in reality not without foundation in the subject, and found an ally in the disposition of the Israelites, which painfully opened up old wounds. Its principal subject, the contrast between their assertion that they were the beloved people of the Lord, and their sad and miserable condition, served therefore to increase their despair, and made the battle by which they had to reach the divine mercy, in spite of the visible signs of divine displeasure by which they were surrounded on all sides, still more difficult for them.

If we consider the internal condition of the exiles, it is impossible not to see that there was a great difference between them and those who had remained behind in Jerusalem, as well as those who had fled to Egypt, who, according to Jer. xliv., gave themselves up to idolatry with almost frantic zeal, and instead of attributing their misfortune to ungodliness, attributed it to the neglect of idolatry. Jeremiah, in chap. xxiv., speaks of them as the seminary, the hope of the kingdom of God. This difference is not due solely to the wholesome influence exercised on them by the exile,—no sorrow contains in itself any improving power, but is just as likely to make a man worse as to make him better, as we see from the example of those Egyptian exiles; we may apply to sorrow the proverb, "To him that hath shall be given; but whosoever hath not, from him shall be taken away even that which he hath,"—but its first ground, to which the other passage of Jeremiah gives a clue, lies deeper, in the fact that it was exactly the better part of the nation that was carried away into captivity, while the worse remained in the country, and were either destroyed there by the judgments of the Lord, or escaped to Egypt, and were there overtaken by them. At the first glance, it seems quite incomprehensible that there should have been such a difference, but on nearer consideration we can discover the reason of its origin. First, it is not improbable that the ungodly, who mocked the prophets and their threats respecting the total destruction of the state and the city, and expected speedy help from Egypt, sacrificed everything for permission to remain in their fatherland; while those who feared God, knowing, especially from the constantly-repeated announcements of Jeremiah, that the destruction of the town was inevitable, and formed the indispensable condition of restoration, voluntarily obeyed the first summons, and joyfully entered on the death which was the sole gate to life,—just as the Christians fled from Jerusalem to Pella before the destruction by Rome. But the main thing is, that the victors recognised in the theocratic principle the Israelitish nationality, and therefore made it their special object to carry away the representatives of this principle, well knowing that their removal would necessarily lead to the dissolution of the nation, and that those who remained would no longer be dangerous to them; for in fact, throughout the whole history of the Jews, we find no other courage than that which had a theocratic basis. Those who were inwardly infected with the spirit of heathenism would necessarily be unable to offer any effectual external resistance to this spirit. They had no longer any sanctuary for which to strive; they contended only for accidents. It is not mere conjecture that the conquerors were led by this principle in their choice of captives, but we can prove it by definite facts. From Jer. xxix. 1 it appears that already, in the first great deportation under Jehoiakim, principally priests and prophets were led away. Among those who returned from exile, the proportion of priests to people is such, that in a total of 42,360 there were not less than 4289 priests, the priests making a tenth part of the whole. This proportion cannot be explained from the fact that a comparatively far greater number of the priests returned than of the others. The proportion of those who returned to those who were led away does not allow the assumption inseparable from such an explanation, viz. that a considerable remnant remained behind in the lands of exile. The preponderance of priests can be explained solely on the assumption that the Chaldees carried away mainly the priests; and since the only reason of this can be that the priests were regarded as the principal representatives of the theocratic principle, it is impossible not to believe that the Chaldees were well acquainted with the inner relations of the Jews, as their considerate treatment of Jeremiah shows, and were at other times influenced in the choice of their captives by regard to the theocratic tendency.

One sign of the good disposition of the exiles is to be found in the reverence with which the elders of the community gather about Ezekiel in order to hear his prophecies; comp. Ezek. viii. 1, xi. 25, xiv. 1, xxxiii. 31 ff. On the last passage adduced Vitringa remarks: " Supponit deus in tota hac oratione sua ad prophetam, populum solitum esse statis vicibus ad Ezechielem venire, coram ipso considere, ipsius coargutiones recipere cum reverentia, et ab ipso solenniter instrui cognitione viarum dei." These passages are quite sufficient to refute the theory advanced by Hitzig and Ewald, that Ezekiel was condemned by the circumstances of the time to lead the life of a private student, " a dim, quiet life in the law and in recollection." Everywhere we find Ezekiel surrounded by a corona of zealous hearers. He is a public orator just as much as any of the earlier prophets. Another circumstance which speaks in favour of the exiles is, that in the time succeeding the exile the state of religion is far more in conformity with the divine law than it had been before,— that idolatry and the tendency to heathenism seem to have disappeared all at once, and only regained their ascendency among a portion of the people some centuries later, in the times when Syria was subject to Greek rulers, and then only with a small minority, so that the nation must have energetically put away this tendency as anti-national.

Since it is plain that the first foundation for this remarkable change was laid already in our period, we shall here enter somewhat more closely into its causes. Many have occupied themselves with the examination of these. This has been most fully done in two treatises which have appeared in Holland: Suringar, *de causis mutati Hebræorum ingenii post reditum e captivitate Babylonica*, Leyden, 1820; and Gerritzen, *comm. de quæstione, cur Hebræi ante exilium se ad idolorum cultum valde propensos, postea autem vehementer alienos ostenderint,* Utrecht.

The change has frequently been attributed to false causes. Joh. Dav. Michaelis, *Mos. Recht,* i. § 32, and others lay great emphasis on the opinion that the Israelites during the time of exile entered into closer relations with the enlightened Persians. Not the smallest proof, however, can be adduced that the Persian religion exercised any such influence on the Israelites. The prophets at least were far from giving it a preference over other heathen religions. Ezekiel speaks with horror of its practices, chap. viii. 16. It becomes more and more evident that the idea of the Persian religion, which lies at the basis of this assumption, is an incorrect one. Stuhr, in his *Religious Systems of the East,* has tried to prove that the Persian religion, as represented in the writings still extant, is a late composition of very heterogeneous elements; that it was originally the pure worship of nature; and that the ethical elements, loosely laid over the physical, which still decidedly preponderated in the later form, are borrowed from the Jews, and, in the latest books, even from Christianity. At the same time, the assertion that the Jews were led by foreign influence to the more determined maintenance of their national religious principle is at variance with all analogy and probability. In all other cases the Israelites are led to apostasy from without; the reaction against it, all reformation, invariably proceeds from within. The relation which, according to chap. vi., Daniel holds towards Darius the Mede, is also unfavourable to this view. Here, as formerly in relation to Nebuchadnezzar and Belshazzar, Daniel is not the recipient, but the donor. He, the worthy representative of exiled Judaism, stands firm and immoveable in faith on Jehovah, and by this faith so influences the Medish king, that he makes a proclamation commanding that the God of Daniel shall be feared and shunned throughout the whole extent of his kingdom. Herodotus says with respect to the Persians, that they betray unusual willingness to accept strange customs, B. i. chap. 135. Spiegel, in his *Elaboration of the Avesta,* i. p. 11, remarks, "In this historical time the Persians certainly borrowed much from their more civilised Semitic neighbours;" and in p. 270 lays down the canon: "If a Persian idea have a foreign sound, we may in most cases assume that it is borrowed."

The true fundamental reason is contained in that which we have already proved, viz. that it was the ἐκλογὴ of the nation who were carried away into exile. If this be so, we cannot properly speak of a revolution in the national mind. Even before the exile, the nation as a whole had never been addicted to idolatry. At all times, even the darkest, there was still an ἐκλογὴ by whom idolatry was utterly abhorred. The difference lay solely in this, that the ἐκλογὴ, who could formerly only occupy the position of a party, were now, under the providence of God, more or less identical with the nation, their principle being absolutely dominant. Many other causes also contributed to this end, strengthening those who already belonged to the ἐκλογὴ in their faithfulness towards the Lord, and quickening their zeal against all contamination by idolatry, and at the same time leading many of the ungodly who had been carried away into exile to repent and renounce all heathen vanity. What they suffered from the heathen destroyed their earlier sympathy with heathenism, just as in our day French sympathies were completely rooted out by the French tyranny, just as the sorrows of the year '48 quite cured many of their democratic tendencies. The more decidedly all hope in human aid disappeared, the more certainly the nationality of Israel was, humanly speaking, destroyed for ever, the greater was the attention paid to the promise already given in the law side by side with the threat, and continually repeated by the prophets, that the Lord would redeem His captive people, the more earnest was the striving to fulfil the God-given condition of this redemption: putting aside all idolatrous practices, the nation turned to the Lord with true repentance. The promises were believed with a readiness proportionate to the accuracy with which the threats had been fulfilled, and the opportunities they had had of learning by painful experience the veracity of God. Zechariah says, chap. i. 6: "But my words and my statutes, which I commanded my servants the prophets, did they not take hold of your fathers? and they returned and said, Like as the Lord of hosts thought to do unto us, according to our ways, and according to our doings, so hath He dealt with us."

The fall of the heathen nations and religions with which Israel had previously been connected, and especially the last great event of this kind, the fall of the apparently invincible Chaldean power, made them suspicious of the power and religion of the world generally, at the same time quickening their faith in the deity of their God alone, who had foretold all these changes by His prophets, and had pointed to Himself as their author. Considerable influence was exercised on the people by those proofs of election which they continued to receive in the midst of their misery, but they were still more strongly affected by their deliverance from exile. A no less part in the great change must certainly be attributed to the long and powerful activity of the highly-gifted Ezekiel, about whom the exiles gathered as their spiritual centre. But misery itself exercised the strongest influence, not indeed upon rude minds, which sorrow only the more hardened, but upon those in whom grace had already begun its work, to whom, as we have already seen, most of those who had been led away captive belonged. In what they suffered they recognised what they had done, and awoke to μετάνοια. "What all the better kings and prophets had never been able perfectly to accomplish in the fatherland," Ewald says, "was now done in a short space of time by the inextinguishable earnestness of these times, in a strange land, without much assistance from man."

But it is necessary not only to explain the fact that the religious consciousness of the nation was much more distinctly opposed to heathenism in the times immediately succeeding the exile than it had been before it, as we have already done, but also to show how it was that this impression was so lasting,—quite different in this respect from the reformations before the exile, which scarcely ever extended their influence beyond the reign of one single king. With reference to this we may remark generally, that the impulse which the nation received by the exile was far stronger than any former one, and that the change in the national consciousness which took place during the exile was also far deeper and more universal, and therefore more lasting. And if love towards God soon again died out among the masses, yet it was impossible to throw off the fear of God with equal facility.

We must also take into consideration the position occupied by the priesthood in the time subsequent to the return from captivity, which was essentially different from their former one. Their very number must have given the priests considerable influence in the new colony, and still more the circumstance that the civil government was in the hands of heathen oppressors. The priesthood was now the sole remaining truly national dignity, and it was quite natural that the eyes of the nation should be directed towards them as to the centre of national consciousness. We see the very same thing among the Greeks before the emancipation. Under the Turkish supremacy, the hierarchy there acquired influence, even in civil affairs, such as they had not formerly possessed. Among the Israelites, until the time of the exile, there had been a theocracy without a hierarchy. Even before the establishment of royalty, the priests had, properly speaking, no political position. The political influence which they exercised here and there was invariably free, and even this disappeared with the establishment of the kingship. After the exile, on the other hand, theocracy gradually developed into hierarchy. The influence of the priesthood extended into every sphere of civil life, and was great in proportion as the heathen oppressors did not endeavour to put everything into the hands of their officials. It is easy to see the importance of this change. The priesthood, now so influential, was bound by all its interests to the Mosaic constitution. Its revenues, its influence—in short, its whole existence—depended on its adhering to this, and endeavouring to keep it in respect with the nation. At the same time, a better spirit had at all times subsisted in this body. Even at the time of the greatest degeneracy of the nation, which would naturally have some influence on them, this spirit was not quite dead. The priesthood had never quite ceased to be the salt of the nation. Prophetic denunciations of their crimes, which at first seem to testify to the contrary, as, for example, Mal. ii. 5 ff., when looked at more closely, confirm our statement. They could not have demanded so much from the priests, nor have been so indignant respecting their errors, if the institution had been quite degenerate,—had it not contained a beautiful fund of the true fear of God. Owing to the increased influence of the priests, the better spirit which had animated them now passed over to the masses. The higher position of the priests and their increased influence had indeed its dark side also. If it formed a powerful antidote to the tendency to idolatry, yet, on the other hand, it gave an impulse to the spirit of externality, to justification by works, and to Pharisaism, which were the forms of sickness peculiar to the priestly nature. We find that these appeared in the new colony in proportion as the tendency to idolatry disappeared; they are the principal enemies combated in Malachi and in Ecclesiastes.

Moreover, we must also consider that the heathen consciousness did not at first meet those who returned from exile in a very powerful form, and hence offered small temptation. The neighbouring nations, the Ammonites, Moabites, Edomites, and Phenicians, and, in the opinion of the old world, also their gods and religions, were trodden under foot by the victories of the Chaldees. The Chaldees, with their religion, received the death-blow by the victory of the Persians, who stood on a much lower step of cultivation than the Israelites. Their religion had throughout an uncertain, misty, vacillating character. Soft as wax, it yielded readily to every impression from without, never properly attaining to any finality, but remaining always in a state of transition; hence it was itself incapable of making any impression on other religions. Things assumed a very different aspect, however, when the Greeks and Romans took the place of the Asiatic oppressors. The heathen principle then again met the Israelites in a form which was really seductive. Their oppressors had the superiority in science and in culture, no less than in power. The national spirit of the conquerors had constituted itself the spirit of the world, and pronounced its curse on the little people that refused to submit to its utterances. It then became clearly evident that the external faithfulness to the Lord, which had formerly characterized the new colony, had its foundation to some extent only in the weakness of the temptations. In the time when Syria was under Greek rule, whole bands apostatized to the heathen principles; even priests served the heathen idols. And though this apostasy called forth a powerful and successful reaction, yet it was never fully set aside,—it merely assumed a more honourable garb, and appeared as Sadduceeism. The circumstance that it was obliged to assume such a garb shows, indeed, that there was still a fundamental difference between the time preceding the exile—when heathenism appeared in the most shameless way, often for long periods completely suppressing the public worship of God—and the time subsequent to the exile, in which the theocratic principle was, on the whole, absolutely predominant among the nation. The reason of this change is probably to be sought partly in the fact that heathenism, even in its more powerful forms, had already begun to bear a character of decrepitude, at least as a religion. Its seductive power lay only in its worldly wisdom and its culture, and therefore had no influence on those deeper minds for which religion was a necessity. In proof of this we have the numerous secessions to Judaism, such as had never occurred in the time before the exile. The decline of heathenism, which called forth these secessions, must have made it easier for those who were at all well-disposed among the Israelites to adhere to the religion of their fathers.

Let us now return to our observations on the internal condition of the exiles. Though we have given them a decided preference before those who had remained behind, yet this must in all cases be looked upon as merely relative. This is self-evident; but it may also be proved, by many decided passages, that even during the exile there was no lack of sin on the part of Israel, and consequent lamentation from the faithful servants of the Lord. God was obliged to make the forehead of Ezekiel as an adamant, harder than flint, that he might not fear them, nor be dismayed at their looks, for they were a rebellious house, chap. iii. 9. With earnest censure he comes before the people, who, though they listened to the words of the prophets, did not obey them, chap. xxxiii. 30 ff. Even among the heathen, whither they went, they profaned the holy name of God, and continued to practise the abomination of murder, and to defile every one his neighbour's wife, so that it was said of them, "Are these the people of the Lord that are gone forth out of this land?" chap. xxxiii. 26, xxxvi. 20, 21. Even the vanity of false prophecy was not confined to Jerusalem, but had spread to the exiles, which could not possibly have happened if the better spirit had held absolute sway among them. Jer. xxix. 20-22 enumerates a few of these exiled pseudo-prophets. These misleaders of the people flattered them with vain hopes of a speedy release, and by this means readily incited them to pernicious revolt, leading them away from the sole work which was incumbent on them, and formed the only means of salvation, viz. repentance. The threat expressed against them by Jeremiah in his letter addressed to the exiles, that God would deliver them into the hand of Nebuchadnezzar that he might slay them before the eyes of all, shows that even the Chaldees were well aware what a spirit of restlessness prevailed among those who had been led away captive, and that they carefully watched every manifestation of this spirit.

If we consider the many weaknesses and sins of the exiled people, who had dwelt among a nation of unclean lips, and whose love had been cooled by the spread of unrighteousness; if we remember how great were their temptations to apostasy,—cast out into the midst of the heathen world, on which the idolatrous spirit of the time was impressed with fearful power, robbed of their sanctuary and their worship, and of so many other pledges of the divine grace; if we consider that the exile, in accordance with the first threatenings of it in the law, comp. Deut. iv. 30, xxx. 2 ff., though, on the one hand, intended as a punishment, was, on the other hand, destined to serve as a means of grace: we shall à priori be led to expect that proofs of the divine election of Israel will not be wanting at this period,—that the love of God will find an expression as well as His anger, for its complete absence would involve the nation in frivolity and despair, two equally dangerous enemies of salvation. Such manifestations on the part of God were the more necessary, since without them the judgment respecting the great catastrophe of the Israelitish state, even in the heathen world, would be entirely incorrect, and would tend to the decided detriment of the God of Israel, being inevitably regarded as a proof of His weakness.

The series of signs of continued election for the captive community begins with the writing already mentioned, sent to them by Jeremiah,—doubtless a very weak beginning. A second sign was the continuance of sacred psalmody in Israel, to which the three psalms composed in exile, Ps. civ.-cvi., bear testimony. These psalms could not fail to make a deep impression on the nation. The first bases confidence in the destruction of the heathen power and the deliverance of Israel, on the greatness of God's works in nature; the second, on the greatness of God's works in history, especially on that which God had done for the fulfilment of the promise of Canaan given to the fathers. The third, by pointing to the pardoning mercy of God, sets aside the last enemy who threatened to deprive the nation of the assistance promised to them by nature and history, and to prevent their returning to their country. A far more important fact was, that God raised up Ezekiel to be a prophet to them, who was of priestly origin and himself a priest, and had been carried away in the deportation under Jeconiah. In the fifth year of his captivity, after having completed the thirtieth year of his age,—at the same time, therefore, when, under other circumstances, he would have begun his priestly functions in the outer sanctuary,—he began his office among the exiles on the river Chebar in Mesopotamia, more than six years before the final downfall of Jerusalem, so that his activity among the exiles ran parallel for a considerable time with the activity of Jeremiah among those who had remained. This circumstance tended not a little to strengthen the impression produced by their discourses. The spirit which foretold the very same thing in Babylon and in Judea appeared as something more than human. We can follow the traces of Ezekiel's activity, whose beginning was occasioned by the formation of the anti-Chaldaic coalition, up to the twenty-seventh year of his captivity, the twenty-second of his call to the prophethood. The twenty-fifth year gave birth to that exalted vision of the second temple in chaps. xl.–xlviii., the figurative representation of the glorious exaltation of the people of God, by which, at a future time, their deepest humiliation was to be followed, —one of the most glorious monuments of the faith which sees the thing that is not as if it were, in its form revealing the priestly mind and character of Ezekiel, like so many other of his prophecies. In the twenty-seventh year the announcement of the great victory of Nebuchadnezzar over Egypt was made, chaps. xxix., xxx. At this time the divine mission of Ezekiel, the Godhead of Jehovah, and the election of Israel, were confirmed by the fulfilment of a number of Ezekiel's prophecies, viz. those which referred to the final overthrow of the Jewish state, in which the minutest circumstances had been foretold; comp., for example, the prediction of the fate of Zedekiah in chap. xii. 12 ff., and that respecting the destruction of the city, chap. xxiv., as well as what is said with reference to the neighbouring nations. Not long before, Nebuchadnezzar, by taking Tyre, had verified the prophecy concerning that insular city, which had already been connected with the mainland by a dam. That this did really happen has been proved in my work, *De Rebus Tyriorum*, Berlin, 1832, in Hävernick's *Commentary on Ezekiel*, and in Niebuhr's *History of Assyria and Babylon*, p. 216. In these prophecies Ezekiel often states the exact time, giving year, month, and day of the divine revelation (comp., for example, chap. i. 1, 2, viii. 1, xx. 1, xxiv. 1, xxxiii. 21), in order to escape all suspicion of a *vaticinii post eventum*; by which assumption rationalistic criticism, as exemplified in Hitzig, has in vain tried to escape the embarrassment of making Ezekiel a deceiver. But not merely these special prophecies, referring in most cases to the immediate future, and passing into fulfilment before the eyes of the exiles, but also the whole mission of Ezekiel, afforded a proof that the Lord was still among His people. Truly he preached in manifestation of the Spirit and of power;

he is a spiritual Samson, who with a mighty arm grasped the pillars of the idol-temple and shook it to the ground,— a gigantic nature, and by this very circumstance adapted to offer effective resistance to the Babylonian spirit of the time, which delighted in powerful, gigantic, grotesque forms. In him we have a remarkable union of Babylonish form and Israelitish nature. "If he has to contend with a people of brazen forehead and stiff neck," says Hävernick, "he on his side is of an inflexible nature, meeting iniquity with undaunted and audacious courage, and words full of consuming fire." Ewald's and Hitzig's subjectivity is nowhere more plainly to be seen than in the fact that they try to transform this very prophet into a timid, retiring student.

Daniel as well as Ezekiel, and in a still higher degree, arrests our attention. He did not, like Ezekiel, exercise a personal activity among the exiles, for which reason the book of Daniel is not ranked among the prophetic writings (we here assume the genuineness of this book to be proved in the introduction to the Old Testament); he was not a prophet by office, but stood in the service of the court. Nevertheless the eyes of the people were directed to him from the beginning, as we learn from the passages Ezek. xxviii. 3 and xiv. 14, where it is assumed that his deep piety and his almost superhuman wisdom are universally known, though he had then only entered on years of manhood. His position at court was necessary for the fulfilment of his mission. How important this was, already appears from the circumstance that the historical portion of his book, which gives us isolated facts from his life, is in fact the only historical account that we possess relative to the period of the captivity. This period as a whole was not an object of sacred historiography, just because it is sacred, though Israel at this time was in the main rejected by God and cast out. This period bears the same character as the last thirty-eight years of the march through the wilderness. It was only necessary to record those separate events which revealed the love concealed behind the anger, the election concealed behind the rejection; and in these events Daniel had a principal part. In order to understand the historical portion of the book of Daniel, it is necessary, above all, to keep the object of it clearly in sight. All the separate narratives seem intended to show that the God of Israel, the nation that was despised and trodden in the dust, was the only true God; that He would not suffer those who despised Him, and were at enmity with His people, to go unpunished, but would help His servants in every time of need. This aim dominates not merely the narrative, but also the facts themselves. If they were subservient to it, they must necessarily abound in comfort and strength for the exiled people who were exposed to such great temptation, and deprived of so many former wholesome influences, at the same time forming an encouragement to repentance, since the isolated signs of continued election quickened the hope of its future complete manifestation. But besides this principal aim, which is far from appearing strange when we recognise the reality of the kingdom of God in Israel, but is rather what might have been expected, and seems quite natural and in order, the events which happened were also intended to make the outward lot of the Israelites tolerable, since by the high position in which they placed Daniel, they enabled him to work for his people; again, they were intended to prepare the way for the release of Israel under Cyrus, in which in all probability Daniel had a considerable share; and, finally, to awaken the heathen to a wholesome fear of the God of Israel, and to set limits to their proud contempt of Him, which had been greatly increased at that time by the weakness of His people. The prophecies of Daniel must likewise be regarded as a sign of the continued election of Israel. Their great significance already appears, from the fact that New Testament prophecy, from the prophetic revelations of the Lord to the Apocalypse, attaches so much importance to them. Their fundamental idea is the final victory of the kingdom of God, predicted with absolute confidence. Kingdoms fall, and new kingdoms rise up in their place; the people of God have much to suffer; but let them take comfort, for their God will overcome the world. and on the ruins of the kingdoms of the world the eternal kingdom shall finally be established. By these prophecies, therefore, the people of God were set as it were on a high mountain, from which they could see the confusion on the plains far below their feet.

Keeping in view what we have said with reference to the signs of the continuing election of God during the captivity, it will easily be seen how very different this exile was from that in which the Jews are now. In the latter such signs are completely wanting; hence the foolishness of the Jews in always expecting to be delivered from it. Deliverance is only conceivable where these signs have continued even during the time of misery. Israel received such signs during the last thirty-eight years of the march through the wilderness, in the continued presence of Moses, in the pillar of cloud and of fire, etc. Where the signs are wanting, there can be no election; and where this does not exist, the hope of redemption is vain. Of this we have already a proof, in the fact that for eighteen hundred years this redemption has failed to come, while the former mere suspensions of the relation of grace lasted only for a comparatively short time. The position of orthodox Judaism becomes daily worse; and we can almost make a mathematical calculation respecting the time when its end will come. The Jews profess to be the chosen race, and during a period of eighteen centuries can point to no way in which this election has been manifested; they hope for redemption, and all the termini which they have appointed for it from century to century have passed away without the expected result. The untenableness of the position occupied by orthodox Judaism is shown also by its undeniable internal hollowness and inconsistency, nor can the Jew conceal this fact even from himself.

With respect to the external worship of God, the offering of sacrifices necessarily ceased entirely during the time of exile. For, according to the law, sacrifices could only be offered in the national sanctuary, Deut. xii., and this no longer existed. By later revelations from God, it was also established that Jerusalem was destined to be the seat of the sanctuary for ever (comp. for example, Ps. lxxviii. 68, cxxxii. 13, 14), and therefore only the worship there offered was acceptable to God; so that there could be no idea of building a new sanctuary in the place of banishment. On the contrary, it must have been evident that it formed part of the punishment of the nation to be deprived of the opportunity of offering sacrifices. The author of the book of Baruch indeed tells how, in the fifth year after the destruction, the exiles sent the sacred vessels which had been carried away by Nebuchadnezzar to Jerusalem to the high priest Jehoiakim, together with money to procure sacrifices. But this is a palpable fiction, for the book does not pretend to give history, but only poetry. According to the books of the Kings, Jerusalem was completely laid waste; according to the book of Ezra, the high-priestly race was in exile; and in the same book, chap. i. 7, we read that the sacred vessels were first given back by Cyrus; and the book of Daniel tells of their desecration by Belshazzar, the last Chaldee king. The zeal for prayer shown by the Jews in exile was very great, if we may take the example of Daniel as a criterion of all the rest, and was probably increased by the want of a sacrificial worship. Just as it was customary in prayer to turn the face towards the sanctuary of the Lord at the time when the sanctuary was still standing, comp. Ps. v. 8, xxviii. 2, cxxxviii. 2, thus indicating a turning not merely to the Deity, but to the revealed Deity, the God of Israel; so it was habitual to turn towards Jerusalem during the period of exile, Dan. vi. 10. Even the places where the temple had stood, where a temple was again to be erected, remained sacred. The Jews could think of no better way to symbolize the turning of the mind to the God of Israel than by turning the face to the place where He had formerly manifested Himself as such, and would again manifest Himself, as they confidently hoped, trusting in His word. According to the same passage from the book of Daniel, it was customary to pray three times a-day,—doubtless, as in former times, morning, noon, and evening; comp. Ps. lv. 18. At the principal turning-points of the day, prayer rose up to the Lord of life. Morning and evening prayer was offered up at the same hour in which daily morning and evening sacrifice had been presented in the temple as long as it stood. This sacrifice was itself an embodied, symbolic prayer; and that it was customary to associate verbal prayer with it is shown by Ezra ix. 5, where Ezra begins his prayer, a spiritual sacrifice, at the time of the evening oblation. From Dan. ix. 21, where Gabriel appears to Daniel when he is praying at the time of the evening sacrifice, we learn that during the exile, when verbal prayer only was possible, the time of the presentation of offerings at least was preserved. From this we see that the exiled Jews recognised the closeness of the relation of sacrifice to prayer, and must therefore have looked upon the removal of sacrificial worship as an incentive to greater earnestness in supplication. The favourite place of prayer, as appears from Dan. vi. 10, was the most lonely part of the house, in the upper room, where, according to 1 Kings xvii. 19, Elijah also retired to pray. The manner and substance of the prayer of those who truly feared God is best seen in a petition uttered by Daniel in the name of the whole nation, given in Dan. ix. The substance is concentrated in vers. 15 and 16, in the words, "And now, O Lord our God, . . . we have sinned, we have done wickedly. O Lord, according to all Thy righteousness, I beseech Thee, let Thine anger and Thy fury be turned away from Thy city Jerusalem, Thy holy mountain; because for our sins, and for the iniquities of our fathers, Jerusalem and Thy people are become a reproach to all that are about us." The joys and sorrows of the individual were absorbed in the great hopes and sorrows of the community. The whole Church of those who feared God prayed more at this time than at any other. Just as the cessation of sacrifice gave rise to greater zeal in prayer, on the one hand, so, on the other, it must have increased the zeal in keeping holy the Sabbath, the neglect of which Ezekiel frequently enumerates among the causes which had brought the divine judgments on Jerusalem, chap. xx. 12 ff., xxii. 8, etc. The keeping of the Sabbath was now the only universally visible mark by which to distinguish the worshipper of Jehovah, the only national acknowledgment of their God which the Israelites could make amid the heathen, and at the same time also the sole outward means of awakening the religious national feeling.

We have already referred to those passages which show that it was customary to gather about the prophets in order to hear their revelations. Whether there were regular religious meetings besides, representative of the sacred assemblies in the temple, we have no certain testimony. It is very probable, however: in favour of it we have a strong argument in the existence of the exile psalms of which we have already spoken, which proceed collectively out of the soul of the Church. It is almost inconceivable that a people of God should have existed for so long a period without any divine worship. Even before the exile, though the temple was the only place of sacrifice, yet assemblies for divine service were by no means confined to it. We cannot, indeed, place any reliance on the statement of the Talmud, comp. Buddeus, ii. p. 861, that the exiles built synagogues. In accordance with the universal character of such statements in the Talmud, it is a mere conjecture, and has not the weight of historical testimony.

The succession of the high-priesthood was not interrupted during the exile. The last high priest before the captivity was Seraiah. His son Jehozadak, who succeeded him, was carried away captive, 1 Chron. vi. 15. The son of Jehozadak was Joshua, who returned with Zerubbabel, and was the first high priest in the new colony; comp. Ezra ii. 2, Zech. iii. 1 ff. From the position which Joshua at once takes in the new colony, we are led to infer that the high priests exercised considerable influence over the nation, even during the captivity.

Another ray of hope illuminating the existence of the exiles was the continuance of the Davidic race, with which such great hopes were connected, and which could not have perished without powerfully undermining faith. The son of Jeconiah the king of Judah, whom Evil-merodach had released from captivity, was Salathiel, or Shealtiel (for many reasons supposed not to have been a true son, but a son by adoption; also, however, of Davidic origin); the son of Salathiel was Pedaiah, whose son Zerubbabel was the leader of those who returned under Cyrus; comp. 1 Chron. iii. 19. This continuance of the Davidic race formed a centre for the national consciousness of the nation, a foundation for its hopes. That the confidence in a glorious future for this race, resting on the word of God, was unbroken even during the exile, is shown by 1 Kings xi. 39. These books were composed in exile, at the time of the deepest humiliation of the race of David. The same thing appears also from the Messianic prediction of Ezekiel; comp. chap. xvii. 22-24. The hope in the future is so strong in Ezekiel, that in chaps. xxxviii., xxxix., not satisfied with predicting the restoration of Jerusalem, which was then lying in ruins, and the fall of its present oppressor, he foretells even the glorious victory of the redeemed over those enemies of the future who were not yet at the scene of action.

We shall now consider the way in which the condition of the Israelites, which has hitherto occupied our attention, came to an end. The deliverance of the Israelites did not quite coincide with the fall of the Chaldee power. The latter took place already at the close of the sixty-eighth year of the Babylonish captivity. The king of the Medes, who was the next ruler of the Babylonian monarchy, did nothing to bring the prophecies respecting the deliverance of Israel nearer to their fulfilment. In the Scriptures (Dan. chap. vi.) he bears the name Darius of Media; in profane history (in the *Cyropedia* of Xenophon) he is called Cyaxares,—a difference which may be explained from the fact that the names of the Medish and Persian kings were mostly only titles, and were therefore many and variable. On this subject Niebuhr has made exhaustive researches, p. 29. He thus gives the result of his examination:—" The same king may appear under several different names—(*a*) under his original personal name, (*b*) under the name taken as king on ascending the throne, (*c*) under one or several surnames, (*d*) under the universal title of the king of his country." In recent times many have questioned the existence of a Medish king of Babylon; but the completely independent agreement of two important testimonies is a sufficient guarantee, all the more since the only argument to the contrary is drawn from the silence of Herodotus and Ctesias, which proves nothing. A full discussion of this question may be found in the

Beiträge, vol. i., Hävernick, *Commentary on Daniel*, and his later *Examination of the Book of Daniel*, Hamburg, 1838, p. 74 ff., Auberlen, *Daniel and the Apocalypse*, and last of all, Pusey in his copious work *on Daniel*. When Niebuhr, p. 61, speaks of Cyaxares, the mythical hero of Xenophon, he forgets that the proof lies not in the historical credibility of the *Cyropedia* in itself, but in its remarkable agreement with Daniel. His assertion that, apart from Daniel, our only knowledge of a Medish king of Babylon is derived from the legendary *Cyropedia*, is incorrect. Æschylus, in *The Persians*, also speaks of such a one; and Abydenus even designates him by the same name as he bears in the book of Daniel.

In Dan. ix. we have a vivid representation of the mind of the exiles (of the ἐκλογή among them) after the great blow had been struck, when Babylon the proud had fallen, and the storm which the Lord had foretold by His servants the prophets at a time when the sky was perfectly clear, beginning in a little cloud, had gradually risen higher and higher in the heavens, and had finally discharged itself with a fearful crash. This chapter contains a vision which was revealed to the prophet in the first year of Darius the Mede, and therefore in the sixty-ninth year of the captivity. At this time Daniel is occupied with Jeremiah, and his mind is deeply affected on reperusing the prophecies so familiar to him, according to which the misery of the covenant-nation is to last for seventy years, and then to be followed by the return and the commencement of the rebuilding of the city and the temple. By the fulfilment of the one great prediction of the prophecies of Jeremiah, faith gained a visible support with reference to the other. Now ensued a time of great suspense, prayer was zealously offered up, and all were moved by a powerful impulse to intercede earnestly for the nation, the temple, and the city of the Lord. Doubtless many prayers, such as that of Daniel, rose up to the Lord, and the words of this prayer, "We do not present our supplications before Thee for our righteousness, but for Thy great mercies," no doubt express the universal feeling at that time. In Ps. cvi. we have a supplement to Dan. ix., which we judge from ver. 46 was sung when the prospects of

Israel had already assumed a brighter aspect, after the Lord had given His people favour with their oppressors.

Darius was already aged when he began to rule over Babylon; and when he died, after a reign of two years, the kingdom passed over to Cyrus the Persian. In many respects this king stands alone in the whole history of the old world. He is the only conqueror who shines equally in sacred and in profane history. Profane history represents him as a monarch characterized by great mildness and love of justice, a helper of the oppressed. So Xenophon in the *Cyropedia*, whose ideal description has an historical basis throughout, and Herodotus in Book iii. chap. 89. In prophecy (in the second part of Isaiah, to which he probably owes the name by which he is familiar to us) he is characterized in a way which almost places him in the rank of theocratic rulers, as the anointed of the Lord, who will not merely accomplish His will on Babylon, but will also redeem His captive people, and that as a servant who knows the will of his lord. In sacred history he appears as one who had acquired a deeper knowledge of the God of Israel, a knowledge essentially distinct from that which had impressed a Nebuchadnezzar, a Belshazzar, or a Darius Medus, without having a deeper root in the mind. While the heathen monarchs had hitherto served only as instruments for the humiliation and punishment of Israel, *he* serves God in the realization of His thoughts of peace towards His people. In the God of Israel he recognises the author of his victories, and proves his gratitude by the benefits which he confers upon His people. His position in this respect has a symbolic-prophetic character. It awakens in us a presentiment that the hostile position which the power of the world had hitherto occupied with respect to the community of God would be altered, that the prophecy of Isaiah would at a future time be fulfilled in a wide sense, according to which kings would be their nursing-fathers and nursing-mothers. He is a foreshadowing, and therefore a prefiguration, of the future removal of the former rude contrast between the kingdom of God and the kingdoms of this world.

At this period we are met everywhere by manifold indications that the time foretold by the prophets of "the gathering of the heathen" is at hand. The most remarkable preparation for this is to be found in the relation of the Jews in the mother country to the Jews in the διασπορὰ, which was formed under the guidance of divine providence. Remembering this, we see clearly that the carrying away of the nation into exile was intended not only as retributive punishment and a salutary incentive to repentance, but had other aims also which were wider and higher. Judah is carried into exile in order to gather the scattered sheep of Israel, to reanimate the spirit of true piety among the exiled citizens of the ten tribes, which had become nearly extinct, and to effect a reunion of the ἐκλογὴ with the Church of God. When this object is attained, and *one* Israel again exists, the nucleus and stem of the nation return, that the Israelitish religious life may find a centre in the new temple. The whole nation, however, does not return, but a considerable number remain in exile. These are kept from sinking into heathenism by the close connection in which they continually stand with the centre. In them a great mission is organized among the heathen, which by divine providence becomes more and more extended in later times, the Jews being scattered over all the countries of the earth. Thus the attention of the heathen world was directed to the light which was already in existence, the true God has witnesses everywhere; and, what is of most importance, care is taken that when the perfect light appears in Israel, it should at the same time be visible to all the nations of the earth. The Babylonish exile thus forms the necessary presupposition of the founding of Christianity among the heathen; and what apparently destroyed the supremacy of the Lord even in the small corner which it had reserved to itself, became a means in His hand of extending it over all the nations of the earth.

Many hypotheses have been laid down respecting the motives by which Cyrus was influenced in his treatment of the Jews. We are led into the right track by a consideration of the contents of the decree which he issued respecting them. This is given to us in Ezra i. 1-4; and that the account is a faithful one appears from Ezra vi. 1-5, according to which, a document was found in the time of Darius, in the archives at Ecbatana, which fully agreed with the import of this edict. In this edict Cyrus acknowledges Jehovah, the God of Israel, as the universal Lord of heaven and earth, confesses that this Jehovah has given him all the kingdoms which he has conquered, and states that He has commanded him to build Him a temple at Jerusalem in Judah. In the two latter points there is an unmistakeable reference to the second part of Isaiah; comp., for example, chap. xlv. 13: "I have raised him up in righteousness, and I will direct all his ways: he shall build my city, and he shall let go my captives, not for price nor reward, saith the Lord of hosts;" chap. xli. 2-4, 25, xliv. 24-28, xlv. 1-6, xlvi. 11, xlviii. 13-15. The reference of the edict to these passages in Isaiah is sometimes verbally exact; comp. the proof given in Kleinert, *The Authenticity of the Prophecies of Isaiah*, p. 142 ff. It is the less to be regarded as an interpolation on the part of the author of the book of Ezra, since he does not expressly indicate that the prophecies exercised an influence of this kind on Cyrus. To the fact that Josephus, *Ant.* xi. chap. i. § 1, 2, explicitly states that Cyrus was influenced to the publication of this edict by those prophecies, we attach little weight. Only on the edict itself do we found our assumption that this was really the case, that the wonderful agreement of the prophecies with the past dispensations of his life called forth in Cyrus the determination to do the will of this great, almighty God, who had taken so great an interest in him even before he knew Him, and in gratitude to give glory to His name (Isa. xlv. 4, 5).

If in this way we have discovered with certainty the immediate cause for the determination of Cyrus, we can at least find probable reasons for a more remote cause. The fact that the prophecies made such an impression on Cyrus, presupposes that he had already attained to a certain knowledge of the true God, and that he had received these prophecies from a credible source. Here everything points to Daniel, formerly one of the most illustrious servants of the Chaldee state, and now of the Medo-Persian. He had already influenced the Chaldee rulers to acknowledge the

God of Israel to be the Lord of all lords, and the God of all gods; Darius the Mede, who had raised him to the highest dignity, had been led by him to express his recognition of the God of Israel in a public edict. What is more natural than to assume that he, with his ardent longing for the deliverance of his people, should likewise have influenced Cyrus to the promulgation of his edict, partly by virtue of the great respect in which he was held by him on account of all that had happened under the previous reigns, and partly because he laid before him the prophecies in question, which were confirmed by his authority?

All other solutions of the problem have either no historical guarantee, or else they are insufficient to explain the facts. This was formerly the case even when the mere release of the Israelites was in question; but here there is more at stake, and therefore more than ordinary motives are required. It is necessary to explain how Cyrus came to the consciousness that *Jehovah* had given him all the kingdoms of the earth, and had commanded him to build Him a temple; how it was that he not merely generously gave up the numerous and valuable vessels of the temple, but also laid a tax in behalf of the building of the temple on his heathen subjects, from whose midst the Israelites had gone forth, and encouraged them to give voluntary contributions to it. We must also explain how it was that the result was so directly and without any interposition attributed to Jehovah the God of Israel, whose co-operation must therefore have been evident; comp. Ps. cxxvi. 1.

The edict of Cyrus has reference not merely to Judah, but to the whole nation, and was made known, according to Ezra i. 1, in the whole kingdom, and not merely in the provinces in which the Judaites dwelt. Nor are proofs wanting that the new colony on the Jordan consisted not merely of Judaites, but also of members of the ten tribes, although in the first great expedition the Judaites no doubt made by far the greater number; which is easily explained from the circumstance that they were the more God-fearing portion of the nation, and also from the fact that the ten tribes, during their much longer abode in the lands of exile, had struck far deeper roots. The very fact that there are twelve leaders of the first expedition of the exiles, ten besides Zerubbabel and Joshua,—in Ezra ii. 2 only nine, but the tenth is added in Neh. viii. 7,—plainly referring to the twelve tribes, shows us that the consciousness of the unity of the whole nation was again present; and this presupposes that the wide distinction between Israel and Judah had ceased during the time of exile. We are also led to the same result, by the fact that on the consecration of the new temple a sin-offering of twelve bulls was presented for all Israel. It is evident that at the time of Christ the inhabitants of Canaan were by no means Judaites alone, but rather belonged to all the twelve tribes, from the designation given to the nation in Acts xxvi. 7, τὸ δωδεκάφυλον ἡμῶν, and again from Luke ii. 36, according to which Anna was of the tribe of Asher, as Saul was of the tribe of Benjamin.

The whole relation is probably to be understood thus:—The prophets, with one consent, give expression to the hope that the great common misfortune impending in the future will put an end to the melancholy breach between Judah and Israel, that both will in consequence repent and become reconciled to God. The fact that this hope is to be found in undiminished strength in Jeremiah, comp. chap. iii., xxxi., and in Ezek. chap. xxxvii., shows that even at that late period the members of the kingdom of the ten tribes had in the main kept themselves strictly separate from the heathen, and had not succumbed to the destroying influences of heathenism. This hope was fulfilled. With the destruction of the kingdom of the ten tribes, the main hindrance to reunion was done away. The separation was mainly due to political reasons, to which also its continuance must be attributed. The religious element in it was only subordinate. The strength of the desire of the Israelites for reunion with respect to religion, appears from the fact that all the Israelitish rulers of the various dynasties despaired of conquering it by considerations of a purely political character, and endeavoured by the maintenance of an Israelitish state-religion to keep the balance, to awake religious antipathies which paralyzed it. Nevertheless they were unable to prevent the whole God-fearing portion of the nation, who gathered about the prophets, from constant sorrowful regrets on account of the separation, from looking upon it as having no internal existence, and longing for its outward abolition. Nor could they prevent continual emigrations to Judea, which were especially numerous at all times when the Lord glorified Himself in the Davidic kingship. With the destruction of the kingdom of the ten tribes the artificial wall of separation which had been built up fell into complete ruin. The cause which had for a considerable period prevented all external approach, viz. the great local distance, fell away when Judah too was led into exile. The hearts of the Judaites were softened by misery, and they made loving advances to their brethren who were in similar affliction, upon whom the revival of piety which had taken place among the Judaites exercised a beneficial influence. They felt that in this respect the Judaites occupied a higher standpoint, and willingly submitted to them, attaching themselves to them. Judah therefore became the centre, during the exile, about which the whole Church of God again collected. The ten tribes in their separation entirely ceased to exist. All its members who retained any Israelitish religiousness entered into the union, which was the more easily done, since the illegal Israelitish priesthood was in no sense animated by a religious *esprit de corps*, but was rather a pure state-institution, which would necessarily perish with the destruction of the state; while the Jewish priesthood, even in exile, still formed a compact mass, and presented an excellent centre round which the whole nation might assemble. Those individuals of the ten tribes in whom the Israelitish consciousness was completely destroyed, the reformed Jews of that time, were lost among the heathen. When the edict of Cyrus was promulgated, it was therefore quite natural, for reasons already given, that in the beginning the members of the ten tribes should only have returned in comparatively small numbers. By this circumstance it came to pass that Judah became still more decisively the centre of the whole, so that all were collectively called by the name of this tribe. The erection of the new temple necessarily served to consolidate the union still more. The eye of the Israelites who had remained in exile was directed to it no less than that of the Judaites. They fully recognised that the temple, with all that pertained to it, was the sole support for the Israelitish national consciousness. Great numbers set out for Judea after the new colony there had become consolidated, principally, perhaps, in the centuries between Nehemiah and the Maccabees, which are shrouded in almost total historical darkness. Even those who remained behind entered into close connection with the temple, sent their gifts to it, and undertook pilgrimages thither.

Another argument in favour of the correctness of this view is, that the great number of Jews whom we afterwards find in Judea, and no less in the diaspora—a great many millions—can scarcely be explained if we assume that they were all descendants of the Jewish exiles. So also the passage 2 Chron. xxxiv. 9, which shows that after the fall of the Israelitish state, the remnant of the Israelites who had remained in the land were driven back into religious fellowship with Judah. All that can be said of those who remained behind is equally applicable to the exiles also. Again, we have the passage Jer. xli. 5–8, where we are told that, after the destruction of Jerusalem, eighty men from Sichem, Shiloh, and Samaria, from the centres of the former kingdom of the ten tribes, journeyed to the place of the former temple, there to lament over the destruction, and to present their offerings.

If our idea be established, it is evident that the many researches which have been made, even to recent times, respecting the abode of the ten tribes, who have always been looked for as a separate nationality, are quite in vain. Grant, an American, whose work appeared in a German translation at Basle, 1842, thought he had discovered the ten tribes in the independent Nestorians in the mountains of Kurdistan, and for a long time it was a favourite idea to look upon the Indians in North America as their descendants. Many identify them with the Afghans, who, having been subject to Jewish influences, regard themselves as descendants of the ten tribes. All these, however, are mere fancies. The remnant of the ten tribes, subsequent to the dispersion, assumed a Jewish character, and afterwards became amalgamated with the Jews who had gone out into the heathen world from the time of Alexander, and especially after the destruction of Rome. The complete fruitlessness of all attempts hitherto made,—in every case where an apparent discovery of the ten tribes has been made, either a Jewish element has subsequently appeared, or it has become manifest that nothing Israelitish existed,—which was to be expected *à priori*, forms another argument in favour of our view, which is of no little importance with respect to many questions. Josephus has already led the way to that error regarding the ten tribes, remarking, *Ant.* xi. 5. 2, that even in his time they dwelt in countless multitudes beyond the Euphrates. So also the author of the fourth book of Ezra, who, according to chap. xiii., imagined the Israelites to be peacefully living in a far-distant land, situated to the north-east. The fact that such opinions could arise, may be explained from the circumstance that the amalgamation of the Israelites with the Judaites took place very gradually and imperceptibly.

Cyrus appointed Zerubbabel to be the leader of those who were returning, and governor of the new colony. In Ezra i. 8 he appears under the Persian name Sheshbazzar; the name Zerubbabel, scattered to Babylon, he bore as the native representative of the nation that had been carried away into captivity. There is no doubt respecting the identity of the two. Cyrus confirmed in his dignity the man who was the native ruler of the Jews, and enjoyed the greatest respect among them. Already he was prince of Judah, and now he became Persian governor, פחה. As such he stood immediately below the king. The Persian governors in Samaria were expected, however, to keep a watchful eye on the new Jewish colony, to frustrate all plans of rebellion, and to give information of all that was suspicious. The Samaritans, as native heathen, looked upon the Persian court as their natural ally against the Jews, which proves that only very extraordinary motives could have influenced them to relinquish to this nation a province so important in a political and strategical aspect. The whole position which the Persian government assumed towards the new colony shows that ordinary motives could not have sufficed in this case, that the walls of policy must here have been broken through by higher considerations. But where anything of this kind happens, it does not generally continue long. Ordinary policy soon reasserts itself, and so it was in this case. The heart of Cyrus, awakened to faith in the God of Israel, had permitted the return, and all that it involved. But the further development of the matter fell to the judgment of his counsellors, and there Israel fared badly.

It is plain that Cyrus intended to confer a benefit on the Jews by giving them a leader out of their midst; but it certainly proved less effective than the Jews expected. They thought that their redemption was inseparably connected with the re-establishment of the race of David, although they had received no special grounds for this idea from the predictions of the prophets, in which nothing is ever said of kings of David's race after the exile, but at this time prominence is invariably given to the kingdom of the Messiah. Doubtless they thought that Zerubbabel would at least have the title of king. But in God's plan it was otherwise ordained. Even the dignity of governor did not remain in the family of David. Zerubbabel was the first and the last who held this position. Persian policy did not suffer it to be otherwise. We see that it was only necessary to give an indication respecting the family of David at the beginning of the new development, with reference to the later grand position which they were to occupy in it; it was not yet intended to raise them to this position. First, they were to sink lower and lower, in order that the exaltation might plainly appear as the work of God. This course of events had also been foretold by the prophets. The burden of their teaching throughout is, that the Messiah should proceed from the family of David at a time when it had sunk into complete obscurity. Comp., for example, Isa. xi. 1, " There shall come forth a rod out of the stem of Jesse, and a Branch shall grow out of his roots," where the cut stem of Jesse denotes the Davidic race robbed of their kingly dignity, and involved in complete obscurity, now no longer remembering their regal, but only their rustic ancestor;—and again, Isa. liii. 2, "For He shall grow up before Him as a tender plant, and as a root out of a dry ground,"—in which passage, it is true, only the humiliation of the servant of God is directly spoken of, but this presupposes the humiliation of his race ;—also Ezek. xvii. 22–24, where the Messiah appears as a small, thin branch, which the Lord has taken from a high cedar and planted upon a high mountain, and which grows into a proud tree, under which all the birds of the air find a dwelling-place. In Jeremiah and Zechariah (iii. 8, vi. 12) the Messiah is called *The Branch*, with reference to the image of a cut stem of the branch of David employed by Isaiah.

All the silver and golden vessels of the temple, which had been kept in the temple of Belus at Babylon since the time of Nebuchadnezzar, and whose number was very great, according to Ezra i. 11, were unhesitatingly given up to Zerubbabel. Just as Zerubbabel stood at the head of civil affairs, so Joshua the high priest stood at the head of religious matters. Among those who returned there must have been comparatively many with means. We see this from the great number of men-servants and maid-servants, from the rich contributions to the building of the temple, and from passages such as Hag. i. 4, according to which many built themselves ceiled houses at the very beginning. The attempt made by some to represent those who returned as a pauper nation is therefore quite unhistorical. It is a complete misapprehension of the power of the religious principle, and is an insult to the human race, to suppose that only those went forth who neither possessed nor could hope to gain anything in exile. It is remarkable that, according to Ezra i. 4, 6, the heathen in whose midst the Jews dwelt responded to the demand of Cyrus by bringing rich presents for the building of the sanctuary, and for those who were returning. This shows us that at that time there was a powerful movement among the heathen in favour of Judah, of the God of Judah and His sanctuaries, and is a prefiguration of the future complete change in the position of the heathen world with respect to the kingdom of God predicted by the prophets, of the time when kings and queens should be the nursing-fathers and nursing-mothers of the kingdom of God; comp. Isa. xlix. 22 ff., lx. 8–10, lxi. 5–11. This movement culminated in many transitions.

§ 2.

THE NEW COLONY ON THE JORDAN TO THE COMPLETION OF THE BUILDING OF THE TEMPLE; OR, ZERUBBABEL AND JOSHUA.

The principal source for this period is the first part of the book of Ezra, chap. i.–vi. This, however, does not contain a complete history; but the author, whose object it is to write sacred history, limits himself to that which is at this time its sole object,—the proper theme which had been given to him, viz. the restoration of the temple. While the book of Ezra gives us a statement of the facts which occurred during this period, the writings of the prophets whose activity belongs to it—of Haggai and Zechariah—give us a clear representation of the mind of the Israelites and their spiritual condition. In the latter respect, great importance is also due to a number of psalms which were composed for use in the restored worship of God. Of these, Ps. cvii. deserves special mention. It celebrates the gathering of Israel from the four ends of the earth, and, according to vers. 22 and 32, was sung at a great thanksgiving feast of the nation, probably at the first celebration of the feast of tabernacles after the return, on which occasion all Israel flocked to Jerusalem, and sacrifices were offered up to the Lord on the newly-erected altar; comp. Ezra iii. 1 ff. And again, Ps. cxi.–cxix., a cycle of psalms sung with the preceding Davidic trilogy on laying the foundation-stone of the new temple. Also the ten anonymous psalms in the collection of pilgrim-songs in Ps. cxx.–cxxxiv., which collectively refer to the melancholy circumstances in which Israel was involved by the machinations of the Samaritans. Finally, the group Ps. cxxxv.–cxlvi., sung after the successful completion of the temple, and probably at the time of its consecration, consisting of three new psalms at the beginning, and one at the end, with eight Davidic psalms between. All the psalms from cvii. to cxlvi., therefore, serve as a source for this period, only excepting those which have been inserted in the various cycles and applied to the relations of that time, which bear the name of David in the superscription.

The company of those who returned found the land empty on their arrival. The last Jewish inhabitants had fled to Egypt on the murder of Gedaliah, and none of the surrounding heathen nations had ventured to anticipate the occupation of the trans-Euphratic rulers by taking possession of it; for they still expected that the conquerors would send a colony into the land, just as the land of the ten tribes had only been colonized a considerable time after the inhabitants had been led away into captivity. And these nations had the less inducement to make the attempt, since they themselves had been very much weakened by the campaigns of Nebuchadnezzar, and were quite satisfied with their dwellings. It is not improbable that they roamed through the land, and employed it as pasture for cattle; but when they heard of the command of Cyrus, they at once retreated in fear. Bertheau, in his treatises *on the History of the Israelites*, p. 382 ff., has indeed laid down the hypothesis that a great number of the Judaites remained behind in the land, the deportation being only partial. But this assumption has no foundation. The desolation and depopulation of the country is everywhere represented as total; for example, in Jer. xliv. 6, 22, 2 Chron. xxxvi. How earnest the Chaldees were in carrying away all Judah, appears from the notice in Jer. lii. 30, according to which Nebuzar-adan carried away 745 Jews into captivity in the twenty-third year of Nebuchadnezzar, such, no doubt, as had by degrees reassembled in the land. The returning exiles find a country completely desolate and uncultivated (comp., for example, Ps. cvii.), and not the smallest trace appears of their finding any inhabitants there. The book of Ezra everywhere proceeds on the assumption that those who returned were the sole inhabitants of the land.

Immediately after their arrival in the land, which had now lain waste for more than half a century, the returning exiles distributed themselves in the various cities, according to their tribes and families, and began to rebuild their houses and to cultivate again their pieces of ground. It was necessary, owing to the small number of those who returned, to choose only a limited number of cities at first to settle in, the preference being given to such as lay in the vicinity of Jerusalem, the centre,—a circumstance from which Ewald has falsely inferred that only these cities were ceded to the Jews in the edict of Cyrus. But the first consideration was to restore the service of God, of which they had so long and so painfully been deprived. They erected a new temporary altar for burnt-offering in the ruins of the temple at Jerusalem, in the same place where the old one had stood. On this provisional altar, and in the temporarily-erected sanctuary, the daily offerings prescribed in the law were offered up. It was consecrated on the first celebration of the feast of tabernacles. Ps. cvii., which was sung at that celebration, enables us to realize the mind of the Israelites at that time: everything in it breathes a spirit of joy, of thankfulness for the glorious mercy of the Lord. We see that the people are celebrating their feast of restoration. They began at once to make every preparation for the rebuilding of the temple. In these preparations the first year passed away. In the second month of the second year they laid the foundation amid great solemnities. But the old men who had seen the first temple lamented, and their loud weeping mingled with the rejoicings of the youth; comp. Ezra iii. 12, 13. Everything seemed to them so small and poor— not a trace of the former glory; and this difference affected them the more painfully, since they looked upon it as a sign that the grace of God had not fully returned to them, and felt themselves still in a state of partial exile. We also gain some clue to the disposition of Israel at that time, by the psalms which were sung on the laying of the foundation-stone of the temple. It is one of soft and quiet melancholy, finding comfort in God. On the one hand we find exultation on account of the help already vouchsafed by the Lord; but on the other hand a striving against sorrow and anxiety is perceptible, caused by a recollection of the misery which still remains, of the small number of the people of God (Ps. cxix. 86, 87), of the oppression of the mighty heathen world under which they sighed (ver. 51), and of the ignominy which rested upon them. By these things the people are impelled to cling more closely to their God, and to form a vivid conception of His former deeds and His glorious promises (comp. Ps. cxi.-cxiv.), to resolve by true observance of the command of the Lord to prepare the way for His salvation. The strange mixture of jubilee and mourning, which, according to the book of Ezra, took place at the consecration of the temple, meets us in these psalms.

But even their joy on account of the weak beginnings of the restoration of divine grace was soon disturbed. When they had begun to rebuild the temple, the Samaritans turned to the rulers of the people with the proposal, "Let us build with you: for we seek your God as ye do; and we do sacrifice unto Him since the days of Esar-haddon king of Assur, which brought us up hither." And when the chiefs sent them the answer, "Ye have nothing to do with us to build an house unto our God; but we ourselves together will build unto the Lord God of Israel, as king Cyrus the king of Persia hath commanded us," they were embittered by it, and did all that they could to hinder the building of the temple, and for a length of time were successful.

In order to understand this event, and the whole subsequent relation of the Jews and Samaritans, we must here necessarily enter into the question of the origin of the Samaritans. On this subject there are two opposite views. According to one, the Samaritans were originally a purely heathen nation, who at first included Jehovah in the number of their gods, because they looked upon Him as the national deity, and worshipped Him together with the gods which they had brought with them, but by degrees, specially under the influence of their relations to the Jews, came to worship Him alone, renouncing their other gods. The other view, on the contrary, makes the Samaritans a mixed nation, consisting not only of a heathen element, but also of a very strong Israelitish element, members of the former kingdom of the ten tribes,—part of them having remained in the country at the time of the Assyrian destruction, while the remainder had returned to it by degrees out of banishment.

The former of these views is undoubtedly the correct one. In favour of the latter we have only the assertion of the later Samaritans themselves, who maintain that they are descended from Israel,—an assumption, however, which has no weight, because it is met by a recognition on the part of the older Samaritans of their purely heathen origin; comp. Ezra iv. 9, 10, where they call themselves "the nations whom the great and noble Asnapper brought over and set in the cities of Samaria;" and again, Ezra iv. 2, where the Samaritans make no attempt to found their demand for participation in the building of the temple on their Israelitish origin. Moreover, they acknowledged their purely heathen origin at a later time, when it became their advantage to do so; comp. Josephus, *Ant.* ix. 14, § 3, xi. 8, § 6, xii. 5, § 5. Hence it follows that the pretension to Israelitish extraction is only one of the many lies by which the later Samaritans tried to make themselves of equal birth with the Jews; while the latter made the purely heathen origin of the former the basis of their assertion, that notwithstanding their worship of Jehovah, they had no part in Him and in His kingdom.

On the other hand, the assumption of the purely heathen origin of the Samaritans has the strongest arguments in its favour, besides the earlier utterances of the nation itself. In 2 Kings xvii. the heathen colonists appear as the sole inhabitants of the land. According to ver. 26 ff., they besought the king of Assyria to give them an Israelitish priest, because they had nobody in their land who could give them even the rudest conception of the way in which the God of the country was to be worshipped. Those prophets who lived after the destruction of the kingdom of the ten tribes universally represent its members as having been completely carried away, only to be brought back at a future time; comp. Jer. xxxi. 5 ff.; Zech. x. In Matt. x. 5, 6, our Lord places the Samaritans on a level with the heathen, and together contrasts them with the Jews. In John iv. 22 He characterizes their religion as subjective throughout, and their piety as self-invented—an ἐθελοθρησκεία: they know not what they worship, *i.e.* they have no essential knowledge of the object of the religion of God, no participation in His revelation, from which alone such knowledge can spring; in short, they are ἄθεοι ἐν τῷ κόσμῳ no less than the heathen. The Saviour would never have denied all essential knowledge of God to the ten tribes, nor have excluded them from participation in the kingdom of God. To these arguments we might readily add a number of others, but regard it as unnecessary. The latest defenders of the view that the Samaritans were a mixed nation—Kalkar in *Pelt's Theological Researches*, iii. 3, and Keil in the *Commentary on the Books of the Kings*, on 2 Kings xvii.—have quoted in their own favour the passage 2 Chron. xxxiv. 9, according to which there was at Joshua's time still a remnant of Israel in the cities of Manasseh and Ephraim, from whom the Levites collected money for the restoration of the temple. But this passage proves the very contrary from what it is intended to prove. It shows that the remnant of Israel, which no doubt existed, strove against intermixture with the heathen colonists, binding themselves closely to the temple at Jerusalem, and entirely giving up the separation. Probably they afterwards went over completely to Judah,—an hypothesis which would serve to explain the passages already quoted, presupposing the total evacuation of the land by its former inhabitants. Or if this were not the case, they must at least have been so unimportant that they could be entirely overlooked. In any case they prove nothing in favour of a mixed nation.

If what we have advanced with respect to the Samaritans hold good, we must regard the position which Zerubbabel and the rulers of the Jews assumed towards them as fully justified, without our finding it necessary to appeal to arguments such as that recently revived by Ewald, that they were at that time partially addicted to idolatry, and that union with them would therefore have been fraught with great danger to the Jews. If Samaritan individuals as such had asked to be received into the community of Israel, their request would certainly have been granted without hesitation. But here the case was very different. The Samaritans demanded that the Jews should recognise them as the second division of the nation of God: they thought it was enough to serve Jehovah in order to be His people. They had no idea that it was necessary before all to be chosen and called of God, and to have His revelation in the midst of those who were chosen and called. If the Jews had not opposed this pretension, they would have shown that their own piety was an ἐθελοθρησκεία, that their own religion was subjective. Our Lord's statement in John respecting the nature of the Samaritan worship of God, already cited, forms the best apology for the conduct of the Jewish rulers, which Ewald has very superficially attributed to a narrow scrupulousness. If the Samaritan religion were such as it was there described, the Jews could not do otherwise than deny them all part in the building of the temple. The reverse would have been an injurious anticipation of the times of the New Testament, in which the narrow limits of the revelation of God were removed, and the revelation was extended to all the nations of the earth.

Just as the correct view of the origin of the Samaritans throws light upon this separate fact, so also upon their whole subsequent relation to Judaism. From this time the most bitter enmity existed between the Jews and Samaritans, occasioned by this event. On the side of the Jews, we find the cause of it in the unfounded claim made by the Samaritans to belong to the people of God, and, on the side of the Samaritans, in the fact that the Jews would not recognise this claim. The attempt to prove and justify their pretensions, to make themselves of equal birth with the Jews, gradually became the fundamental principle of the nation. In favour of it they banished all idolatry from their midst; they obtained the Jewish law, and followed even its most burdensome ordinances,—for example, those with respect to the sabbatical year; they built a temple on Gerizim, and invented a multitude of lies in order to place it on a par with that at Jerusalem; they received every Jewish priest who fled to them for refuge with the greatest joy,—first of all the priest Manasseh, to whom they assigned the highest priestly dignity.

The machinations of the Samaritans against the Jews

must have been the more dangerous to the latter, since the Samaritans, as native heathen, would be more fully trusted by the Persian court, and moreover the Persian officers in Samaria had from the beginning been invested with a kind of supremacy over the Jews.

They first succeeded in frustrating the well-meaning designs of Cyrus towards the Jews, for they gained over his counsellors to their side. In this way the Jews missed the help which had been promised to them in building the temple. They were discouraged, and relinquished the work. Their zeal was not great enough to outweigh the continual hindrances and annoyances. That there was no absolute hindrance, appears from the fact that Haggai and Zechariah afterwards reproached them severely with their neglect in carrying on the building of the temple. The assumption that the Jews were prohibited from continuing to build the temple by a formal edict of the Persian king is based on a false presupposition. Ezra iv. 4, 5, contains the sole reference to the hindrances in building the temple: "Then the people of the land weakened the hands of the people of Judah, and troubled them in building; and hired counsellors against them, to frustrate their purpose, all the days of Cyrus king of Persia, even until the reign of Darius king of Persia." Vers. 6-23 form a parenthesis, in which we are told how afterwards the Samaritans, under Ahasuerus, Xerxes, and Artaxarta, Artaxerxes, combined against the building of the city wall in a similar way. Ver. 24 returns to vers. 4 and 5. It was not until the second year of Darius, after Haggai had severely censured them for their neglect, that they recommenced the work with zeal, and this zeal was powerfully quickened by the encouraging and comforting predictions of Haggai and Zechariah. Haggai and Zechariah are the only prophets whose activity stands in connection with the building of the second temple. To them only is there a reference in the passage Zech. viii. 9, on which Ewald founds his false assumption that numerous prophets assembled about the sanctuary which was rising out of its ruins. In the third year of Darius there was a new interruption. The royal officers in Samaria commanded the

Jews to cease for a time, until they would have laid the matter before the Persian court, and have received directions respecting it. These officers, however, quite unlike those who had probably been deposed, seem to have been men of a just spirit, who were satisfied with the mere duties of their office. They notified to the king that the Jews appealed to the edict of Cyrus, and begged that the archives might be examined whether there were really such an edict. This was done; the edict was found and ratified by Darius in the beginning of the fourth year of his reign, in so far that a part of the cost of the building was to be defrayed from the royal coffers, from the revenues of the territories in the cis-Euphratic lands, and at the same time the Jews were to receive means to enable them to carry on their worship: comp. Ezra vi. 8, 9, a passage which is perfectly clear in itself, and could only be used by Bertheau in favour of a totally unfounded hypothesis by forcible misinterpretation. The restoration of the temple stands in immediate connection with this edict of Darius, which appears the less strange, since we elsewhere find in him traces of that magnanimity towards prisoners and subordinates which characterized Cyrus. In consequence of this edict, the building of the temple made rapid progress, so that it was quite finished within a period of three years. It is remarkable that just as there were seventy years from the first occupation of Jerusalem by the Chaldees to the first year of Cyrus, so there were exactly seventy years from the destruction of the temple to the edict of Cyrus; just as there were eighteen years between the beginning of the destruction and its completion, so also between the beginning of the restoration and its completion. It is remarkable, also, that soon after that edict, in the fifth year of Darius, heavy punishment fell upon Babylon in consequence of its revolt, by which means it was brought considerably nearer to its complete overthrow. Judgment and mercy, which are placed in close connection by the prophets, especially by Jeremiah, xxv. 12, 13, kept equal pace in history also. The end of the two periods of seventy years shows us in like manner both connected. The final completion of the temple, which in Ezra vi. 17 is expressly characterized as the common sanctuary for Israel in all the twelve tribes, took place in the sixth year of Darius. The consecration was very solemn, the people gave themselves up to lively joy.

But the newly-built temple was not only very inferior to Solomon's externally, but was also deficient in very important things which the latter possessed. The following are mentioned as such by the Jews :—1. The Urim and Thummim. Externally, indeed, this was still present: the high priest wore the breastplate with the precious stones even under the second temple, but no divine answers were imparted through it. That the Urim and Thummim had really lost its significance under the second temple, is evident from Ezra ii. 63, Neh. vii. 65, where the determination of a difficult case is deferred to the time when a priest should again stand up with the Urim and Thummim. This loss, however, was not simultaneous with the destruction of the first temple. Already, after David's time, the Urim and Thummim disappears completely out of the history; and there is little doubt that this is due to its cessation, and not to the mere fact of its not being mentioned. The cause is to be looked for in the fact that the immediate higher illumination, of which the answers through the Urim and Thummim were the result, withdrew more and more from the priests and confined itself to the prophets. The more powerfully the prophethood asserted itself as a special institution, the more completely the prophetic elements which had formerly characterized the priesthood disappeared from it; the priestly and the prophetic spirit gradually became purely antithetic. We can only attribute the loss to the time after the exile in so far as it then actually took place, partly because the priestly principle then universally acquired absolute supremacy, partly because, owing to the political position taken by the high priests in the new colony, spiritually-minded men were far less frequently found among their number than had been the case previous to the exile. According to the Jews, the second temple wanted (2) the ark of the covenant. There can be no doubt that this really was wanting. It does not appear on Titus' arch of triumph, which is still in Rome. That which was by many for a long time supposed to be it, has since been unanimously recognised as the table of shew-bread. Moreover, Josephus makes no mention of it in his description of the triumph, *De Bell. Jud.* l. 7, 17, in which it would necessarily have appeared if it had existed, since it was the first sanctuary of the nation. He, the eye-witness, speaks of three things which were carried before the conqueror—the table for shew-bread, the golden candlestick, and the law; he says explicitly that the holy of holies was quite empty. Those who maintain that the ark of the covenant was present even in the second temple, appeal mainly to the idea that it is inconceivable how the Jews should have erected a new altar for incense, a new table for shew-bread, and a new candlestick, in the place of that which had been destroyed, and not have made a new ark of the covenant. But this argument has no weight. With the ark of the covenant the case was quite different. Among all sanctuaries it was the only one whose preparation the Lord had not left entirely to the people. The writing on the tables of the law had a mysterious origin, according to the Pentateuch; and if it were impossible to procure such tables again, it would be useless to restore the ark which was destined to conceal them. Herein lay a definite indication that God would not have the ark restored. Again, it has been said that if the ark of the covenant were wanting, there would no longer have been any reason for separating the holy of holies from the holy place by a curtain; for this separation had no meaning except in relation to the ark of the covenant. But here the sign is confounded with the thing signified. The latter, God's presence in the holy of holies, was still there, only its outward symbol was wanting. The loss of the ark must have been extremely painful to the nation. This alone justified the words spoken by Haggai in chap. ii. 3, that the second temple was as nothing in comparison with the first, which refer chiefly to external things. The author of the book of Cosri, in part ii. § 28, says very truly that the ark with the mercy-seat and the cherubim was the foundation, the root, the heart, and the seal of the whole temple and of the whole Levitical worship. The way in which everything holy under the Old Testament was connected with the ark of the covenant already proved that the ark of the covenant was made before everything else. 'Arca fœderis,' says Wits. *Miscellanea Sacra,* tom. i. p. 439, 'veluti cor totius religionis Israeliticæ primum omnium formata est.' It was esteemed the most costly treasure of the nation. This, the place where God's honour dwelt, Ps. xxvi. 8, where He manifested Himself in His most glorious revelation, was called the glory of Israel; comp. 1 Sam. iv. 21, 22, Ps. lxviii. 61. It is true that in a spiritual sense the ark of the covenant still existed under the second temple, as we have already intimated; to the eye of faith it was still visible in the empty holy of holies. If this had not been so, there could never have been any thought of building the second temple. The God of heaven and of earth was still in a special sense the God of Israel; the temple had still a *numen præsens.* But the visible pledge of this presence which He had formerly given to the nation was now wanting, the support which He had formerly vouchsafed to their weak faith was taken away; and hence it must have been far more difficult to rise to the consciousness of His mercy. If we inquire into the reasons of this withdrawal, we see that on the one side it was continued punishment for the sins of the nation. The non-restoration of the pledge of the presence of God in the nation showed the people that their repentance, and therefore their reconciliation with God, was incomplete, and threatened them with the total cessation of this presence, unless they became truly reconciled with the Lord. Hence it forms the link between the Chaldee and the Romish destructions. In this respect the loss of the ark of the covenant stands on a level with so many other signs of the incompleteness of the restoration of the grace of God, of the melancholy external condition of the nation, etc. This was what the want of the ark of the covenant testified to the mass of the people. For them it was an actual punishment and threat. But the circumstance had a different meaning for the ἐκλογή. In the kingdom of God there is no decay without compensation. The decay of the old forms a guarantee of the approach of the new and more glorious. In order to make the longing for this the more intense, the old was taken away considerably sooner, before the new was given; just as it was necessary for the Davidic race to lose the glory which it already possessed, before it could attain to its true and perfect glory. It must have been the more easy to recognise this meaning in the circumstance, since Jeremiah had already foretold that at a future time the Lord would manifest Himself in a far more real way than by the ark of the covenant, so that the loss of the most glorious thing that they possessed would seem to be their gain; comp. the remarkable prophecy, chap. iii. 16: " And it shall come to pass, when ye be multiplied and increased in the land, in those days, saith the Lord, they shall say no more, The ark of the covenant of the Lord; neither shall it come to mind, neither shall they remember it, neither shall they visit it, neither shall that be done any more."

The third thing which, according to Jewish writers, was wanting in the second temple was the Shekinah, the habitation of God,—a cloud of fire which, according to Jewish tradition, is said to have floated constantly in the space above the mercy-seat between the two cherubim. This visible presence of God ceased with the destruction of the temple of Solomon. But the theory of a constant visible presence of God in the tabernacle of the testimony, and in the first temple, proves, on nearer examination, to be a Jewish figment. It is only in so far true, that the presence of the Lord in the tabernacle of testimony and in the first temple, which was generally invisible, sometimes on extraordinary occasions manifested itself also in a visible way, as Vitringa rightly perceived, *Obrs. S. T.* p. 169. The principal passage, Lev. xvi. 2, does not speak of a constant visible presence, but of isolated appearances; of these, however, it speaks most distinctly, so that only the most forced interpretation, such as Bähr has attempted, p. 396, can take this meaning out of it. And, moreover, in every other place where mention is made of a visible presence of the Lord, on the consecration of the tabernacle of testimony and of the temple of Solomon, it appears as something extraordinary and momentary. The defenders of the Shekinah—among whom Rau, Professor in Herborn, is the most learned and is the author of a whole book on the subject, *de Nube super Arcam Fœderis*, Utrecht, 1760—appeal to the fact that Ezekiel saw the glory of the Lord above the cherubim rise out of the temple before the destruction, chap. xi. 22. But this argument has no weight. We have to do with a vision, which by its nature must necessarily drag the invisible into the sphere of the visible, and materialize the spiritual. If, therefore, the presence of the Lord had, as a rule, been spiritual even in the tabernacle of testimony, and under the first temple, it follows that in this respect there was no difference between the first temple and the second, for the same presence continued even under the second temple.

The fourth blessing in which, according to the Jews, the second temple was deficient, is the spirit of prophecy. They believe that Haggai, Zechariah, and Malachi only prophesied until the time of the completion of the temple, and then all three died in one year. With the completion of the temple prophecy entirely ceased. On the other hand, we must remember that Malachi did not appear until some time after Zechariah and Haggai, and was contemporary with Nehemiah. There are arguments of considerable weight for supposing that Ezra is concealed under the name of Malachi, which is taken from the prophecy itself. On the whole, however, there is no doubt with regard to the correctness of the Jewish opinion. Haggai, Zechariah, and Malachi were plainly the only prophets of their time, and the last of the old covenant. They hold the same position with respect to the prophethood under the first temple, as the dominion of Zerubbabel to the earlier Davidic kingship. In their isolated appearance they are rather to be looked upon as suggestive of the prophethood, pointing to its absence and its future impending glorious restoration, than as representing the prophethood in themselves. This cessation of the prophethood, which continued till the time of the manifestation, is intelligible from the whole character of the post-exile time. It is characteristic of this period that Ezra, the scribe, plays so important a part in it. Scholarship now took the place of prophecy. The period bears throughout the character of dependence, of a leaning upon the former, which is perceptible even in the few prophets who still come forward.

These, by the statement of the Jews, are the most important things in which the second temple was deficient. Let us now look once more at the mind and spirit of the nation during this period, which we recognise intuitively from Haggai and Zechariah. Those who returned were inspired with a universal and lively enthusiasm. The beginning of the salvation which had been foretold by the prophets before the exile, was now at hand; and since these prophets had made no separation between the beginning and the end, but rather, in accordance with the nature of prophecy, had depicted the salvation in its whole extent without temporal separation, the nation had no doubt that the accomplishment would soon follow, that the kingdom of God was on its way to glorification, while the power of the world was near its overthrow. But the reality by no means corresponded to this expectation,—it rather offered a direct contrast. Israel remained under the dominion of the heathen, a poor, wretched, despised nation; it was still without a capital; there could be no thought of restoring the walls of Jerusalem, for this would at once have aroused the suspicion of the heathen rulers,— it was an open village; the house of God, which they had begun to build, presented a very meagre appearance in comparison with the former splendid edifice, and even the completion of this tabernacle was for a long time prevented by the machinations of the enemy, so that the nation seemed to be partially deprived even of that which the Lord had given them through Cyrus. Heathenism, on the other hand, still continued in the bloom of its power, full of pride in its own might and that of its idols, scarcely deigning to bestow a glance on Israel and its God.

In this state of things the thoughts of hearts were laid open. Two separate parties now appeared, which had formerly been undistinguishable, owing to the all-absorbing enthusiasm. The first consisted of those who truly feared God. These justly recognised in the state of things an actual declaration on the part of God that the repentance of the nation was still incomplete, that it was not yet ripe for a higher stage of redemption. But in thus directing their glance towards the sin, they were in danger of losing sight of the mercy; they thought the guilt and sinfulness of the nation were so great that the Lord could never again have mercy on them; they were almost in despair. The Lord comforts them by His servants; He gives them the assurance that all the glorious predictions of the prophets will at a future time be fulfilled; especially He directs their glance to the Redeemer, through whom the Lord will simultaneously put an end to the sins and the sorrows of His people. The Messianic prophecies of Zechariah are the most important, the clearest, and the most characteristic of all, next to those of Isaiah. This mission was given not only to the prophets, but also to a man who was singularly gifted in the department of sacred song, the author of the anonymous psalms of degrees, more correctly pilgrim-songs, Ps. cxx. ff., in which the burden is comfort to all. Among these psalms the reference to the time of the origin is most clearly stamped on the first, Ps. cxx., which calls God to help against evil calumny (the machinations of the Samaritans) in confident expectation of His assistance. Again, the same object characterizes also the group of psalms which were sung at the dedication of the new temple, Ps. cxxxv.-cxlvi. The tendency to comfort and raise up the people of God is common to the whole group. Ps. cxxxv. cxxxvi. point to the glorious works of God in nature and history. Ps. cxxxvii. quickens the hope in the impending judgment on the enemy. Ps. cxlvi. represents the Lord as the omnipotent and faithful helper of His suffering people. The interpolated psalms of David occupy themselves chiefly with the glorious David and the promise given to the nation of the eternal kingship of his race; they carry the Davidic race and the nation comfortingly through all the changes of the world which threaten to bring this promise to nought, and conclude with a solemn " We praise thee, O God, for the final glorious fulfilment of this promise."

The second party consisted of the hypocrites. These did not hesitate to seek the cause of the delay of the salvation in God, instead of in themselves. Ignorant of true righteousness, they thought that because the nation had renounced gross idolatry, all had been done on their side that could be required of them. They murmured and forgot even the slight external fear of God which they had still retained. For them also the prophets, especially Zechariah, describe the future blessings of God, in order by this means to give them an incentive to true repentance. But at the same time they make it distinctly understood that without this repentance they can have no part in the blessings; they recall the judgments which befell those who mocked the warning of the earlier prophets, and threaten new judgments, equally terrible. Here also the psalms of this time are closely connected with the prophets. In Ps. cxxv. 4, 5, we read, " Do good, O Lord, unto those that be good, and to them that are upright in their hearts. As for such as turn aside unto their crooked ways, the Lord shall lead them forth with the workers of iniquity: but peace shall be upon Israel."

§ 3.

EZRA AND NEHEMIAH.

The sources for this period are the second half of the book of Ezra, in which we have an account by Ezra himself of his activity until the coming of Nehemiah, and the book of Nehemiah, with a statement of what he did for the welfare of the new colony, but also giving a very full account, in chaps. viii.-x., of an event in which Ezra had the *primas partes*. Parallel with the book of Nehemiah, giving remarkable disclosures respecting the mind and disposition at that time, we have the prophecy which bears the name of Malachi, a name which in all probability was not a proper name but a symbolical one, borrowed from the prophecy itself. The four psalms, cxlvii.-cl., which were sung at the dedication of the walls, under Nehemiah, also serve as a source. Finally, the book of Ecclesiastes, which undoubtedly belongs to this period, whose historical presupposition is the deep humiliation of the people of God, and their bondage to the power of the world, and whose tendency is to give comfort on the one hand, and on the other to expose the moral religious evils of the time, and to urge their removal. Among these we find especially moroseness, avarice, and a righteousness merely external and apparent, the first beginnings of Pharisaism.

With respect to chronological relations, this period is not immediately connected with that which precedes it, but they are separated by a considerable interval, which is passed over in sacred history because it offers no material. The former period comprised the twenty years from the first year of Cyrus to the sixth year of Darius. Our period begins with the march of Ezra to Canaan in the seventh year of Artaxerxes. Between them therefore lie the remaining thirty years of the thirty-six years of Darius and the whole reign of Xerxes, regarding the duration of which there is a difference of opinion, some maintaining that it was twenty-one years in length, while others, on the contrary, assert that it was only eleven. Finally, six years of Artaxerxes. These forty-seven years are completely passed over in our first important source, the book of Ezra. In chap. vii. 1 ff. the events which follow are connected with the words, "And after these things Ezra went up." Among the remaining books Esther alone supplements it. The history narrated in this book belongs, as is now universally acknowledged, to the time of Xerxes, and he is the Ahasuerus of the book. It is necessary for an introduction to the Old Testament to occupy itself much more fully with this book than Old Testament history. The latter has merely to indicate the principal point of view from which this event must be regarded. The centre of it is formed by the great deliverance vouchsafed to the Jews in the diaspora, outside Palestine, in a danger where no human help was available, into which they had fallen by their faith in Jehovah and their acknowledgment of Him; for Mordecai refused to worship on religious grounds, and Haman based his proposal to punish the whole nation on a religious motive.

This incident contains an important doctrine, viz. this, that the government of God was not confined to the colony on the Jordan, but that the diaspora was also an object of His special oversight; and it is evident that the Jews took this meaning out of the event, from the circumstance that the feast of Purim, which perpetuated the memory of it, was introduced into the colony on the Jordan no less than the diaspora. If we consider the event and the doctrine contained in it, we recognise that the diaspora was destined in the future for the realization of important designs of God; that we are not to seek the cause of its origin only in the indifferentism of the great mass of the Israelites, but must rather direct our attention to the divine causality.

With respect to the condition of the colony on the Jordan in the time between Zerubbabel and Ezra and Nehemiah, we have only one single incidental notice which contains any information. From Neh. v. 15 we learn that the new governors who were placed over the people after the death of Zerubbabel did not consider what was best for the people of God in the discharge of their office, but only consulted their own interest. It is true that Zerubbabel had sons, but none of them succeeded him on the throne. Here we read: "But the former governors, that had been before me, were chargeable unto the people, and had taken of them bread and wine, besides forty shekels of silver; yea, even their servants bare rule over the people: but so did not I, because of the fear of God." How little these governors, who were probably heathen officers, did for the good of the people, is apparent from the melancholy external condition in which Nehemiah found affairs on his coming. And we perceive that even internally everything had become worse after the death of Zerubbabel and the two prophets Haggai and Zechariah, from the great abuses which Ezra finds on his arrival.

Many scholars, after the precedent of Josephus, c. *Ap.* i. § 22, believe they find a notice referring to the Jews in this interval, in a passage which he has preserved from the poet Choerilus, who, in describing the march of the various nations of which the army of Xerxes consisted, says: "Then followed a nation of peculiar physiognomy and dress, speaking the Phenician language. They inhabit the mountains of Solyma, along which there is a great sea." The Phenician language, the name Solyma resembling Jerusalem, the mountains, the sea (the Dead Sea),—everything in this description appeared to point to the Jews. But nevertheless Bochart, *Geog. Sacr.* P. ii. l. 1, chap. 2, has shown by overwhelming arguments that the Solymi in Pisidia are meant.

Let us now turn to the events of our period. It begins with the mission of Ezra. The most important thing here is to establish the correct view with respect to the authority of Ezra, which is given in Ezra vii. 11 ff., and also with regard to his whole position, resting upon it. The common view, recently brought forward again by Auberlen, is that his authority extended to all ecclesiastical and civil matters; that it gave him not merely the rights of a spiritual reformer, but also the dignity of a Persian governor,—the position previously occupied by Zerubbabel, and afterwards by Nehemiah. But this view is undoubtedly false, and has given rise to much perplexity and erroneous thought. The following is the correct view:—Ezra's mission was only such as became a priest and scribe. It was limited to the sphere of religion. The only passage which is quoted in favour of a more comprehensive mission is chap. vii. 25, "And thou, Ezra, after the wisdom of thy God that is in thine hand, set magistrates and judges, which may judge all the people that are beyond the river, all such as know the laws of thy God; and teach ye them that know them not." But since this refers only to matters in which the determination was taken from the law of God, it was quite natural that some authority should be conceded to Ezra in this department also, even if he were simply a spiritual reformer. This was the only passage under the Mosaic legislation where the priests took part in civil affairs, while they were quite exempt from administration and government. Nothing appears elsewhere in his authority which would lead to the inference that Ezra had any political position. Against this hypothesis we have the fact that he is always called "the scribe," a name denoting the character of his office, and never "the governor," like Zerubbabel and Nehemiah; and, again, all his transactions of which we have any account relate to the sphere of religion in Israel. Moreover, Nehemiah would not have expressed himself as he does, in chap. v. 15, respecting his predecessors, if Ezra had immediately preceded him in his office;

the passage presupposes that besides the office of Ezra there was also the office of a governor. Nor can we explain the melancholy state in which Nehemiah found the civil affairs of the colony, if Ezra had received royal authority to ameliorate it; and there is nowhere the slightest indication that Nehemiah, who worked along with Ezra for a considerable time, interfered with him in his office, but, on the contrary, they worked peaceably together without any contact between their respective spheres of activity, holding the same relation towards one another as Zerubbabel and Joshua. According to the more recent view, Ezra must have been partially deposed.

Ezra did not come to Judea alone, but with a considerable number of his countrymen. His first important undertaking was the removal of foreign wives. The main thing here is to ascertain the relation of this measure to the Mosaic law. If Ezra put away all the strange wives with their children, it appears at the first glance that he went beyond the Mosaic law. In the Pentateuch, for example, there is no prohibition against marriage with Canaanitish women and the heathen generally, in itself, but only against a certain kind of marriage, where the native heathen remained heathen. Wherever we find any ordinances of this nature, the prohibition is only against such marriages as are the result of a covenant with the inhabitants of the land. Heathen women who were captured in war, and were therefore removed from all national intercourse, might be married by Israelites, according to Deut. xxi. 10–14. Hence it would appear that Ezra might have been satisfied with insisting that the heathen wives should renounce all heathen practices. But, on nearer consideration, it is evident that under existing circumstances the command against unequal marriages was to be regarded as absolutely forbidding all marriages with heathen wives, and involved the unconditional dissolution of all such marriages. For, owing to the circumstances of the time, marriages with heathen wives must necessarily have borne more or less a character of inequality, and it was impossible to remove the deeply-rooted heathen spirit except by the dissolution of these marriages. The great number of heathen women in the new colony was in itself calculated to strengthen individuals in their heathen faith. And, again, it was much less probable that a heathen woman would renounce her heathen consciousness when the nation into which she entered had sunk so low, and was in a state of such deep degradation. Finally, at that time heathen wives had much greater facility in communicating with their kindred. The heathen nations from whom they were descended and the Judaites were both subjects of the Persians, and the case was therefore very different now from the time when the state was independent and flourishing, when a heathen woman who married an Israelite was, *eo ipso,* cut off from all external communication with heathenism. In this state of things the conduct of Ezra will be found to have been in perfect conformity with the law and the spirit of the lawgiver. The very fact that so many were married to foreign wives, shows how much contact there must have been with the heathen, and under these circumstances it would have been most dangerous to have prepared a hearth for heathenism within the state itself. The heathen woman could have worked more effectively for the spread of heathenism in Israel than any mission. The question was of the existence or non-existence of the people of God; and it redounds to the great honour of Ezra, and to his everlasting credit, that he did not suffer himself to be deterred from vigorous measures by any false sentimentality.

The prayer uttered by Ezra on this occasion is characteristic of his whole standpoint, and of the spirit of the post-exile piety generally. In speaking of it, Hess says with some justice, *Rulers of Judah after the Exile,* part i. p. 367: "A prayer which almost forces upon the reader the conviction that, notwithstanding all his well-meant zeal, the man was not the most spiritual suppliant. It is characteristic of the religious history after the exile, that those who were the most zealous observers of the Mosaic customs were proportionately deficient in the spirit of freedom and heartiness. But we cannot therefore accuse an Ezra either of hypocrisy, or of that small-minded tendency to strange tradition and scholastic lore with which religion was afterwards overladen." The prayer is certainly calculated to show us the difference between a scribe, however pious, and a prophet, whose place was now filled by the scribes. The tension of extremes had ceased, the religion of Jehovah had gained the victory; but the spirit was not yet so powerful under the old covenant, as to be able to dispense with the powerful impulse which had been given to it by the struggle against a mighty opposition. Under the new covenant the case is different. The spirit then required nothing more for its invigoration than friction and external incentives generally.

Of the other efforts of Ezra until the coming of Nehemiah we know very little, and of the time which followed it we have only an account of his participation in one single important act. From his authority, and from the analogy of that first undertaking, which betrays an important personality and a determined zeal for the carrying out of the Mosaic law, which could not possibly have been satisfied with one single performance, we must conclude that he made every exertion to promote the public observance of the ordinances of the Mosaic law, even to its minutest details. That his activity in this respect was extremely important, successful, and regulative for centuries, also appears from the great respect in which he was held by the later Jews. He could not have been so highly esteemed if he had not done far more than he tells us himself in his book. Even Mohammed thought that the Jews looked upon Ezra as the son of God. They do, in fact, call him the second Moses, the chief of the scribes; compare the eulogiums in Buxtorf, *Tib.* c. 10, § 99 ff. The so-called third and fourth books of Ezra represent him in mythic glorification.

The most enduring merit of Ezra is for what he accomplished for the canon of the Old Testament,—a merit which is unanimously ascribed to him by Jewish tradition. But this must be more fully treated in the introduction to the Old Testament.

In order to show that the activity of Ezra, and other men who worked in the same spirit and had a similar mission, was not enough, but that the appearance of a man like Nehemiah was absolutely necessary,—one who would occupy the same position with respect to civil affairs as Ezra had occupied with regard to spiritual matters,—we shall here examine into the condition of Jerusalem, the civil and religious centre of the nation, on whose strength and importance so much still depended at the time of Ezra, and until the coming of Nehemiah. It is also of importance to realize this condition, because a knowledge of it best enables us to understand the very depressed feeling of the God-fearing in Israel, and the murmuring defiance of the hypocrites, with which the three post-exile prophets, Haggai, Zechariah, and Malachi, have everywhere to do. As long as the head was sick, all the members must feel sick ; and this feeling of sickness led either to the verge of despair or to defiance, according to the respective dispositions of the individuals.

Our view of the condition of Israel until the time of Nehemiah, which teaches us at the same time the importance of his mission and the mercy which was shown in it to the nation, is briefly as follows :—Until the twentieth year of Artaxerxes, the nation had properly no capital. Jerusalem was in a state similar to that of Athens before the Greek war of freedom. It was an open, thinly-inhabited village, exposed to all the attacks of its neighbours. In the wide space covered with the ruins of former splendour, a few isolated dwellings were lost among the rubbish. This lay in such great heaps about the city, that the way round it was impassable.

We must first set aside the arguments which have been brought forward against this view of the condition of Jerusalem and in favour of a more advantageous one. In the first place, Hag. i. 4 is appealed to. The prophet there, in the beginning of the reign of Darius Hystaspis, reproaches the inhabitants of Jerusalem for dwelling in ceiled houses while the house of the Lord lay waste. But nothing more can be inferred from the passage than the existence of a number of better built houses in Jerusalem, which no one doubts. On this supposition alone the prophet had sufficient foundation for making the contrast palpable, for applying to the whole what in reality applied only to a part. If he had spoken as an historian, he would have said, "While the people of the Lord already dwelt in houses, of which many were even ceiled, the habitation of the Lord still lay in ruins." Again, appeal is made to Ezra iv. 12, where the enemies of the Jews write to Artaxerxes, that the Jews, with rebellious intent, are restoring the walls of the city. But here the allusion is to an unsuccessful attempt to restore the walls, made in the earlier time of Artaxerxes. Immediately after its beginning, a strict prohibition came from the Persian court, at the instigation of the enemies of the Jews. The passage shows, on the contrary, that Jerusalem was an open village very shortly before the coming of Nehemiah. Only a misunderstanding of the passage Ezra ix. 9 has led Auberlen to quote it in favour of a restoration of the walls before the time of Nehemiah. The allusion there is not to the restoration of the walls, permitted by the grace of God, but to a hedge. The hedge is an image, borrowed from Isa. x. 5, of the protection which hovered over Israel. Finally, appeal is made to Neh. i. 3, where those who had come from Jerusalem to Nehemiah say, "The remnant that are left of the captivity there in the province are in great affliction and reproach: the wall of Jerusalem also is broken down, and the gates thereof are burned with fire." On the presupposition that it was necessary for these strangers to tell Nehemiah something quite new, some have concluded from the passage that the town was already built up again before the time of Nehemiah, and was provided with walls and doors, but that it was again destroyed by the surrounding enemies, and that the only merit due to Nehemiah is that of having obviated the consequences of this destruction immediately after it had taken place. But this presupposition is certainly false. What Nehemiah heard from the strangers he knew very well, but it had probably never affected him so deeply as now, when he heard it from eye-witnesses, who spoke with an emotion drawn from their own painful experience, of the misery, of the deep humiliation of the people of God; for in them he saw, as it were, the delegates sent to him by the ruins of Jerusalem. The destruction of the walls and gates here spoken of, is no other than the Chaldee. Nowhere do we find the slightest trace of any other. The enemies of the Jews, in Neh. iv. 2, know only of one. The book of Ezra contains no allusion to the walls having been restored. No edict of any Persian king, previous to that issued by Artaxerxes in his twentieth year in favour of Nehemiah, gave them the slightest vestige of permission to undertake the work; and surely no one will maintain that this permission was taken for granted. The contrary is evident, from the fact that the enemies of the Jews could find no more effective accusation against them than that they were building the walls. It was a different thing to give an unarmed nation permission to return, and to give this same people permission to fortify their capital. The Persians still vividly remembered how much this capital had troubled the Chaldees, their predecessors in the supremacy over Asia; and if they had forgotten it, they would have been reminded of it by the hostile neighbours of the Jews. Only the closeness of the relation in which Nehemiah stood to Artaxerxes had power to overcome the suspicion common to all Asiatic rulers, who were well aware that their power rested solely on the weakness of their subjects.

In positive confirmation of our view we may adduce the following arguments. In Zechariah, the condition of Jerusalem appears throughout as provisional. Those who mourned over the melancholy present he comforts with a prediction of the impending future restoration; comp., for example, chap. ii., vi. 13, viii. 5. That this condition lasted until the time of Nehemiah, we learn from his own book. In chap. ii. 3, 5. for example, Nehemiah says to the king of the Persians, "The city, the place of my fathers' sepulchres, lieth waste, and the gates thereof are consumed with fire. Send me unto Judah, unto the city of my fathers' sepulchres, that I may build it." According to ver. 17 of the same chapter, he says, in Jerusalem itself, to the inhabitants, "We see the distress that we are in, how Jerusalem lieth waste, and the gates thereof are burned with fire." Neh. vii. 4 is also very significant: "How the city was large and great, but the people were few therein, and the houses were not builded,"—a passage which refers to the time immediately after the completion of the city walls. These had been restored in their old extent, for it was not necessary to make an absolutely new erection, but only to repair the old. The walls were of course not completely thrown down, but only very much broken, and the few houses were completely lost in the great area.

We have a remarkable contrast to this condition of the city before Nehemiah, in what we are told by some heathen writers respecting its condition after Nehemiah; and here let us refer to them, in order by this contrast to throw light on the whole significance of the mission of Nehemiah, and to show how great things the Lord did for His people by His invisible activity. The most remarkable accounts are contained in Herodotus. That the Cadytis which he mentions was Jerusalem we consider fully established, notwithstanding the contradiction of Hitzig, who tries to prove that it is Gaza. The conviction forces itself upon every unprejudiced reader, and has therefore always been upheld by the greater number of critics and the most important authorities. Among the earlier ones we shall name only Prideaux, i. p. 106 ff., and Cellarius, ed. Schwarz, ii. p. 456; and among the later, Dahlmann, *Researches*, Part ii. p. 75, and Bähr on Herodotus, 1. 922, where other literature is also found. Herodotus mentions the town Cadytis in two passages. The first, ii. 159, "After the battle he took Cadytis, which is a large city in Syria," refers to the occupation of Jerusalem by Pharaoh-necho, therefore to the time previous to the Chaldee destruction. Yet Herodotus describes Jerusalem as a city which was very large, even in his day. But the second passage, iii. 5, is far more important. He here speaks of Cadytis, "a city of the Syrians, which is called Palestine," in his opinion not much smaller than Sardis. But even under the Persian supremacy, and after it had ceased to be the residence of the Lydian kings, Sardis was so important a town, that in antiquity it was always called The Great. While these passages in Herodotus refer to a time which bordered closely on that of Nehemiah, the account of Hecataüs of Abdera, a writer of the time of Alexander and of Ptolemy Lagi, has reference to the condition of the city about a hundred years later, but nevertheless possesses no small interest for our purpose. It is to be found in a fragment in Josephus, l. 1, c. *Ap.* § 22, and in Eusebius, *præp.* ix. c. 4. "The Jews," we there read, "have many citadels and villages in their territory; but they have one fortified city, of about fifty stadia in circumference, inhabited by nearly twelve myriads of men. They call it Jerusalem."

The maturity of the Israelitish nation had begun at the time when David raised it to be the capital of the kingdom, and enabled it really to fulfil this its destination. Nehemiah was not able to do as much for Jerusalem, and, through it, for Israel, as David had done. The nation remained in subjection to the Persians; yet the national consciousness was very much strengthened by what he did, while a foundation was given for Israelitish piety. Hence Jesus Sirach justly exclaims, in chap. xlix. 13: $Νεεμίου ἐπὶ πολὺ τὸ μνημόσυνον, τοῦ ἐγείραντος ἡμῖν τείχη πεπτωκότα καὶ στήσαντος πύλας καὶ μοχλοὺς, καὶ ἀνεγείραντος τὰ οἰκόπεδα ἡμῶν$ (has restored our waste places, our ruins). Only a false, unpractical spiritualism can mistake the importance of acts such as those of Nehemiah, or object that he did not possess the same spiritual maturity which we find in other servants of God, whose mission was more immediately directed to spiritual things, while his only aim was to place them on a secure foundation.

With regard to the personal relations of Nehemiah we know but little. His ancestors must have dwelt in Jerusalem, for in chap. ii. 3 he says that the graves of his fathers are there. But we know neither his race nor his tribe. His father Hachaliah had not availed himself of the permission to return to the fatherland, withheld probably by possessions and honours acquired in the land of captivity. It appears that he dwelt at Susa, and that it was he who opened up to his son the path to the influential position which he occupied. Nehemiah was namely one of the cup-bearers at the court of Artaxerxes,—a very important post, since it gave an opportunity of being often about the king, and of taking advantage of his favourable humours. This position also gave him an opportunity of increasing the considerable fortune which he probably possessed originally,—a circumstance which afterwards very much facilitated the success of his mission, since he did not set his heart on riches, but willingly and joyfully employed them in the interest of his calling. In spite of his great fortune, he was not a rich man.

Although born and educated in a strange land, yet his heart clung to Zion. His constant wish to be able to do something for it became a definite resolve, when the melancholy condition of affairs there was brought home to him by people who came from Jerusalem. He began to carry out this resolve by making an earnest petition to the Lord for Israel, His people, and for the sanctuary of His choice, having first fasted,—the symbolic expression of the repentant heart under the old covenant,—and Nehemiah here regarded himself as the representative of the whole nation. Having assured himself of help from above, he turned to the earthly king. Looking at the matter from a merely human point of view, he had some reason for hoping to prevail with his request. For Artaxerxes—called The Long-handed by Grecian historians, because he could touch his knees with his hands when standing upright—was a magnanimous and gracious prince, and the special favour in which he was held by him already opened up and prepared the way for his mission before he received it. The king himself gave him an opportunity of preferring his request. He noticed his melancholy, and inquired into the cause of it. Nehemiah answered, that he mourned for Jerusalem, and begged to be sent there with authority to do what was best for it. At once a decree was issued, commanding the restoration of the walls and gates of Jerusalem, and Nehemiah was invested with the dignity of a governor of Judea, and charged with the carrying out of this decree. The king gave him a military escort, sent instructions to the royal governor on this side of the Euphrates to give him every assistance, and commanded the head overseer of the royal forests in that district to supply him with as much wood as he required. Nehemiah retained his position at court. He was to return there as soon as he had finished his work. But it seems that his patriotism, which had its root in piety, did not permit him to return as soon as the king expected, according to chap. ii. 6, but that he remained twelve full years in the new colony without undertaking a journey to the court; and even when he did set out on this journey, in the thirteenth year, he did so with the determination to return to his sphere of activity in Jerusalem, for he recognised that the fulfilment of this was the true task of his life, while he attached no importance to his position at court except as a means to an end.

Nehemiah encountered not a few difficulties on his arrival at Jerusalem. He had first to deal with foreign enemies, whose heads were Sanballat the Samaritan, Tobiah the Ammonite, and Geshem the Arabian. The surrounding nations were bent upon forcing the people of the Lord to relinquish their obstinate exclusiveness, and heathenizing them; and an undertaking such as that of Nehemiah, which consolidated the nation in itself, must necessarily interfere with this plan. Moreover, there was a heathenizing party even in the nation itself, who combined with the enemy outside in making every effort to hinder the undertaking, and even attempted to work on the people by false prophets. In almost every period we find a heathenizing party of this kind among the covenant-nation, which was, *à priori*, only to be expected. How powerful they were at this time, we already see from the many mixed marriages which Ezra found, as well as from the fact that the vigorous measures which he instituted against it proved effectual for so short a time. There does not, however, seem to have been any actual idolatry at that time. The broken power of heathenism is seen in the circumstance that the heathenizing tendency within Judaism after the exile, as a rule, shares only the heathen scepticism, but holds aside from heathen superstition. That heathenizing party, which powerfully reasserted itself during the subsequent absence of Nehemiah, rightly saw in the external openness of Jerusalem to the heathen a symbol and pledge of the abolition of the inner wall of partition. This explains their opposition.

But Nehemiah would not be discouraged by these difficulties. He urged on the work with such zeal, that it was accomplished in fifty-two days. It would have been impossible to have finished it in so short a time if it had been necessary to build up an entirely new wall. That very important remains of the former city-wall were still standing, is not merely probable, but can be demonstrated by positive proof, so that there was nothing more to do than to fill up the gaps. Owing to the machinations of the enemy, it was necessary for one part of the nation to remain under arms while the other built, and even those who were building had their weapons at hand, that they might seize them at the first signal,—a fact which has often been regarded as having symbolic significance, as an individualization of the truth that in every reformation of the people of God which is to raise them from a deeply degraded condition, the building and the struggling activity must go hand in hand. This necessity has its basis in the fact that important interests are invariably attached to the maintenance of the old wickedness, of the old man, of the world, of Satan, who cannot bear to see the kingdom of God flourish; therefore it is impossible to recover in a peaceful way from a state of decay.

The first great work of Nehemiah was therefore now finished, that which has always been regarded by the Jewish nation as the principal object of his mission, as we learn from the passage quoted from Jesus Sirach. The consecration of the walls and gates was performed with great solemnity. The psalms sung on this occasion, which have already been pointed out, the last of the whole collection, are distinguished from all others belonging to the post-exile period by their tone of unqualified rejoicing, without any background of sadness. The nation here first exhibits renewed joy in its existence. In Ps. cxlix. we even meet with a warlike tone again. At the building of the wall Judah had again raised the sword against the heathen for the first time since the Chaldee destruction, and with a happy result. This taking up of arms awakened in the nation the new and lively hope of future victory over the servile heathen world,—a hope which was first of all externally fulfilled in the victories of the time of the Maccabees, whose success had their foundation in what was done by Nehemiah; but infinitely more gloriously when Israel in the time of the Messiah took up the sword of the Spirit, and with it executed the most noble revenge on the heathen conquerors.

Nehemiah now proceeded to provide for the civil welfare of the city, leaving the care of spiritual affairs, in so far as they did not directly interfere with civil matters, to Ezra, who held the same relation towards him which Joshua had formerly held towards Zerubbabel. The next thing which he did was to make regulations respecting the way in which the re-fortified city was to be guarded. His attention was then drawn to the small population of Jerusalem, which would necessarily make its defence a matter of far greater difficulty; and he saw clearly how the strength of the national consciousness was dependent on the strength of the centre. He first persuaded the heads of the nation to build themselves houses in Jerusalem, and to dwell there. Others followed their example, and voluntarily resorted to the capital, whose good fortification, in the view of many, outweighed the advantages offered by a residence in their country possessions. Of the remainder, every tenth man was to move into the city. What most strikes us here is the proportion of priests and Levites who determined to repair to the city to those who remained. After all who had resolved to become citizens had carried out their determination, the number of grown up men was 468 of the tribe of Judah, 928 of the tribe of Benjamin, 1192 members of the priesthood, and 456 Levites. The cause is easily understood. The vicinity of the sanctuary must have been especially attractive to the priests and Levites; but in its consequences the circumstance was necessarily very significant. The preponderance of the priesthood in the capital must infallibly act as a powerful incentive to the priestly spirit in the nation, which had already made great progress even apart from this. Not only would the priests by this means obtain a direct influence in affairs of government, but by their strength in the very centre of the nation they must necessarily exercise a far more powerful influence on its spirit.

One circumstance which very much facilitated the official

activity of Nehemiah was his freedom from material interests, and his considerable fortune, which enabled him to renounce all those advantages to which his external position gave him a just claim. His predecessors, who had probably belonged to the great families who combined against Nehemiah with his foreign enemies, had taken advantage of their position to enrich themselves. They demanded a very considerable salary. But Nehemiah took nothing; and of his own means provided free tables, generally containing 150 covers. This disinterestedness could not fail to tell in his favour, especially in the reform which he undertook respecting matters of debt. By his example he put to shame the rich men who practised usury contrary to the law, who had taken possession of the lands of the poor, and even of their persons; and he succeeded so far as to obtain the remission of all debts, and the emancipation of possessions and persons.

By all these ameliorations of their outward condition the people were rendered very susceptible, and their chiefs thought it would be unjustifiable to allow this favourable moment to pass by without trying to make a deeper impression on them. What use they made of it we learn from a section of Nehemiah, chaps. viii.-x., which in recent times, after the example of Joh. Dav. Michaelis, has generally been taken out of the connection in which it there stands, and made to refer to the time previous to the coming of Nehemiah, on the utterly false ground that, according to Josephus, Ezra did not live to see the coming of Nehemiah. This testimony of Josephus has no weight whatever against the testimony of the book of Nehemiah, which represents Ezra as having performed that religious act under the civil rule of Nehemiah. It is a strange *quid pro quo* to correct the book of Nehemiah by Josephus.

Ezra, on whom, as the spiritual head of the nation, the direction of the solemnities devolved, appointed on the civil new-year's feast, and on the feast of tabernacles which also fell in the seventh month, a great public reading of the law, connected with a translation of it into the Chaldee language,—a circumstance from which we gather that Hebrew was at that time quite unintelligible to the mass of the nation, who had brought the Chaldee language with them out of exile. This reading made a very deep impression on the nation, which is not to be explained on the assumption that the law had hitherto been unknown to them, but solely and alone from the circumstances under which they now heard it. The proofs of faithfulness to the covenant which the Lord had just given them had touched their heart, and the reading of the law made them painfully conscious of their own unfaithfulness. Ezra and Nehemiah, discerning this repentant spirit, ordained a fast, *i.e.* a fast-day, two days after the feast; and on this day a solemn act was undertaken, by which the nation bound itself thenceforward to try and keep the law inviolable. This covenant was signed and sealed by the most important members of every class, Nehemiah at the head. In particular, they pledged themselves to keep certain prescriptions of the law which had been most frequently neglected in the times after the exile, as appears from the prominence here given to them, as well as from other reasons, viz. to avoid all mixed marriages, and to keep the sabbaths and sabbatical years, to pay the annual taxes to the temple, and also the tithes to the priests and Levites, from whose payment avarice was so prone to try and escape, as we learn from Malachi.

The good impression which the reading of the law produced on this occasion called forth the determination that in future the law should be read in every city by the most learned Levites, or other scholars who had studied it well. This reading, like that of Ezra, may have taken place at first in the open air. But the inconveniences connected with this mode soon made themselves felt; the reading was transferred to tents or houses, and thus the institution of synagogues reached its full development, though its germs go back into far earlier times; comp. Acts xv. 21.

After Nehemiah had held his office for twelve years, he undertook a journey to Persia, which took place, therefore, in the thirty-second year of Artaxerxes. We have already seen that he had not been finally dismissed from Persia, but had only received temporary leave of absence. It might be of consequence to him to re-establish himself in the favour of the king, whose assistance he needed so much in the face of powerful opposition both at home and abroad. It is uncertain when Nehemiah returned from this journey. In Neh. xiii. 6 we read that it happened לקץ ימים. It is evident that this expression must be translated "after some time," thus leaving the length of the absence undetermined, and not, as most translate it, "after the expiration of a year," for the abuses which he found on his return were too great and numerous for so short an absence. After his return, he applied himself with the greatest zeal to the removal of the abuses which had crept in. The most important of these was the renewed prevalence of mixed marriages. The fact that this should have recurred so soon after the activity of Ezra, which was directed against it, and who must have died before the departure of Nehemiah, or at least soon after it; that it should have recurred so soon after the formal obligation to refrain from such marriages, which the nation had undertaken on the occasion already named,—shows how strong a temptation to such marriages lay in the relations of that time, and how difficult it then was to maintain the Israelitish national consciousness upright. The other abuses also belong mostly to the same department, and are due to a weakening of this national consciousness, to a removal of the barrier between Israel and heathendom. We see, therefore, how important it was that this evil should be opposed in the most energetic way. A false spiritualism would here have led to the destruction of the covenant-nation. We learn how deeply-rooted the evil was, from the fact that even the family of the high priest was tainted with it. One of the sons of Jehoiada the high priest had married the daughter of Sanballat the Horonite, a native of Horon or Beth-horon, a city formerly in the tribe of Ephraim, now in Samaria, who, according to Josephus, was Persian governor in Samaria. Nehemiah acted with great severity. He obliged all those who had taken strange wives either to separate from them or to leave the country. The son and brother of the high priest, called by Josephus Manasseh, preferred the latter. He repaired to his father-in-law in

Samaria, who made him high priest in the temple on Gerizim, built on the occasion of his going over; so that the measures of Nehemiah against mixed marriages produced most important results. But here we must enter somewhat more closely into an important difference which occurs between Nehemiah and Josephus respecting this marriage of a son of the high priest, since the determination of the time of the building of the temple at Gerizim depends on it.

In Neh. xiii. 28, 29, we read, "And one of the sons of Joiada, the son of Eliashib the high priest, was son-in-law to Sanballat the Horonite: therefore I chased him from me. Remember them, O my God, because they have defiled the priesthood, and the covenant of the priesthood, and of the Levites," *i.e.* of the covenant which Thou hast concluded with them. God had given glorious promises and prerogatives to the priests and Levites, but He had also imposed sacred obligations upon them. They were to set a pattern to the whole nation in their observance of the law, in their fulfilment of the command, "Be ye holy, for I am holy." According to this, the event belonged to the time of Nehemiah, and therefore occurred under Artaxerxes. In Josephus, on the other hand, *Ant.* xi. 8. 4, it is related that Sanballat, who was made governor of Samaria by the last Darius, married his daughter to a distinguished priest of the Jews; his son-in-law was deprived of the priesthood and banished from Jerusalem on account of this marriage, which was forbidden by the law. Sanballat then got permission from Alexander, whose party he espoused at the time of the siege of Tyre, to build a temple on Mount Gerizim, close to Samaria, after the pattern of the one in Jerusalem, and to appoint his son-in-law as high priest. After Sanballat, at the head of 8000 men, had personally assisted Alexander in this siege and that of Gaza, he died about the time when the latter place was taken.

There is therefore a difference of more than a hundred years.

The usual way of obviating this difficulty is by assuming that Nehemiah and Josephus spoke of a different event,—that there were two Sanballats. But this explanation is quite inadmissible. The Sanballat mentioned in the last chapter of Nehemiah is the same who frequently appears in the first chapters as the great adversary of Nehemiah, who sought to thwart every attempt for the deliverance of his people. And this Sanballat of Nehemiah is also identical with the one spoken of in Josephus. The Sanballat of Nehemiah was governor of Samaria, according to chap. iii. 34; so also was the Sanballat of Josephus. Each was a great enemy of the Jews. Each gave his daughter to a distinguished Jewish priest. The authority of Josephus must indeed be extraordinarily great, if it were able to set aside such convincing arguments as these which speak for the identity, or to justify the assertion that the error is due to the author of the book of Nehemiah, which is the less admissible, since Nehemiah himself speaks in this passage; and all critics, even those who hold that the book contains later elements, and did not come from Nehemiah in its present form, agree in this, that all the passages in which Nehemiah himself speaks, do really belong to him. But in Josephus the history of the Persian period is full of the most palpable errors. For example, he speaks of a second return of the Israelites under Darius Hystaspis, of which the Scriptures know nothing. No less than 4,008,680 men are said to have returned on this occasion, but he gives them only 40,740 wives and children. The events narrated in the book of Esther he places under Artaxerxes instead of Xerxes; and, on the other hand, represents Ezra and Nehemiah as having come to Jerusalem under Xerxes instead of under Artaxerxes; he makes Ezra die before Nehemiah arrives, and places the coming of the latter in the twenty-fifth year instead of in the twentieth, while he makes the building of the walls to have lasted for three years and a half instead of fifty-two days, etc. When such is the character of his statements, how can it be a matter of surprise that in this case also he should have taken events out of their true connection, and have placed them in a fictitious one? The confusion is probably due to the fact that Josephus held the opinion common to nearly all Jews, that the Darius whom Alexander dethroned was the son of Ahasuerus (in his opinion, of Artaxerxes) and of

Esther. From Artaxerxes he suddenly passes over in his history to Darius Codomannus, without saying a word of those who reigned in the interval.

But however great the inaccuracy of Josephus be, yet his account is of essential value to us. Nehemiah carries his history no farther than the expulsion of the priest who had allied himself by marriage with Sanballat. The consequences of this expulsion had probably not begun to appear at the time when Nehemiah concluded his book. We learn what they were from Josephus, who throws light on the connection between that expulsion by Nehemiah and the building of the temple on Gerizim. This connection is quite natural. Owing to the whole tendency of the Samaritans, to the insecurity of a bad conscience which everywhere characterizes them, it must have been a matter of great rejoicing to them that they could oppose something analogous to the Jewish priesthood which was consecrated by the law. Not until they were able to do this did they summon courage to establish a Samaritan sanctuary in opposition to the Jewish one. Probably by the advice of Manasseh, they built it on Mount Gerizim, because this mountain, according to Deut. xxvii. 12 and Josh. viii., had been made sacred by the circumstance that the blessing on the faithful observance of the law had been pronounced there by the direction of Moses, after immigration into the land. To this real dignity they added a stolen one, by changing Ebal, which occurs in ver. 4 of the same chapter in Deuteronomy where the stones on which the law was written are commanded to be set up on Mount Ebal, into Gerizim.

The example of Manasseh found many imitators. Not a few members of the heathenizing party, among them even priests, were attracted by the freer tendency of the Samaritans, who could never deny their origin, and, going over to them, were received with open arms. To these renegades (and not to the kingdom of the ten tribes) we must attribute the Israelitish element presented by Samaritanism, and even the language of the Samaritans. By this Jewish influence the last remnants of idolatry were banished from their midst. The

Jewish hatred did not, however, diminish on this account, but acquired still greater intensity. It burned far more violently against the Samaritans, who were regarded as heathen that laid claim to the dignity of the people of God, than against the heathen themselves. It even went so far that all intercourse with them was forbidden; all the fruits of their land, and all that belonged to them, especially food and drink, was pronounced to be defiled, and equally unclean with pork; while all the members of this nation were for ever excluded from the right of being accepted as proselytes. So also they were excluded from all participation in eternal life after the resurrection from the dead. Compare the compilation in Lightfoot, *Opp.* i. p. 559. Jesus Sirach, chap. l. 26, 27, speaks of "the foolish nation at Sichem as the most detestable of all nations;" and in the New Testament, John viii. 48, the Jews employ the phrases, "Thou art a Samaritan," and "Thou hast a devil," almost indiscriminately.

There is scarcely a doubt that it was Manasseh who first brought the Mosaic book of the law to the Samaritans, and introduced it among them. The idea that they possessed the Pentateuch at a much earlier time, and that it was transmitted to them from the kingdom of the ten tribes, is connected with the very erroneous opinion that the Samaritans were to a great extent descendants of the Israelites. Even the Israelitish priest who was sent to them, according to 2 Kings xvii. 28, by Asarhaddon, to teach them how they should fear the Lord, probably did not take them the law. At that time they were still too rude to have wanted it. Even towards the close of the exile, according to the testimony of the author of the books of the Kings, they united the worship of their old idols with the worship of Jehovah, which could scarcely have been the case if the Pentateuch had been publicly recognised among them. Their later acceptance of the Pentateuch rested, it seems, on the same ground as their joyful readiness to receive Jewish priests, and to entrust them with the guidance of their sacrificial offerings; which also accounts for their lying assertion that they were descendants of the ten tribes, viz. the endeavour to make themselves of equal birth with the

Israelites, which may be regarded as the centre of the Samaritan nationality. The first legitimization for a nation which laid claim to a part in the covenant was the possession of the book of the covenant, and the regulation of their lives according to it.

In observing the precepts of the Pentateuch, the Samaritans displayed no little zeal, though this had its origin in the external reasons already given, more than in any of an internal nature. The Jews themselves are obliged to bear testimony to this; comp. the passage from Maimonides in Reland, *de Samarit.* p. 10. Even the most troublesome ordinances, such as that with respect to the sabbatical year, were practised among them. Josephus tells that they entreated Alexander that he would remit their taxes, like those of the Jews, in the seventh year. But we recognise the continuance of a heathen background in the Samaritan consciousness, in the fact that they eagerly adopted every freer tendency which appeared among the Jews. Thus they borrowed the Sadducee doctrine respecting angels, and held that they were mere powers which emanated from God and returned to Him. The Sadducee denial of the resurrection also found acceptance with them. The striving of the Alexandrian Jews to avoid everything anthropomorphic and anthropopathic likewise passed over to them, for they were especially dependent on Alexandrian-Jewish theology, on account of its greater tendency to freedom. But no sooner was a freer view or tendency separated from the Jewish consciousness as heretical and heathenizing, than they also timidly drew back from it, fearing that by retaining it they would give a handle to their opponents, and injure their claim to belong to the people of God. Though they always went as far as those who went farthest among the Jews, yet they fell back as soon as they were forsaken by their models, which accounts for the fact that we find no more trace among the later Samaritans of the denial of the personality of angels or the resurrection.

The other sacred books, besides the Pentateuch, were not accepted by the Samaritans; which may be explained from the circumstance that the post-Mosaic sacred literature had its centre in the temple at Jerusalem. With the Pentateuch it is quite different. It speaks very frequently of the future place of the sanctuary, but never designates it more exactly. The Samaritans interpreted these passages as referring to their sanctuary on Gerizim. Some of the later sacred books, such as Joshua and Judges, like the Pentateuch, are free from all allusions to Jerusalem as the relative centre of the nation. But if the Samaritans had accepted these, they would have rendered their rejection of the remaining ones suspicious. Hence they could only do this with plausibility by laying down the principle that the divine Lawgiver alone was to be heard.

Among the Samaritans, however, we find in full development even those Old Testament dogmas which are so faintly indicated in the Pentateuch that they could scarcely have been drawn from it alone; for example, the doctrine of the resurrection and of the Messiah. This may be explained from the dependence of the Samaritans on the later Jewish theology, which had taken these doctrines from the later sacred writings. This theological and religious dependence of the Samaritans on the Jews is universal. Nowhere do we find among them any trace of peculiar and independent development. Their whole virtuosity consists in the invention of lies by which they seek to pervert the true relation, and to ascribe the priority to themselves.

So much for the temple at Gerizim and the Samaritans. The information respecting Nehemiah comes to an end with the account of his reformation after his return from the Persian court. We know neither how long his activity still continued, nor when he died.

With respect to the political condition of the Jews in the time of Nehemiah, there was still much to be desired, even after the great benefits which God had conferred upon His people through his instrumentality. It was still far removed from what Moses had promised to the nation in event of the faithful observance of the law, Deut. xxviii., and therefore formed a strong and real accusation against them. In Neh. ix. 36, 37, we have a very vivid description of this state: "Behold, we are servants this day; and for the land that Thou gavest unto our fathers, to eat the fruit thereof, and the good thereof, behold, we are servants in it: and it yieldeth much increase unto the kings whom Thou hast set over us because of our sins: also they have dominion over our bodies, and over our cattle, at their pleasure; and we are in great distress." It appears from this that the Jews were obliged to pay a very heavy tribute to the Persians, and that even the favour in which Nehemiah was held by Artaxerxes had brought them no alleviation in this respect. In harmony with this, we have the allusions contained in the book of Ecclesiastes respecting the state of matters at that time. According to the beginning of chap. iv., the people of God were in deep affliction; heavy misfortune had come upon them; everywhere the tears of the oppressed; the dead more to be praised than the living. According to chap. vii. 10, they lamented bitterly that the former days were better than the present. According to ver. 21, Israel was derided and insulted by the heathen; those who, by the law of God and justice, ought to have been servants of the nation which, in its first beginning, had been called to the supremacy of the world, were exalted. It was a time when, to judge from the beginning of chap. ix., the facts of life threw great stones of stumbling in the way of faith, since it led to perplexity respecting God and His just rule upon the earth; for the lot of the righteous and of the wicked was entangled together.

That this condition was no contradiction of the law, but rather a remarkable confirmation of it—the outward misery being a true representation of the inner wretchedness, consistently with the statement of the law, that God could not give more than He did give; that He was not hard towards the nation, but that the nation was hard towards itself;—all this we learn from the prophecy of Malachi, which, as we have already seen, was contemporaneous with the last reformation of Nehemiah. The very superscription, "The burden of the word of the Lord to Israel," points to the retributive and threatening character of the prophecy, allowing no anticipation of good. Even Zechariah found occasion to announce a new and heavy judgment on Judah, to take place after the ungodliness, which was already germinating in his time, would have struck deeper roots and have thrown out branches; comp. chaps. v. and xi. In the interval between him and Malachi, the development of the germ made rapid progress, as the prophecy of the latter shows. Only on the form in which the ungodliness manifested itself did the exile still continue to exercise any great influence. There was no return to gross idolatry, although doubtless there still existed a not insignificant heathenizing party in the nation, the forerunner of later Sadduceeism. The main tendency, however, was towards the later Pharisaism; and this, in its fundamental features, is to be found in Malachi. Characteristic of this externally pious, inwardly godless party, or rather national tendency, we have the complete want of a deeper recognition of sin and righteousness, the boasting of the external fulfilment of the law, the eagerness for judgments on the heathen, who can only be regarded as the object of the divine retributive justice, and the murmuring against God, which is always to be found where the punishment of sin coincides with a want of the recognition of sin. It is remarkable that Malachi, the last of the prophets, concludes with the words, that unless the nation repent, the Lord will come and smite the land with a curse. In describing the moral condition of the people, the book of Ecclesiastes runs side by side with Malachi. In it also we find no traces of idolatry in its description of the internal defects of the nation, but, on the contrary, we are everywhere met by a tendency to the later Pharisaism,—a hollow righteousness, which sought to compensate for the want of a lively fear of God and inward resignation by miserable outward works, empty sacrifices (iv. 17), copious prayers (v. 1, 2),—the murmuring spirit which always accompanies a spiritless piety and a soulless righteousness when deceived in their speculations,—the avarice which can only be destroyed where there is a true impulse of the soul towards God, such as pharisaic piety cannot take away, but only excites—an avarice which proves itself especially seductive in troublous times: here lies the danger of constant accumulation.

Yet even at this time, as at all periods prior to every infliction of the curse, there was still an ἐκλογὴ in the nation which was advancing towards its destruction. They are expressly mentioned in Mal. iii. 16: " Then they that feared the Lord spake often one to another: and the Lord hearkened, and heard it; and a book of remembrance was written before Him for them that feared the Lord, and that thought upon His name." The vindication of God by the truly pious though small community is here placed in opposition to the godless but seemingly pious masses. In ver. 9 the whole nation is represented as murmuring. In ver. 17 the Lord gives a comforting promise to the faithful: the day of judgment on the ungodly will at the same time be the day of salvation for the godly.

With respect to the worship, we may already infer, from the national tendency to Phariseism, that the regulations of the Pentateuch regarding it were more strictly observed at this time than at any former one. Nehemiah strengthens the observance of the Sabbath, which was far more closely kept immediately after the exile than it had been before it, by new and stricter regulations; comp. chap. xiii. 15 ff. From Neh. x. 31 we learn that even the sabbatical years were kept; and the more burdensome this ordinance is, the better can we argue from the observance of it, to that of the other ordinances. At this time there was an addition made to the feasts in the establishment of Purim. According to the book of Esther, this was introduced into those districts which had been the scene of the events it was intended to perpetuate, immediately after these events. Whether it was also observed in Palestine or not, we are not told; but if we consider the way in which the feast was celebrated in later times, we can scarcely look upon its establishment as a gain. The celebration had a profane, sensuous character. It gave bold prominence to the worst sides of the Jewish national character, viz. national pride and revenge. How completely it left the ethical-religious ground of the old Jewish feasts, and lost itself in heathenism, already appears from the fact that drinking was on this occasion regarded as meritorious; it was the custom to drink until it became impossible to distinguish between "Blessed be Mordecai" and "Cursed be Haman." But the very circumstance that the feast bore this carnal character gave it the greatest importance in the eyes of the carnally-minded nation, which was especially the case when, by the destruction of the temple, the three principal feasts lost a portion of that dignity which distinguished them from all the rest.

We have now only to speak of two institutions which Jewish tradition ascribes to this period, viz. the Synedrium magnum and the Synagoga magna. Of the former we find just as little trace at this time as in earlier ones. At this time, as before, we meet with elders of the nation under the name of שרים, and heads of families, who were consulted by the royal governors on important occasions. But nowhere do we find any trace of a Synedrium. Here the *argumentum e silentio* has great significance, since the Synedrium must necessarily have been mentioned had it been in existence. The most important things are done, and the Synedrium has no part in them. On the renewal of the covenant, which is described in Neh. viii.-x., the document is signed by many of the most distinguished of the nation, priests and Levites, but no mention whatever is made of a Synedrium.

While the Synedrium is an actual Jewish institution to which Jewish tradition attributed far greater antiquity than belonged to it, only for the purpose of giving it additional glory, the so-called Great Synagogue is a pure Jewish fiction, invented in the interest of pharisaic propositions. This was already pretty universally acknowledged when the work of Joh. Eberh. Rau, entitled *De Synagoga magna*, appeared at Utrecht, 1726. But to this work, which may be regarded as a model of critical research, the merit is due of having finally settled the matter, and completely destroyed the authority of the tradition. Many, indeed, have subsequently given credence to the tradition, but only because the work was unknown to them. Ewald has in vain sought to re-establish it on a historical basis; it is his way never to acknowledge truth without fiction, nor fiction without truth. The substance of Jewish statement respecting the Great

Synagogue is as follows :—In the time of Ezra, and under his superintendence, there was a college of 120 distinguished men, which, under public authority, preserved, inculcated, and transmitted the so-called oral law, *i.e.* the pharisaic statutes, which had been handed down to them from the prophets. This was the main business of the Great Synagogue, and is attributed to it alone in the oldest passages which refer to it, in the Pirke Aboth, chap. i., where we read, "Moses received the (oral) law on Mount Sinai, and transmitted it to Joshua; Joshua to the elders; the elders to the prophets; but the prophets (whose chain ended in the time of Ezra and Nehemiah) to the men of the Great Synagogue." In later Jewish writings other occupations also are ascribed to the Great Synagogue. Thus it is said to have done meritorious work for the Holy Scriptures, and especially to have written out those books whose authors lived out of the Holy Land, where no sacred book could have been written, such as Ezekiel, Daniel, and Esther; then again, to have added the *K'ris*, the vowels and accents to the text, and to have divided the Pentateuch into sections, and the text generally into verses, besides having composed certain formulas of prayer, given regulations with respect to Purim, and so on. Evidently the Great Synagogue was a depositary for everything that was difficult to dispose of otherwise.

The tradition is already sufficiently refuted by the circumstance that the alleged main business of the Great Synagogue, care for the oral law, will not suit the time of Ezra. Of this oral law we find no trace whatever in Ezra and Nehemiah. Their whole endeavour seems rather directed to the enforcement of the ordinances of the Pentateuch. But the silence of all credible sources regarding this institution, which is said to have been so magnificent, is decisive. We do not read a word of it in the books of Ezra and Nehemiah. Even Josephus knows nothing of it. The first trace of it is to be found in the Pirke Aboth. In this state of affairs it is no longer worth the trouble to prove, from the separate employments of the Great Synagogue, that we have to do with a mere fable.

We learn the origin of this fable from the oldest passages

referring to it, viz. those in the Pirke Aboth. The task was to prove an unbroken succession of trustworthy depositaries for the so-called oral law. A link was wanting between the prophets and the rabbis, the pharisaic teachers of the law, and this empty space must be filled up by the men of the Great Synagogue. After the Great Synagogue had thus come into existence, a multitude of other things were attributed to it for which there was no authority, however much it might be desired. But, owing to the gross historical ignorance of the later Jews, they were unable to invest the fiction with even the semblance of truth. They represent as members of the Great Synagogue men such as Mordecai and Daniel, who were never at Jerusalem. Haggai, Malachi, and Simon the Just, separated from each other by comparatively great distances of time, take part in it as contemporaries, etc.

§ 4.

FROM THE DEATH OF NEHEMIAH TO THE TIME OF THE MACCABEES.

This period includes a considerable number of years;—the exact length of time we cannot determine, since we do not know the year of Nehemiah's death. If we reckon from the time when Nehemiah first came to Jerusalem, the twentieth year of Artaxerxes, we have 287 years till the first appearance of the Maccabees,—about two and a half centuries, therefore, after the activity of Nehemiah had come to an end. Of this time about a hundred years (from the twentieth year of Artaxerxes to one hundred and nineteen) belong to the Persian supremacy, while the rest belong to the Greek supremacy.

But in this period our sources are excessively scant and confused, so that, notwithstanding its length, it offers scarcely as much that is noteworthy as one of those that preceded it, which taken all together are far from reaching to the same length. The canonical books of the Old Testament leave us with Nehemiah, from which it appears that this period offered no important gain for sacred history; so that the theologian as such has little to regret in the scantiness of accounts respecting it. The only non-canonical native author who extends over the whole period is Josephus; but with him we are not much concerned. Throughout his history he shows himself incapable, owing to his religious shallowness, of grasping those deeper religious phenomena among his people with which we have specially to do. In addition to this, we have the fact that his work was destined for the heathen, which led him to remain on the surface, without even going as deep as he might have done. Then again we must consider that at this period his sources must have been remarkably meagre. Properly speaking, his work contains no history at all, but only a series of disconnected notices; and even these have an uncertain character. Everywhere we feel that we must be on our guard, that we are on ground where not only ignorance, but intentional dishonesty, has been at work, and false patriotism; we feel that we have entered on that time, so disastrous for historiography, when the national vanity of the peoples who had been subjugated by Macedonian power sought to regain on paper that which they no longer possessed in life.

Of the remaining Jewish works composed at this period, or having reference to it, none are of any importance except the book of Jesus Sirach, properly the only literary monument which affords us a deeper insight into the religious tendency of the Jews at this period. The rest are less calculated to give us any knowledge of the time, than to expose the evil Jewish literary activity which characterized the period of their composition,—an activity which finds its only excuse in the fact that the Jews were not the originators of this literary deception, but only participated in what was universal, and had its principal seat in Alexandria. The story of the seventy interpreters of the Pseudo-Aristeas is a miserable fabrication, in which even a basis of historical truth has been looked for in vain. The same may be said of the third book of the Maccabees. This book contains an account of the persecutions which Ptolemy Philopator is said to have inflicted on the Jews in Egypt, and therefore does not mention the times of the Maccabees. Nevertheless it is justly entitled to its name. There can be no doubt that its origin must be explained by the endeavour, which arose after the appearance of the Maccabees, to multiply as much as possible the number of persecutions and deliverances experienced by the people of God: it is an invention copied from what in the time of the Maccabees was reality. The completely fabulous character of the book must be clear to every one who reads it. Authentic history contains no indication whatever that the Ptolemies had any tendency to religious persecution.

Even in heathen authors we find but little information respecting the history of the Jews at this time. Their testimony is important only in so far as they contain the history of the kingdom in whose fate the Jewish nation was implicated. Respecting the Jews themselves they give but little special information; and where this does occur, we are obliged to be extremely cautious, lest we fall into the hands of Jewish deceivers, who, from motives of false patriotism, have palmed their inventions on heathen authors. Among these the most important, and at the same time the most secure from the suspicion of such deceptive supposititiousness, are the fragments of Hecatæus of Abdera, who is said to have written a separate book about the Jews under Ptolemy Lagi. These are given by Josephus, *c. Ap.* l. 21, and published in a separate work by Zorn, Altona, 1730. He professes to derive his knowledge of the Jewish nation principally from the accounts of the high priest Hezekiah, who resided with him at the court of Ptolemy. According to the first book of Origen *c. Celsum*, the fact of his being favourable to the Jews was already brought forward by Herennius Philo as an argument against the composition of the book by the historian Hecatæus. This argument, however, cannot be regarded as decisive, and is outweighed by others in favour of the genuineness, especially this, that a Jew would scarcely relate that many myriads of Jews had been transplanted to Babylon by the Persians;—an argument, however, which is not conclusive, since the Persians may probably mean the Asiatic power in general, the designation being borrowed from the nationality which wielded this power immediately before it passed over to the Greeks, a supposition favoured by the connection. Again, Alexander is said to have given even the territory of the Samaritans to the Jews on account of their loyalty and honesty,—a statement so palpably at variance with historical truth, that it could scarcely have been asserted by any Jew. But neither is this argument conclusive, for liars and boasters often go to extremes, and the masked Jew might fancy that in his heathen garb he could irritate and annoy the Samaritans with impunity. But it cannot fail to arouse actual suspicion, when Hecatæus says of the Jews that they were so devoted to their laws and their religion, that, notwithstanding the opprobrium which they hereby incurred from neighbours and strangers, and even the ill-treatment which it drew down upon them from the kings and satraps of Persia, they refused to depart from their principles, choosing rather to suffer the most cruel martyrdom and death than to renounce the law of their fathers. Here there seems almost to be an allusion to the religious oppressions of Antiochus Epiphanes. At the time of Ptolemy no actual religious persecution had yet been inflicted on the Jews. The persecution instigated by Haman cannot exactly be called a religious one. Moreover, the circumstance which Hecatæus relates immediately afterwards is somewhat suspicious, viz. that Alexander wished to rebuild the temple of Belus at Babylon, and commanded his soldiers, the Jews among others, to assist with the work, but when the Jews refused, and the king found that no punishments were of any avail, he gave them a dispensation. In this we seem to see that Jewish imagination which received a powerful impulse by the events of the time of the Maccabees.

In other cases the deception is undeniable and lies on the surface. This may be said, for example, of the passage which Josephus, *c. Ap.* l. § 22, professes to take from the book of Klearch, a well-known pupil of Aristotle. Here Aristotle himself narrates how in his travels he made an acquaintance, which proved of great importance to him, with a man of an extremely regular and wise manner of life. This was a Judaite from Cœlesyria, a nation descended from the philosophers in India. Philosophers were there called Calani, but among the Syrians, Judaites. This man entered into friendly relations with him and other students of philosophy, and inquired into their sciences, but gave more than he received. It is scarcely comprehensible how Hess, who thinks that "this foreign monument is to be reckoned among those which are authentic," and others could have fallen into so great a snare. Evidently the narrative cannot be isolated, but must be regarded as in connection with the many other attempts by which the Jews sought to secure for themselves the honour of priority in philosophy, since the time when they themselves had entered into connection with it, especially in Alexandria. It seemed a disgrace to them that the people of revelation should concede this priority to the unenlightened heathen. They themselves were *à priori* persuaded that it belonged to them; but this did not satisfy them, their vanity demanded an acknowledgment on the part of the heathen also, and with this object they had recourse to the arts of deception, which, according to the remarkable passage of Galenus in Dähne, *Jewish-Alexandrian Philosophy of Religion* (1834), i. p. 82, had its first origin and its principal seat in Alexandria, and was so prevalent there, that moral feeling was almost blunted where it was concerned. That alleged passage of Klearch was fabricated in the same forge as the great number of verses which have been attributed to Orpheus, the Sibyl, to Linus, and other honoured names; or as the statement of Aristobulus, that Plato took the most and the best of what he wrote from Moses, as well as much else. Comp. Dähne, *l.c.* p. 76 ff.

After these introductory remarks, let us now turn to the events themselves. The whole period, comprising about a hundred years, which the Jews still spent under the Persian supremacy, remains unnoticed, with the exception of one single event, which, though unimportant in itself, yet deserves mention on account of a conclusion which may be drawn from it. Under the reign of Artaxerxes Mnemon, a strife arose between the high priest Jochanan and his brother Jesus. The latter tried, with the help of the Persian general Bagoses, who was friendly towards him, to usurp the high-priestly dignity. Jochanan, being informed of it, slew him in the temple. Bagoses then came to Jerusalem to avenge his friend. In spite of all opposition, he penetrated to the temple, and laid a tribute on the nation as a punishment.

This event is remarkable, in so far as it shows us that the position of the high priest was even at that time one of great political importance. It seems that after the death of Nehemiah no more civil governors were appointed by the Persians, but the highest civil dignity devolved upon the high priest, who was at the same time responsible for the payment of the taxes. This change can only be regarded as detrimental. The union of the civil position with the spiritual, which Moses had most carefully avoided, led to a deterioration of the high-priesthood, such as had never taken place in former times. We now very seldom find an able, truly spiritual-minded man among the high priests; the dignity is the object of ambition, and not unfrequently we find crimes committed in order to obtain or preserve it. The great catastrophe under Antiochus Epiphanes, which threatened the Jewish nationality and religion with complete destruction, had its first foundation in this secularization of the high-priesthood, as we shall see in the course of this history.

Leo has already drawn attention to the fact that the condition of the Jews at this period was in many respects analogous to that of the Greeks at the time when they were still quietly subject to the Turks. The nation, he says, had throughout no true political existence, just as little as the Greeks, but, like the Greeks, they had a religious existence. The consequence naturally was, that all common interests found their organ in the priests, that all interests were drawn into the circle of spiritual jurisdiction, and were thus settled independently, without the intervention of the Persians. It was the same with the Greeks before the revolution: the clergy took cognizance of all common interests of the nation, and the nation was represented before the emperor by the patriarch in Constantinople, who was therefore esteemed the head of the nation. Thus the high priest of the Jews became at this time more and more the head of the nation.

The two hundred years of the Persian supremacy had on the whole been one of prosperity for the Jews, if we except the oppressed feeling which invariably accompanies the desire for independence, and was peculiarly strong in this people, who, in the first beginnings of their existence, were impressed, under divine authority, with the idea that they were absolutely free, and were subject to no ruler but God, and who therefore necessarily regarded oppression as a heavy punishment, the sign of an angry God. They owed their temple and their walls to the good-will of the Persians, under whom they had enjoyed perfect religious freedom; and several Persian kings had done homage to the God of Israel. The condition of the nation at the end of the Persian rule was essentially different from what it had been at the beginning. The thickly-populated land, the flourishing capital, bore witness to the comparative clemency of the rulers. No wonder, therefore, that the Jews were in no haste to throw themselves into the arms of the rising Greek supremacy. It would have been equally unwise and ungrateful.

With respect to the manner in which the Persian supremacy gave way to that of the Greeks, Josephus gives us a full account, *Ant.* xi. 8. The substance is as follows:— The Tyrians got their grain and their provisions principally from the neighbourhood, especially from Judea and Samaria. When Alexander undertook the siege of Tyre, his attention was directed to the same districts; and by his ambassadors he sent a summons to the Jews to surrender, and to provide his army with the means of subsistence. The Jews, however, refused, appealing to the oath of fidelity which had been made to them by Darius. Alexander was exasperated by this, and determined to punish the Jews most severely for their obstinacy, after the conquest of Tyre. In this danger the nation, with the high priest Jadduah at their head, turned in zealous prayer to God. Jadduah had a vision in the night, in which he was commanded to advance to meet the conqueror in his high-priestly garments, accompanied by the priests in their official vestments, and the nation clothed in white. In obedience to this command, they repaired in procession to a height, viz. Sapha. Alexander was amazed on perceiving the high priest. Full of awe, he advanced to meet him, and bending, greeted him. This unexpected acknowledgment caused universal astonishment; and to Parmenio's question respecting the cause of it, Alexander answered that at Dion in Macedonia, when he was absorbed in thinking of the war against the Persians, this same man, in the same garb, had appeared to him in a dream, and had told him to have no fear, but only to advance boldly to Asia, for God would be his leader in this campaign, and would give him the kingdom of the Persians. Alexander then manifested a friendly disposition towards the Jews, and presented offerings in the temple. Jadduah showed him the prophecies in Daniel foretelling the destruction of the Persian kingdom by a king of Greece. Alexander then commanded the Jews to ask a favour before his departure. They requested freedom in the exercise of their religion, and exemption from taxation in the seventh year, which was granted. Scarcely had Alexander left Jerusalem, when the Samaritans sent a deputation to him with a request that he would visit their temple at Gerizim also. (Josephus here contradicts himself, for he asserts elsewhere that the temple on Gerizim was built in consequence of the permission given by Alexander at the siege of Tyre, in which case it could not have been ready at this time.) The Samaritans had at once submitted to the demand made on them by Alexander at the siege of Tyre, and had not merely sent him provisions, but also an auxiliary force of 8000 men. Hence they thought they had far greater claims on the favour of the king than the Jews, and confidently entreated him to come to their city also; and when Alexander explained that there was now no time to do so, they begged that they too might have freedom from taxation in the seventh year. Alexander inquired whether they were then Jews. They answered that they were Hebrews, and observed the same law as the Jews. Alexander, however, delayed his examination into the matter and his decision respecting it until his return.

There is nothing to throw suspicion on the perfect historical certainty of this whole narrative, except the fact that it appears in an author such as Josephus, and in a part of his work where suspicion is most natural, having to do with a subject where the disfigurement due to his false patriotism is especially prominent. With this exception, everything is in favour of its credibility and nothing against.

In the first place, the event narrated suits the connection. All historians of Alexander mention that after the battle of Issus he besieged Tyre for seven months, and went from it to Gaza. Arrian says that Judea voluntarily surrendered. We cannot maintain that Alexander did not, as Josephus asserts, march from Tyre to Gaza, and from Gaza to Jerusalem, but from Tyre to Jerusalem, and from Jerusalem to Gaza. The strong citadel of Gaza seemed to be of much more consequence. The subjection of Jerusalem was regarded only as a secondary object. Hence the more important was accomplished first. The favour shown by Alexander towards the Jews, to whom, after the founding of Alexandria, he granted the same privileges as to the Macedonians, is confirmed by history, and seems to demand some such cause as that given in the narrative of Josephus.

That which has no express historical sanction commends itself by its internal truthfulness. For example, the conduct of Alexander is in striking harmony with his historical character. Everywhere we find in him a tendency to employ religion as a means to serve his ends, and to represent himself as favoured by deity. He knew the power which religion exercised on the oriental spirit, and sought to derive advantage from it, while in secret he scoffed at all religion. It was his aim to be declared the favourite of the gods by the most various voices; and the attainment of this object cost him exertions and sacrifices, compared with which the favours granted to the Jews were as nothing. Thus, in order to procure for himself the same advantages which the Persian kings enjoyed by their divine dignity, he undertook the wearisome, difficult, and dangerous journey to the temple of Jupiter Ammon, in which he almost perished with thirst, together with his whole army. He humbly submitted to the requirements of the priests that none but himself should enter the temple. At a time when his power was already much more firmly established, he restored the temple of Belus at Babylon at an immense cost.

But however much may still be said in favour of the narrative of Josephus, yet there remains always this one great objection, the want of a valid external authority, and we must therefore leave uncertain how much it contains of truth and how much of fiction.

On the disposition of the provinces after the death of Alexander, Judea was first united with Syria. But only four years afterwards it was conquered by Ptolemy Lagi, the regent of Egypt, and Laomedon was taken. Ptolemy took Jerusalem on the Sabbath, knowing that he was certain to meet with no opposition on this day. Until the time of the Maccabees, the Jews were of opinion that it was not right to do anything, even in defence of life, on the Sabbath. With respect to this conquest, we have the credible witness of a heathen author, Agatharchides of Cnidos, given to us by Josephus, which runs thus: "There is a nation called the Jews. This people looked on while their strong and great city of Jerusalem was occupied by Ptolemy, and, owing to their untimely superstition, they refused to take up arms, preferring rather to be subject to a hard master."

According to Josephus, Ptolemy took an immense number of captive Jews back to Egypt with him. But it is plain that he here follows no other authority but that of the Pseudo-Aristeas, who only represents Ptolemy Lagi as having carried away 100,000 Jews, in order that Ptolemy Philadelphus might be able to release that number. Moreover, what Josephus says of the distinctions which Ptolemy conferred on the Jews in his army, because he regarded them as people who never broke their oath of fealty, is subject to well-founded suspicion. It is certain, however, that Ptolemy granted the same privileges to the Jews who wished to repair to Egypt, and especially to Alexandria, as had already been bestowed on them by Alexander. Under these circumstances, it was natural that the Jews should settle there in ever increasing numbers. The unity of the government must have tended to increase this very much. To explain the fact, we require neither measures of compulsion on the part of Ptolemy, nor a special predilection for the Jews. The Jews had already left Egypt in great numbers for Cyrene and Libya. In vain does Josephus try to bring in Ptolemy here again, maintaining that he felt the more secure in his possession of this district the more Jewish inhabitants it contained. The Jewish inclination for trade, which had even then shown itself, affords a better explanation. We see, however, how with Alexander the spread of the Jews, which formed the necessary condition for the realization of their world-historical destination, had reached its second stadium. But however much this extension increased, yet the temple at Jerusalem always remained the religious centre of the nation, and Judea, in a certain measure, the fatherland. The Jews in the διασπορὰ looked upon themselves as all strangers and pilgrims.

It was of great importance for the Jews that Seleucus took possession of Syria, and founded a kingdom which extended to the Indus. By this means Judea fell into the same fatal position which it had formerly occupied when the Egyptian and Assyrian, and afterwards the Chaldee monarchy, had been at variance among themselves. Palestine, with its richly-wooded Lebanon and the sea-coast, was the natural apple of contention between the kingdom of Egypt and the great Asiatic monarchy; yet these collisions did not take place in the immediate future. Palestine still remained for a considerable space of time in undisturbed possession of Egypt; for we cannot maintain, with Usher and Hess, on the most unsatisfactory authority of Sulpicius Severus, that Seleucus added Palestine to his dominions during the lifetime of Ptolemy Lagi. On the contrary, Antiochus the Great was the first who conquered Palestine, after it had remained for more than a hundred years under Egyptian supremacy.

But Seleucus held an important position with regard to the Jews, in so far as he granted them the same privileges in the numerous cities which he built as the Macedonians, probably because he regarded them as natural allies against the natives. They were especially numerous at Antioch; comp.

Josephus, xii. 3, § 1. But they were scattered everywhere throughout all Syria and Asia Minor.

The reign of Ptolemy Philadelphus is only remarkable in so far as it is the scene of the romance of the Pseudo-Aristeas respecting the origin of the Alexandrian version of the Pentateuch. That in this professedly authentic account we have really only a romance, is now universally acknowledged. It is proved by the most palpable arguments: thus, for example, the author, though he represents himself as a Greek, always speaks as a Jew; then, again, the enormous sums given by Ptolemy Philadelphus to obtain a mere translation of the Jewish law-book, etc. In this point, also, theologians agree that the object of the invention is partly the glorification of the Jews, and partly the glorification of the Alexandrian version. Most, however, try to preserve at least some measure of historical truth. Some think they have already done enough when they have struck out thirty-six of the seventy-two translators, and so also in other things (so Parthey *on the Alexandrian Museum*); others think that the narrative contains at least this basis of fact, that the translation was made and placed in the library at Alexandria under Ptolemy, and at his desire. But we must question even this. The desire of Philadelphus, it is assumed, follows naturally from his zealous endeavours to complete his library. But here the position in which the Greeks stood towards the Jews and their sacred literature is not enough considered. Of all the Greek and Latin authors that have come down to us, not one has thought it worth his while to cast even a glance into the religious book of the Jews, although it existed in the Greek language, and would therefore have been so readily accessible. For the whole literary heathen world the Alexandrian version, a hundred years after its composition, was still as good as non-existent. How then can it be considered probable, even necessary, that a heathen monarch, whose exertions it is plain were only directed to the literature of the world, should have given the first impulse to the composition of this translation? The nature of the translation itself also speaks against this view. Everywhere it bears evidence of having been composed by Jews for Jews,—not for the satisfaction of heathen literary curiosity, but to supply the religious need of Greek-speaking Jews. We cannot even tell the time when the translation was made with any certainty from the writing of Aristeas. In the sphere of literature, Ptolemy Philadelphus has become a sort of mythical personage. His name as the great promoter of learning is interwoven in a multitude of literary fictions. Thus, for instance, the author of an Egyptian history, or rather a historical romance, who wrote under the name of Manetho in the time of the Romish supremacy, represents himself as a distinguished Egyptian priest of the time of Ptolemy Philadelphus, who wrote his work at the request of the king, and dedicated it to him.

The following is undoubtedly the correct view of the origin of the Alexandrian version:—The Jews, who dwelt in Alexandria in great numbers from the time of Alexander, and especially since the reign of Ptolemy Lagi, soon adopted Greek as the prevailing language, just as their forefathers had done with Chaldee in the period of their exile. Thus arose the want of a translation of the sacred books. First the Pentateuch was translated, for which there was a specially urgent demand, because it was generally read aloud in the synagogues. The necessity of the Jews requires that this translation should have been made not later than the time of the first Ptolemies. The other books followed gradually. According to the prologue of Jesus Sirach, the whole must have been completed about the year 130 B.C. at the latest.

We learn from the nature of the translation that it was not composed by Palestinian Jews brought for the purpose, but by Alexandrian Jews. It contains not a few traces of an Alexandrian-Jewish tendency, the result of the existing relationship between the Jewish population and the heathen, who were superior to the former in number and in scientific culture. It already shows that the philosophic mode of thought and instruction, which prevailed among the heathen population in Alexandria, exercised a certain influence upon the Jewish population also. Not unfrequently anthropomorphisms and anthropopathisms, which did not harmonize with the refined religious mode of thought, are set aside, although in this respect the translators are not altogether consistent. In other respects also a rationalizing tendency makes itself evident in many places. But when Dähne, in his *Jewish-Alexandrian Philosophy of Religion*, part ii. p. 3 ff., maintains that the authors of the Alexandrian version were already familiar with the maxims of the Philonic philosophy, he asserts far more than he is afterwards able to prove.

The more widely the Jews became scattered, the more the importance of the Alexandrian version increased. At last it came into ordinary use even in Palestine, where Greek had already taken very deep root at the time of Christ; but it was through Christianity that it first attained its full dignity. The very fact of its frequent use in the New Testament served to recommend it. All the Grecian churches made use of it; the Latins, until the time of Jerome, had only a Latin translation made from it. Not a few converted nations made it the basis of translations into their own language. But just in proportion as it rose in Christian estimation did it fall in the estimation of the Jews, and it was not long before it fell into complete disuse.

Jadduah was succeeded in the high-priesthood by his son Onias, who was again succeeded by his son Simon surnamed the Just, a designation bestowed on him, according to Josephus, on account of his piety towards God and his benevolence towards his countrymen. There is a brilliant eulogy on him in Jesus Sirach, in chap. l. 1 ff., which, however, gives no true indication of the spirit that characterized him, whether he was a man of true reflective tendency and of a spiritual mind. He is said to have rendered great service by a series of buildings, and again he is lauded on account of the solemn state with which he conducted his office: "How honoured was he in the midst of the people, in his coming out of the sanctuary! He was as the morning-star in the midst of a cloud, and as the moon at the full, as the sun shining upon the temple of the Most High," etc. In later Jewish tradition he appears in mythic glorification; so also in the Mishna, and still more in the Gemara. But what is told of him is too absurd to be worth quoting.

From this time the history offers nothing of any value for

our object till Antiochus the Great. Under him Judea threw off the dominion of Egypt, to which it never reverted, and became subject to Syria. In the very beginning of the war against King Ptolemy Philopator, Antiochus was on the point of taking Judea. But the victory which Ptolemy obtained over him at Raphia, not far from Gaza, put a limit to his conquests. To this actual fact of the victory at Raphia, the author of the third book of the Maccabees attaches his romance. Ptolemy is represented as having visited Jerusalem after the victory. Notwithstanding the most active opposition on the part of the whole nation, he persisted in carrying out his determination to penetrate into the interior of the sanctuary, and did actually reach the second court; but there God struck him with sudden fear, so that he had to be carried out half-dead. He left the city thirsting for revenge against the Jews, and first directed his rage against those in Alexandria; but these were saved from the impending destruction by immediate divine intervention. How little this narrative deserves credence, appears from the fact that Josephus in his *Antiquities* says nothing of all this. In the book *against Apion* brief mention is made of a similar event, but it is placed under the reign of Ptolemy Physkon, a considerable time later. It is plain that we have to do with an uncertain tradition, which had its origin in the time of the Maccabees, and whose first germ, though certainly found by the author of the third book of the Maccabees, was extended and embellished by his hand. The date of this book cannot be determined. At the time of Josephus it seems not yet to have been in existence. Its position is also in favour of its later origin, after the two first books of the Maccabees, although it describes events which in point of time are earlier than the first book of the Maccabees. The second book of the Maccabees is also of a comparatively later date. The first who mentions the third book is Eusebius in the *Chronicon*. In the Latin Vulgate it was not received; in consequence of which it has also been rejected by most ecclesiastical translations into modern language since the Reformation.

After the death of Philopator, Antiochus made use of the

opportunity which presented itself in the minority of his surviving son, Ptolemy Epiphanes, to invade Cœlesyria and Phenicia, and took possession also of Judea. But Scopas, the general of the young king, reconquered Judea. Soon, however, Antiochus again acquired the upper hand. The Jews, as soon as he approached their land, hastened to offer their allegiance. When he came to Jerusalem, the priests and elders went in procession to meet him, received him with the greatest demonstration of joy, and helped him to drive out the Egyptian garrison which Scopas had left in the castle. We do not know whether this conduct on the part of the Jews had its foundation in oppressions experienced in the latter time of the Egyptian supremacy, or whether it was due only and solely to the great aversion with which the nation always regarded heathen dominion, and which might make the change in so far agreeable, as it gave them an opportunity of revenging themselves on their former oppressors, in so far, also, as the secession to the new ruler was an act of freedom, a sort of prelude to a fuller exercise of it. Respecting the favourable disposition of Antiochus towards the Jews, called forth by this ready advance, Josephus has plenty to say. He communicates several edicts that were made in their favour; among others, one in which all who were not Jews were forbidden to enter the temple, to bring into the city the flesh of animals that were impure according to the Mosaic law, or to keep such animals in the city. Whether these edicts really were published in the form in which we find them in Josephus, is doubtful. One of them at least is somewhat suspicious from internal reasons, viz. the command to Zeuxis, an old general of his, to transplant, with great favour, two thousand Jewish families from Mesopotamia and Babylonia into Lydia and Phrygia, in order that the inhabitants, who were inclined to rebellion, might be the better kept within bounds. The passage in this work, " I have confidence in them, that they will watch faithfully over our rights, on account of their religiousness, and because, as I well know, they inherit the reputation of faithfulness and of willing obedience from olden times," sounds somewhat Jewish.

All things considered, however, it must à *priori* seem very probable that Antiochus made every exertion to attach the Jews to his interest, in order by this means to give greater security to his uncertain conquest. This conquest took place in the year 198 B.C.

Antiochus the Great was succeeded first by his elder brother Seleucus Philopater, who showed equal favour towards the Jews, and then by his son Antiochus Epiphanes. The high-priesthood was occupied at that time by Onias III. According to Josephus, l. xii. chap. 4, § 10, this high priest received a writing from Areus, a king of Sparta, to this purport: " Since there was a written monument, according to which Spartans and Jews were descended from the same ancestor Abraham, he offered every act of friendship to the Jewish nation, and expected the same from them in return." Besides the reference to this event contained in Josephus, it is mentioned not only in the second book of the Maccabees (2 Macc. v. 9), but also in the first (chap. xii. 7, 8), which speaks also of another event which necessarily presupposes the former, viz. the writing which Jonathan sent to the Spartans. Hence there can be no doubt with regard to the accuracy of the fact, if we take into consideration the weight of authority belonging to the first book of the Maccabees. One thing only remains doubtful, viz. the date. Josephus places the event under Onias III. The first book of the Maccabees, on the other hand, calls the high priest Onias without any closer designation; and from the circumstance that in the letter of Jonathan to the Spartans there given, it is stated that a long time has already elapsed since that letter to Onias, Onias III. seems to be excluded, for he died only twelve years before Jonathan entered upon his office. Moreover, history proves that at the time of Onias III. the Spartans had no king of the name of Areus, or Darius, as he is called in the first book of the Maccabees, by a confusion of the less common name with the more common. Yet these arguments have but little weight. "Αρειος, from "Αρης, Mars, may have been an honorary title of the Spartan kings.

Great trouble has been taken to explain how the idea of

relationship with the Jews could have originated among the Spartans, and what was the writing upon which they based it. But if we take into consideration the whole mass of Jewish productions which collectively have the one object of making the Jews beloved and respected among the heathen nations, we can scarcely doubt that the Spartans, who were not well versed in literary intelligence, were here the victims of a Jewish literary deception. The fact of their claiming relationship with *this* nation has its natural foundation in the great fame which the Spartans enjoyed in olden times, even after the fall of their state, and in the honour which it must therefore bring to be recognised by them as brethren. Moreover, the Jewish deception certainly did not emanate from the Jewish nation as such, but only from a single individual, a Jewish Simonides. We cannot, however, exempt the rulers of the Jews from the imputation of having accepted the error of the Spartans *utiliter*. They must have known from their sacred books that the Spartans were not descendants of Abraham. We have an analogy in the circumstance that not a few of the nationalities of Asia maintain that they are descended from the ten tribes of the Israelites,—an opinion to which they can scarcely have come except through Jewish influence.

There is therefore no difficulty in explaining the fact, nor is there any reason for accepting, with Leo, the assumption of Joh. Dav. Michaelis, that by a misunderstanding a statement was made respecting the Spartans which ought rather to have been understood of the Sepharads, or Jewish exiles who had settled at Sepharad, probably on the Bosphorus, and had there founded an independent kingdom (Mich. on 1 Macc. xii.). The Jew who planned the deception would certainly not thank Michaelis for having thus baffled his intention. Rome and Sparta might well be classed together; but we cannot understand how it could have occurred to Jonathan to send an embassy to Rome and Sepharad at the same time, or how the author of the first book of the Maccabees could have looked upon Rome and Sepharad as in any sense equal.

In the year 175 B.C. Antiochus Epiphanes ascended the

throne. He stands as one branded with a curse, not only in sacred history, but also in profane. Polybius, Livius, Diodorus, all heathen authors, represent him as the incarnation of every crime. The people called him Epimanes instead of Epiphanes.

In order to understand the events which took place under him in Judea, we must premise the following remarks:—By the conquests of Alexander, and the Greek supremacies to which they gave rise, Greek culture, morals, and philosophy were brought into the East, which received impressions with that softness peculiar to the conquered in relation to the conquerors. Even the Jews were unable to withstand Greek influence. The heathenizing party which had always existed among them now became stronger and stronger. They were unwilling to bear the contempt of the heathen any longer, and were anxious to participate in the spirit of the world, ashamed of their antiquated superstition. It was natural that the orthodox, stirred into opposition against this party, who aimed at nothing less than the complete overthrow of Judaism, should be moved to greater and more active zeal for their faith, and should combine the more closely. Matters soon came to such a pitch, that it was necessary for each one to declare himself in favour either of the one party or the other. The orthodox party, however, who took the name of the Chasidim, were decidedly on the decrease; and if matters had gone on progressing quietly as before, the Israelitish principle had everything to fear. But God now intervened. The compulsory measures adopted by the heathen government in connection with the heathenizing party, led many who were already wavering to a decision; the Israelitish-religious interest gained an ally in the Israelitish-national interest; and the issue of the thing was, that the heathen principle, though not entirely thrust out, was obliged to disguise itself in the garb of tame Sadducism.

We can scarcely doubt that the entrance which heathenism found was facilitated by the unspiritual character which had become more and more common to orthodox Judaism during this period. To this time belongs the origin of the so-called oral law. The Pentateuch is not content to lay down the

highest moral-religious maxims, and to impress them on the
mind by exhortation, but wishes to carry the law into the
heart of the national life, and for this purpose gives a
number of special directions, which, however, collectively
flow from the highest principles, and are continually traced
back to them, especially in Deuteronomy, where the command to love God is constantly repeated as the highest
and only real command. In this way, however, a good
handle was given for an external, mere legal spirit; and we
learn how imminent this was, from the solicitude with which
the prophets contend against it. Owing to this opposition,
the tendency never attained to any firm consistency and
dominion. But after the exile, when the prophethood was
extinct, and the spirit was gradually disappearing, it gained
ground. And now, in directing the glance to the external
as such, it soon became evident that the Mosaic law was
most incomplete, and by no means contained an adequate
rule for all external action. Life presented a number of
cases for which there were no regulations; and where such
cases did not actually occur, casuistry was indefatigable in
inventing them. Not content with representing these supplementary laws in their true character, as mere inferences
and applications, the product of scholarly subtlety, the
authors thought it necessary to invest them with a higher
authority, and thus arose the fiction of an oral law, received
by Moses from God along with the written law, and handed
down to the present by a succession of safe depositaries.
Under cover of this, Rabbinical casuistry now weighed down
all life with an intolerable burden of commands, which descended to the very minutest details, and gave Judaism a
character of unspirituality which must have been very revolting, especially to the young. Yet Rabbinical sophistry
was still far from its height at the end of this period, and
was only consolidated in its tendency by the victory which
the orthodox party afterwards gained over heathenism, of
which the result was the manifestation of developed Pharisaism, which had just as little existence before the time of
the Maccabees as Sadducism. The Chasidim, whom we encounter towards the end of this period, possessed the elements

not merely of the sect of the Pharisees, but also of that of the Essenes, to whom their name descended.

After these preliminary remarks, we shall consider those events at the close of this period which paved the way to the beginning of the following. We have already shown how the political position which devolved on the high priest in the times after the exile necessarily had the most injurious effect, leading worldly ambition to make this dignity the object of its strivings. This was the case here also. Soon after Antiochus came to the throne, a brother of Onias the high priest, called Jesus, a name which he afterwards changed into Jason, the Greek equivalent, offered him a large sum if he would appoint him to the dignity of his brother. The proposition was accepted, the God-fearing Onias was deposed, and the godless Jason installed in his place. Owing to the character of Jason, and the way in which he obtained his office, he was naturally at variance with all that was in any way attached to the religion of the fathers. In order, therefore, to maintain his position, he made it his object to introduce heathenism more and more among his people. By encouraging heathenism, he hoped at the same time to make himself very popular at the heathen court. He offered the king 150 talents more for permission to establish a gymnasium in Jerusalem, a theatre for combat and other athletic sports for the youth, in accordance with the Greek custom. He also obtained permission from the king to bestow the very valuable freedom of the city of Antioch, and conferred it only on those who joined the Greek faction. These measures led to important results. Even priests left the temple to take part in the games and diversions of the gymnasium. Jason had even the audacity to send ambassadors with presents to the feast of Hercules in Tyre. But he soon lost his dignity in the same way in which he had obtained it. He had sent a certain Menelaus to the king at Antioch, for the purpose of paying him the tribute due, and of treating with him on important matters. According to Josephus, this Menelaus was a brother of Jason, the third son of Simon the high priest. The author of the second book of the Maccabees, on the contrary, says that he was a brother of Simon the Benjamite. This latter view is the more probable. The former probably had its origin in the fact that Jewish authors found it difficult to reconcile themselves to the idea that a man who was not of the high-priestly family should have occupied the position of high priest. But Menelaus may have been of priestly origin, notwithstanding the fact that he is called a Benjamite; for the Levites were counted as belonging to those tribes among whom they dwelt. Menelaus now asked the king for the priesthood, offering a larger sum for it than Jason had paid. His request was granted. But the mere payment did not suffice. He required strong military support in order to dispossess Jason. To obtain this, he and his adherents made a declaration to the king that they renounced the laws of their country, and accepted the religion of the king and the worship of the Greeks. The king now supplied him with troops, and, accompanied by these, he took possession of his office without any opposition. The hope of retaining it could only rest on his zeal in the promotion of heathenism. Only in this way could he remain in favour with the court, or rely on the assistance of the heathenizing party; he could have no hope of winning over the Chasidim, the pious party, and must therefore make it his aim to destroy them. In full confidence he took the way that was opened up to him by circumstances. He publicly renounced the law of Moses and embraced the religion of the Greeks, making every effort to lead others to the same apostasy. In order to pay the sum promised to the king, he sold a great number of the vessels belonging to the temple. The legal (but deposed) high priest Onias was slain by Andronicus, a court officer, bribed by Jason, under circumstances so revolting, that even Antiochus was filled with indignation when he heard of it, and commanded Andronicus to be executed on the spot where the crime was committed.

The object which Antiochus followed with the most strenuous zeal was the possession of Egypt. He undertook three great expeditions against this kingdom. On the third, an end was put to all his ambitious projects, for he received a definite command from the Romans to keep within the limits of his kingdom. Josephus has mixed up together the things that Antiochus did on his return from the second expedition and on his return from the third; but the books of the Maccabees discriminate exactly what was done on each occasion. From them we learn that after the second expedition Antiochus himself carried out his measures of persecution, but that after the third he left their accomplishment to Apollonius, his commander-in-chief. Between these two events lies a period of two years. The former took place in the year 170 B.C., the latter in the year 168 B.C.

When Antiochus was in Egypt on the second expedition, a false report arose in Palestine that he was dead. Jason thought it necessary to take advantage of this opportunity. He came to Jerusalem with a small military force, and, with the assistance of his party there, drove out Menelaus, who retired to the palace, and perpetrated the greatest cruelties. When Antiochus heard an account of all this, he was greatly enraged, principally because the inhabitants of Jerusalem had received the news of his death with the greatest demonstration of joy. He marched at once to Jerusalem, and took the city by storm, κατὰ κράτος, according to the account of the second book of the Maccabees and of Diod. Sic., with which Josephus also is in harmony in *De Bell. Jud.* i. 1, but in the *Ant.* xii. 7 he contradicts himself, and states that the city was taken ἀμαχητί. He instituted a great massacre; 40,000 persons are said to have been slain, and an equal number sold as slaves to the surrounding nations. He penetrated to the interior of the temple, sacrificed a pig on the altar of burnt-offering, and sprinkled every part of the temple with the blood of this unclean animal. He carried away the altar of incense, the table of shew-bread, the golden candlestick, and other vessels of the temple, together with the spoil of the plundered city. Jason fled on the news of the arrival of Antiochus, and died at Sparta in the greatest misery.

On his return from the third expedition, Antiochus, filled with displeasure on account of the failure of his projects, determined to revenge himself on the Jews, although they had given him no cause for anger. On his march through

Palestine he sent Apollonius with 22,000 men against Jerusalem. This general executed his bloody commission on the Sabbath, when the nation was peacefully assembled in the synagogues. He commanded his troops to slay all the men, and to take the women and children prisoners, and sell them into slavery. After the massacre they plundered the city, and set fire to it in several places. A number of houses were pulled down, and a fortress was built of the materials opposite to the temple, and commanding a view of it. In this fortress there was placed a strong garrison, which attacked all those who went to worship in the temple. The temple was defiled in every way. The morning and evening sacrifices, and the worship of God generally, now ceased, until three and a half years later, when Judas rescued the temple from the hands of the heathen, and purified it. Jerusalem was almost entirely deserted by Jewish inhabitants.

Antiochus now issued a decree that all the nations of his states should abandon their old religious customs, and embrace the religion of the king. This decree was given with special reference to the Jews, notwithstanding its comprehensive form. Its aim was the complete destruction of their religion and nationality. We best learn the motive which here influenced Antiochus from 1 Macc. i. 43. He was anxious that all his subjects should be one nation,—the same motive which led Louis XIV. to murder the Protestants. He acted less from heathen fanaticism than in the interest of his own despotism. Every observance of a particularity in his kingdom he regarded as an infringement of his rights. The Jewish religion must have been odious to him, in proportion as it placed the will of another higher King in opposition to his will, in proportion to the decision with which the professors of this religion asserted the principle of obedience to God rather than man, a principle which had no footing in heathenism. Doubtless also the Jewish apostates helped to increase the animosity of the king. They continually assured him that no reliance could be placed on the submission of the Jews so long as they retained their own religion, but that they would take the first opportunity of making themselves independent; and there may have been various manifestations of a restless political spirit in the orthodox party to offer a foundation for such accusations.

The conduct of the Samaritans on this occasion is highly characteristic, and affords great insight into their whole religious position. We here see that they were self-constituted worshippers of Jehovah, that they had chosen Jehovah without His having chosen them, without His having revealed Himself to them or having taken form among them; so that to them Jehovah was in fact an idol. For it is characteristic of all idolatry (with which rationalism is on a par) that the initiative belongs to man, who worships a God who has not revealed Himself, while all true worship of God can appear only as an answer on the part of the Church. Formerly the Samaritans had taken every opportunity of representing themselves as the followers and descendants of the ten tribes. Now, when the pretended relationship with the Jews seemed likely to prove injurious to them, they came out with the truth. They declared that they were originally heathen, who had only resolved to pay a certain homage to the God of the country in order to avoid certain evils. But they were quite willing to comply with the command of the king, and only begged that they might not be involved in the same punishment with the criminal nation of the Jews. They besought permission to dedicate their temple on Gerizim, which had hitherto been consecrated to a God without a name, to the Greek Jupiter, and because they were strangers in the land, to Jupiter Xenios. In saying that their God had until now been without a name, they spoke the truth, although with the intention of deceiving, for in the biblical sense their God was indeed without a name,—He had done nothing among them from which a name could have arisen in a living way.

Among the Jews also many obeyed the law of the king, not from fear alone, but also from inclination. These apostates then became more violent in persecuting their brethren than the heathen themselves.

The king now sent a commission, with Athenæus at their head, to Judea, for the purpose of carrying out his law. With the help of the Syrian soldiery, these men made it their first aim to destroy every trace of the Jewish religion in the capital. Circumcision was forbidden, and the observance of the Sabbath; every copy of the law that could be found was destroyed; the temple was dedicated to Jupiter Olympus, whose statue was erected on the altar of burnt-offering, and to whom sacrifices were presented. A similar course of action was adopted in the other cities. Once in every month, on the birthday of the king, the inhabitants were compelled to sacrifice on the heathen altars, which were erected everywhere, and to eat the flesh of swine and other unclean animals that were presented as offerings. Many, however, gave up their life for their religious convictions. The author of the first book of the Maccabees, chap. i. 62, 63, only makes this general statement; but the author of the second book gives us a full history of many such martyrdoms, in which, however, we are unable to distinguish how much is historical truth and how much embellishment. What Josephus relates in the book *de Maccabœis* is mostly taken from the second book of the Maccabees.

Hence we see how everything was at stake. And the more trying the time was for those who feared God in Israel, the more natural must it appear that God should have given them consolation in the prophecies of Daniel long before the consolation itself appeared; the more natural, since prophecy itself was at this time completely extinct, so that the consolation could not proceed from the midst of themselves. Daniel pointed out that the object of this dispensation was the trial and purification of the nation. We see how necessary this was from what has already been said.

Before turning to the succeeding period, we must speak of a literary production belonging to this time, which serves not a little to throw light on the better tendency of Judaism which prevailed in it. This is the book of Jesus Sirach, which, together with the book of Wisdom, the book of Tobias, Baruch, and the first book of the Maccabees, forms the kernel of the Apocrypha. This book received the name of Ecclesiasticus from the circumstance that, although possessing no canonical authority, it was yet in ecclesiastical use. The (merely) ecclesiastical books are opposed to the canonical; and because Jesus Sirach occupied the first place among these, having the greatest authority, and being the most read in the Church, it was called κατ' ἐξοχὴν Ecclesiasticus. Among the Church fathers we find it also under the names πανάρετος and πανάρετος σοφία, which form an excellent indication of its contents. In determining the age of the book, we have a double date at our service. First, the high priest Simon is described in a way which suggests the idea that the author must have seen him in his official activity. But there can scarcely be a doubt that this was Simon the Just, elsewhere so celebrated, who lived in the last quarter of the third century B.C., and not the obscure Simon the Second, who lived in the second quarter of the same century. The author knows only one Simon. If he had meant Simon the Second, he must have distinguished him from the famous Simon the First. Then again the translator, the grandson of the author, says that he came to Egypt under the reign of Ptolemy Evergetes, in the thirty-eighth year. Of the two Ptolemies who bore the name Ptolemæus Evergetes, the first from 246–241 B.C., the other about the middle of the second century, we have in favour of the former, agreement with the first chronological date. On the other hand, it has been asserted that the first Evergetes did not reign for thirty-eight years; but it is not stated that the translator came to Egypt in the thirty-eighth year of *Ptolemy*. Many, among others Winer, *Disputatur de utriusque Siracidæ ætate*, Erlangen, 1832, have justly supposed that reference was made to the thirty-eighth year of the translator's age, just as in the superscription of Ezekiel the thirtieth year means the thirtieth year of the prophet. According to this, the composition of our book must not be placed in the first half of the second century, as is now generally done, after the example of Eichhorn, and has been recently by Fritzsche in his commentary, Leipzig, 1859, but rather in the first half of the third century,—a view which has lately been defended by Hug, in a special treatise, in the Journal for the archbishopric of Freiburg, in vol. 7. The book was originally written in the Hebrew language, as the grandson of the author states in the preface. There is also another Jewish book of Proverbs, by a certain Ben Sira, which has been frequently edited. This Ben Sira is without doubt no other than Jesus Sirach. Not only is the name in favour of this view, but also the agreement of many sentences. The book, however, is not the original, but a free elaboration after the Greek, bearing the same relation to the true Jesus Sirach as Josephus Ben Gorion bears to the true Josephus. Of the author of the book we know nothing more than what we can gather from the book itself. The way in which he speaks of the γραμματεῖς in chap. xxxviii. 25-xxxix. 1-15, the decision with which he gives the preference to this calling before every other, makes it highly probable that he was himself a scribe. From that description, however, and the example of the author himself, we learn that among these scribes, who in themselves were regarded only as literati, but from whose midst all public teachers and officials were chosen, there were most honourable men; that at that time the pharisaic propositions had not yet supplanted the deeper and devoted study of Holy Scripture, which here appears as the highest task of the scholar. In estimating the book, a false criterion has only too frequently been applied. We ought not to compare it with Isaiah and the Psalms in the Old Testament, or with the Gospel of John in the New Testament, but with the Proverbs in the Old Testament, and perhaps with the Epistle of James in the New Testament. There will still, no doubt, be a considerable difference—the difference between an apocryphal and a canonical book—but we shall yet have sufficient reason for rejoicing in the work of the author, regarding it as a beautiful memorial of Israelitish piety and recognition of God. Those who look upon Christ only as a moral teacher have no reason to place Him much higher than Jesus Sirach, who continued to work on the foundation laid by Solomon, and whose moral maxims are frequently in striking harmony with those of the New Testament. "With respect to the forgiveness of injuries," says Hess, "and the hope built upon it of finding grace with God; with respect to freedom from the spirit of revenge; regarding benevolence and the best mode of practising it;

conjugal fidelity, etc.,—probably nothing was written before the time of Christ which more nearly resembled His mode of thought, although not quite conformable to so high a standard."

§ 5.

THE TIME OF THE MACCABEES.

The most important sources for the beginning of this period, the time of the true struggle for freedom, are the books of the Maccabees, the first of which, the only one that can lay claim to perfect credibility, leads us down to the time of John Hyrcanus. From these two books, on which we possess an excellent monograph by Wernsdorf, 1749, Josephus has drawn; perhaps also from a fourth book of the Maccabees, containing the life of John Hyrcanus, which is said to have been seen as late as the sixteenth century. For the remaining time we have only Josephus and the scattered accounts of heathen authors. The whole period comprises 125 years, of which sixty years passed away under the ethnarchy of the Maccabees, forty-two under their kingship, and twenty-three under the ethnarchy of Hyrcanus, under whom the supremacy was only nominally with the race of the Maccabees.

Those who form the centre of Jewish history at this period bear a twofold name—the Hasmonians and the Maccabees. Many, in imitation of Josephus, have derived the former designation from an individual of this name. But there can be no doubt that the name is the Hebrew השמנים, optimates, Ps. lxviii. 32, and a title of honour which was conferred on the family. The name of Maccabee was first borne by Judas alone, as the bravest of the brethren, and is probably derived from מקב, hammer, the hammerer; comp. Jer. xxiii. 29, where the word of God, of which Judas was an instrument, is compared to a hammer that breaketh the rock in pieces. It then passed over to the whole race of heroes, especially in the Christian Church, and was even employed in a still wider sense, being applied to all those who resembled them in zeal for the defence of the true religion.

It is not our intention here to enter into the details of the struggles which led to the release of the Jews. For these we must refer to the first book of the Maccabees.

The principal, almost the only, personages who attract our attention at this time are Mattathias the son of John, a priest of the tribe of Joarib, who first rose against the heathen persecutors in the hill city Modin, and soon collected the Chasidim about him, but died only a year afterwards; and three of his five sons, Judas, Jonathan, and Simon, who successively came to be leaders of the nation, and all died in the service of their country.

It is quite evident that these men, and the Chasidim under their leadership, manifest a truly heroic spirit; yet we must not overlook the fact that the final success of their undertaking, the emancipation, is attributable just as much to the state of the Syrian kingdom at that time, as to this spirit of heroism. One change of government followed another. In many cases the various pretenders made every effort to attach the Jews to their interest. It is very remarkable how often, just when matters had come to the worst, a change of this kind in the Syrian kingdom rescued the Jews from the threatened destruction. This concurrence of what the world calls chance was not sufficiently considered by the Jews, when, trusting to their success in the time of the Maccabees, they afterwards rebelled against the Romish power. The destruction which they met at the hands of this power may be regarded as the natural consequence of their success against the Syrians. It was at the same time a righteous judgment on them, because they had not shown their gratitude in the right way for the salvation which God had granted them at that time. Hence, in this case, the salvation was changed into destruction.

In the first twenty-three years of this period, under Judas, who stood for six years at the head of affairs, and Jonathan, who held the reins for seventeen years, the condition of the nation was on the whole a melancholy one, glorious victories alternating with defeats,—matters having frequently gone so far that all hope was apparently lost, the country being laid waste by hostile armies, who raged cruelly against the

Chasidim. The six years of Judas, in which Antiochus Epiphanes died a miserable death, were especially wretched. We find one bright spot in the restoration of the worship of God in Jerusalem, after the heathen abominations had been done away and the temple had been purified. It was an event which gave occasion for the founding of a yearly feast, the Encænia, which, according to 1 Macc. iv. 59, was kept for eight days, beginning on the twenty-fifth of Casleu or December. From John x. 22 we learn that this feast, the only one besides the feast of Purim that was introduced after the Mosaic time, was still observed at the time of Christ. It was called also λυχνοκαία, the feast of candles, because lights were then kindled everywhere, as a sign that God would allow the light of His salvation to appear in the darkness of the misery.

A happier time began under Simon, who was distinguished alike for bravery and wisdom, and who accomplished the work of emancipation in the first year of his primacy. From this time the Syrian kings themselves had dealings with the Jews, as with their φίλοις συμμάχοις, and the nation remained in possession of freedom, until the unfortunate disputes of Hyrcanus and Aristobulus regarding the supremacy led to interference on the part of the Romans, which resulted in a new servitude of the Jews.

According to Josephus, xii. chap. 17 and 19, Judas already held the office of high priest, having been raised to this dignity by the people; but from 1 Macc. ix. 54, 55, it follows that Judas died before Alcimus, the ungodly high priest; and Josephus contradicts himself, for in xx. chap. 8, he says that after the death of Alcimus the nation was seven years without a high priest. The correct view is that Jonathan only attained to the dignity of a general, as well as that of a high priest, six years before his death; comp. 1 Macc. x. 20. In all probability the nomination was first made by the nation, and the actual appointment by Alexander Balas, the Syrian king.

Alcimus, however, did not belong to the family in which the high-priesthood had remained for centuries; and when this office now passed over to the Maccabees, they lost all expectation of regaining the dignity. A descendant of this family, Onias, sought to indemnify himself for what had been lost, and, with the permission of Philometer, the Egyptian king, built a temple in the district of Heliopolis, where the worship of God was performed by priests according to the Mosaic ritual. This temple was only closed under Vespasian.

At first sight, there is something very strange in this circumstance. We cannot understand how Onias could have had such presumption, in the face of the strict ordinances of the Pentateuch with regard to the unity of the sanctuary, and the later declarations of God respecting the exclusive choice of Zion. We have a presentiment beforehand that Onias had some other authority by which he thought he could defend himself against this, which was actually the case. Doubtless he appealed to the passage, Isa. chap. xix. 18–21, where the prophet foretells the future conversion of Egypt to the true God, and the erection of altars there to His name. It is quite evident that the passage could not really serve as a justification of his undertaking. It refers not to a sanctuary for Jews, but for converted Egyptians. We must not forget, however, that his undertaking did not by any means receive the approval of the nation, but in all probability his temple was only recognised and visited by a small schismatic party. Josephus expressly condemns his undertaking: οὐκ ἐξ ὑγιοῦς γνώμης ταῦτα ἔπραττεν, he says, de Bell. Jud. 1. vii. chap. 10, § 3. Nor must we neglect to point out that this attempt to effect what God had reserved to Himself to accomplish in the Messianic time, is by no means a solitary one. The circumcision which John Hyrcanus forcibly imposed on the Edomites belongs to the same category, and the restoration of the temple attempted by Herod, which latter was occasioned by the prophecy of Haggai. But when the true fulfilment began, these apparent fulfilments were revealed in all their meagreness.

Judas had received the dignity of a general, and Jonathan that of a general and high priest, only as a personal thing; but Simon received from the nation and the council the formal and solemn assurance of the hereditary primacy as well as the high-priesthood. In 1 Macc. xiv. 35 ff. we have the decree of the council and nation. It was engraved on tables of brass, and hung up on the wall of the sanctuary. From this alone we see that the position of the Maccabee princes was a very difficult one, and subsequent history confirms the view. The decree is based on the presupposition that the power was properly only with the nation and the council, the power of the prince being merely a *potestas delegata*,—the prince and high priest appointed purely by favour of the people, and the people purely by the favour of God.

With absolute power the nation decides what dignities are to be united in the prince, and what insignia he is to bear. A power which has originated in this way cannot be independent even after its establishment; and every attempt to make it so—and there can be no lack of such attempts, at least in an oriental state—must entail severe conflicts. There was a stronger motive to opposition at this time, since the priestly-pharisaic party at the head of the nation must soon become cognizant of the evils caused by the formerly unheard-of union of the high-priestly dignity and the highest civil power. This union had been the result first of the necessity of the times, and afterwards of gratitude; when the necessity was over and the gratitude extinct, many scruples arose. Thus, immediately after the happy termination of the external struggle, and even during it, the foundation was laid for an internal conflict, equally injurious to the nation and the rulers.

The determination contained in ver. 41, that Simon should be their governor and high priest for ever, ἕως τοῦ ἀναστῆναι προφήτην πιστόν, is remarkable. The Maccabee time, notwithstanding all its zeal for the law, was yet conscious of having been forsaken by the Spirit. It had no prophets to make known the hidden decrees of God; comp. 1 Macc. ix. 27, which is in perfect agreement with the fact that in the sole authentic source, the first book of the Maccabees, we find nothing in what occurred like a miraculous intervention on the part of God, but everything seems rather to depend on natural ground, while the second book of the Maccabees strenuously endeavours to destroy this character. It was hoped, however, that this state, so little in unison with the idea of a people of God, would be only temporary;

that in the future God would enter into closer and more immediate connection with His people. In this expectation only a provisional character was given to the most important determinations. Here there was a special reason for giving prominence to the thought, and pointing to the possibility, that the decree might at a future time be reversed by divine authority. The kingdom had been given and confirmed to the race of David by a series of prophetic oracles; that it should permanently be taken away from this race was inconceivable. From it the Messiah was to proceed at a future time, who, according to Ps. cx. and the prophecies of Zechariah, should combine the dignity of high priest and king. Hence, when the kingly and the high-priestly dignity were transferred to a race not proceeding from David, it could only be done with the consciousness that it was a momentary concession to the force of circumstances, which called loudly for such a measure, but that the elevation could have only a temporary character, and this race, as an intermediate one, would, at a future time determined by God, have to yield again to the only legitimate one.

In all probability the firm constitution and the consolidation of the supreme tribunal at Jerusalem, composed of seventy members and a president, which bore the name συνέδριον, סנהדרין, took place in the time of the struggle for freedom against the Syrians. This Greek name itself is an argument against those who attribute its origin to a far earlier date. It was not merely the highest judicial court, but also legislated for the whole religious community. The less definitely the boundaries of this and the princely power were marked out, the more readily must quarrels arise; and nothing was more probable than that the pharisaic-priestly party, who were always supreme in this council, should make it a means of concentrated opposition against the princely power.

It is probable that the constitution of the synagogue also received its fuller development during the struggle for religion and freedom; its beginnings date back to the earliest times, and are as old as the Mosaic law. In proportion as the zeal for the religion of the fathers increased, it was thought necessary to erect synagogues in every place where the Mosaic law was taught. According to the statement of the Jews, there were more than four hundred synagogues in Jerusalem alone; and from the gospel history we learn that in Galilee there were synagogues even in the smaller places. The Jews maintain that synagogues were erected in every place where there were ten men of distinction and wealth who had leisure to attend divine service daily. At the time of the Syrian oppression, we are told, it became the custom to read sections from the prophets as well as from the law. For at the time of Antiochus Epiphanes the reading of the Mosaic law had been forbidden, and instead of it selections were made from the prophets, called Haphtharas. These were afterwards retained along with the Parashas. But the correctness of this Jewish statement may well be doubted. The selection of passages from the prophets as well as from the law is so natural, that we can scarcely believe it could have been occasioned by a cause so purely external. Respecting the constitution of the synagogues we have a classic work by Vitringa, *de Synagoga*, lib. iii.

Simon was treacherously assassinated by his son-in-law Ptolemy, after a reign of only eight years, a time of great prosperity for the nation. Coins with his stamp are still in existence. They bear the name שמעון נשיא ישראל, together with the first, second, etc., year of the redemption of Israel. The genuineness of these coins was triumphantly proved in the contest between Tychsen and the Spanish scholar Bayer (principal work, *de Numis Hebr. Samaritanis*, Valentia, 1781, 4to); compare the full account of this dispute in Hartmann's *Oluf Gerhard Tychsen*, ii. 2, pp. 295–495.

Ptolemy's plot to slay John Hyrcanus also, the heir to the throne, was unsuccessful, and the latter succeeded to the dignity of his father, which he held for twenty-nine years. His reign also was beneficial to the nation. He knew how to make himself feared by the surrounding nations. He took possession of Sichem, and destroyed the temple on Gerizim, which was never rebuilt; and at the time of Christ the Samaritans had no longer any temple,—a fact which is often overlooked. Yet the mountain still served them for a sanctuary. He then conquered the Idumeans, and compelled them to be circumcised,—not, as many affirm, to adopt the rite for the second time. The assumption that they had formerly been circumcised, and that the rite had only been discontinued from the time of Antiochus Epiphanes, is quite untenable. We have already indicated the motive by which he was led. He had the prophecies of the future conversion of the heathen before his eyes, and intended, as far as was possible to his limited understanding, to accomplish it by force. From this time the Idumeans were reckoned as Jews. But the deed bore bitter fruit for the Jews. It led to the supremacy of the family of Herod the Idumean.

It is of special importance to note that it was under Hyrcanus that the Pharisees and Sadducees first appeared prominently in history. Josephus states that hitherto Hyrcanus had always advocated the principles of the Pharisees, and had shown favour to this party. But it now happened that one of this party publicly called upon him, in a hateful and dishonourable manner, to renounce the dignity of high priest; and the way in which the heads of the party behaved on this occasion led Hyrcanus to suspect that the individual was only the organ of the whole party, and that the mode alone in which he asserted the party-feeling was peculiar to him. That Hyrcanus was not deceived in this opinion, we have already shown. The union of the highest civil with the highest spiritual power must have appeared highly hazardous to the Pharisees. From a high priest who was at the same time prince they could not expect such unconditional devotion to the strictest ecclesiastical maxims; and if he were to act in opposition to these principles, their defenders would be without protection and centre. Hyrcanus now went over to the side of the Sadducees.

This is the place to treat somewhat more fully of the three principal sects of the Jews, of which the two former especially play so important a part in the following history. First with regard to the Pharisees, there can be no doubt as to the meaning of their name. פְּרִישׁ, as the Pharisees are called in Aramæan, viz. in the Syrian translation of the New Testament, is the participle *Pail* of the verb פרש, to separate, corresponding to the Hebrew participle *Paul*. Separatists, this was the name adopted by the members of this party, because they were distinguished by an especially strict observance of the law, particularly of the ceremonial parts, from the great mass of the nation, who were more lax and careless in this respect, and probably still more because they anxiously avoided all nearer contact with them, fearing lest they should be contaminated with their uncleanness. Elias Levita, in his dictionary Tisbi, says: "These are they who are separated from the ways of this world, like the Nazarites;" so also Suidas, Φαρισαῖοι, οἱ ἑρμηνευόμενοι ἀφωρισμένοι, παρὰ τὸ μερίζειν καὶ ἀφορίζειν ἑαυτοὺς τῶν ἄλλων ἁπάντων; and the author of the Talmudic dictionary Aruch, "A Pharisee is one who separates himself from all uncleanness and from all unclean food, and from the common people, עם הארץ, who pay no particular attention to the distinction of meats." That the name is characteristic of the thing, when thus interpreted, appears from passages such as Luke xviii. 11, Mark vii. 7.

Respecting the origin of the Pharisees there are many different opinions. According to Josephus, *Ant.* l. xviii. chap. 1, § 2, the three sects of the Jews were known from very early times, ἐκ τοῦ πάνυ ἀρχαίου. He first mentions them in the history of Jonathan the Maccabee, when in his latter years he made a covenant with the Romans and Spartans. At that time, he says, *Ant.* xiii. 5, 9, there were three sects among the Jews, without meaning that they first originated at that time. Their first important appearance occurs in the time of Hyrcanus. We get a middle course between the different views, by distinguishing between Pharisaism as a tendency and as a party. As a tendency, Pharisaism was very old,—in its most general outlines almost coeval with the giving of the law. Even in the times previous to the exile, we find not only the openly godless, heathenizing disposition, but also another, which sought by external piety to conceal the inner estrangement from God, or godlessness, not only from others, but also from itself and from God. The prophets declaim against them in many passages; for example, Isaiah in chap. i. and lxvi., and the author of Ps. l. After the return from the captivity, this form of godlessness became the prevailing one, and remained so until the influence of the Greek supremacy raised the other, the heathenizing tendency, to new importance. As a party, however, Pharisaism is young. In this respect its roots only lie in the time of the Maccabees. It owes its origin to the machinations of the heathenizing party to destroy the paternal religion. In consequence of this, all those who remained true to the religion of their fathers—the Chasidim of the books of the Maccabees—formed a close union among themselves. But when the continuance of their religion was secured, those among them who differed internally separated into the two parties of Pharisees and Essenes, of whom the former were by far the more important in number and influence. From this time the Pharisees, though possessing no external bond of union, yet formed a kind of order, whose members were so well known that they could be counted, and who, after the manner of the Jesuits, made every effort to acquire and retain supremacy in the state for the Israelitish-religious principle, according to their conception of it, and for themselves as its representatives. With this object in view, they placed themselves in the closest contact with the masses, and, relying on their support, thought they could set at defiance those rulers who placed themselves in opposition to their interest. The necessary presupposition of the continuance of this party was that heathenism possessed an influence with respect to Israel both internal and external. If this influence had disappeared, the party, as such, would also have disappeared, and only the spirit could have remained in existence. Moreover, by the fact that the Pharisees formed themselves into a party, Pharisaism as a tendency was considerably modified. All its lines were more sharply drawn; the more distinctly and prominently the Pharisees appeared in public as representatives of the Israelitish-religious principle, the more they sought to legitimize themselves in this capacity by the strictest, and at the same time the most public, fulfilment of the commandments. At the same time a number of most unworthy members joined the party, who could not have participated in the tendency, because this had reference only to the satisfaction of personal religious wants, while the party offered abundant satisfaction to ambition and other passions. The gross hypocrisy which sounded a trumpet before it, etc., must have been greatly encouraged by the circumstance that Pharisaism as a party never lost sight of its position with respect to the people, always striving to impose upon them and to gain glory in their eyes, knowing well that without the assistance of the nation it was powerless.

If we now proceed to inquire into the main peculiarities of Pharisaism, we must first of all designate it a form of Israelitish piety which refused to acknowledge the forgiveness of sins and the Holy Spirit, and therefore regeneration. That this characteristic was present even in the noblest Pharisees, we learn from our Lord Himself, when He says to Nicodemus, " Verily, verily, I say unto thee, except a man be born again, he cannot see the kingdom of God;" and " Except a man be born of water and of the Spirit, he cannot enter into the kingdom of God."

All piety without regeneration seeks a substitute in order to silence the demands of the conscience, at least in some measure. The Pharisees found this substitute in the observance of the external Mosaic commands, especially of those which treat of legal purity and impurity. In all these matters, that could be performed while the heart was still unregenerate, they were most scrupulous. The better of them, however, were not content with observing the mere externalities of the Mosaic law, but strove to fulfil it in its whole extent; and the impossibility of reaching this goal from their standpoint involved them in conflicts such as those which Paul, the former Pharisee, describes in Rom. vii. from his own experience.

But this was not the rule. On the contrary, superficiality and perversion of the Mosaic law belong to the characteristics of the party, just as we invariably find a tendency in those minds which recognise neither forgiveness nor the Holy Ghost, to deaden the law, in order to escape from its accusations. From the polemic which our Lord directs against them in the Sermon on the Mount, we learn that they placed sin only in the sphere of action, in striking contrast to the Mosaic law, and made its banishment from this sphere their sole aim. But even with respect to action they had divers expedients for allowing free scope to the sinful inclination that was kept down by the law. Thus Matt. xv. 4 ff. shows how, by their doctrine of the collision of duties, they paralyzed the command regarding the reverence due to parents, to which Moses assigned so high a place. How great the blindness of Pharisaism was respecting the true sense of the law, is shown by the answer of the Pharisee youth when our Lord referred him to the ten commandments: πάντα ταῦτα ἐφυλαξάμην ἐκ νεότητός μου, τί ἔτι ὑστερῶ; They thought they could not only fulfil the law, but could do even more than the law required. Thus D. Kimchi, on Ps. ciii. 7, defines the חסיד as one who does more than is commanded. What they took away on one side they added to the other. The so-called oral law was fostered and cherished by the Pharisees, and its validity formed a great subject of dispute between them and the Sadducees. They were well satisfied with the exchange. It is true that every oral law imposed a number of burdensome obligations, but it did not invade the life of the natural man, and the idea of obtaining merit with God indemnified them for sacrifices and deprivations.

Again, self-righteousness is a peculiar characteristic of Pharisaism, and is found wherever religiousness exists without forgiveness and the Holy Spirit. Their doctrine of the powers of the human will was subservient to this self-righteousness. If not entirely Pelagian, it was more than semi-Pelagian. The doctrine of the Pharisees respecting the providence of God, of His influence and His co-operation in the actions of men, and of the freedom of the human will, are mentioned by Josephus in three passages, *Antiq.* xiii. 5. 9, and xviii. 1. 3, and *De Bell. Jud.* ii. 7. In all these passages he makes use of the word εἱμαρμένη, fate, but in a different sense from that of the Greeks,—not in the sense of a blind fatality, but of an influence exercised by God on human affairs. The expressions of Josephus are not quite clear, and want doctrinal accuracy. He does not sufficiently discriminate between the actions and the destinies of men. This much, however, is clear, that with reference to the former question, the Pharisees, after the manner of the rationalists, only attributed an uncertain co-operation to God, and regarded virtue as well as vice as properly the work of man, allowing only supervision, punishment, and reward to God, while the Sadducees denied Him even this. From this it is self-evident how superficial their knowledge was with reference to human sinfulness. They are characterized by all the faults invariably connected with self-righteousness, by want of love generally, and especially towards their fallen brethren (Matt. ix. 11), by carnal aims, and many other defects.

The remaining doctrines said to be peculiar to them were common to them with all those who adhered to the religion of their fathers. Thus, for example, the doctrine of the resurrection, whose denial, however, was characteristic of the Sadducees. They would only have been peculiar with respect to the doctrine of the resurrection if they had taught the transmigration of souls. But this idea is based only on an intentional ambiguity, which Josephus employs for the eyes of his Greek readers. He says, *De Bell. Jud.* ii. 7. 14, the Pharisees maintain that souls pass into another body, μεταβαίνειν εἰς ἕτερον σῶμα, but only the souls of the pious; those of the ungodly are appointed to everlasting punishment. The words are so placed that they may be understood of resurrection with a glorified body, in harmony with the doctrine of the Old Testament. In 1 Cor. xv. the resurrection-body is described by Paul as different from the present body. But Josephus has avoided expressing himself more definitely, because the doctrine of the resurrection of the body was offensive to the heathen philosophers, and to those educated in their schools; comp. Acts xvii. 32 and 1 Cor. xv. From Acts xxiii. 8 and Luke xx. 39, it is certain that the Pharisees did not teach the transmigration of souls, but the resurrection in the biblical sense. And there can be no doubt that their further ideas of eternal life were regulated by their moral condition, just as with us. The ordinary Pharisees, having their treasure upon earth, conceived of eternal life as analogous to this. Their carnal ideas were ridiculed by the Sadducees, and generally employed as the foundation for attacks against the doctrine of the resurrection; comp. Matt. xxii. 24 ff.

In Matt. xxiii. 15 the striving of Pharisaism to make proselytes appears to be peculiar to it. This it has in common with every self-made piety. Indifferentism is entirely free from it. So also is the true faith which is the work of the Holy Spirit, though for a very different reason. This faith knows from experience that nothing can be artificial in the sphere of religion, but everything must be given from above. The mere form of religion, which is all that proselytism can produce, is nothing in itself.

The Pharisees were not, like the Essenes, a close corporation under rulers, but only a party. As such, however, they held closely together, and this very union, increased by the powerful opposition against which they had to contend, formed their greatest strength. A kind of free organization had formed itself among them, but only by the force of habit. The youth were very respectful towards their elders, and dared not contradict them. In Josephus the heads of the party are termed οἱ κρῶτοι τῶν Φαρισαίων, to distinguish them from the rest who in the New Testament are called μαθηταὶ τῶν Φαρισαίων: comp. Matt. xxii. 16. It is scarcely necessary to state that many adhered outwardly to the party of the Pharisees only on political grounds.

The Pharisees were held in high esteem by the nation, and for this reason their influence in public affairs was very great. They owed this partly to their actual piety, partly to the appearance of godliness which they displayed. Not only did they make it their systematic object to gain this esteem, but they also knew how to take advantage of it. This relation towards the nation was very injurious to Pharisaism. It must have served as a strong encouragement to hypocrisy, to which there is already a tendency in every self-made piety. In all that they did, they considered the nation more than God.

In the New Testament we not unfrequently find Pharisees and scribes spoken of in connection. The scribes were the literati of the nation. Many teachers, as well as judges and officials, went out from their midst. Since the Pharisees were the ruling party, and enjoyed the favour of the people, it was natural that most of the scribes should attach themselves to their interest. The Sadducees were conscious that as scribes—teachers or officials—they must occupy an untenable position; moreover, constant occupation with Scripture and the propositions connected with it was distasteful to them. Yet the Sadducees were not entirely excluded from public offices. Thus the Sanhedrim in Jerusalem consisted principally of Pharisees, learned γραμματεῖς and unlearned; yet, according to Acts xxiii. 6 ff., there were also assessors of the party of the Sadducees, and, according to Josephus, *Antiq.* xx. 9. 1, Ananus the high priest himself was a Sadducee: the Sadducees, however, were obliged to embrace Pharisaism when they held public offices.

According to the statement of the Jews, the Sadducees took their name from a certain Zadok; but the accounts are too late, and the analogy of the Pharisees and Essenes speaks against the derivation from an individual. The most probable view is, that it is a title of honour which they themselves adopted. They called themselves צדיקים or צדוֹקים, the righteous, in contradistinction from the חסידים and the פרישים, the pious and the separated, taking righteousness not in its comprehensive Israelitish, but in its limited Grecian sense. No reliance can be placed on the fable that they derived their wisdom from an individual. If we consider what the books of the Maccabees relate respecting the open apostasy to heathenism in the time of Antiochus Epiphanes; if we consider that a tendency of this kind could not have disappeared so soon, least of all when it was so greatly favoured by outward relations; there can be no doubt respecting the origin of Sadduceeism. They are nothing more than the same heathen, godless party in Israelitish clothing. The Israelitish element which characterizes them seems to be mere accommodation. There is nothing that would lead us to infer that they had any closer internal sympathy with the Israelitish principle. So far, at least, as the great mass was concerned, they remained internally at the standpoint of the ἀσεβεῖς of the books of the Maccabees. It is a mistake to try to identify them with the Karaites, a Jewish sect which does not appear until the eighth century after Christ. This attempt has originated in purely Jewish ground. Their rejection of the oral law was the result of a true recognition of the written law; while the Sadducees in their heart recognised the written law just as little as the oral one, and only took up the standpoint of belief in the word for the more effective refutation of their opponents, just as many among us when they want to attack the creeds. It has frequently been asserted that the Sadducees, like the Samaritans, acknowledged only the Pentateuch. The correct view, however, is that the Sadducees externally acknowledged the whole canon, though internally they acknowledged the five books of Moses just as little as the rest. When our Lord, in Matt. xxii. 31, 32, refutes the Sadducee denial of the resurrection from the writings of Moses, although the other books offered far more convincing arguments, He does this only because they had drawn their argument from these writings, and because the Mosaic writings were the most important for every Jew. And when Josephus, *Antiq.* xiii. 10, says that the Sadducees held only to what had been written by Moses, he does not place the Pentateuch in opposition to the other books, but rather contrasts the written and the oral law. The Sadducees boldly advocated such doctrines as they could with any plausibility bring into harmony with the writings of the Old Testament; where this was not possible, they kept them to themselves. What they openly defended, however, sufficiently proves that they had lost the substance of the divine teaching. The doctrine which they most confidently contested was that of the resurrection. Here, so far as the Pentateuch was concerned, they could easily embarrass their opponents. The plainer passages in Isaiah, Ezekiel, and especially in Daniel, they probably explained away by giving them a figurative meaning. According to Acts xxiii. 8, they also denied the existence of angels. Josephus makes no mention of this; but the denial of this doctrine stands in the closest connection with the denial of the resurrection. The denial of the resurrection was with them a result of their materialism. The soul exists only in and by virtue of its connection with the present body. Hence they must also deny the existence of angels as incorporeal beings. Doubtless they did not come into direct opposition with the Pentateuch, but professed to acknowledge what was there said of the appearance of angels, and then proceeded to explain that these were only divine intelligences,—a view which gains plausibility by the way in which Holy Scripture speaks of angels. According to Acts xxiii. 8, they taught that there was no spirit, πνεῦμα. The same thing necessarily follows from what Josephus says of them in his *Antiq.* xviii. 1. 4, that in the opinion of the Sadducees the soul ceased at the same time with the body; so also, *de Bell. Jud.* ii. 7, the Sadducees deny the resurrection of the soul and retribution in the lower world. As materialists, they could neither accept the doctrine of the resurrection nor the doctrine of angels, nor yet the doctrine of God, though they did not venture to deny the last.

It must have been difficult for them to bring the denial of the divine providence into harmony with Holy Scripture. Yet Josephus, *Antiq.* xiii. 5, § 9, so distinctly states their denial of this doctrine, that they must have propounded it openly: "They maintain that everything proceeds from us, that we acquire what is good, and draw down evil upon ourselves by wicked actions;" comp. *de Bell. Jud.* ii. 8. Probably they here availed themselves, like rationalism, of an accommodation or condescension.

Josephus, *De Bell. Jud.* ii. 8, states that even in their intercourse with one another they were excessively rude and uncourteous. This is only what must be expected *à priori.* Their tendency was so egotistic throughout, they were so completely wanting in all spirituality, that they were not even able to organize themselves into a true party. According to Josephus, the most distinguished and the wealthy belonged to the sect of the Sadducees. This may be explained from the fact that these, by their position, were brought into closer connection with heathen society and culture.

Finally, the Essenes. That these are of far less importance than the two other parties, already appears from the circumstance that they are not mentioned in the New Testament. This shows that they had no importance for the sumtotal of national life, but were a mere sect. Among the various derivations of the name, only two deserve consideration. According to one of these, the name comes from the Syriac אסא, to heal. Some of the defenders of this view take the healing in its ordinary sense, appealing to Josephus, according to whom the Essenes occupied themselves with the preparation of medicines, probably boasting, like so many theosophs, of a deeper insight into nature. Against this view, however, we have the fact that this activity was very partial, and was practised only by a few individuals. Others, on the contrary, understand the אסא spiritually, as those who are intent on the practice of virtue, worshippers of God. But, spiritually taken, the name could only denote the physician of souls, the spiritual physician for others; and this name seems unsuitable. It would be a strange thing in any case for a sect to call itself after the conversion of others, and, moreover, the tendency of the Essenes was not in this direction; they did not enter into connection with others, but separated themselves as much as possible from the world. According to the other derivation, the name of the Essenes had its origin in חסידים—Esseni softened from Esdeni. We have already shown that in the time of the Maccabees the Essenes were connected with the Chasidim. From the Chasidim arose the Pharisees and the Essenes; and while the Pharisees adopted a new name more distinctively characteristic, the general name of חסידים continued with the Essenes. Respecting the origin of the Essenes, it is a problem not yet solved whether they sprang up only on Jewish ground, or arose through heathen influence, by means of the Alexandrian-Jewish philosophy of religion. The latter view has been advocated especially by Dähne. But the traces of heathen influence are by no means so certain. Only two doctrines can with any great probability be reckoned as such: firstly, the doctrine of the body as the prison of the soul,—comp. Josephus, *De Bell. Jud.* ii. 8. 11, according to whom they taught immortality but no resurrection, while on Israelitish soil both are united; and, secondly, their existence as an order, and their adoption of mysteries, which is very remote from the Israelitish standpoint, and vividly recalls heathen analogies, especially Pythagorism. According to Philo and Josephus (the latter alone serves as an historical source; Philo idealizes too much), the Essenes amounted to about 4000, and were scattered throughout the whole land; and when the elder Pliny names a district beside the Dead Sea as their exact place of abode, we can only take this to mean that they had an important settlement there. From the Therapeutæ in Egypt, who were essentially the same sect, they were distinguished only by the fact, that while the former devoted the whole day to contemplation, these occupied a part of it in manual labour, and did not altogether withdraw from human society; they did not all forswear matrimony, nor did they entirely renounce riches, but had only community of goods. On superficial consideration, the Essenes must appear to be worthy of great honour, as Christians before the time of Christ, so that many, indeed, have derived Christianity from Essenism. But, on deeper consideration, the matter assumes quite a different aspect. A spirit of piety cannot be denied. How superior they were to the Pharisees and Sadducees in this respect, appears from their doctrine that everything is under the supervision of God, or under the εἱμαρμένη (Josephus, *Ant.* xviii. 2), by which we are not to understand a blind fate, but the will of God, in opposition to the godless assumption of Pharisaism, which ascribed all action to man, and of Sadduceeism, which ascribed both action and passivity to man. But on the other hand there are also dark shadows. First, we find a large residuum of bare externality, which contrasts strangely with the false spiritualism shown in the doctrine of the resurrection. They regarded the use of oil, which belongs to oriental custom, as unworthy, and considered it honourable to wear a white garment, not putting it off until it was quite worn out; they observed the Sabbath with scrupulous accuracy; so also the washing before meat; they not only avoided all the heathen, but within the sect itself the members of a higher grade avoided all contact with those of a lower: comp. Josephus, *de Bell. Jud.* ii. 8, § 4. Essenism was a developed separatism; and its strict retirement from the world is quite at variance with Christianity, which announces itself as leaven that is to leaven the whole lump, whose aim it is to overcome the whole world, and to be of service to it. Our Lord says, "Go forth, and teach all nations." Essenism destroyed even the relations towards one's own nation. The Essenes looked upon it as unlawful to present offerings in the temple, fearing lest they should contaminate themselves by association with the worldly crowd who were less rigorous in their ablutions. According to Josephus, they presented sacrifices in their private dwelling-houses; while, according to Philo, they offered only spiritual sacrifice, which is the more probable. In thus isolating themselves so completely from church-life, they not only cut themselves off from all comprehensive activity, but also shut themselves out from a number of wholesome influences, their heart became contracted, and their views more and more one-sided. Essenism had not merely the faults of a sect, but also those of an order. The greatest slavery was formally sanctioned; the saying, "Thou shalt be no man's servant," was quite disregarded; and blind submission to the ruling power prevailed. Even when they wished to do good to a relative, they were obliged to ask permission from the rulers first. Theosophic trading in secrets also prevailed among them. On their inauguration they were obliged to take an oath—at other times they were not allowed to swear —and, among other things, to swear that they would tell to none the angel-names imparted to them. Then they had secret books. With all this it was not easy for the Essenes to become Christians after the manner of Christ. In one aspect Essenism was less accessible to Christianity than Pharisaism, because the latter did not shut itself up in the same way.

It is commonly supposed that every Jew belonged to one of the three sects named. But the very germ of the nation, the ἐκλογὴ, stood outside these sects, having only a more or less intimate connection with the Pharisees, because the latter represented themselves as defenders of the nationality and the faith. These people, the Israelites without guile, were the quiet of the land; and if we had only Josephus, who confines himself to the noisy element, we should scarcely suspect their existence. But in the New Testament we encounter their lovely forms, Zacharias, Simeon, Joseph, Nathanael, Elisabeth, Hannah, the three Marys, etc. We learn what a treasure of hungering after salvation and childlike surrender still had a place in the nation, from the example of the apostles in the first days of their relation to Christ, and the attachment with which the ὄχλοι met Christ. Perhaps there never was a deeper religious life in the nation than at this time, in which we are everywhere met by traces of the greatest moral confusion. But when Christianity attracted that genuine Israelitish element to itself, the nation became a shell without a kernel. Authors such as Josephus and the heathen were in their place, but the destruction of the nation was near at hand, and the eagles were gathering about the carcase.

John Hyrcanus was succeeded in the year 105 B.C. by his corrupt son Aristobulus, who signalized the beginning of his reign by several infamous acts. He assumed the title of king, but died after a reign of only one year. His brother Alexander Jannæus succeeded him on the throne. We are far more interested in the internal conflicts which raged violently under this king, than in the wars which he carried on against his neighbours. In the year 94 the hatred of the people, which his father had brought upon himself and his family by going over to the sect of the Sadducees, broke forth. For a moment the rebellion was suppressed by Alexander, who instituted a great massacre by his hired soldiers among the rebels; but a defeat which the king suffered in the following year, in a war against the Arabs, gave occasion for a new insurrection, which became a violent struggle against the king, and lasted for six years. Finally peace was restored by the most inhuman cruelties against the rebels. After several campaigns, Alexander died in the year 77, in the twenty-seventh year of his reign. By his means the territory of the Jews had been considerably augmented. After his death his widow Alexandra assumed the reins of government, and was able to retain her position by showing favour to the Pharisees, and making them the ruling party,—a course of action to which she had been advised by her dying husband. Her eight years' reign was peaceful. After her death, which took place in the year 69, her younger son Aristobulus took possession of the throne, having defeated his elder brother Hyrcanus, who was supported by the Pharisees. Hyrcanus remained quiet for some years; but in the year 64, at the instigation of Antipas or Antipater, the father of Herod the Great, a distinguished Idumean, he concluded a treaty with Aretas, the king of the neighbouring Arabs, and, accompanied by Antipas, fled to him for refuge. According to Josephus, Antipas was the original name of Herod's father, most appropriate for a contentious Idumean, an Idumean bandit, and he assumed the name of Antipater afterwards as his official title. Aretas now accompanied Hyrcanus back to Judea with a large army; Aristobulus was defeated, Judea taken. But when all appeared to be lost, the king, who had taken refuge in the temple, purchased the help of the Roman general Scaurus, who was then at Damascus. Owing to his threats, Aretas was obliged to retreat, but was overtaken by Aristobulus, and suffered a great defeat. Aristobulus then sent an embassy to Pompey, who had arrived at Damascus, to demand his recognition of him as king, while Hyrcanus turned to Pompey through Antipater. Pompey summoned both brothers to Damascus, without, however, giving any decision. Aristobulus, foreseeing that the result would be unfavourable to him, turned back and made preparations for war. Irritated by this, Pompey invaded Judea. Aristobulus surrendered and was put in chains, while Jerusalem was conquered and made the scene of a great massacre. This happened in the year 63 B.C. Pompey threw down the walls, but left the treasure of the temple and the sacred vessels untouched, and commanded the restoration of divine worship. Hyrcanus was appointed prince and high priest, a dignity in which he was afterwards confirmed by Julius Cæsar, who appointed Antipater to be his $\epsilon\pi\iota\tau\rho o\pi o\varsigma$. Yet the country lost its independence and became tributary to the Romans. It is remarkable that here also the first interference of the Romans in Jewish affairs, to which the Maccabees had incautiously approached very near, originated with the Jews themselves. The end was already contained in the beginning. The Romish thirst for power could not rest until the nation had been brought into complete subjection; and the Jewish national pride, which rested on a pseudo-religious basis, and was increased by memories from the time of the Maccabees, could not submit to such subjection. If matters were to come to open warfare, there could be no doubt as to the result. The enemy with whom the Jews had now to deal was very different from their former enemy, as only blind fanaticism can fail to see. The hard disposition of the Romans gave just as little hope of a mild lot for the conquered as of a tender sparing of their sensibility before the war. Hence we can already foresee the destruction of Jerusalem and the dispersion of the nation, and history has little more to do than to answer the question: When will this come to pass?

§ 6.

THE JEWS UNDER THE SUPREMACY OF THE ROMANS.

Antipater now made himself of more and more consequence, which was not difficult, owing to the indolence of Hyrcanus. He made his elder son Phasael governor of Jerusalem, and his second son Herod governor of Galilee. Later, at the recommendation of Hyrcanus, they were both appointed tetrarchs of Palestine by Antonius. Soon afterwards the Parthians, under the leadership of Pacorus, took possession of Syria, and were induced by a large sum of money to raise Antigonus, the youngest son of the former king Aristobulus, who had previously come to Judea, but had been defeated by Herod, to the supreme power in Judea. After both parties, Antigonus and his Parthian auxiliaries on the one side, and on the other side Herod and Phasael, who supported the cause of the indolent Hyrcanus,—Antipater had already been slain,—had fought for some time with changing fortune, without any great advantage having been gained on either side, Phasael and Hyrcanus were taken prisoners by the Parthians by means of a stratagem. Herod escaped while there was yet time with his family and his treasures to the mountain fortress of Masada on the western side of the Dead Sea, where he left a garrison of 800 men under the command of his brother Joseph. He himself went to Alexandria, and there embarked for Rome. Jerusalem and the surrounding district was now plundered by the Parthians, and Antigonus established as king. Phasael committed suicide in the prison; and Hyrcanus, with his ears cut off, was led away by the Parthians to Seleucia on the Tigris.

In the meantime, Herod, favoured by Antonius and Octavianus at Rome, was appointed by the senate to be king of Judea, an honour which he had never sought. On his return to Palestine, the Parthians had already been driven back by the Romans beyond the Euphrates. Nevertheless he found it no easy task to occupy the country. It was not until the year thirty-four, after having obtained a large force of Romish troops through Antonius, that he conquered Jerusalem, where the Romans, exasperated by the obstinate resistance with which they had met, instituted a great massacre against his wish. The king Antigonus surrendered, and was executed at the command of Antonius. With him the Hasmonæan or Maccabee dynasty came to an end; and Herod, who was descended from an Idumean family, though allied to a wife of the Hasmonæan house, a granddaughter of Hyrcanus, obtained the crown. We must content ourselves with a few general remarks respecting his character and position. The position of the Hasmonæan rulers had already been one of great difficulty. Every attempt on their part to exercise the kingly power in its full extent was anxiously and jealously watched by the nation, or rather by the pharisaic party, who had the nation in their power. But the position of Herod was one of far greater difficulty. The Maccabee rulers had been of ancient Jewish blood, and the nation could never quite forget their obligations to their family. Herod, on the other hand, was of Idumean extraction, and the Idumeans, though received into Israel by circumcision, were yet by no means regarded as brethren. It was looked upon as a disgrace to have such a king, more especially since he did not hold his kingdom, like the Maccabees, in fee from the nation, but from the heathen, the Romans. And the position, in itself so difficult, was made still more so by the personal disposition of Herod. He was born a despot, and submitted willingly and gladly to be dependent on the Romans, only because he well knew that without their assistance he was lost; the idea of rights pertaining to the nation apart from his interest he found insufferable, and could scarcely prevail upon himself to leave even a shadow of importance to the Sanhedrim and the high-priesthood. Moreover, Herod was not only heathen by descent, but also in feeling; and he had a twofold reason for giving prominence to this heathen disposition, partly because he thought he could in this way make himself popular with the Romans, partly because, like the apostate high priest in the time of the Maccabees, he hoped by encouraging heathenism in the nation to break the power of the orthodox principle that was hostile to his supremacy. His predilection for heathenism went so far that he erected heathen temples in the land of Jehovah. The animosity to which this gave rise on the part of the nation, and especially among the Pharisees, had no bounds; and it availed him little that he proved his love of splendid buildings by embellishing also the temple at Jerusalem. There arose a violent and long-protracted struggle, which served to reveal more and more fully the badness of both parties, and at last made Herod an object of horror, of whose like history affords but few examples. In recent times many attempts have been made to justify him. His whole position, it is alleged, necessarily made him a tyrant. The despotic power which he exercised only appears as a consequence of the continual mortifications offered to him by the Pharisees. It was only through the instrumentality of this hostile pharisaic party that he was led to execute one member of his family after another—for the Pharisees eagerly supported all that were dissatisfied—Aristobulus, Mariamne, Alexandra, and Hyrcanus, and finally his own sons. This fact alone made them dangerous, and gave them the boldness and proud confidence with which they opposed Herod until he put them to death. In all his severity, his cruelties and persecutions, Herod fought only against this one party. It is no wonder if, under such circumstances, the noblest man were to become a hyena. But if this mode of justification be universally admissible, it may be applied also in favour of the Pharisees. The cause for which they fought was after all a better cause than that of Herod, who had no higher object in view than his own personal interests. And if they contended for their partially good cause in a bad disposition and with bad means, if their baseness developed his and brought it to maturity, his baseness had just as much to do with the development of theirs. This mode of looking at history leads to the abrogation of all human responsibility. On the contrary, we must firmly maintain that although circumstances may tend to the development and maturity of evil, they can never create it; that all things must work for good to them that love God; and that faith is the victory that overcometh the world. Whoever fails to recognise this, has a very low conception of man as well as of God.

The more completely the earthly prosperity of the people of God decreased, and the deeper those sank who had staked their existence on its restoration, until every truly pious mind shrank with horror from the deeds which they performed for the alleged glory of God, the more earnest did the longing in such minds become for a spiritual salvation, the more completely in their case did that mist disappear which concealed the true form of the promised future Redeemer from the mass of the people, and the more joyfully did they welcome Him. Shortly before the end of the reign of Herod the Saviour was born. This ending was a fearful one. It is impossible to read it in Josephus without horror. In the very face of death he altered his will, and appointed his son Archelaus to be his successor in the kingdom, Herod Antipas to be tetrarch of Perea and Galilee, Philip to be tetrarch of Batania, Gaulonitis, Trachonitis, and Paneas.

Archelaus hesitated to assume the title of king until he would have received confirmation of it from Rome. Immediately after his accession to the throne, the long-suppressed dissatisfaction of the nation broke forth. A formal rebellion arose, in which three thousand men perished, and the insurrection became still more fearful when Archelaus had set out for Rome. Sabinus, procurator of Syria, had during the time taken forcible possession of the treasures, strongholds, and royal palaces, and had even plundered the temple of its treasures. The nation, who were assembled in Jerusalem in great numbers at the feast of Pentecost, attacked Sabinus, and kept him closely surrounded, with his troops. At the same time all Judea became agitated; the land was filled with bands of rebels, each having their own king. This state of things continued until the Roman general Varus marched into the country and restored peace by the most severe measures. He left a legion as a garrison in Jerusalem. Notwithstanding the objections and complaints of the Jews, who demanded that Palestine, as a Roman province, should be annexed to Syria, Augustus persevered in carrying out the will of Herod, though refusing to give Archelaus the title of king, instead of which he gave him that of ethnarch. Archelaus now took possession of his ethnarchy. But his hard rule caused the Jews and Samaritans to make new complaints to Augustus, in consequence of which he was deposed in the twelfth year of Christ, and banished to Vienne in Gaul. Judea and Samaria were now annexed to Syria, while the two brothers of Archelaus, Herod Antipas and Philip, remained still in possession of their tetrarchies. The census, which was taken in the very beginning by Quirinus for the purpose of regulating the taxation, led to an insurrection, headed by Judas the Gaulanite or Galilean, for the nation regarded it as a violation of their dignity as the people of God: Acts v. 37. Although this insurrection was put down at the time, yet the seed then sown continued to grow until the final rebellion.

It is no longer a part of our task to describe in detail how this rebellion continued to spread more and more widely; how, after a series of separate revolts, it burst forth fully, and led to the destruction of the city and the temple. We have already given the leading outlines, and there can be no charm in the details unless given with that fulness with which they are described by the eye-witness Josephus in his books *De Bello Judaico*.

INDEXES.

I.—TEXTS OF SCRIPTURE ILLUSTRATED OR EXPLAINED.

GENESIS.								
	VOL.	PAGE		VOL.	PAGE		VOL.	PAGE
ii. 14,	i.	98	xvi. 22-30,	i.	301	xvii. 14-20,	i.	366
iv. 2, 3,	i.	229	xvii. 16,	i.	308	xviii. 15,	i.	318
ix. 24,	i.	104	xix. 6,	i. 323, 369,	383	xxiv. 16,	i.	424
ix. 27,	i.	126	xix. 22,	i.	336	xxv. 18,	i.	308
ix. 26, 27,	i.	213	xxii. 10,	i.	338	xxxi. 11, 12,	i.	368
x. 11,	i.	97	xxiii. 21,	i.	208	xxxii.	i.	95
x. 14,	i.	106	xxiv. 17,	i.	281	xxxiii. 16,	i.	255
xi. 29,	i.	131	xxxi. 13-17,	i.	305			
xii. 3,	i. 125,	145	xxxii. 22,	i.	340	JOSHUA.		
xiii. 14,	i.	134	xxxiv. 6, 7,	i.	341	ii. 16,	i.	409
xiv.,	i.	136	xxxiv. 30,	i.	342	vii. 26,	i.	421
xiv. 7,	i.	110	xxxviii. 30,	i.	363	ix. 1,	i.	433
xiv. 10,	i.	150				x. 12-15,	i.	435
xiv. 19,	i.	121	LEVITICUS.			xix. 1,	i.	456
xv. 2,	i.	129	x. 3,	i.	359	xxiv. 2,	i.	120
xv. 15, 16,	i.	128	x. 17,	i.	349	xxiv. 27,	i.	461
xvi. 7, 11,	i.	207	xvii. 7,	i. 123,	245			
xvi. 22-30,	i.	231	xxiv. 8,	i.	357	JUDGES.		
xvii. 18,	i.	144				i. 19,	ii.	12
xix. 24,	i.	154	NUMBERS.			ii. 7,	i. 467; ii.	5
xx. 7,	i.	141	v. 5,	i.	351	iii. 19,	ii.	26
xx. 13,	i.	131	x. 9,	i.	29	viii. 22,	ii.	40
xxii. 10,	i.	355	x. 35,	ii.	54			
xxiii. 16,	i.	206	xi. 9,	i.	301	1 SAMUEL.		
xxiii. 18,	i.	137	xi. 25,	i.	378	ii. 22,	ii.	52
xxx. 11,	i.	121	xii. 2,	i.	141	iii. 1,	ii.	49
xxxi. 19, 30, 35,	i.	120	xii. 6-8,	i.	380	v. 6,	ii.	54
xxxii. 2,	i.	186	xiii. 29,	i.	102	vi. 19,	ii.	55
xxxii. 7,	i.	187	xiv. 20,	i.	110	x. 25,	ii.	60
xlvii. 22,	i.	122	xv. 27-31,	i.	350	xiv. 14,	ii.	61
xlvii. 52,	i.	114	xvi. 17,	i.	383			
xlviii. 16,	i.	209	xvi. 32,	i.	384	2 SAMUEL.		
xlix. 10,	i.	200	xxi. 4,	i.	385	i. 18,	i.	438
			xxiii. 10,	i.	247			
EXODUS.			xxiv. 7,	i.	110	1 KINGS.		
i. 10,	i.	241	xxiv. 20,	i.	308	xvi. 34,	i.	420
iii. 14,	i.	259	xxvi. 52-56,	i.	449	xxii. 17,	ii.	194
iv. 24, 25,	i.	253	xxvii. 21,	i.	364			
xii. 40,	i.	401				2 KINGS.		
xiii. 21,	i.	281	DEUTERONOMY.			viii. 10,	ii.	227
xv. 11,	i.	211	iii. 11,	i.	113			
xv. 27,	i. 300,	309	iv. 24,	i.	284	2 CHRONICLES.		
xvi. 4,	i.	31	viii. 2-5,	i.	294	xxxii. 31,	ii.	244
			xi. 10-12,	i.	128			

EZRA.		
	VOL.	PAGE
iv. 5,	ii.	299
vii. 25,	ii.	311

NEHEMIAH.		
xiii. 28, 29,	ii.	327

JOB.		
xxxi. 26–28,	i.	117

PSALMS.		
xx. 7,	i.	447
xxviii. 2,	i.	307
xl. 8,	i.	323
xlviii. 11,	i.	127
lxxvi. 2,	i.	137
cxxxvii.,	ii.	260, 261
cxxxix.,	i.	356

ISAIAH.		
iv. 5, 6,	i.	383
xix. 18–21,	ii.	369
xli. 24,	i.	266

JEREMIAH.		
iii. 16,	ii.	304
ix. 25,	ii.	220
xv. 1,	ii.	148
xxv. 29,	ii.	152
xxix. 1,	ii.	263
xxix. 10,	ii.	253

EZEKIEL.		
v. 5,	i.	129
xx. 38,	i.	295
xxiii. 14–18,	ii.	245

DANIEL.		
i. 1,	ii.	250
ix.,	ii.	281
ix. 21,	ii.	278
xii. 24,	i.	328

HOSEA.		
	VOL.	PAGE
xii. 4,	i.	189
xiv. 2,	i.	227

AMOS.		
i. 11,	i.	189
v. 25, 26,	i.	245, 383

HABAKKUK.		
iii. 11,	i.	442

ZECHARIAH.		
xii. 11,	ii.	249

MALACHI.		
ii. 5,	i.	369

SIRACH.		
xlvi. 5,	i.	435
xlix. 13,	ii.	319

MATTHEW.		
v. 17–19,	i.	326
viii. 22,	i.	357
xix. 28,	i.	6
xxii. 23,	i.	214

LUKE.		
ix. 55,	i.	348
xviii. 1,	i.	308

JOHN.		
iii. 14, 15,	i.	387
iv. 22,	ii.	296, 297
viii. 56,	i.	170

ROMANS.		
ii. 28, 29,	i.	96
viii. 32,	i.	164
xi. 17–24,	i.	7
xii. 1,	i.	356
xiii. 1,	i.	316

1 CORINTHIANS.		
	VOL.	PAGE
viii. 5,	i.	266
x. 4,	i.	307
x. 16–22,	i.	266

2 CORINTHIANS.		
iii. 17, 18,	i.	342

GALATIANS.		
iv. 9,	i.	319

EPHESIANS.		
iii. 15,	i.	316

1 TIMOTHY.		
ii. 8,	i.	308
vi. 9,	i.	160

2 TIMOTHY.		
iii. 8,	i.	276

HEBREWS.		
v. 7,	i.	189
vii. 3,	i.	136
xi. 24,	i.	252
xii. 16,	i.	177
xii. 29,	i.	255

JAMES.		
i. 2, 12,	i.	160
ii. 23,	i.	170

1 PETER.		
iv. 17,	i.	359

2 PETER.		
ii. 7,	i.	152

JUDE.		
Ver. 9,	i.	404

APOCALYPSE.		
i. 10,	i.	306
iii. 20,	i.	356

II.—HEBREW WORDS EXPLAINED.

	VOL.	PAGE		VOL.	PAGE
אהל מועד,	i.	345	חֲמוּשִׁים,	i.	287
איים,	ii.	62	כְּבוֹד יהוה,	i.	283
ברית,	i.	311	מכחיש,	ii.	63
זונה,	i.	405	נביא,	i.	141

PRINCIPAL SUBJECTS, PERSONS, AND PLACES. 395

	VOL. PAGE		VOL. PAGE
נתינים,	i. 432	שׁאל,	i. 270, 276
עפלים,	ii. 54	שׁלמים,	i. 353
צדיקים,	i. 324	שׁועלים,	ii. 62
קרבן,	i. 347		

III.—PRINCIPAL SUBJECTS, PERSONS, AND PLACES.

AARON, meets Moses on his return to Egypt, i. 262; the conduct of, in the affair of the golden calf, 340, 341; death of, 375; and Miriam, contend with Moses, 380.

Abiathar, escapes from the slaughter of the priests at Nob, ii. 97; and Zadok, 115; deposed by Solomon, 127.

Abijah, son of Jeroboam, ii. 152.
Abijah, son of Rehoboam, ii. 156.
Abimelech and his confederates, the Nemesis which overtook, ii. 42, 44.
Abner, goes over to David, ii. 108; murdered by Joab, 108, 109.
Abomination of the Egyptians, the, i. 123.
Abraham, the call of, i. 124-127; why led just to Canaan, 127-130; in Egypt denies his wife, 130-134; separation of, and Lot, 134, 135; expedition of, against the kings, 135; meeting of, with Melchizedek, 136-140; God's covenant with, 140; and Hagar, 143; promise of Isaac to, 144; change of name, 145; visited by angels, 146; intercession of, for Sodom, 148; Isaac born to—expulsion of Ishmael, 158; tempted to offer up Isaac, 159-166; death of his wife, 165; his death, 167; estimate of his character, 169-172.
Absalom, his conspiracy, ii. 119; murders Amnon, 120.
Abydenus, i. 75.
Achan, i. 421, 423, 424.
Achish, David goes to, ii. 101.
Adonijah, ii. 127.
Adoram stoned, ii. 145.
Adullam, David in the cave of, ii. 98.
Africa, varieties among the inhabitants of, i. 92.
Agag, ii. 86.

Agriculture, the antiquity of, i. 90, 91.
Ahab, his character, ii. 165; under Jezebel's influence, 167; challenged by Elijah to decide between Jehovah and Baal, 175; war with Benhadad, 186-190; covets and takes possession of Naboth's vineyard, 190, 192; Elijah denounces, 192; forms an alliance with Jehoshaphat against the Syrians, 193-196; his death, 197.
Ahaz, ii. 242.
Ahaziah, unites with Jehoshaphat in building a merchant fleet, ii. 203, 204; sends to consult Baal-zebub, 205; sends to apprehend Elijah, 206, 207.
Ahaziah, king of Judah, ii. 230.
Ahijah, the prophet, his prediction of the separation of the tribes, ii. 140, 144; Jeroboam sends his wife to—his answer, 152, 153.
Ahimelech, the high priest, receives David, and is slain by Saul's orders, ii. 95, 96.
Ai, defeat of Israel at, i. 422; capture and destruction of, 424-426.
Ajalon, i. 444.
Alexander the Great, the favour shown to the Jews by—its cause, ii. 344, 345; makes religion subservient to his projects, 346.
Alexander Jannæus, ii. 386.
Alexandra, queen of Jerusalem, ii. 386.
Alexandrian version, the, of the Old Testament—pseudo-Aristeas' account of, ii. 349; the true account of, 350; the importance of, 351.
Altar, the, built by the trans-Jordanic tribes, i. 460-462.
Amalekites, the, the descent of, i. 109-111; attack Israel, 307;

Saul's disobedience in the case of, ii. 86, 87.
Amaziah, conquers the Edomites, ii. 235; ensnared by Edomite idols, 235, 236; makes war on Joash, 236; dethroned, 236.
Ammonites, David subdues the, ii. 112.
Amon, king of Judah, ii. 247.
Angel of Jehovah, the, i. 207-211; did the Israelites identify him with the Messiah? 211-214; all grace and revelations given through, 213, 214; the appearance of, to Joshua, 415, 416, 417.
Animal worship in Egypt, i. 122, 123.
Anquetil du Perron's *Zendavesta*, i. 76.
Antiochus, joyfully received the Jews, ii. 353; alleged command of, to his general Zeuxis, 353.
Antiochus Epiphanes, his character, ii. 355, 356; his attempts on Egypt, 359; takes Jerusalem, 360-363.
Antipas, or Antipater, ii. 387.
Apocryphal books of the Old Testament, as a source of Old Testament history, i. 53-59.
Apotheosis, i. 119.
Arabs, the Bedouin, the government, as illustrative of patriarchal life, i. 202-205.
Arch of Titus, the, at Rome, i. 78, 79.
Aretas, ii. 387.
Aristeas, pseudo, his account of the Alexandrian version of the Old Testament, ii. 349.
Aristobulus, ii. 387.
Ark of the Covenant, the, mistaken confidence in, and captivity of, ii. 54; sent back by the Philistines, 55; the separation of, from the sanctuary, 115; wanting in the second temple, 301-304.
Artaxerxes, ii. 320.
Asa, the reformation effected by, ii. 157, 158; defeats Zerah, 158, 159; buys off Benhadad, 161; his death and funeral, 162.
Asarhaddon, or Asnapper, colonizes the land of the ten tribes, ii. 241.
Asher, the lot of, i. 457.
Ashera and Astarte, ii. 23.
Asnath, meaning of the name, i. 122.
Ass, the, of Balaam, speaking—how to be viewed, i. 394-396.
Ass, Samson's use of the jawbone of an, ii. 63.

Assyrian, history, i. 73, 74; kingdom and kings, 239, 240; host, destroyed miraculously, 243, 244; kingdom, and Babylon, how related, 244, 245.
Astarte and Baal, the worship of, established in Israel by Ahab, ii. 166, 167; the prophets of, 168.
Athaliah, ii. 228, 233.
Atonement, the great day of, i. 329.
Azariah, ii. 159.
Azazel, i. 329.

Baal, the worship of, introduced by Ahab, ii. 166; the prophets of, 168; the priests of, contest with Elijah, 176-180.
Baal-berith, ii. 41, 42.
Baal-shalisha, a man from, brings a present to the sons of the prophets, ii. 220.
Baal-zebub, or Baal-zebul, ii. 205, 206.
Baasha, attacks Judah, ii. 160; fortifies Ramah, 161; slays Nadab, 163; the destruction of his house threatened, 163.
Babylon, an embassy sent from, to Hezekiah, ii. 244; relation of, to Assyria, 244, 245; Judah carried captive to, 250, 251.
Babylonia, i. 96.
Babylonians and Chaldæans, history of the, i. 73, 74.
Bagosis, ii. 342, 343.
Bahr, his *Symbolik des Mosaischen Cultus*, i. 88, 89.
Balaam, sought for by Balak to curse Israel, i. 390; character of, 391; compared with Simon Magus, 393; journey to Balak, 394-396; prophecies of, 396-398; his end, 398.
Barak and Deborah, ii. 28-31.
Barbarism, not the original condition of man, i. 90, 91.
Barley-cake, the symbolism of, ii. 39.
Bashan, i. 450.
Bathsheba, ii. 118.
Bauer, E. Sor., his *Handbook of the History of the Hebrew Nation; Hebrew Mythology;* and *A Hermeneutic of the Old Testament*, i. 24, 83, 84.
Bees found by Samson in the lion's skeleton, ii. 60.
Belshazzar, who, ii. 256, 257.
Benhadad, bought off by Asa, invades Israel, i. 161; invades Israel under Ahab, 186; defeat of, by Ahab, 187, 188; invades

Israel again, and is again defeated, 188, 189; is spared by Ahab, 189; besieges Samaria, 225.
Benjamin, the lot of, i. 455; war of the tribes against, ii. 17-20; the left-handed, 23.
Berosus, as an historian, i. 74.
Bethel, Jacob's vision at, i. 181-183.
Beth-horon, Upper and Lower, i. 433, 434.
Beth-shemesh, the people smitten at, for looking into the ark, ii. 55.
Blessing, Isaac's, i. 178; Moses', 400.
Bloodless sacrifices, i. 356, 357.
Blood-revenge, the custom of, how met and restrained by Moses, i. 457-459.
Blumenbach quoted respecting national varieties, i. 93.
Brazen serpent, the, a type, i. 386, 387.
Breastplate, the, of the high priest, and Urim and Thummim, i. 363, 364.
Buddæus, his *Historia Ecclesiastica Veteris Testamenti*, i. 80.
Burning bush, the, i. 255, 256.
Burnt-offerings, i. 352.

CADYTIS, ii. 249.
Caleb, the inheritance of, i. 450, 451.
Calf, the golden, i. 339.
Calves, the, set up by Jeroboam, ii. 146, 147.
Canaan, son of Ham, why cursed, i. 104.
Canaan, the land of, Abraham led to, i. 127, 128; the division of, among the tribes, 449, etc.
Canaanites, the, i. 99-101; tribes of, 102, 103; were the Israelites blamable for not driving out? ii. 12; oppress Israel, 27, etc.
Caphtor, and Caphtorim, i. 106-109.
Captivity, the Babylonish, ii. 250, 251; the chronological relations of, 252-255; the Chaldee rulers during the period of, 255-257; outward, internal, and religious condition of the Israelites in, 258-262; the Israelites cured of their tendency to idolatry in—causes of this, 264, etc.; position of the priesthood in, 268, etc.; signs of continued election given to Israel in, 272; distinguished men during, 274; external worship of God during, 276; difference between, and the present exile of the Jews, 276; continued succession of the high-priesthood and Davidic race during, 279; God's design in, 283; way in which it came to a close—motives of Cyrus, 283, 284; edict of Cyrus for the return from, includes the whole nation, 285; Cyrus appoints Zerubbabel leader of the people returning from, 289.
Captivity, the, of the ten tribes, ii. 241.
Carmel, mount, ii. 175, 176.
Casluhim and Caphtorim, the, i. 106.
Ceremonial law, the, the relation of, and the Moral, i. 325; continuation, yet abrogation of, 326, 327; aim and signification of, 327, etc.; not a useless circumlocution involved in, 330-332; how far, if at all, derived from the heathen, 332-335.
Chaldees, the, ii. 248.
Cherith, the brook, ii. 171.
Cherubim, the, i. 346, 347.
Chronology, of the history of the patriarchs, i. 200-202; of the abode of Israel in Egypt, 401, 402; of the book of Judges, ii. 1-10; of the captivity, 252-255.
Circumcision, i. 216; was it given to Abraham as a new custom? among the Egyptians, 217-221; aim and meaning of, 222; relation of, to the Passover, 226; renewed at Gilgal, 411; why not observed in the wilderness, 411-415.
Cities of refuge, i. 458.
Clean and unclean, i. 369, 370.
Climate, the influence of, on men, i. 92, 93.
Commerce, the, of Solomon, ii. 129, 130.
Condescension of God, the, which pervades the Old Testament, i. 18.
Corruption, the, which set in after the flood, i. 115, etc.
Country, the influence of, in modifying the physical condition of men, 91, 92.
Covenant, i. 2, 3; the, with Abraham, 141, etc.; at Sinai—meaning of the word, 311, etc.; the giving of the law in connection with the, 321, etc.
Credibility of the books of the Old Testament, i. 26, etc.
Cushan-rishathaim oppresses Israel, ii. 23.
Cuthites, the, ii. 241.
Cyaxares, ii. 280, 281.
Cybele, the worship of, ii. 177.

Cyrus the Persian, the character of, in sacred and profane history, ii. 282; the symbolical position of, 282; motives which influenced him in his treatment of the Jews, 283–285.

DAGON, ii. 54.
Dan, the lot of, i. 457.
Daniel, his character, position, and prophecies, ii. 265, 274.
Darius the Mede, ii. 265, 280.
Daughter, the, of Pharaoh, adopts Moses, i. 250.
Daughters, the sale of, i. 183; among the patriarchs could not inherit, 204.
David, anointed king, ii. 89, 90; first brought to court, 91; slays Goliath, 92; friendship with Jonathan, 92; receives the plaudits of the Israelitish women, 93; Saul attempts to kill, 94; goes to Nob, 95; repairs to Gath, 96; repairs to the cave of Adullam, and organizes a band, 98; moves from place to place, 98; in Engedi, 99; spares Saul in the cave, 99; in the wilderness of Paran, 100; goes to the land of the Philistines, 101, 102; recovers the captive people of Ziklag, 103; after Saul's death repairs to Hebron, 107; becomes king of all Israel—takes, enlarges, and beautifies Jerusalem, 110; his officers, 110; his wars, 111, etc.; brings up the ark to Jerusalem, 113, 114; reproached by Michal, 114; his intention to build a temple—Nathan's message to, 116, 117; his sin in the case of Bathsheba, and consequent misfortunes, 118; his sin in numbering the people, 120, 121.
Dead Sea, the, i. 154–156; and sea of Gennesareth contrasted, 156.
Death, the uncleanness of, i. 370.
Deborah, incites Barak to take the field against the Canaanites, ii. 28, etc.; the song of, 31.
Decalogue, the, ii. 322.
Devil's apple, the, ii. 219.
De Wette, his *Kritik der Israelitischen Geschichte*, and *Lehrbuch der Hebr. und Judischen Archäologie*, i. 24, 50.
Dew as a symbol, ii. 37.
Diodorus Siculus, i. 72.
Disobedient prophet, the story of the, ii. 150–152.

Dispensations, i. 2, 3.
Dius, i. 73.
Doeg murders the priests at Nob, ii. 96.
Dream, the, of the barley-cake, ii. 39.
Drought, the, in the days of Ahab, ii. 173.

EBAL and Gerizim, i. 427; the blessings and the curses recited on, 430.
Ecclesiastes, the book of—its description of the condition of Israel under Persian rule, ii. 333.
Ecclesiasticus, an account of the book of, ii. 363–366.
Edomites, the, refuse Israel a passage, i. 376; conquered by David, ii. 112.
Egypt, i. 113–115; religious state of, in the time of Abraham and Moses —the animal worship of, 120-123; Abraham in, 130; why was it necessary that Israel should be transplanted from Canaan to? 191–196; the deliverance of Israel from, 264; the gods of, 265, 266; the plagues of, 267; how far the ceremonial law of the Jews was borrowed from, 332–335; the reproach of, 414.
Egyptian antiquities, the bearing of, on the confirmation of Old Testament history, i. 28.
Egyptian history, its meagreness and uncertainty, i. 69–72.
Egyptians, the, cause of their hatred of the Jews, i. 71, 72; existence of circumcision among, 222–226; oppression of the Israelites by, 240, etc.; spoiling the, 276, 277.
Ehud, ii. 25.
Elah, ii. 164.
Eli, ii. 46, 47; destruction of the family of, 54.
Elijah, his character, ii. 169; obscurity of his early history, 169, 170; announces an impending drought, 170, 171; fed by ravens, 171, 172; sent to Zarephath, 172, 173; meets Ahab, 175; contest of, with the priests of Baal, 176–180; flees from Jezebel, 181; his journey to Horeb, 182, 183; appearance of God to, 183–185; calls Elisha, 185; confronts Ahab in Naboth's vineyard, 192, 193; sends back Ahaziah's messengers, 205; his *habitus*—destroys two captains sent to take him, 206; presents himself to Ahab, 207; the miracles of, com-

pared with those of the Mosaic and New Testament history, 207; accompanied by Elisha, visits various places, 208; translation of, 210; his body foolishly sought for, 211; letter of, to Jehoram, 229, 230.
Elim, i. 209, 210.
Elisha, called by Elijah, ii. 185; accompanies Elijah to the last, 208; asks a double portion of Elijah's spirit, 209; witnesses the rapture of Elijah, 210; divides the waters of the Jordan, and heals the brackish water of Jericho, 210, 211; mocked by boys, 212; promises a supply of water, 214; the miraculous deeds of—remarks on, 217; at Shunem—restores the Shunammite's child to life, 217, 218; at Gilgal—rectifies the poisonous mess, 219; miraculously feeds a number of men, 220; recovers the lost axe, 220; heals Naaman's leprosy, 221, 222; smites Gehazi with leprosy, 224; on his death-bed, visited by Joash, 234, 235.
Elkana and Hanna, ii. 49.
Emir, an Arabian, i. 202.
Endor, the witch of, and Samuel, ii. 104, 105.
Engedi, wilderness of, ii. 99.
Esau, the birth of, i. 174; character of—loved by his father, 175, 176; despises the birthright, 176, 177; defrauded of his father's blessing, 178-180; Jacob's fear of, 187, 189.
Essenes, the, described, ii. 282-286.
Esther, the credibility of the book of, i. 28, 29; time to which it belongs, contents, and aim, ii. 309, 310.
Ethbaal, or Ithobalos, ii. 167, 168.
Eusebius, his *Chronicon*, and *Præparatio Evangelica*, as sources of Hebrew history, i. 68.
Evil-Merodach, ii. 255, 256.
Ewald, his *History of the People of Israel* characterized, i. 84.
Ezekiel among the captives in Babylon, ii. 264, 272.
Ezra, the mission of, ii. 311; compels the Jews to put away their foreign wives, 312; his prayer, 313; other efforts of, before the coming of Nehemiah, 314; reads the law to the people, 324, 325; is he concealed under the name Malachi? 305.

FABRICIUS, *Codex Pseudepigraphia Veteris Testamenti*, i. 66.

Faith, the, of the patriarchs, i. 215, 216.
Famine, the, in Samaria, 225, 226.
Fire, the use of, and how to produce, known to all nations, i. 94; God's appearance under the symbol of, 143; the pillar of, its nature and symbolical significance, 281-286.
First-born, the, consecration of, i. 280, 281.
Flood, the corruption which set in after the, i. 115, etc.
Forty, the number, 336, 337.

GEHAZI, smitten with leprosy, ii. 224, 225.
Gennesareth, the sea of, contrasted with the Dead Sea, i. 156.
Genesis, the book of, not mythical, but genuine history, i. 31.
Gerizim and Ebal, i. 427, 430; a temple built on the former, ii. 327, 329.
Gibeonites, by stratagem make a league with Israel, i. 430; made slaves, 432, 433; attacked by a confederation of Canaanites, are relieved by Joshua — battle of Gibeon, 433, 434.
Gideon, i. 33-41.
Gilead and Bashan, i. 451.
Gilgal, the circumcision of Israel at, i. 411, etc., 413, 414; camp of Israel at, 430; Saul inaugurated at, ii. 81.
God, the hidden and the revealed, i. 207, 209-211; the condescension of, in making a covenant with man, 311, 312; the lawgiver of the theocracy, 313; not only the source but the basis of right to the covenant people, 315; all power in Israel, an efflux from, 315; punishes disobedience to His laws, 316; takes care that His will shall be known, 317, etc.; dwelt among His people, 319; the sole land-owner in Israel, 361.
Gods of Egypt, the, i. 265, 266.
Goliath, ii. 92.
Goshen in Canaan, i. 445.
Gourds, wild, ii. 219.
Government, civil, the beginning of, i. 95.
Graves of lust, the revolt of Israel at the, i. 377.
Greek and Roman authors as sources of Jewish history, i. 67, 69.
Grimm, his *Commentary on the First Book of the Maccabees*, i. 54.

HAGAR and Abraham, i. 143.
Hanani, the prophet, reproves Asa, ii. 161.
Hands, the imposition of, i. 232; lifting up the, its significance, 307, 308.
Hardening Pharaoh's heart, i. 262, 263.
Hasse, his *History of the Old Testament*, i. 88.
Hävernick's *Lectures on the Theology of the Old Testament*, i. 89.
Hazael, ii. 226-228.
Hazor, i. 446.
Heaving and waving, the custom of, peculiar to the thank-offerings, i. 355, 356.
Heber, Bishop, quoted respecting the inhabitants of Hindostan, i. 92, 93.
Hebrew nation, the, distinctive characteristics of, as compared with all other nations, i. 41, 42.
Hebron, i. 445; David's reign at, ii. 107, 108.
Hecataeus of Abdera, his testimony respecting the Jews, ii. 340, 341.
Heeren quoted respecting the inhabitants of Africa, i. 92.
Herod the Great, ii. 387-391.
Herodotus, i. 71, 72.
Hess, Joh. Jac., his *History of the Israelites before the Time of Jesus*, i. 85.
Hezekiah, ii. 243-246.
Hiel builds Jericho, ii. 170.
Hierarchy and theocracy distinguished, i. 367, 368.
Hiram, king of Tyre, ii. 110, 135; the riddle-contest between him and Solomon, according to Syrian tradition, 174.
Holy of holies, the, i. 346.
Honey, why prohibited in sacrifices, i. 358.
Horites, the, i. 111, 112.
Hornets, i. 465.
Horses, i. 206; Solomon's trade in, ii. 133.
Hoshea, ii. 240.
Hyde, *De Religione Veterorum Persarum*, i. 76.
Hyksos, the, who were they? i. 237-240.
Hyrcanus and Aristobulus, ii. 387.

IDOLATRY, the fundamental principle and stages, i. 116-120; how far advanced in the time of Abraham, 120-123; first step towards, 339;
Israel cured of, in the Babylonian captivity, ii. 264, etc.
Images, the worship of, i. 339.
Immortality, the doctrine of, known to the Israelites, i. 214, 215.
Isaac, promised to Abraham, i. 144; the birth of, 158; marriage of, 166; events of the life of—character, 172.
Isaiah, ii. 242.
Ish-bosheth, ii. 107-109.
Ishmael, i. 144.
Israel, the people of, why sent down into Egypt, i. 191-196; the condition of, in Egypt before Moses, 234, etc.; increase of, in Egypt, 235, etc.; proved to be the Hyksos of Manetho, 237-240; treatment of, in Egypt, 240; religious and moral condition of, in Egypt before Moses, 243; deliverance of, from Egypt, 264, etc.; the route God took them, 286; mode of their departure from Egypt, 287; their passage of the Red Sea, 288, etc.; march through the wilderness, 293, etc.; make a golden calf at Horeb, 339; leave Sinai, 394; rebellion of, in the wilderness, and consequent exclusion from Canaan, 376, 377, etc., 381-383; length of their sojourn in Egypt, 401, 402; state of, in captivity, ii. 258, etc.; state of, under Ezra and Nehemiah, 292-336; parties among, after the captivity, 306, 307; under Persian rule, 332, 333, 342-344; external worship among, 334; state of, from the death of Nehemiah to the time of the Maccabees, 338; state of, under the Maccabees, 366, etc.
Issachar, the lot of, i. 456.
Ithobalos, or Ethbaal, ii. 167, 168, 173.

JABIN, king of Hazor, i. 446, ii. 27, etc.
Jacob, the birth of, i. 174-186; wrestles with an angel, 186-190; crime of his sons at Sichem, 190.
Jadduah, the high priest, and Alexander the Great, the credibility of the story of, ii. 344, 345.
Jael, the wife of Heber, murders Sisera, ii. 30, 31.
Jannes and Jambres, i. 276.
Jasher, the book of (Book of the Just), i. 438.
Jason, the high priest, ii. 258, 259.
Jawbone of an ass, Samson's—did the well spring from? ii. 63.

PRINCIPAL SUBJECTS, PERSONS, AND PLACES. 401

Jehoahaz, ii. 250.
Johoiada, ii. 233.
Jehoiachin, ii. 251.
Jehoiakim, ii. 250.
Jehoram, ii. 228, 230.
Jehoshaphat, ii. 193-217.
Jehovah (Javeh), meaning and significance of the name, i. 258, 259; the theocratic name of God, 260.
Jehu, ii. 230-232.
Jehu, the prophet, predicts the destruction of the house of Baasha, ii. 163, 164.
Jephtha, his vow and its fulfilment, ii. 44-46.
Jeremiah, ii. 272.
Jericho, the situation of, i. 404; capture of, 417-419; the builder of, laid under a curse, 419, 420; rebuilt by Hiel, ii. 170; the bad waters of, healed by Elisha, 211.
Jeroboam, king of Israel, ii. 141-152.
Jeroboam II. of Israel, ii. 238.
Jerusalem, anciently Salem, i. 137; taken by David, and beautified, ii. 110; the ark brought to, 113, 114; taken by the Chaldean army, 250; state of, at the coming of Nehemiah, 315-319; Herodotus and Hecatæus quoted respecting, 318, 319; taken by Ptolemy Lagi, 347.
Jesus Sirach, the book of [see Ecclesiasticus].
Jethro, i. 253.
Jews, the [see Israel].
Jezebel, her parentage and character, ii. 167, 168; her hypocritical murder of Naboth, 191, 192; slain by Jehu, 230.
Joab, murders Abner, ii. 108, 109.
Joash, king of Judah, ii. 233.
Joash, king of Israel, visit of, to Elisha on his death-bed, ii. 234.
Jochanan, and his brother Jesus, the strife between, for the high-priesthood, ii. 342, 343.
Jonathan and David, the friendship of, ii. 92.
Joram, ii. 212.
Jordan, Israel crosses, i. 407-411.
Joseph, the object of God's peculiar leadings of, i. 191-196; his conduct in Egypt justified, 196; treatment of his brethren justified, 198, 199.
Joseph, the lot of the tribe of, 454.
Josephus, his personal history, i. 59, 60; books of the *Jewish Wars*, 60, 61; *Archæology*, 61-64; *De Vita*

Sua, 64: *Contra Apion*, 64, 65; how received by Jews and Christians, 65; editions of the works of, 65, 66; blunders of, respecting Persian history, ii. 328.
Joshua, original name, and character of, i. 403; prepares to lead Israel into Canaan, 404; advances to the Jordan, 407; marches against Jericho—appearance of an armed warrior to, 415, 416, 417; how he acts in the case of Achan's transgression, 422, etc.; takes and destroys Ai, 424-426; raises an altar on Mount Ebal, 427; makes a league with the Gibeonites, 430, 431; address of, to the sun and moon, 435; his conquest of Canaan in detail, 445; sends men to survey the land, 455; twice calls the people together to exhort them, 462, 463; alleged heathen confirmations of the history of, 466; observations on the history of religion in the time of, 466-469.
Joshua, the book of, i. 32.
Josiah, his reign, ii. 247-249.
Jotham, ii. 242.
Judah, the lot of the tribe of, i. 454.
Judith and Tobit, the books of, i. 59.
Judges, the, of Israel—the civil constitution of Israel in the time of, ii. 67, etc.; the nature of their office, 69, etc.; the condition of religion in the time of, 71, etc.
Judges, the book of, i. 32; the chronology of the book of, i. 1-10.

KENITES, the, i. 397.
Kern, his *Doctrine of the Kingdom of God*, i. 85, 86.
Keturah, i. 168.
Kibroth Hattaavah, the revolt of Israel at, i. 377.
King, God the, of Israel, i. 315.
King, the people ask for a, ii. 66, 67.
Kings and Chronicles, the books of, i. 33.
Kingship, provided for by the Mosaic law, i. 366, 367.
Kir-hareseth, ii. 216.
Klearch, a pupil of Aristotle, his supposed testimony respecting the Jews, ii. 341.
Korah, the revolt of, i. 383.
Kruger, his *History of the Assyrians and Iranians*, i. 77.
Kurtz, his *Compendium of Bible History*, i. 87, 88.

LABAN, i. 184-186.
Laborosoarchad, ii. 256.
Law, the revelation of, to Israel, i. 322; the main object of the giving of the, 223-225; the relation of the ceremonial and the moral, 325; the continuance yet abrogation of, 326, 327; the aim and significance of the ceremonial, 327-330; is there in the ceremonial a useless circumlocution? 331, 332; the locality of the giving of the, 335, 336.
Lawgiver, God the, in the theocracy, i. 313.
Leaven, the symbol of corruption, i. 357, 358.
Leprosy, the uncleanness of, i. 371; a type of sin, ii. 224.
Levirate law, the, i. 203.
Levites, the, the revenues of, i. 360; cities appointed for, 459; divided into courses by David, ii. 115, 116.
Lot, his separation from Abraham, i. 134; in Sodom, 152-158.

MAACAH, ii. 157.
Maccabees, the name, ii. 366; Judas and Simon, 367-372.
Maccabees, the books of, as a source of Old Testament history—the first book, i. 53; the second book, 56; the third and fourth books, 58; character of the third book of, ii. 352; character of the first and second books, 366.
Machpelah, the cave of, i. 165.
Magicians of Egypt, the attempts of the, to imitate the miracles of Moses, i. 273-276.
Magistracy, the ordinary, among the Israelites, ii. 305.
Makkedah, the conquest of, i. 445.
Malachi, who, ii. 305.
Man, alleged progress of, from a state of uncivilisation, i. 90, 91; unity and varieties of the race, 92-94.
Manasseh, king, his wickedness and repentance, ii. 247.
Manasseh made high priest in Samaria, ii. 326, 327.
Manetho, who, i. 70.
Manna, what, and how produced, i. 299-301; a double quantity of, falls on the Sabbath, 302.
Marah, the waters of, i. 298, 309.
Marriage, among the patriarchs, i. 203, 204.
Meat-offerings, i. 356-358.
Megiddo, the battle of, ii. 249.

Melchizedek meets Abraham, i. 136-139.
Menahem, king of Israel, ii. 239.
Menelaus obtains the high-priesthood by bribery, ii. 258, 259; driven out, 360.
Merodach-Baladan, ii. 243.
Mesopotamia, i. 99.
Messiah, the knowledge of the, among the Israelites, i. 211-214.
Micah and his house of idols, ii. 16.
Micaiah, the prophet, called before Ahab and Jehoshaphat—his prediction, ii. 193-196.
Michaelis on the first book of Maccabees, i. 54.
Midianites, the, seduce Israel, i. 398; oppress Israel, ii. 32.
Mincha, the, i. 356, 357.
Miracles, in Egypt, i. 269, 270; magicians attempt to imitate, 272-276; of Elijah and Elisha, ii. 207.
Miriam and Aaron contend with Moses, i. 380.
"Mixed Multitude," the, which went up with Israel out of Egypt, i. 377, 378.
Moabites, the servitude of the Israelites to, ii. 25; the subjugation of, by David, 111, 112; defeated by Jehoshaphat and Joram, 212-217; the king of, sacrifices his son, 216, 217.
Mohammedanism, i. 144.
Money in the time of the patriarchs, i. 206.
Moses, the call of, i. 248, etc.; the deliverance of, in childhood, 249; adopted by Pharaoh's daughter, 250, 251; alleged campaign of, against the Ethiopians, 251, 252; visits his brethren, and slays an Egyptian, 252; flees into Midian, 253; occurrences to, on his return to Egypt, 253, 254, 261; called to the service of God at Mount Sinai —his vision of the burning bush, 254-256; on the Mount, 336, 337; permitted to see God, 341, 342; the glory of his face, 342; his command to the Levites to slay their idolatrous brethren, 342, 343; builds the tabernacle, 344; chooses the seventy elders, 378; Miriam and Aaron contend with, 380; the blessing of, 400; his death, 400, 401.
Mythical theory, the, respecting Old Testament history refuted, i. 23, etc., 42-50.

PRINCIPAL SUBJECTS, PERSONS, AND PLACES.   403

Myths, the, of the heathen, and Old Testament history, i. 43, etc.

NAAMAN, cured of his leprosy, ii. 221-224.
Nabi, i. 141.
Nabopolassar, ii. 250.
Nabonned, ii. 256.
Naboth, the story of, ii. 190-192.
Nadab, king of Israel, ii. 162.
Nadab and Abihu, i. 358.
Nahash, the Ammonite, defeated by Saul, ii. 81.
Naomi, ii. 33.
Naphtali, the lot of, i. 457.
Natalis, Alexander, his *Historia Ecclesiastica Vet. et N. Testamenti*, i. 80.
Nathan, ii. 116; reproves David for his sin, 118, 119.
Nazarites, and the institution of the Nazirate, ii. 49-52.
Nebuchadnezzar, ii. 256.
Nehemiah, ii. 319-328.
Neriglossar, ii. 255, 256.
Nethinim, the, i. 432, 433.
New Testament, the, in the Old, and the distinction between the two, i. 19.
Nimrod, i. 96, 97.
Nob, David flees to, ii. 95, 96.
Nomadic life, the, i. 205.
Numbering the people, David's, and its punishment—wherein the sin of, consisted, ii. 120-124.
Numbers, the symbolism of, i. 336-338.

OBADIAH conceals and feeds the prophets of Jehovah, ii. 174, 175.
Obed-edom, ii. 114.
Offerings, for sin, i. 348, etc.; trespass, 351, 352; burnt, 352; peace, 353; thank, 354.
Og and Sihon conquered, i. 338.
Oil, the symbolism of, i. 327, 328, 358.
Old Testament, history, nature, extent, and name, i. 1-6; divisions of, 9; aim, object, and import of, 10, etc.; uses of, 11-16; the consistent mode of treating, 16, 17; fundamental idea which pervades, 18; sources of, 21, 22, 50, 53, 59, 67; the mythical view of, 23; credibility of the books of, 26, etc.; the canon of the, sanctioned by Christ, 26; harmony between, and the history of other nations, 27; the antiquity of the books of, 29; close agreement of, with the historical references in the Prophets and Psalms, 34; agreement of the occurrences related in, 34, 35; aim of, 35; free from false patriotism, 35; no magnifying of the priesthood in, 37-41; mythical theory respecting, baseless, 42-50; aids to, 79, etc.

Omri, ii. 165.
Onias builds a Jewish temple in Egypt, ii. 369.
Onias III., communication received by, from Sparta, ii. 354.
Orgiastic worship, ii. 177.
Othniel, ii. 24.

PALESTINE, the inhabitants of, in the time of Abraham, i. 99; its central position, 129.
Pantheism, i. 116, 117.
Pareau, J. H., *De Mythica Sacri Codicis Interpretatione*, i. 25.
Particularism, the groundlessness of the charge of, against the Old Testament, i. 140.
Passover, the, instituted—the nature of, i. 278-280; the feast of, at Shiloh, ii. 20.
Patriarchs, chronology of the history of, i. 200-202; mode of life followed by, 204; wealth of, 205, 206; religious knowledge of, 207, etc.; glimpse of, into the future, 211, 212, etc.; the faith of, 215, 216; external worship of God among, 216, etc.
Peace-offerings, i. 353.
Pentecost, relation of the Old and New Testament, i. 323.
Peor, the iniquity of, ii. 468.
Persians, the, the history and antiquities of, i. 75-78; supposed influence of, on the Israelites, ii. 265; Israel under the rule of, 333; how the supremacy of, over the Jews gave way to that of the Greeks, 344.
Petavius, *De Doctrina Temporum*, i. 82.
Pharaoh, the hardening of the heart of, 262, 263; his proud challenge, and God's treatment of, 265-267.
Pharaoh-necho, ii. 248-250.
Pharisaism, the tendency to, among the Jews in the time of Ezra and Nehemiah, ii. 334.
Pharisees, the, when they first became prominent, ii. 373, 374; origin of, 374; main peculiarities of, 376; their love of proselytism and popularity, 379.

Philistines, the, their origin and period of the immigration of, to Canaan, i. 105-107; language of, 109; defeated by Shamgar, ii. 83, etc.; by Samuel, 65, 68; by Saul, 85; by David, 111.
Philo, ii. 66; his translation of *Sanchuniathon* characterized, 73.
Phinehas, his avenging deed, i. 398, 399; mission of, to the trans-Jordanic tribes, 462.
Phœnicians, the, the history of, i. 72, 73, 99-101; Solomon's alliance with, ii. 129, 130.
Pillar of fire and cloud, the, i. 281-286.
Plagues of Egypt, the, 267, 269, 270; the bearing of, on Pharaoh, 270-273; imitation of, attempted by the magicians, 273-276.
Plank's *Genesis of Judaism*, i. 42.
Polygamy, i. 143; among the patriarchs, 203, 204.
Polytheism, i. 117.
Pompey invades Judea, ii. 387.
Potiphar, meaning of the name, i. 122.
Prideaux's *Connection of the Old and New Testaments*, i. 83.
Priesthood, the, the position of, during the captivity, ii. 268, etc.
Priests and Levites, the, the position of, under the Old Testament, i. 37-40; the consecration of, 358; for whom allowed to mourn, 359; the separation of the order of, defended, 360, etc.; the power of, 362-369.
Prophecy, the spirit of, wanting in the second temple, ii. 305.
Prophet, the disobedient, ii. 150-152.
Prophet class, the, i. 40, 41, 71; meaning of the word, 141.
Prophets, the, the writings of, as a source of Old Testament history, i. 50, 52; the schools of the, ii. 73, 74.
Psalms, the, as a source of Old Testament history, i. 50.
Ptolemy Lagi takes Jerusalem, ii. 347.
Ptolemy Philadelphus, ii. 349.
Ptolemy Philopator, ii. 352.
Punishments under the old covenant and the new, i. 342-344.
Purifications, i. 232.
Purim, the feast of, ii. 335, 336.

QUAILS, Israel supplied with, i. 379.

Queen of Sheba, her visit to Solomon, ii. 128.

RAAMSES, i. 309.
Rachel steals her father's teraphim, i. 185.
Raguel, i. 253.
Rahab, her conduct in regard to the spies, i. 405-407; received into the covenant nation, 420.
Rambach, his *Collegium Hist. Eccles. Vet. Test.* characterized, i. 80, 81.
Rationalism, its contributions to the elucidation of the Old Testament, i. 83-89.
Rebecca gives birth to Jacob and Esau, i. 174.
Red Sea, the passage of the, i. 287-293.
Reformation period, treatment of Old Testament history in the, i. 79-82.
Rehoboam, revolt of the ten tribes from, ii. 139-145; attacked by Shishak, 153.
Rephites, the, i. 112, 113.
Reproach of Egypt, the, rolled away, i. 414.
Reuben, the territory assigned to, i. 450, 451; return of, to their possessions, 460.
Revenues, the, of the priests and Levites, i. 361.
Revolt of the ten tribes, the, ii.
Rezin, ii. 242.
Romans, the, the beginning of the authority of, in Judea, ii. 387; the Jews under the supremacy of, 388-392.
Royalty, the establishment of, in Israel, ii. 66-75.
Ruth, the book of, as a picture of domestic life, ii. 72.

SABAISM, i. 117.
Sabbath, the, i. 230, 231; double quantity of manna on, 302; the institution and main design of, 302-305; in its essence, eternal, 305; and the Lord's day, 306; observed in the Babylonian captivity, ii. 278.
Sacrifices, among the patriarchs, i. 226-230; of the law, 347; distribution of the, 348.
Sacrificial meals, i. 356.
Sadducees, the, the rise and opinions of, ii. 270, 380-382.
Salem, i. 137.
Salt, its symbolical significance, i. 358.

PRINCIPAL SUBJECTS, PERSONS, AND PLACES. 405

Samaria, the great famine in, ii. 225, 226.
Samaritans, the, the origin of, ii. 241, 242, 295-297; ask to take part in the rebuilding of the temple, 295, etc.; enmity between the Jews and, 298, 330; many Jews join, 329, 330; how they received the sacred books, 330; the zeal, yet free tendency of, 331; the dogmatic views of, 332; ask from Alexander the same privileges he had granted to the Jews, 345; conduct of, in the time of Antiochus Epiphanes, 362.
Samson, the birth of, i. 52; his mission, 56, 57; fallen condition of, 58, 59; slays a lion, 60; his riddle, 61; delivered to the Philistines—he slays 1000 men, 62, 63; carries away the gates of Gaza, 64; pulls down a Philistine's temple—death of, 64, 65.
Samuel, a second Moses, ii. 11; name and presentation of, at the tabernacle, 52; his important position, 53, 54; defeats the Philistines, 65, 66; demand of the people to, for a king, 66; was he deceived in the choice of Saul? 76; dealings with the people in reference to a king, 81, 82; his judgment on Saul's first act of disobedience, 84, 85; anoints David, 89, 90; was he raised by the witch of Endor? 104-106.
Samuel, the books of, i. 32, ii. 79.
Sanballat, ii. 326, 327, 328.
Sanchuniathon, i. 73.
Sanctuaries, many, i. 464; two, in David's time, ii. 115.
Sanhedrin, the probable origin of the, ii. 371.
Sarah, and Sarai, i. 145; the death of, 165.
Sarepta, the widow of, ii. 172, 173.
Saul, made king of Israel, ii. 75; his family, and low stand-point, 76, 78; changed, 79; proclaimed, 79, 80; his humility, 80; solemn inauguration of, 81; beginning of his reign, 83; his first act of disobedience, and Samuel's judgment on it, 84, 85; defeats the Philistines—his foolish oath, 85, 86; his disobedience in case of the Amalekites, 86, 87; rejection of, 87, 88; troubled by an evil spirit, 91; his jealousy excited against David, 93; goes to Nob, 95; has the priests of Nob slaughtered, 96; his life spared by David, 99; his miserable state, 101; forsaken by God, he resorts to the witch of Endor, 103, 104; his death, 106.
Satan, i. 195.
Schools of the prophets, the, ii. 73, 74, 219, 220.
Scribes, i. 366.
Seleucus conquers Syria, ii. 348.
Sennacherib, the miraculous destruction of his host, and death, ii. 242, 243.
Septuagint [see Alexandrian version].
Serpent-charmers, i. 387.
Serpents, the Israelites bitten by, i. 385-387.
Seventy, the, chosen by Moses, i. 378.
Shallum, ii. 238.
Shalmaneser carries away Israel into captivity, ii. 241.
Shamgar slays 700 Philistines with an ox-goad, ii. 26, 27.
Sheba, the queen of, ii. 128.
Shekinah said to be wanting in the second temple, ii. 304, 305.
Shemaiah, the prophet, ii. 145.
Sheol, i. 215.
Sheshbazzar, ii. 289.
Shew-bread, i. 357; David eats the, ii. 95.
Shimei put to death, ii. 127.
Shiloh, i. 200, 454, 455, 463; the feast at, ii. 20.
Shishak invades Judea, ii. 155, 156.
Shunem and the Shunammite, ii. 217, 218.
Sichem, the blessing and the curse pronounced at, i. 427; Joshua assembles the people at, 463, 464; the importance of, in Ephraim, ii. 43.
Simeon's lot, i. 456.
Simon the Just, ii. 351, 352.
Sinai, Mount, i. 254, 335; the covenant of, 311, etc.; other occurrences on, 336, etc.; departure of Israel from, 374, etc.
Sin-offerings, the, i. 330, 349, 350, 351, 352.
Sodom and Gomorrah, the judgment on, i. 147, 148, 151; the region of, 149; agencies employed in the destruction of, 153.
Solomon, succeeds David, ii. 124; wisdom and piety of, 126; first measures of, 127; knowledge and literary ability of, 128; visit of

the queen of Sheba to, 128, 129; his buildings, 129; his alliance with the king of Tyre, 129, 130; the peaceful and prosperous condition of the nation under, 131; the apostasy of, 132; did he ever repent? 134; the alleged riddle-contest between Hiram and, 174.
Spartans, the, a letter from the king of, to the Jewish high priest, ii. 354; how the idea of a relationship between the Jews and, originated among, 354, 355.
Spies, the, sent by Moses—the report of, and its consequences, i. 381; sent by Joshua, and harboured by Rahab, 404–407.
Spirit of the Lord, the coming of the, on a person, ii. 24.
Spirit, the lying, in the mouth of Ahab's prophets, ii. 195.
State-Churchism, not God's institution, i. 8.
Stones, the anointing and consecration of, i. 231, 232.
Strauss' *Life of Jesus*, i. 23, 25.
Sun, did Joshua stay the, in its course? the whole question fully investigated, i. 435–444.
Symbolism, the, of the law, i. 327, 328; the tendency towards, in the East, 330; how it has sometimes led to idolatry, i. 330.
Synagoga Magna, the, ii. 336–338.
Synagogues, ii. 371, 372.
Synedrium Magnum, the, ii. 336.

TABERNACLE, the erection, furniture, and divisions of, i. 344–347.
Tabernacles, the feast of, i. 328, 329.
Talmud, the, i. 66.
Temple, the, David's intention respecting, ii. 116; built on Mount Moriah, 135; size, arrangement, and splendour of, 136, 137; rebuilt after the captivity, 294, 300; in what the second, was said to be deficient, 301–306.
Temptation, the, of Abraham, i. 159, 160; of Israel in the wilderness, 294, etc., 297, etc.; the tenth, and its fearful consequences, 381, 382.
Tents, the, of the Arabs, i. 204.
Ten tribes, the, carried into captivity, ii. 241.
Terah, i. 124.
Thank-offering, the, i. 354.
Theocracy, the, i. 67; the prophets of the, 313–319; the duration of, 319–321; and a hierarchy, distinguished, 367, 368.
Tiglath-pileser, ii. 242.
Tithes, i. 231.
Titus, the arch of, at Rome, i. 78, 79.
Tobit and Judith, the books of, i. 59.
Trespass-offering, the, i. 351, 352.
Tribes, the, and their respective inheritances, i. 454, etc.; the revolt of the ten, ii. 141–145; the reunion of the twelve, 285–288; research after the supposed lost, vain, 288, 289.
Tyre, Solomon's alliance with the king of, ii. 129, 135.

UNCLEANNESS, various kinds of, i. 370–373.
Unity and varieties, the, of the human race, i. 92–94.
Ur of the Chaldees, i. 124.
Uriah, ii. 118.
Urim and Thummim, what, i. 363, 364; the use of, 365; the history of, 365; said to be wanting in the second temple, ii. 301.
Uzzah, the breach of, ii. 114.
Uzziah, his long and prosperous reign, ii. 236, 237; invades the priesthood and is smitten with leprosy, 237.

VARIETIES of the human race, the, how they originated, i. 92–94.
Vision, i. 141.
Vow, Jacob's, at Bethel, i. 183; the Nazarite's, ii. 50.

WEALTH, the, of the patriarchs, i. 205, 206.
Wilderness, the, Israel's march through, and trials in, i. 293, etc.; the locality of, 295; the adaptation of, to God's object in reference to Israel, 297; the way of Israel through, to Sinai, 308–310; the revolt of Israel in, 376–384; the condition of Israel in, during thirty-eight years, 381–383.
Wife, Lot's, i. 156.
Wives, foreign, Ezra compels the Jews to put away, ii. 312.
Women, holy, at the sanctuary, ii. 44, 52.

YEAR, the law respecting the beginning of the, i. 277.

ZEBULUN, the lot of, i. 456.
Zechariah, king of Israel, ii. 238.
Zechariah, the prophet, slain, ii. 234.
Zedekiah, king, ii. 251.
Zedekiah, the calf-prophet, ii. 194, 195.
Zerah, an Ethiopian king, defeated by Asa, ii. 158, 159.

Zerubbabel appointed leader of the returning captives, ii. 289, 290.
Zeuxis leads a colony of the Jews into Lydia and Phrygia, ii. 353.
Zimri, king of Israel, ii. 164, 165.
Zipporah, her character, i. 253, 254; sent home, i. 261.
Zobah makes war on David, ii. 112.
Zoroaster, i. 76, 77.

THE END.

www.ingramcontent.com/pod-product-compliance
Lightning Source LLC
Chambersburg PA
CBHW032008300426
44117CB00008B/940